HANDBOOK OF RESEARCH ON CLUSTER THEORY

Handbook of Research on Cluster Theory

Edited by

Charlie Karlsson

Professor of the Economics of Technological Change, Director of CISEG (Centre for Innovation Systems, Entrepreneurship and Growth), Jönköping International Business School, Jönköping University and Guest Professor of Economics, University West, Uddevalla, Sweden

HANDBOOKS OF RESEARCH ON CLUSTERS SERIES, 1

Edward Elgar
Cheltenham, UK • Northampton, MA, USA

Published by
Edward Elgar Publishing Limited
The Lypiatts
15 Lansdown Road
Cheltenham
Glos GL50 2JA
UK

Edward Elgar Publishing, Inc.
William Pratt House
9 Dewey Court
Northampton
Massachusetts 01060
USA

A catalogue record for this book
is available from the British Library

Library of Congress Control Number: 2008927947

ISBN 978 1 84542 516 6 (cased)

Printed and bound in Great Britain by MPG Books Ltd, Bodmin, Cornwall

Contents

Contributors   vii
Preface   xvi

1   Introduction   1
    Charlie Karlsson

PART ONE   AGGLOMERATION AND CLUSTER THEORY

2   Agglomeration economics   23
    Philip McCann

3   The analysis of location, colocation and urbanization economies   39
    Börje Johansson and Ulla Forslund

4   The knowledge spillover theory of entrepreneurship and spatial clusters   67
    David B. Audretsch and T. Taylor Aldridge

5   Knowledge-based clusters: regional multiplier models and the role of 'buzz' and 'pipelines'   78
    Harald Bathelt

6   Clusters formation from the 'bottom-up': a process perspective   93
    Andrew Atherton and Andrew Johnston

7   Cluster life-cycles: an emerging synthesis   114
    Edward M. Bergman

8   Clustering in space versus dispersing over space   133
    Karen R. Polenske

PART TWO   CLUSTER RESEARCH METHODS

9   Industrial clusters in the input–output economic system   153
    Michael Sonis, Geoffrey J.D. Hewings and Dong Guo

10   Clustering using wavelet transformation   169
    Abdullah Almasri and Ghazi Shukur

PART THREE   CLUSTERS IN DIFFERENT SPATIAL CONTEXTS

11   Industrial districts: theoretical and empirical insights   189
    Giulio Cainelli

12   Cluster renewal in old industrial regions: continuity or radical change?   203
    Michaela Trippl and Franz Tödtling

13 The reciprocal relationship between transnationals and clusters: a literature
    review   219
    Filip De Beule, Daniël Van Den Bulcke and Haiyan Zhang

14 Diversity and the case against specialized clusters   234
    Pierre Desrochers, Frédéric Sautet and Gert-Jan Hospers

PART FOUR   SECTORAL CLUSTERS

15 Clustering in financial services   249
    Naresh R. Pandit, Gary A.S. Cook and G.M. Peter Swann

16 Spatial clustering of culture   261
    David Emanuel Andersson and Åke E. Andersson

17 Clustering in the broadcasting industry   274
    Gary A.S. Cook and Naresh R. Pandit

18 Tourism clusters   292
    Ewen J. Michael

Index   305

Contributors

T. Taylor Aldridge is a Research Fellow in the Entrepreneurship, Growth and Public Policy division at the Max Planck Institute and is a PhD student at the University of Augsburg.

Abdullah Almasri is Associate Professor of Statistics at the Karlstad University, Sweden. He received his PhD at the Lund University in 2003. He has spent research periods at the University of Washington in the US, University of Birmingham, UK and Växjö University in Sweden.

Åke E. Andersson is a Professor of Economics and was born in Sweden in 1936. He received his degree in economics at the University of Göteborg, and thereafter worked for the City of Stockholm, the Nordic Institute of Planning in Stockholm (Nordplan), the University of Göteborg, the University of Pennsylvania, the International Institute for Applied Systems Analysis (IIASA) in Laxenburg, Austria, the University of Umeå, the Swedish Institute for Futures Studies, the Royal Institute of Technology in Stockholm, and currently as Professor of Economics at the Jönköping International Business School. In 1995, Professor Andersson was awarded the prestigious Japanese Honda Prize for his work on dynamic analysis in the fields of regional economics and regional planning. In 2005, Professor Andersson received the European Prize in Regional Science from the European Regional Science Association at the organization's 45th Congress in Amsterdam. His first research interests were oriented to programming models of regional and industrial models with a focus on integer variables and other non-convexities as consequences of economies of scale and economic interdependencies. Later on he became focused on theories and models of regional and industrial economic growth and the role of infrastructure in the regional and urban economies. This led him towards the role of knowledge in the economic growth process and the first formal models were published in the early 1980s. In recent years he has been working on the economics of experiences, entertainment and arts.

David Emanuel Andersson is a Research Fellow in the Department of Urban Planning at National Cheng-Kung University, Tainan, Taiwan and Adjunct Professor in the Department of Business Management at National Sun Yat-Sen University, Kaohsiung, Taiwan. He holds a PhD in Regional Planning from the Royal Institute of Technology (KTH) in Sweden. Previously, he was a Visiting Research Fellow at Taiwan's Academia Sinica as well as at the Chung-Hwa Institution of Economic Research. He is co-author of *The Economics of Arts, Experiences and Entertainment* and co-editor of *Gateways to the Global Economy*. Both books are published by Edward Elgar. He is also a co-editor of *Asia-Pacific Transitions*, which is published by Palgrave. David Emanuel Andersson is the author of a forthcoming book entitled *Property Rights, Consumption and the Market Process*, which is to be published by Edward Elgar.

Andrew Atherton is Pro Vice Chancellor Strategy and Enterprise and Professor of Enterprise and Entrepreneurship at the University of Lincoln, UK. He is also founder of the Enterprise Research and Development Unit (ERDU), which is the University's focus for research and development in enterprise and SME development. Before joining the university in October 2002, he was Executive Director of the Foundation for Small and Medium Enterprise Development at the University of Durham. Andrew has degrees from the School of Oriental and African Studies, University of London, and Yale. Current research interests and areas of activity include enterprise and SME policy; innovation and entrepreneurship; learning, knowledge and cognition; the social dynamics and aspects of entrepreneurship; and new venture creation.

David B. Audretsch is the Director of the Entrepreneurship, Growth and Public Policy Division at the Max Planck Institute of Economics in Jena, Germany. He also serves as a Scholar-in-Residence at the Ewing Marion Kauffman Foundation, an Honorary Professor at the Friedrich Schiller University of Jena, Research Professor at Durham University, the Ameritech Chair of Economic Development and Director of the Institute for Development Strategies at Indiana University, an External Director of Research at the Kiel Institute of International Economics and is a Research Fellow of the Centre for Economic Policy Research (London). He has previously served as the Director of West European Studies at Indiana University and as Acting Director at the Wissenschaftszentrum Berlin für Sozialforschung (Science Centre Berlin). Audretsch's research has focused on the links between entrepreneurship, government policy, innovation, growth and economic development and global competitiveness. He has received support for his research from a broad spectrum of foundations and government agencies, including the Ewing Marion Kauffman Foundation, the Advanced Technology Program (ATP) of the National Institute of Standards and Technology (NIST), the National Academy of Science, U.S. Department of Education, and the National Science Foundation. His research has been published in over one hundred scholarly articles in the leading academic journals. His books include *Entrepreneurship and Economic Growth*, with Oxford University Press in 2006, and *The Entrepreneurial Society*, also with Oxford University Press, in 2007. He is co-founder and co-editor of *Small Business Economics: An Entrepreneurship Journal*. He was awarded the 2001 International Award for Entrepreneurship and Small Business Research by the Swedish Foundation for Small Business Research. He has consulted with the World Bank, National Academy of Sciences, U.S. State Department, United States Federal Trade Commission, General Accounting Office and International Trade Commission as well as the United Nations, Commission of the European Union, the European Parliament, the OECD, as well as numerous private corporations, state governments and a number of European Governments. He is a member of the Advisory Board to a number of international research and policy institutes, including the Zentrum für Europäische Wirtschaftsforschung (ZEW, Centre for Economic Research), Mannheim, the Hamburgisches Welt-Wirtschafts-Archiv (HWWA, Hamburg Institute of International Economics), Deutsche Telekom Foundation and the Swedish Foundation for Research on Entrepreneurship and Small Business.

Harald Bathelt is Professor in the Department of Political Science at the University of Toronto, Canada, where he holds the Canada Research Chair in Innovation and Governance. He is also cross-appointed as Professor in the University of Toronto's Department of Geography and Research Associate of the Viessmann Research Centre at Wilfrid Laurier University in Waterloo, Canada. He received both his PhD and

Habilitation (post-doctoral degree) at the University of Giessen, Germany in 1991 and 1997, respectively. Before joining the University of Toronto in 2006, he was Professor of Economic Geography at the University of Frankfurt/Main, Germany (1998 to 2002) and Professor of Geography at the University of Marburg, Germany (2002 to 2006). He was also Visiting Professor at Wilfrid Laurier University and East China Normal University in Shanghai, China. His research interests are in the areas of industrial and economic geography, political economy and methodology. Specific areas which provide the focus of his research activities include the analysis of long-term social and economic development, industrial clustering and the socio-economic impacts of regional and industrial change.

Edward M. Bergman As Professor at Vienna University of Economics and Business Administration since 1995, Bergman directs the Institute of Regional and Environmental Economy (formerly Professor, University of North Carolina, 1972–1995). He is European Coordinator of the NEURUS research network and co-directs the Chapel Hill–Vienna Regional Research Seminars, while maintaining an active research programme, ranging from basic to policy studies for organizational sponsors and partners such as the European Commission, UNIDO, OECD, Austrian Ministries, City of Vienna. Recent research and publication focus upon technological diffusion, industrial cluster dynamics, innovation networks and systems, and regional spillovers. Active editorial board service includes Annals of Regional Science, Regional Studies, and European Planning Studies, while also serving on research proposal, doctoral and faculty promotion review panels in several EU countries and the US. He has been the recipient of Woodrow Wilson, National Science Foundation and Fulbright competitive scholar awards and serves on the Austrian–American Fulbright Commission in Vienna.

Giulio Cainelli is Professor of Economics at the Faculty of Law of the University of Bari, Italy. He is also a Research Associate at the National Research Council (CNR), Milan. Before joining the University of Bari, he was Research Fellow at IDSE-CNR, Milan (1997–2001), at the National Statistical Institute (ISTAT), Rome (1995–1997); at the Economics Research Department of the Regional Agency for Development of the Region Emilia Romagna (ERVET), Bologna (1991–1995); at NOMISMA, an Economics Research Institute, Bologna (1988–1991); and at PROMETEIA, an Econometrics Research Institute, Bologna (1989–1991). He has been a Visiting Professor at the Catholic University of Milan, at the University of Bologna and at the University of Ferrara. Professor Cainelli has published several articles on spatial agglomeration, industrial districts, regional development, technological innovation and economic statistics in international journals such as the *Cambridge Journal of Economics, Regional Studies,* the *Review of Income and Wealth, Industry and Innovation, Revue d'Economie Régionale & Urbaine* and *Revue d'Economie Industrielle.* He has also published two books on these topics with international editors.

Gary A.S. Cook is Senior Lecturer in Applied Economics and Director of Undergraduate Studies at the University of Liverpool Management School, UK. He gained his PhD in 1993 from Manchester Business School, where for many years he was Visiting Fellow in Economics. He is the author of numerous journal articles, book chapters and reports in the areas of industrial clustering, small firm insolvency, entrepreneurship and vertical integration and vertical restraints. He also writes regularly on the wood, paper, printing and publishing industries.

Filip De Beule is Associate Professor at the Lessius University College Belgium, and Guest Professor at the Catholic University of Louvain and at the University of Antwerp, where he received his PhD in 2003, on Belgian Subsidiary Management in China. He is an Affiliate Researcher at the Centre for Institutions and Economic Performance (LICOS) at the Catholic University of Louvain. His main research focus is on multinational corporations and on emerging markets such as China and India. He is the national representative for Belgium at the European International Business Academy.

Pierre Desrochers is Assistant Professor of Geography at the University of Toronto, Canada. He received his PhD in Geography from the University of Montreal in 2000 and was Research Director of the Montreal Economic Institute between 2001 and 2003. His main research interests are in the areas of technological change and business–environment interactions. The author of several publications on these and other topics, he maintains a detailed website at http://eratos.erin.utoronto.ca/desrochers/.

Ulla Forslund holds a licentiate degree from the Royal Institute of Technology. During the past ten years she has been a Researcher at Jönköping International Business School and Assistant to the Editor of the *Annals of Regional Science*. Her publications cover fields such as multi-regional interdependencies, technology diffusion across urban regions, spatial product cycles, leads and lags of regional change processes, and location dynamics. She has also participated in comparative studies of road pricing in metropolitan regions in Europe.

Dong Guo is a Research Fellow at the Centre National de la Recherche Scientifique in France, working at the Université de Bourgogne on the issues of urban and regional economic development and policy in Europe. She received her PhD from the University of Illinois at Urbana-Champaign in 2005. In 1995, she joined the National Bureau of Statistics of China in Beijing and engaged in GDP accounting, input–output accounting and applications, and macroeconomic and regional economic analysis in China.

Geoffrey J.D. Hewings is Director of the Regional Economics Applications Laboratory at the University of Illinois in Urbana-Champaign. He is also a Professor of Geography and Regional Science, of Economics and of Urban and Regional Planning and in the Institute of Government and Public Affairs. His research focuses on models for urban and regional analysis and his work has explored alternative methods for examining structural change. Applications range from the Midwest of the US to Brazil, Japan, China, Indonesia and Korea. He has been a Visiting Professor at institutions in China, Japan, Korea, Australia, Chile and Israel. He is one of the co-editors of the series, *Advances in Spatial Sciences*.

Gert-Jan Hospers (1974) is Assistant Professor of Economics at the University of Twente (UT) in Enschede, the Netherlands. In 2004, he defended his PhD thesis, 'Regional Economic Change in Europe: a Neo-Schumpeterian Vision' at the same university. He is editorial board member of the magazine *Regions* and several Dutch policy-oriented magazines on regional and urban issues. Gert-Jan is interested in the economic geography of European regions and the economics of clustering and innovation. He has published in the field of innovation studies, regional cluster policy, creative cities and the economic development of old industrial regions (e.g. Twente, the Ruhr Area and the Øresund). Meanwhile, Gert-Jan has been Visiting Fellow at the Regionalverband Ruhrgebiet (Germany) and the Universities of Münster (Germany), Riga (Latvia), Aalborg

(Denmark) and Toronto (Canada). He is an active member of the Regional Studies Association.

Börje Johansson is Professor of Economics at the Jönköping International Business School (JIBS), Guest Professor at the Royal Institute of Technology (KTH), Stockholm, and director of CESIS (Centre of Excellence of Science and Innovation Studies) at KTH. He received his PhD at the University in Gothenburg in 1978 and was Acting Professor in Regional Economics at the University of Umeå in 1979. At the same university he has been Director of the Centre of Regional Science. In 1982, he joined the international institute IIASA in Laxenburg, Austria and was in charge of the Regional Development Program. Later he was appointed Professor at the University of Trondheim in Norway and Adjunct Professor at the KTH in Stockholm. He has spent research periods at the Tottori and Kyoto Universities in Japan, at CSIRO (Melbourne) and the University of Western Australia (Perth) in Australia and Boston University, USA. He has also been host scientist of the Japan Society for the Promotion of Science (JSPS grant). Börje Johansson is also editor of the international journal *Annals of Regional Science*.

Andrew Johnston is a Research Associate based in the Centre for Regional Economic and Enterprise Development (CREED), which is located within the Management School at the University of Sheffield. He received his PhD from the University of Sheffield in 2005 and his research interests focus on regional economic development, clusters, knowledge spillovers and the economy of cities.

Charlie Karlsson is Professor of the Economics of Technological Change at Jönköping International Business School (JIBS), Sweden and Guest Professor of Economics at University West, Sweden. At JIBS he is Director of the Institute of Industrial Research and of JIBS/CESIS (Centre of Excellence for Science and Innovation Studies). He is also Associate Professor in Regional Planning at the Royal Institute of Technology, Stockholm. He holds a BSc and an MSc in Economics from Gothenburg University and a PhD in Economics from Umeå University. During his career he has been Assistant Professor of Economics at Gothenburg University, Karlstad University College, and Jönköping University College, an expert on workers' co-operatives at the Ministry of Industry in Stockholm, Research Leader for the Regional Science Research Unit, Karlstad University College, and Senior Research Fellow at the Centre for Regional Research at Umeå University (CERUM) and at the Institute for Futures Studies in Stockholm. He has also served as a Researcher for the Delegation for Metropolitan Development at the Prime Minister's office between 1988 and 1990. Between 1990 and 1994 he worked full-time as Project Leader for the project that led to the establishment of Jönköping International Business School in 1994. From 1994 to 2000 he served as Associate Dean at JIBS, responsible for developing internationalization including agreements on student exchange with foreign universities. He has for many years worked as an independent consultant on regional and industrial development. In his research, he has focused on infrastructure economics, urban economics, the economics of technological change, economic growth, regional economics, spatial industrial dynamics, entrepreneurship and small business economics, and the economics of R&D and higher education. Charlie Karlsson has published articles in the *Papers of the Regional Science Association, Entrepreneurship and Regional Development, Engineering Economics, Regional Studies, Environment and Planning A,*

Growth and Change, Journal of Evolutionary Economics, The Annals of Regional Science, Research Policy and *Small Business Economics*. He has also contributed with more than 25 chapters in edited books and he has served as an editor for more than 15 books published by international publishers, such as Springer Verlag, Edward Elgar, Routledge, Cambridge University Press and special issues of international scientific journals.

Philip McCann is Professor of Economics at the University of Waikato, New Zealand, and Professor of Urban and Regional Economics at the University of Reading, UK. In recognition of his research in 2002 he was given the Hewings Award by the North American Regional Science Association. Philip is the only non-North American based scholar to win the award. Philip was also awarded the 2006 Moss Madden Memorial Medal by the British & Irish Section of the Regional Science Association for the best paper in regional science. He was educated at Cambridge University. He has subsequently taught at University of Pennsylvania USA, 1993–1995, University of Reading UK 1995–2005, and University of Waikato, New Zealand since 2005. Philip has previously also been Visiting Professor of Economics at Thammasat University, Bangkok, Thailand, and at the University of Tsukuba, Japan. He is currently Visiting Research Professor at the Regional Economics Application Laboratory, University of Illinois Urbana-Champaign. Philip is the Pacific Editor of *Papers in Regional Science*, Co-editor of *Spatial Economic Analysis*, and Series Editor for the Edward Elgar series of *New Horizons in Regional Science*.

Ewen J. Michael is an Associate Professor and Director of Tourism and Hospitality in the School of Sport, Tourism and Hospitality Management, within the Faculty of Law and Management at La Trobe University, Melbourne Australia. He is also the Deputy-Director of the La Trobe University Research Centre for Public Accountability and Governance. On completion of his undergraduate studies he spent more than a decade working as a policy analyst in the transport industry before returning to university to complete a doctorate in Economics. Over the past decade his research interests have focused on tourism and the development of niche markets in small communities and the role that public sector decision makers can play in this process. His two most recent publications are particularly pertinent to the broad issues surrounding the development of cluster theory, viz: *Public Policy – The Competitive Framework*, Oxford University Press (2006), and *Micro-Clusters and Networks: the Growth of Tourism*, Elsevier (2007).

Naresh R. Pandit is Professor of Management and Director of Research at Norwich Business School, University of East Anglia. His research focuses on the link between business clustering and economic performance and has been funded by grants from the British Academy, Corporation of London, DTI, ESRC, European Union, Institute of Chartered Accountants, and the North West Regional Development Agency. He was the recipient of the 2002–3 Manchester Business School/AT Kearney Lecturer of the Year Award and has worked as a consultant for a number of companies, including Asda/Wal-Mart, Cambridge Econometrics and PricewaterhouseCoopers.

Karen R. Polenske is Professor of Regional Political Economy and Planning in the Department of Urban Studies and Planning at the Massachusetts Institute of Technology (MIT). Prior to joining the MIT faculty in 1972, she taught in the Department of Economics at Harvard University. In the 1960s, Professor Polenske pioneered in the development of a US multiregional accounting framework comparable to that used at the national level for the analysis of changes in the gross national product. Currently, Professor Polenske is conducting international as well as domestic research. The international projects include: (1) A comparison of energy-intensity trends in Brazil and China. Because Brazil and China are two of the 10 largest energy consumers in the world, this is an especially important study that can contribute to understanding some of the climate-change issues; and (2) Regional restructuring implications of land-recycling in China to examine China's widespread urban industrial restructuring and land-use transformation efforts. The domestic project is to examine two US food and related energy issues. First, determining methods to prevent or manage the impact of major disruptions to the US food supplies regionally and nationally due to a sudden energy-related disruption in food production or to transportation and distribution networks. Second, examining the distributional burdens on households caused by increased energy requirements for food production and distribution and from volatile energy prices. She teaches classes on regional economic accounting and growth and socioeconomic modelling. She is past President of the International Input–Output Association. In 2005, Professor Polenske was selected to be a Fellow of the Regional Science Association International, and in 2007, a Fellow of the International Input–Output Association. She won the 1996 North American Distinguished Scholar Award and the 1999 Associated Collegiate Schools of Planning Margarita McCoy Award for outstanding service. Her publications include eight books, the latest of which are *The Technology–Energy–Environment–Health (TEEH) Chain in China: A Case Study of Cokemaking* (Kluwer Academic Press, 2006) and *The Economic Geography of Innovation* (Cambridge University Press, 2007), and numerous articles in key economic and planning journals.

Frédéric Sautet is a Senior Research Fellow at the Mercatus Center at George Mason University. He is also a member of the Graduate Faculty at George Mason University. Prior to joining Mercatus, Frédéric was a Senior Economist at the New Zealand Commerce Commission and a Senior Analyst at the New Zealand Treasury, where he focused on economic transformation, entrepreneurship, utility development and tax policy. Frédéric holds a doctorate in Economics from the Université de Paris Dauphine and did the course work for his doctorate at the Institut des Etudes Politiques in Paris. He also studied at New York University as a post-doc. Frédéric's current work focuses on entrepreneurship, institutions, and social change. He is the author of *An Entrepreneurial Theory of the Firm* and the editor of the Mercatus Policy Series.

Ghazi Shukur is Professor of Statistics at Jönköping International Business School (JIBS), Sweden. He is also Professor of Statistics at Växjö University, Sweden. He received his PhD at Lunds University, Sweden in 1997, and then became Associate Professor in Statistics at Göteborg University, Sweden, in 1999.

Michael Sonis is Professor Emeritus of Geography, at Bar-Ilan University, Israel, and Distinguished Research Professor at the Regional Economics Application Laboratory, University of Illinois, USA. Recent research interest focus is on spatial socio-economic and behavioural sciences: mathematical, theoretical and computer approaches. He received his BSc degree (Mathematics and Physics), 1958, from the Pedagogical Institute, Odessa, Ukraine; his MSc degree (Mathematics and Mechanics), 1961, from Leningrad State University and his PhD (Functional Analysis and Theory of Functions), 1967, from Moscow State University. He is one of the founders and Honorary Editor of the international multidisciplinary journal, *Discrete Dynamics in Nature and Society*.

G.M. Peter Swann is Professor of Industrial Economics at Nottingham University Business School. He is the author of eight books and around 100 journal articles, book chapters and reports, mostly on the economics of innovation. He has held several advisory positions with government, including as Specialist Adviser to the House of Lords Committee on Science and Technology and as a member of the Academic Panel of the British Government's Innovation Review. He was awarded an OBE in the Queen's Birthday Honours of 2005.

Franz Tödtling is Professor at the Institute for Regional Development and Environment of the Vienna University of Economics and Business Administration. His main research areas are the knowledge economy from a spatial perspective, innovation systems and policy, as well as regional development and policy. He has been involved in a number of international research projects and cooperations funded by the European Science Foundation, the European Framework Program and the US National Science Foundation. Publications include books such as *The Governance of Innovation in Europe* (jointly with P. Cooke and P. Boekholt, Pinter, London, 2000) a large number of articles in edited volumes and professional journals such as *Research Policy*, *Technovation*, *Journal of Technology Transfer*, *Papers of Regional Science*, *Regional Studies*, *Environmental and Planning* and *European Planning Studies*.

Michaela Trippl is a Researcher at the Institute of Regional Development and Environment at the Vienna University of Economics and Business Administration and a Lecturer at the University of Applied Sciences bfi Vienna. She holds an MA and PhD in Economics from the Vienna University of Economics and Business Administration. Her main areas of research comprise spatial aspects of knowledge-intensive industries, regeneration strategies for old industrial regions, regional innovation processes and clustering, and new forms of political governance. Publications include books such as *Regional Knowledge Economies* (jointly with P. Cooke, C. DeLaurentis and F. Tödtling, Edward Elgar, Cheltenham, 2007), and a number of articles in edited volumes and journals such as *Urban Studies*, *Research Policy* and *European Planning Studies*.

Daniël Van Den Bulcke is Emeritus Professor of International Management and Development of the University of Antwerp, Belgium. He is a former Director of the Centre of International Management and Development–Antwerp (CIMDA) and President of the Institute of Development Policy and Management of the University of Antwerp. He holds an MA in international economics from the University of Toronto, Canada, and a PhD from Ghent University, Belgium. He was Scientific Coordinator of the Intercollegiate Centre of Doctoral Studies in Management (1988–1994) and the European Institute of Advanced Studies in Management (EIASM) (1988–1998) for which he organized the doctoral tutorial in international management from 1987 to 2004. He was nominated Titular Professor of EIASM in 1998. He is Chairman of the European International Business Academy (EIBA). He was also Chairman of the Western European Region of the Academy of International Business (AIB) from 1987 to 2006 and Vice President of AIB in 2000–2002. He was elected Fellow of AIB in 1992 and of EIBA in 2003. He has been Visiting Professor at several Belgian universities and abroad (e.g.

the Netherlands, Indonesia, Poland, the Philippines, Thailand, India, China, Bolivia, Vietnam, Cambodia). Daniël Van Den Bulcke is the author and co-author of many books and articles on foreign direct investment issues and the activities of multinational enterprises in Europe and Asia, especially China. He was involved in research projects on behalf of Belgian and international organizations (e.g., UNCTC, OECD, ILO, World Bank, EU). He is Associate Editor of the *International Business Review* and member of the editorial board of several other journals in the domain of international management.

Haiyan Zhang is Programme Director of the Euro-China Centre of the University of Antwerp Management School and a Senior Researcher at the Centre. He holds an MA and a PhD in Public Administration and Management from the University of Antwerp, Belgium. His research interests include international business activities of Chinese and overseas Chinese-owned enterprises, foreign direct investment and management issues of international joint ventures in transition economies, industrial agglomeration in China, etc. He has published in journals such as the *Management International Review* and has contributed to more than ten books on foreign direct investment in China and the internationalization of Chinese multinational enterprises. He is co-author of the book, *European Direct Investment in China – Characteristics, Challenges and Perspectives*, published by Routledge in 2002. He has consulted for several trade associations, government institutions and multinational companies on various topics, such as US direct investment in Belgium, strategic management of bilateral cooperation with Chinese local authorities, and merger and acquisition in China.

Preface

This 'Handbook of Research on Cluster Theory' is intended to provide a comprehensive information source for scientists, students, policy makers and cluster managers keen to have an up-to-date overview of agglomeration and cluster theory, cluster research methods, clustering in different spatial contexts and clustering in service industries. A parallel 'Handbook of Research on Innovation and Clusters: Cases and Policies' will present a similar up-to-date overview of clustering in high-tech industries, cluster case studies and cluster policies. A rich empirical material in both handbooks makes it possible to learn lessons from cluster experiences in many different industries and countries in Europe and North America.

In organizing the two handbooks, I have benefited from getting contributions from a large number of leading scientists in the field, who not only have written well-balanced and content-rich chapters but also have actively participated as referees of each other's chapters. I thank them all for their contributions. I have also been effectively assisted by the staff at Edward Elgar. I thank them all. In particular, I have benefited from the support of licentiate Ulla Forslund-Johansson, who has been responsible for most of the direct contacts with the authors and with the staff at Edward Elgar, as well as for the referee process. She has also gone through every chapter to check that all references are correct. Thank you, Ulla! During the work, I have benefited from financial support from the joint Centre of Excellence of Science and Innovation Studies (CESIS) at The Royal Institute of Technology, Stockholm and at Jönköping International Business School, Jönköping. I thank the board of CESIS for this support.

Charlie Karlsson
Jönköping International Business School
September 2007

1 Introduction
Charlie Karlsson

This handbook presents a comprehensive overview of research on economic clusters, which hopefully will be of interest to scholars as well as practitioners involved in cluster formation and cluster management. In the development of this book, leading writers on clusters from many countries have been attracted. The result is a thorough overview of economic cluster research in terms of agglomeration and cluster theory, methods for analysing clusters, clustering in different spatial contexts, and clustering in service industries. An overview of research on clustering in high-tech industries, cluster case studies and cluster policies is presented in a parallel handbook – 'Handbook of Research on Innovation and Cluster: Cases and Policies' edited by Charlie Karlsson and published by Edward Elgar. The studies cover the developed economies in Europe and North America.

Clusters and clustering have caught the imagination of scholars and policy makers as well as business people. A general search on Google in October 2006 on the concept cluster gave about 116 million hits. An unrestricted search on Google Scholar gave about 1 550 000 hits, while a search restricted to economic and social sciences gave about 206 000 hits. These results clearly illustrate the great general scientific interest in clusters and clustering. The interest in clusters and clustering among researchers in economics and related subjects is also increasing rapidly. Using EconLit of October 2006, we find three hits for clusters in 1969 but 146 hits for clusters in 2005.

The study of clusters and clustering and related subjects is now an integral part of many undergraduate and postgraduate studies in business administration, economics, economic geography and urban and regional planning. At the policy level governments at central, regional and local levels in most developed countries have conducted cluster studies and introduced policies aiming at supporting existing clusters as well as stimulating the emergence of new clusters. The success of these policies has varied substantially but cluster policies seem to have become an integral part of the political thinking on industrial and regional policies. International organizations, such as the OECD, have conducted major cluster studies to support the development of cluster policies (Malmberg & Maskell, 2002).

The growing intellectual as well as political interest in clusters and clustering is the prime motivation for this handbook. The current strong interest in clustering and agglomeration is a culmination of a research tradition that goes back to the nineteenth century and that is associated with names such as von Thünen, Marshall, Weber, Ohlin, Hoover, Christaller, Palander, Lösch, Isard and Beckmann. Even if both economists and economic geographers have contributed to the field it has been mainly economic geographers that have kept the research tradition running. Mainstream economists have largely ignored spatial issues until the early 1990s, when Krugman (1991) suddenly seemed to realize that the most striking feature of the geography of economic activity was concentration – a problem analysed by Hotelling (1929), Christaller (1933) and Lösch (1943). However, since then also a growing number of non-spatial economists have started to take an interest into what has become known as 'New Economic Geography'.[1] Fujita, Krugman and Venables (1999) explain the increased theoretical and empirical interest among economists in where economic activities take place and why they concentrate in space. Their major explanation is that it has to do with its importance for core areas in economics such as urban economics, location theory and international trade theory.

What is an industrial cluster and what do different researchers imply when using the concept? Despite substantial research on clusters, there is still much confusion concerning the proper conceptualization of a cluster, except that it is generally conceived as a non-random spatial concentration of economic activities (Ellison & Glaeser, 1997). Gordon and McCann (2000) have offered some help by providing a comprehensive assessment of various theoretical frameworks in which industrial clusters have been analysed. They have observed that the phenomenon of industrial clustering has attracted researchers from several disciplines and research traditions employing a diverse set of theoretical frameworks and analytical approaches. Varieties of conflicting conceptualizations have been used, which has generated ambiguity. Concepts such as agglomeration, cluster, industrial district, regional economic milieu and industrial complex have been used more or less interchangeably with often very little concern about how to make them operational. Gordon and McCann identify three analytically distinct forms of spatial industrial clustering, each of them subject to logic of its own:

- The classical model of pure agglomeration, referring to job matching opportunities and service economies of scale and scope, where externalities arise via the local market and local spillovers.
- The industrial-complex model, referring to explicit links of sales and purchases between firms leading to reduced transaction costs.
- The club model, also referred to as the social-network model, which focuses on social ties and trust facilitating cooperation and innovation.

Whatever the type of cluster, the phenomena of industrial clustering are evidence of the pervasive influence of interdependently increasing returns (Krugman, 1991). Typical of clusters is the existence of one or several forms of direct and/or indirect interaction between economic agents. Increasing returns obtain when such interaction generates positive externalities for the economic agents belonging to the cluster.

The three cluster notions above may coexist since local markets, local transaction links and local social networks can be integrated in various combinations into functional regions. Thus, even if it is possible to distinguish analytically three 'pure' cluster models, it is important to realize that industrial clusters in reality often exhibit rich but complicated and integrated features, many of which may be difficult to create or influence by policy measures. Many industrial clusters are unique and the result of specific historical circumstances. Cluster models give little guidance for the development of such clusters, since they are the result of specific circumstances, which are more or less impossible to imitate.

1.1   The functional region: the home of clusters
The concept of market potential can be used as a means to describe economic concentration and the opportunities of making contacts within and between such concentrations

(Lakshmanan & Hansen, 1965). There are several strong reasons for making a precise distinction between a region's internal and external market potential. The geographic delineation of a functional region is in a fundamental way related to the identification of its internal market potential. The internal market potential is a measure of the market opportunities existing inside the borders of a functional region.[2]

A functional (urban) region is characterized by its agglomeration of activities and by its intraregional transport infrastructure, facilitating a large mobility of people, products and inputs within its interaction borders. The basic characteristic of a functional region is the integrated labour market, in which intraregional commuting as well as intraregional job search and search for labour is much more intensive than the interregional counterparts (Johansson, 1998). The border of a labour market region is a good approximation of the borders of a functional region. The idea of the functional region has a place in most models of urban economies. In New Urban Economics, for example, an urban region is identified by deriving increasing commuting costs from increasing distance to the city centre, which hosts the majority of all workplaces (Fujita, 1989).

It is a common assumption in regional economics that products vary with respect to the contact or interaction intensity associated with their input and/or output transactions (von Thünen, 1826; Lösch, 1943; Hirsch, 1967). For products with standardized and routine transaction procedures, little or no direct contact between buyer and seller is necessary. Moreover, when the same supplier and customer repeat the same delivery, the interaction between these two actors can be routinized, and hence the contact intensity goes down, causing transaction costs to decline. However, many products are traded under complex (and contact-intensive) transaction conditions, which may involve many transaction phenomena, such as inspection, negotiations and contract discussions, legal consultation and documentation of agreements. Such products may themselves be complex and have a rich set of attributes, but the basic thing is that, from a transaction point of view, they are not standardized, and the interaction procedures are not routine. A special case of a contact-intensive transaction is when a product is customized and designed according to specifications by the customer in a process of supplier–customer interaction. Thus we can assume that the contact-intensity associated with selling and delivering different products varies considerably.

Another common assumption is that interaction costs are much lower for transactions within a functional region than between functional regions. This implies that contact-intensive products can be claimed to have distance-sensitive transaction costs and that these geographic transaction costs rise sharply when a transaction passes a regional border (Johansson & Karlsson, 2001). This also implies that products can be distance-sensitive with respect to input transactions. Similar arguments apply to the labour market in the sense that individuals (firms) search for jobs (labour) mainly inside their functional region. As a result, the interaction frequency associated with distance-sensitive products supplied in a given region including labour can be assumed to decrease with increasing (time) distance from the region's centre (Holmberg, Johansson & Strömquist, 2003). Actually, it is a general result from spatial interaction theory that the interaction intensity is a decreasing function of the time/distance between origin and destination (Sen & Smith, 1995).

For each type of product in each functional region, it is possible to divide the total market potential into the internal (intraregional) and the external (interregional) market potential. Firms wanting to supply distance-sensitive products must find a sufficiently large demand for their sales inside their own region. When internal economies of scale prevail, the internal market potential must exceed a certain threshold if firms producing distance-sensitive products are to be able to make a positive profit; i.e. 'economic density' matters (Ciccone & Hall, 1996; Karlsson & Pettersson, 2006).

The size of the internal market potential in a region is, among other things, a function of its infrastructure provision. Infrastructure for interaction has the role of offering high density combined with low transaction costs, i.e. a large accessibility (Johansson, 1996). This implies that suppliers have a wide accessibility to customers and that producers have a wide accessibility to suppliers of specialized inputs as well as to households supplying specialized labour inputs.

Infrastructure has two fundamental roles (Lakshmanan, 1989): (i) it influences both the consumption and the production possibilities of societies, and (ii) it is intrinsically a collective good in the sense that it is not only common to all households but also common to both households and firms. Thus infrastructure in a basic way will influence the size of the internal and external market potential of a functional region by (i) extending its spatial interaction links, and (ii) creating intra- and interregional accessibility of regions. Infrastructure also extends over time through its durability, which creates sustainable conditions for production and consumption for extended time-periods.

1.2   The emergence and growth of clusters

The traditional analysis of location and clustering emphasizes the relative abundance of resources 'trapped' in a functional region (Ohlin, 1933). This approach is a resource-based theory of location and clustering (and trade). The critical resources have the character of durable capacities which consists, on the one hand, of natural resources and, on the other hand, of the supply of infrastructure in the form of facilities and networks, R&D organizations, existing production capacities with specific techniques, and the supply of different immobile labour categories. Modern resource-based models often emphasize the supply of knowledge-intensive labour as a primary location factor. The durable capacities generate comparative advantages in the sense of Ricardo and influence the potential specialization profile of a functional region. Although these characteristics are more or less exogenously given in the short and medium term, a major part of the durable characteristics (except natural resources) change gradually over time and are to a large extent created by investment and migration-like processes.

The resource-based approach has been challenged in recent decades by scale-based models (Dixit & Norman, 1980; Lancaster, 1980; Krugman, 1979, 1980, 1981; Ethier, 1982; Helpman, 1984). However, this point was already made explicitly by Ohlin (1933). They explain location and clustering (and trade) in a context of internal and external economies of scale and local and external market potentials, where the dynamics of the interdependence between market size and economies of scale is essential. In the short and medium term, the properties of markets are durable phenomena, which create comparative advantages in pertinent regions. It is obvious that, in order to understand the emergence and, in particular, the growth and dynamics of clusters, there is a need to bring the two approaches together. One possible approach to do this is to associate (i) the resource-based advantages with the input market potentials of each sector, and (ii) the scale-based advantages with the customer market potentials of each sector (Holmberg, Johansson & Strömquist, 2003).

The realization of scale economies and the associated potential of division of labour, i.e. decomposition of production, and specialisation are, intrinsically related to the size of the market (Stigler, 1951; Arrow, 1979; Beckmann, 1958; Tinbergen, 1967; Kaldor, 1970). When the decomposition takes place within a firm, the firm takes advantage of internal economies of scale, and when decomposition leads to outsourcing of production, the firm may take advantage of external economies of scale. Internal economies of scale are technological phenomena related to individual firms and imply that the productivity increases (the unit cost decreases) as output gets larger. They may be related to the existence of one or several productivity-enhancing indivisibilities (fixed-cost factors), such as indivisible equipment, knowledge resources including patents, brand names, material and non-material networks or set-up costs including learning how to do it (Koopmans, 1957), i.e. a 'catalyst', which must be present in the production process without being used up (Krugman, 1990). It is not the absolute size of the fixed costs that matters. Instead, the size of the fixed costs should be related to the size of the potential demand (Chamberlin, 1933; Krugman, 1991).

In theories of agglomeration of firms, i.e. clustering, internal economies of scale and the size of the internal and external market potential of regions are used as the principal factors explaining the spatial agglomeration of firms. Internal economies of scale are essential components in all models, which emphasize the role of variety of outputs and inputs, respectively. Firms with internal economies of scale search for functional regions with a large enough market potential to make it possible to produce at a profit, and functional regions in which many firms want to locate develop a large market potential. Some types of goods and many types of services are connected with large geographical transaction costs, which implies that it is the intraregional market potential that determines whether profitable production is possible in a region or not. Thus, it is essential to classify products with regard to their distance sensitivity, where transaction costs are concerned. On the basis of such an approach, one can identify specific categories of products with a potential to develop clusters in small, medium-sized and large functional regions, respectively.

Industrial clustering cannot be explained solely by internal economies of scale. Of equal importance is the existence of external scale-economies, which are vital for a sustainable development of clusters in regions. The first type of external economies of scale – localization economies – is a systems phenomenon, which occurs when several firms, producing similar products, are located in the same functional region, i.e. in the same 'industrial district'. Localization economies are vital for specialization and clustering processes in small and medium-sized regions (when they are not resource-based) (Johansson & Karlsson, 2001). The second type of external economies of scale, urbanization economies, is another type of systems phenomenon, which occurs in large urban regions hosting many different and interacting clusters.

The impact of external economies of scale in the form of location economies was already emphasized by Marshall (1920). A firm operating under constant returns to scale can benefit from positive external economies from the output from other firms in the same region, i.e. from external economies of scale (Chipman, 1970). Localization economies generally play a central role in many models in urban and regional economics as well as in models of spatial product cycles (Mills, 1967; Henderson, 1986; Hirsch, 1967).

According to Marshall's theoretical scheme, there are three sources of the positive industry-specific effects from clusters, i.e. the agglomeration of firms, namely (1) non-traded local inputs, (2) local skilled-labour supply, and (3) information spillovers. The first category may be considered as distance-sensitive inputs. Owing to high geographic transaction costs, these inputs are more expensive when delivered from sources outside the functional region. This implies that proximity becomes an advantage when firms are colocated, since the concentrated demand from the pertinent industry also attracts neighbouring firms, which are input suppliers (of various kinds). These input suppliers have their own internal economies of scale. Thus, it is important for them to have accessibility to a sufficiently large demand, which in this case is provided by the localized firms in the cluster.[3] The desire of specialized input suppliers to be in the same region as their customers is determined by a combination of frequent interactions with their customers and distance-sensitive transaction costs.

The second category of agglomeration economies is related to a firm's labour acquisition costs. In a functional region where a large share of the labour force already has specialized skills, the costs for a firm to expand its labour force may be lower than otherwise. For example, search and training costs can be assumed lower when the labour pool is large in a functional region. At the same time, a cluster of firms can attract to the region a rich variety of labour categories, specialized to suit the industry in question. According to the above arguments, proximity to specialized input suppliers and specialized labour supply will imply that inputs can be acquired at a lower total cost for given quality levels. Because of this, the described phenomena belong to the family of pecuniary externalities.

The third category, the information and knowledge available in clusters, is a regionally available, semi-public good. This phenomenon has the character of a non-pecuniary externality, since it brings benefits that are not provided at a price, except in the form of land prices. Information and knowledge are spread without being priced in the intraregional neighbourhood, because in such an environment with intense face-to-face interaction it becomes prohibitively costly to privatize all information and knowledge. Hence, some of it will spill over, sometimes as the result of a conscious mutual exchange of information. The information and knowledge of importance concerns a wide area, such as information and knowledge about production technique, product attributes, input suppliers, customers, and/or market conditions. The Marshall approach provides an explanation of the sources of agglomeration economies within an individual industry, i.e. in a single-industry cluster.

Another scheme for analysing agglomeration economies was outlined by Ohlin (1933). In contrast to Marshall, Ohlin focused more on how the individual firm is affected by colocation with other firms. In his classification, agglomeration economies have four origins:

- *Internal economies of scale* associated with the production technique or production conditions of the individual firm.
- *Localization economies*, which affect the individual firm as an influence from the industry to which it belongs.
- *Urbanization economies*, which arise from the size of the regional economy and thus are external to the industry and its firms.
- *Inter-industry linkages* of input–output type, where proximity to suppliers of intermediate inputs reduces their price.

Both input and customer market potentials tend to vary with the size of the functional region. This makes it possible to combine resource-based and scale-based models to explain the emergence and growth of clusters. We can assume that the larger the functional region, the larger the potential to combine internal and external economies of scale and the larger the economic density. In particular, for large functional urban regions, scale economies imply a location advantage with regard to all products with a 'thin demand' and thus clusters in these industries will mainly be found in such regions. Thus, large urban regions can specialize in 'cluster diversity' and rely on the double force of internal and external scale economies. However, scale economies constitute an equally important phenomenon for industrial clustering in functional regions of all sizes. Also smaller regions can develop a specialization, i.e. a cluster, in a self-organised way, but in this case, the development is limited to a set of closely related products in the same industry with low geographical transaction costs supported by localization economies.

In what follows, we present a sketch of how the location of a firm in small and large functional regions, respectively, may release a set of self-reinforcing circular processes, which in an endogenous change process give rise to one or several clusters through what Myrdal (1957) described as 'cumulative causation'. This form of positive feedbacks is in general constrained, on the one hand, by the development of the demand in the region and in its external markets, and, on the other hand, by the existing capacities in the form of built environment, accessibility based on transportation systems, production capacities and labour supply. For certain activities, these constraints may not be binding, whereas other activities require adjustments of the durable capacities. The market potentials can be assumed to adjust on a faster time scale than the durable capacities. In the longer time perspective, regional capacities and the regional economic milieu will adjust through a system of coupled feed-back linkages. The interaction between scale economies and regional durable characteristics has the same nature in both small and large functional regions, although external linkages to other (and larger) regions are more vital in smaller regions. For small and medium-sized regions, the adjustment of durable capacities may be assumed rather specific with regard to the narrow set of sectors which form the specialization nucleus of such regions. Sketching how the location of an individual firm may release a clustering process will be done by referring to (i) a firm's customer market potential, (ii) a firm's input market potential, and (iii) a firm's labour-input market potential. In a similar manner, it is possible for the individual household to identify (i) its job market potential, (ii) its housing market potential, and (iii) its consumption market potential. The interaction infrastructure will function as a support factor in the development process.

1.2.1   Clustering in smaller regions

Owing to the low internal customer market potential in smaller regions, clustering in smaller regions must be based on products with low geographical transaction and transportation costs. Suppose now that a firm producing a product with low geographical transaction costs is established in a smaller region and starts to supply distant markets, taking advantage of the existing external customer market potential. If the firm is successful and starts to grow, information and knowledge about the product, its production process and its market will increase. This might under the right circumstances induce the formation of more firms in the form of both pure start-ups and 'spin-offs' from the original firm producing the same and/or closely related products also to supply distant markets, i.e. the emergence and growth of a cluster.

The growth of the size and number of firms in the same industry will increase the industry's input market potential and labour-input market potential. This will induce the location and growth of input suppliers in the region, in particular those input suppliers supplying distance-sensitive inputs. As the input suppliers have their internal scale economies, growth among the input suppliers will lead to lower input prices for the cluster firms, which makes it possible for them to lower their output prices and thus become more competitive at the distant markets they supply. The increased demand for labour among the cluster firms will lead to the emergence of a labour market supplying the specialized skills demanded through education, in-migration and on-the-job training. The development of a specialized labour supply decreases the labour costs, the recruitment costs and the risks of the cluster firms, which lower their costs and increase their competitiveness. The growth of the number and size of cluster firms naturally increases the availability of information about the actual products, production processes and markets, which reduces the search costs and the R&D costs of the individual cluster firms and contribute to strengthen their competitiveness and growth potential. Thus, we can see how the clustering process and the different sub-processes it induces in a self-organized manner creates an economic milieu, which tend to attract more firms to the cluster thanks to the available localization economies.

If the accessible market is very large, the cluster may grow very large. In such a case, the intraregional market potential may become so large so that clusters emerge both to supply inputs and consumer products with general regional growth as the end-result. However, in many cases the accessible market is limited, which implies that there is a limit for the growth of clusters in many small regions. Regions with such clusters can be described as 'industrial districts'.

1.2.2   Clustering in larger regions

What about clustering in larger regions? Suppose that a new firm is located in a larger region, possibly substituting previous imports to the region (Jacobs, 1969). This will induce the number of jobs and the income in the region to increase, which will increase the customer market potential in the region. If this augmentation is significant, it will stimulate an expansion of activities in existing firms. It may also trigger the introduction of new firms into the regional market. Thus, we can imagine a cumulative process, which expands activities in incumbent firms, stimulating start-up of new firms and increases in the number of jobs and incomes.

For distance-sensitive products, the export flows to other regions are often small. However, as the production grows, in particular in incumbent firms, the cost per output decreases as a result of internal economies of scale. This makes it possible to lower the export prices, which may generate an increase in the export flows. In this way, these companies can take advantage of the market potential in other regions.

In relation to this analysis, one should observe that internal and external scale economies might be present simultaneously. The effect of positive external economies is attraction of firms with activities similar to each other. When firms with similar activities start to locate near each other, i.e. to cluster, their input suppliers are also stimulated to locate in the region, to the extent that their input deliveries are distance-sensitive, which makes it possible for the input suppliers to take advantage of internal economies of scale. Overall, this implies that a large overall market potential in a region can ascertain and stimulate the development of input-market potentials in general. This will further improve the production conditions of the cluster as well as of other activities with similar input requirements. As the input-market potentials increase, falling output prices are generated both for the inputs and for the final products. As the prices of the final products decrease, exports to other regions will be stimulated and the external market potential of the region will grow in importance.

When firms with internal economies of scale locate in a region, the intraregional market potential increases, which makes it possible for more firms with internal economies of scale to locate in the region. Thus, the spontaneous behaviour of firms with internal economies of scale may generate a clustering of firms in regions that offer a large enough market potential. It is important to note that clusters in most cases emerge and develop spontaneously in evolutionary processes. As more and more firms cluster together, various external economies may develop, which further stimulate the clustering of firms.

1.2.3 *Clustering as an entrepreneurial process*

Clustering processes are located and limited to the functional region where the initial entrepreneur or group of entrepreneurs decided to locate a new firm. The emergence of clusters is often triggered by events that make a natural or social asset of a functional region an important location factor for an industry or that encourage a local entrepreneur or group of entrepreneurs to engage successfully in a specific industry (Feldman & Schreuder, 1996). Entrepreneurs function as change agents and, at the same time as they are driven by the possibility of earning an entrepreneurial profit, they also influence the conditions for other entrepreneurs to start and develop firms. They do this by changing the demand and supply conditions in the region as well as over time and develop norms and other informal institutions, which form the entrepreneurial climate in the region. Thanks to their colocation, firms are also able to develop trust-based relationships, not only with other firms in the same industry but also with other important economic agents in the functional region, such as suppliers, customers, public authorities, R&D institutions, and so on (Press, 2006).

Cluster formation processes are not linear processes but can be described as adaptive, self-organizing processes. These processes engage entrepreneurs as well as political decision makers and contribute to the establishment of supporting and governing functions as well as material and non-material infrastructures, often with the help of public resources. This implies that the cluster and the regional specialization created through the activities of entrepreneurs tend to become unique as a result of its history (Krugman, 1991) and thus inherently difficult to copy (Feldman & Martin, 2004).

When entrepreneurs during the cluster formation process decide to start new firms they take advantage of those resources which have accumulated over time, such as customer market potential, input supply potential, financial capital and social capital (Westlund, 2006). Cluster growth is often driven by the start-up of 'breakaway firms' (Jacobs, 1969), i.e. firms started by entrepreneurs with experiences from the same industry. Entrepreneurs with experiences from the same industry create the cluster and contribute to its continued growth (Feldman & Romanelli, 2006).

To the extent that these entrepreneurs are successful, their activities will further strengthen the regional economic milieu, including its institutions and its social capital, and increase the possibilities of taking advantage of internal and external economies of scale as well as establishing new firms. Successful clusters not only create their own resources, institutions and potentials. They also attract resources, such as financial capital, labour and entrepreneurs from other functional regions. However, there is no guarantee that clusters which have developed well in the early stages will continue to grow. There are examples of clusters which, after being successful in the early stages, start to deteriorate long before the mature stage (Feldman & Francis, 2004).

Since entrepreneurs initiate economic activities and build up resources and market potentials, they are a necessary factor in the dynamic cluster formation process. Entrepreneurial processes are mostly localised processes. New firms are to a high extent started in the functional region where the entrepreneur lives and has established commercial and social networks and has access to a customer market potential as well as an input supply potential.

1.3   Efficient versus innovative clusters

The concept of external economies of scale relates to various more or less complex forms of externalities. Johansson (2005) makes a distinction between three aspects of externalities: (1) source, (2) economic nature, and (3) consequence. He distinguishes two externality sources: (i) proximity, which affects transaction costs and facilitates uncharged spillovers, and (ii) link effects, which affect both transactions and information spillovers. As regards the economic nature of externalities we have (i) pecuniary externalities that operate via prices, i.e. via the market (intra-market externalities) or via inter-firm links (quasi-market externalities) and (ii) non-pecuniary, i.e. technological externalities, which operate outside the market: extra-market externalities. The consequences of externalities appear in the following form:

- efficiency externalities, which create static differences between regions with regard to productivity and the costs per unit of output of firms; and
- innovation externalities, which are dynamic phenomena and appear as a change of economic efficiency (new routines) but also in the form of new products, increased product diversity and similar novelties.

As shown in Johansson (2005), the above three aspects of externalities can be complemented by another dimension of importance for understanding clustering, namely a distinction between horizontal and vertical externalities, where vertical externalities can be separated into upstream and downstream externalities. This provides us with a much richer understanding of the various factors generating efficiency and innovation externalities.

1.   *Efficiency externalities*
- Vertical:
   i.   Downstream externalities that affect the price suppliers can charge customers.
   ii.   Upstream externalities that affect the input costs of firms.

- Horizontal:
  i. Formal and informal cooperation between two or more firms in the same industry, e.g. joint marketing and transport solutions of long-distance exports and shared market information.
- Pure demand:
  i. The size of the local demand facilitating exploitation of scale economies for suppliers.
  ii. The size of the local labour demand generating a labour market with a supply of labour with specialized skills.

2. *Innovation externalities*
  - Vertical:
    i. Downstream externalities affecting the knowledge flows from customers to suppliers.
    ii. Upstream externalities affecting knowledge flows from input suppliers to producers.
  - Horizontal:
    i. Formal and informal knowledge flows between firms in the same industry, e.g. joint R&D efforts based upon a cooperation link or pure knowledge spillovers.
  - Pure demand:
    i. Size and diversity of local demand facilitates experiments and communication with customers in the product development process in the early phases of a product cycle.
    ii. Size and diversity of local labour demand generating an inflow of knowledge workers generating a larger and more diversified supply of qualified labour.

Some of these externalities are by definition based upon proximity, while others can be based on either proximity or link effects. However, link effects are dependent on location. Regions with a cluster of firms in a specific industry might over time develop general as well as specialized interregional transport and communication infrastructure, which facilitates the development of link effects. Large regions with many clusters in different industries will normally develop a rich general interregional transport and communication infrastructure, which generally supports the development and exploitation of link effects. Thus, regions may offer proximity or link advantages, or both, to one or several industries, which may result in the emergence of one or several industrial clusters.

What is important with this exposé of various externalities is that it shows that the emergence, development and competitiveness of clusters might be based upon a variety of externalities and not least varying combinations of externalities. This implies that a deep understanding of industrial clustering is dependent upon a clear understanding of various externality phenomena, their sources and their nature and how they may interact with each other. It also implies that different clusters may be based upon quite different mechanisms and that general cluster policies are difficult or even impossible to develop.

What is particularly important is that we can make a simple distinction between what we might term 'efficient and innovative' clusters. We can think of the traditional industrial district as an example of an efficient cluster, while modern phenomena such as Silicon

Valley or Telecom Corridor are typical examples of innovative clusters driven by the continuous development and spread of new knowledge. Depending upon the logic behind different clusters, cluster policies must be adapted to the special circumstances.

1.4   The sustainability of clusters

The market potential variables discussed above represent resources that adjust on a slow time scale, which implies that the growth of clusters is a gradual process. This in turn implies that a functional region's overall market potential, as well as its specific components, plays the same role as infrastructure. The different market potentials of a functional region provide an arena for processes that adjust on a fast and medium-speed time scale. Furthermore, the input market potentials comprise, among other things, the regional supply of capital, labour (with different skills, experiences and education) and built environment, which are all factors emphasized in resource-based models of location and clustering.

It is important to ask questions about the knowledge-intensity of the labour force in different functional regions since there is a strong focus on knowledge-intensive clusters in the cluster literature. Many studies lend empirical support to the assumption that households with a university education and other skill attributes, such as entrepreneurial skills, are attracted to migrate to and stay in regions that offer an attractive household milieu, i.e. large and varied household market potentials (Clark, et al., 2002; Florida, 2002; Glaeser, Kolko & Saiz, 2001). The latter includes natural and artificial amenities as well as climatic attributes. In addition, the household milieu is strongly affected by the functional region's household infrastructure, which comprises its housing market potential and the accessibility it offers from housing areas to (i) the supply of household services, (ii) the supply of amenities of different kinds, and (iii) job opportunities in different workplace areas. This implies that a functional region's household milieu is a partly independent attractor (repellent) of household location and regional labour supply. However, it also implies that regional labour markets adjust by means of a process where firms follow the location of the labour supply, rather than the opposite (Quigley, 1990; Maclellan, 1990). This form of causation is associated with the 'knowledge society' in which the growing economic sectors have a high demand for knowledge-intensive labour, primarily with university education. Under these conditions knowledge-intensive households select residential locations in areas and functional regions with an attractive household milieu and firms with a large demand for knowledge-intensive labour have to adjust their location accordingly. Thus, the supply of knowledge-intensive labour is one factor driving the clustering of firms.

Infrastructure for interaction in a functional region is, primarily, the entire built environment with is various networks for transportation and communication and its various arenas for meetings, negotiations, education, and so on (Batten, Kobayashi & Andersson, 1989; Kobayashi, 1995). It also includes the links connecting the region to other functional regions and the associated external market potentials. The intraregional infrastructure has the function of making it possible to combine a high economic density with low interaction costs for all existing markets.

High density and low geographic transaction costs imply 'thick' markets with large demand, many customers and suppliers and frequent transactions. Moreover, the interaction infrastructure may also enlarge the markets in a functional region in a complementary way by including geographic domains, which previously belonged to other functional regions or even other functional regions as a whole. In this case, extensions and/or improvements of transport infrastructure integrate new geographical areas with the functional region by reducing the travel time distances to these areas. This form of enlargement also implies that the internal market potential of the functional region grows, while it declines in neighbouring functional regions.

The overall market potential of a functional region, i.e. its size and density, is an infrastructure phenomenon in itself. It changes in a process of very slow adjustments and provides collective market opportunities that benefit both households and firms. In growing functional regions, the location of households and firms form a self-reinforcing dynamic process, i.e. a process with positive feedbacks. Over time, the (slow) formation of regional infrastructure affects the process by gradually building up the basic conditions for the household milieu and the economic milieu of firms. Naturally, the economic milieu is partly determined by the job and firm location processes. However, we assume that the economic milieu as a whole changes at a much slower pace than the location of firms and clustering does. Hence, in a limited time perspective, it is possible to treat the milieu characteristics as approximately invariant. The same argument applies to the relation between the household milieu and the dynamics of household location. The regional change process described here has the form of interdependent dynamics such that firms and households mutually adjust to each other.[4]

Economic history shows that creative and innovative clusters can grow and stay competitive for long periods, but it also shows that even the most successful clusters can start to decline and ultimately disappear (Braudel, 1979; Andersson, 1985, 1987; Janick & Toulmin, 1978; Malmberg & Maskell, 2002). Many regions that have faced severe structural problems in recent decades had thriving clusters in their time. This observation raises a number of questions. What are the factors that can end even very successful clusters? Are these factors the same for effective and innovative clusters? Are there cluster configurations that are better or worse for long-term survival? What can active cluster policies do to avoid the deterioration of clusters and to what extent should they? Here it is important to observe that the factors that once enabled a cluster to form and to grow may not necessarily be as important in sustaining it.

Tichy (1998) argues that cluster sustainability is a matter most properly considered over a long development wave analogue to a product cycle, during which a cluster forms, then grows and eventually reaches maturity and even decay. However, it is not given that the development of existing clusters over time is deterministic, as explained by Press (2006, p. 6):

> Empirical evidence on the development of clusters has revealed that despite the dynamics in the spatial distribution of industries, there is no such thing as a deterministic life-cycle running from emergence to exhaustion. Depending on the response of local agents, change events may not shift the industry away from an existing cluster. Instead local decline can be avoided if agents in the cluster are able to accommodate the new situation.

Cluster sustainability may be caused by internal as well as external threats. The internal threats come from what may be termed 'structural rigidities'. These rigidities may develop within the cluster firms in the form of obsolete products and production technologies, but also within their economic milieu in the form of obsolete infrastructure, obsolete labour training and education, obsolete R&D, obsolete institutions and internal or regulatory inflexibilities (Porter, 1990). Conservative investment policies might lead clusters to become locked-in in irreversible development paths that over time prove to lead to a state of obsolescence. From an evolutionary perspective (Nelson & Winter, 1982), one can also imagine clusters specializing in (what in the global selection process turns out to be) inferior or non-preferred technologies. These and other cluster-specific developments, such as, increasing opportunistic behaviours (Maillat, 1998), can reduce agglomeration economies or increase congestion costs, thus making a location in the functional region less advantageous.

External threats include (i) *cyclical disturbances*, (ii) *fundamental technological changes*, i.e. technological discontinuities in product or process technologies, (iii) *fundamental demand changes*, such as changes in quality and quantity of demand, (iv) *cluster-competition effects*, due, for example, to reduced geographical transaction costs as a result of investments in transport infrastructure, and (v) *changes in economic and industrial policies*, for example legislation, tariffs and other trade regulations (Porter, 1990; Karlsson, Johansson & Stough, 2005).

If the internal and/or the external threats become a reality, they may of course be counteracted by actions from the economic agents in the cluster as well as from policy makers in the region. If, for example, the firms in a cluster are threatened by low-cost competition a survival strategy for the cluster firms might be to change from the production of standard goods to the production of non-standard goods based upon design or customization. There are, however, limits to what changes in strategy or policy can achieve under these circumstances and, if the effects of the threats are marginal, it is easy for de-agglomeration or de-clustering cumulative processes to set in that ultimately might lead to the end of a cluster (Myrdal, 1957). Probably, the de-clustering process in many cases might reach new cluster 'equilibria', where a smaller cluster still can be competitive. In other cases, where there are fundamental changes in relative cost conditions between locations, or fundamental technological changes, clusters might very well face extinction.

1.5   The contents of this handbook

It is not possible to do justice to the rich contents of each of the chapters in this handbook. Nevertheless, to assist the reader, this section contains a very brief summary of each chapter. The contributions to the first volume of this handbook is organized in four sections: (i) agglomeration and cluster theory, (ii) cluster research methods, (iii) clusters in different spatial contexts, and (iv) sectoral clusters.[5]

1.5.1   Agglomeration and cluster theory

In Chapter 2, Philip McCann gives an overview of agglomeration theory, stressing the importance of clustering and agglomeration. He describes the relationship between agglomeration, clusters, and innovation and provides an overview of firm types and the nature of transactions in a broad typology of clusters. The chapter ends with a discussion of agglomeration measurement problems.

In Chapter 3, Börje Johansson and Ulla Forslund give an overview of the analysis of location, colocation and urbanization economies. They start by presenting the basic conditions for the location of a firm and continue by examining how colocation externalities make colocation processes self-reinforcing, where distance sensitivity and scale economies generate the externalities. The same model is also applied to illustrate urbanization economies. The authors conclude that it is possible to consider a set of basic principles to describe a firm's location decision in the context of localization and urbanization economies.

David B. Audretsch and T. Taylor Aldridge in Chapter 4 take their starting point from the knowledge spillover theory of entrepreneurship, which has a focus on the generation of entrepreneurial opportunities emanating from knowledge investments in incumbent firms and public research organizations. The creation of a new organization is important because it is an endogenous response to knowledge not completely and exhaustively appropriated in existing organizations. Not only does endogenous entrepreneurship serve as a conduit for knowledge spillovers, but, because such knowledge spillovers tend to be spatially localized, it results in the emergence of localized entrepreneurial clusters.

Harald Bathelt in Chapter 5 also focuses on knowledge-based clusters. He discusses the relation between regional networks and growth and stresses the limited evidence of regional input–output linkages. The chapter contains an overview of three models of regional growth and development: (i) regional multiplier effects in the export-base model, (ii) regional innovation in the milieu school, and (iii) Scott's model of super-clusters. These models are then integrated and extended into a regional model of knowledge generation centred on local buzz and global pipelines.

Cluster formation is the topic of Chapter 6 by Andrew Atherton and Andrew Johnston, where cluster formation is analysed from a bottom-up process perspective. The authors see cluster formation as a business dynamic of relational as well as spatial proximity and they present a taxonomy of clusters emergence. The cluster formation process is described as a five-stage process and they discuss the critical issue of thresholds in clusters development.

Chapter 7, by Edward M. Bergman, takes on the critical issue of cluster life-cycles. He focuses on available concepts that permit better understanding of the way clusters of dynamic firms dominate certain technologies, and why the same dominant clusters may later morph successfully into new combinations, or decline into oblivion. In this chapter, he analyses the different phases of cluster cycles: (i) existence phase, (ii) expansion phase, and (iii) exhaustion phase.

The last chapter of Part one (Chapter 8) by Karen R. Polenske takes as its starting point the existence of agglomeration as well as dispersion economies. The author discusses five major spatial concepts used in location theories emphasizing different types of agglomeration/dispersion economies: (i) industrial clusters, (ii) growth poles, (iii) industrial complexes, (iv) industrial districts, and (v) inter-firm networks. At the end of her chapter, she uses supply chains as an illustration of the importance of dispersion economies.

1.5.2 *Cluster research methods*

Michael Sonis, Geoffrey J.D. Hewings and Dong Guo in Chapter 9 deal with the issue of cluster identification using a set of inter-industry accounts. Their contribution is rooted in the legacy of industrial cluster and complex analysis associated with the work of Czamanksi in the 1970s. It deepens the now more involved cluster-based development strategies described in detail by Bergman and Feser (2000) and the methods linking clusters and innovation presented in Bröcker, Dohse and Soltwedel (2003).

In Chapter 10, Abdullah Almasri and Ghazi Shukur introduce and describe an alternative clustering method using wavelet analysis that has the ability to decompose a data set into different scales. The wavelet algorithm is then used to specify the number of clusters and quality of clustering at each scale. The authors illustrate the successfulness and efficiency of this kind of methodology in detecting clusters under different situations.

1.5.3   Clusters in different spatial contexts

Giulio Cainelli, in Chapter 11, presents theoretical and empirical insights concerning one special type of clusters: the industrial districts. In particular, he examines two different aspects taken up in the research on industrial clusters. The first concerns the widely analysed phenomenon of corporate grouping within industrial districts. The second involves the relationships between technological innovation and industrial districts.

In Chapter 12, Michaela Trippl and Franz Tödtling explore conceptually the role of clusters for economic recovery of old industrial regions. They identify three types of cluster-based renewal, distinguishing between an innovation-oriented adjustment of mature clusters (incremental change), the emergence of new agglomerations in established industries (diversification), and the rise of knowledge-intensive and high-technology activities (radical change).

The reciprocal relationship between transnational corporations and clusters is analysed in Chapter 13 by Filip De Beule, Daniël Van Den Bulcke and Haiyan Zhang. Although both transnational corporations and clusters are broadly thought to affect the host economy positively, the two phenomena have normally been studied separately. In this chapter these two phenomena are studied simultaneously with a focus on the specific reciprocal relationship of transnational corporations and local clusters and, in particular, the role of foreign-owned subsidiaries.

Pierre Desrochers, Frédéric Sautet and Gert-Jan Hospers in Chapter 14 make a strong case for diversity and at the same time make a strong case against specialized clusters. In their contribution they re-examine the case against regional specialization by pointing out that it is more likely to result in economic downturns, to prevent the spontaneous creation of inter-industry linkages, and to hamper the creation of innovative ideas through the combination of existing know-how and artefacts than a more diversified economic base.

1.5.4   Sectoral clusters

Chapter 15, by Naresh R. Pandit, Gary A.S. Cook and G.M. Peter Swann, describes how wholesale financial services production clusters in the City of London. They also examine why wholesale financial services production clusters in the City of London. Existing theory on the reasons for financial services clustering is tested against the findings of a large-scale empirical study of financial services clustering in the City of London. The chapter ends with a discussion of the likelihood of continued financial services clustering in the City of London.

It is a commonplace that creative industries are principally urban phenomena and have a strong tendency to be highly agglomerated within a particular city. David Emanuel Andersson and Åke E. Andersson (in Chapter 16) start with the observation that the cultural sector, i.e. the sector producing arts and entertainment goods, is by tradition heavily concentrated in space. However, the degree of clustering differs between different sub-sectors. In this chapter, the concentration is on the film industry and on centres of cultural heritage, which exhibit different reasons for spatial clustering.

Chapter 17, by Gary A.S. Cook and Naresh R. Pandit, focuses on television broadcasting, which is far more highly concentrated than radio broadcasting. They reflect on a number of key issues and debates in the economic geography literature in respect of which the broadcasting industry offers some relevant evidence. The evidence they present indicates that the nature of clustering in broadcasting in Britain is akin to that identified in Hollywood and typical of that claimed to be characteristic of cultural industries more generally.

Ewen J. Michael, in Chapter 18, which deals with tourism clusters, starts with rehearsing the arguments about what constitutes a tourism activity and the issues that confront its development, before considering how the principles of clustering have been interpreted for application in this field. He then draws attention to the work by tourism analysts in micro-cluster formations and the linkages they have established with network theory. The chapter concludes with some considerations on how these principles are now being applied in practice.

Notes

1. For an overview of the contributions of economic geographers and economists to the study of clusters, see Scott (2004).
2. In a precise analysis one has to define the market potential with regard to each specific group of products or each specific group of economic activities. However, here we want to illustrate the impact of a generalized market potential concept, represented by the size and the density of a functional region.
3. Neighbouring firms may in addition include specialized customers, which are attracted by the concentrated and varied supply from similar firms located in the same region, i.e. from the cluster.
4. A formulation like this is in sharp contrast to the so called 'export base' model, according to which economic activities locate independently, whereas the labour supply of households are assumed to adjust to the demand for labour, partly through in-migration. In this case, households follow jobs. Regional change processes of this kind are usually associated with the 'industrial society' characterized by homogenous labour employed in factories.
5. The *Handbook of Research on Innovation and Clusters: Cases and Policies* will contain three sections: (i) high-tech clusters, (ii) cluster case studies, and (iii) cluster policies.

References

Andersson, Å.E. (1985), *Kreativitet – Storstadens framtid*, Stockholm: Prisma.

Andersson, Å.E. (1987), 'Creativity and economic dynamics modelling', in D. Batten, J. Casti and B. Johansson (eds), *Economic Evolution and Structural Adjustment*, Berlin: Springer Verlag, pp. 27–45.

Arrow, K.J. (1979), 'The division of labour in the economy', in G.P. O'Discroll (ed.), *Adam Smith and the Modern Political Economy*, Ames: Iowa State University Press, pp. 153–64

Batten, D.F., K. Kobayashi and Å.E. Andersson (1989), 'Knowledge, nodes and networks: an analytical perspective', in Å.E. Andersson, D.F. Batten and C. Karlsson (eds), *Knowledge and Industrial Organisation*, Berlin: Springer Verlag, pp. 31–46

Beckmann, M. (1958), 'City hierarchies and the distribution of city sizes', *Economic Development and Cultural Change*, **3**, 343–8.

Bergman, E.M. and E.J. Feser (2000), *Industrial and Regional Clusters: Concepts and Applications*, Web Book of Regional Science, Regional Research Institute, Morgontown, WV (www.rri.wvu/WebBook/Bergman-Feser/contents.htm).

Braudel, F. (1979), *Civilisation matérielle, économie et capitalisme XVe-XVIIIe siècle*, Paris: Colin.

Bröcker, J., D. Dohse and R. Soltwedel (2003) (eds), *Innovation Clusters and Interregional Competition*, Berlin: Springer Verlag.

Chamberlin, E. (1933), *The Theory of Monopolistic Competition*, Cambridge, MA: Harvard University Press.

Chipman, J.S. (1970), 'External economies of scale and competitive equilibrium', *Quarterly Journal of Economics*, **72**, 347–85.

Christaller, W. (1933), *Die zentralen Orte in Süddeutschland*, Jena: Gustav Fischer.

Ciccone, A. and R.E. Hall (1996), 'Productivity and the density of economic activity', *American Economic Review*, **86**, 54–70.

Clark, T.N., R. Lloyd, K.K. Wong and P. Jain (2002), 'Amenities drive urban growth', *Journal of Urban Affairs*, **25**, 493–515.

Dixit, R. and V. Norman (1980), *Theory of International Trade*, Cambridge: Cambridge University Press.

Ellison, G. and E.L. Glaeser (1997), 'Geographic concentration in U.S. manufacturing industries: a dartboard approach', *Journal of Political Economy*, **105**, 889–927.

Ethier, W. (1982), 'National and international returns to scale in the modern theory of international trade', *American Economic Review*, **72**, 389–405.

Feldman, M.P. and J. Francis (2004), 'Homegrown solutions: fostering cluster formation', *Economic Development Quarterly*, **18**, 127–37.

Feldman, M.P. and R. Martin (2004), 'Jurisdictional advantage', *NBER Working Paper* No. 10802.

Feldman, M.P. and E. Romanelli (2006), 'Organization legacy and the internal dynamics of clusters: the U.S. human bio-therapeutics industry, 1976–2002', paper presented at the 2006 DRUID Winter Conference.

Feldman, M.P. and Y. Schreuder (1996), 'Initial advantage: the origins of the geographical concentration of the pharmaceutical industry in the mid-Atlantic region', *Industrial and Corporate Change*, **5**, 839–62.

Florida, R. (2002), 'The economic geography of talent', *Annals of the Association of American Geographers*, **92**, 743–55.

Fujita, M. (1989), *Urban Economic Theory*, Cambridge, MA: Cambridge University Press.

Fujita, M., P. Krugman and A.J. Venables (1999), *The Spatial Economy: Cities, Regions and International Trade*, Cambridge, MA: The MIT Press.

Glaeser, E.L., J. Kolko and A. Saiz (2001), 'Consumer city', *Journal of Economic Geography*, **1**, 27–50.

Gordon, I.R. and P. McCann (2000), 'Industrial clusters: complexes, agglomerations and/or social networks', *Urban Studies*, **37**, 513–33.

Helpman, E. (1984), 'Increasing returns, imperfect markets and trade theory', in R. Jones and P. Kenen (eds), *Handbook of International Economics*, Vol. 1, Amsterdam: North Holland, pp. 325–65.

Henderson, J.V. (1986), 'Efficiency of resource usage and city size', *Journal of Urban Economics*, **19**, 47–70.

Hirsch, S. (1967), *Location of Industry and International Competitiveness*, Oxford: Oxford University Press.

Holmberg, I., B. Johansson and U. Strömquist (2003), 'A simultaneous model of long-term regional job and population changes', in Å.E. Andersson, B. Johansson and W.P. Andersson (eds), *The Economics of Disappearing Distance*, Aldershot: Ashgate, pp. 161–89.

Hotelling, H. (1929), 'Stability in competition', *Economic Journal*, **39**, 41–57.

Jacobs, J. (1969), *The Economy of Cities*, New York: Vintage.

Janik, A. and S. Toulmin (1978), *Wittgenstein's Vienna*, New York: Cambridge University Press.

Johansson, B. (1996), 'Location attributes and dynamics of job location', *Journal of Infrastructure, Planning and Management*, **530**, 1–15.

Johansson, B. (1998), 'Infrastructure, market potential and endogenous economic growth', paper presented at the Kyoto workshop, 1997, Department of Civil Engineering, Kyoto University, Japan.

Johansson, B. (2005), 'Parsing the menagerie of agglomeration and network externalities', in C. Karlsson, B. Johansson and R.R. Stough (eds), *Industrial Clusters and Inter-Firm Networks*, Cheltenham, UK and Northampton, MA, USA: Edward Elgar, pp. 107–47.

Johansson, B. and C. Karlsson (2001), 'Geographic transaction costs and specialisation opportunities of small and medium-sized regions: scale economies and market extension', in B. Johansson, C. Karlsson and R.R. Stough (eds), *Theories of Endogenous Regional Growth – Lessons for Regional Policies*, Berlin: Springer Verlag, pp. 150–80.

Kaldor, N. (1970), 'The case for regional policies', *Scottish Journal of Political Economy*, **17**, 337–48.

Karlsson, C., B. Johansson and R.R. Stough (2005), 'Industrial clusters and inter-firm networks: an introduction', in C. Karlsson, B. Johansson and R.R. Stough (eds), *Industrial Clusters and Inter-Firm Networks*, Cheltenham, UK and Northampton, MA, USA: Edward Elgar, pp. 1–25.

Karlsson, C. and L. Pettersson (2006), 'Regional productivity and accessibility to knowledge and dense markets', *Annals of Regional Science* (forthcoming).

Kobayashi, K. (1995), 'Knowledge network and market structure: an analytical perspective', in D.F. Batten, J. Casti and R. Thord (eds), *Networks in Action. Communication, Economics and Human Knowledge*, Berlin: Springer Verlag, pp. 127–58.

Krugman, P. (1979), 'Increasing returns, monopolistic competition and international trade', *Journal of International Economics*, **9**, 469–79.

Krugman, P. (1980), 'Scale economies, product differentiation and the pattern of trade', *American Economic Review*, **70**, 950–59.

Krugman, P. (1981), 'Trade, accumulation, and uneven development', *Journal of Development Economics*, **8**, 149–61.

Krugman, P. (1990), *Rethinking International Trade*, Cambridge, MA: The MIT Press.

Krugman, P. (1991), *Geography and Trade*, Cambridge, MA: The MIT Press.

Koopmans, T.C. (1957), *Three Essays on the State of Economic Science*, New York: McGraw-Hill.

Lakshmanan, T.R. (1989), 'Infrastructure and economic transformation', in Å.E. Andersson, D.F. Batten and B. Johansson (eds), *Advances in Spatial Theory and Dynamics*, Amsterdam: North-Holland, pp. 241–62.

Lakshmanan, T.R. and W.G. Hansen (1965), 'A retail market potential model', *Journal of the American Institute of Planners*, **31**, 134–43.

Lancaster, K. (1980), 'Intra-industry trade under perfect monopolistic competition', *Journal of International Economics*, **10**, 151–75.

Lösch, A. (1943), *Die Raumliche Ordnung der Wirtschaft*, Stuttgart: Gustav Fischer.

Maclellan, D. (1990), 'Urban change through environmental investments', in *Urban Challenges*, Stockholm: Allmänna Förlaget, pp. 51–76.

Maillat, D. (1998), 'Innovative milieux and new generations of regional policies', *Entrepreneurship and Regional Development*, **10**, 1–16.

Malmberg, A. and P. Maskell (2002), 'The elusive concept of localization economies: towards a knowledge-based theory of spatial clustering', *Environment and Planning A*, **34**, 429–49.

Marshall, A. (1920), *Principles of Economics*, London: Macmillan.

Mills, E.S. (1967), 'An aggregative model of resource allocation in a metropolitan area', *American Economic Review*, **57**, 197–210.

Myrdal, G. (1957), *Economic Theory and Under-Developed Regions*, London: Ducksworth.

Nelson, R.R. and S.G. Winter (1982), *An Evolutionary Theory of Economic Change*, Cambridge, MA: Harvard University Press.

Ohlin, B. (1933), *Interregional and International Trade*, Cambridge, MA: Harvard University Press.

Porter, M.E. (1990), *The Competitive Advantage of Nations*, London: Macmillan.

Press, K. (2006), *A Life Cycle for Clusters? The Dynamics of Agglomeration, Change, and Adaptation*, Heidelberg: Physica-Verlag.

Quigley, J. (1990), 'The quality of housing', in *Urban Challenges*, Stockholm: Allmänna Förlaget, pp. 39–50.

Scott, A.J. (2004), 'A perspective of economic geography', *Journal of Economic Geography*, **4**, 479–99.

Sen, A. and T. Smith (1995), *Gravity Models of Spatial Interaction Behaviour*, Berlin: Springer Verlag.

Stigler, G. (1951), 'The division of labour is limited by the extent of the market', *Journal of Political Economy*, **59**, 185–93.

Tichy, G. (1998), 'Clusters: less dispensable and more risky than ever', in M. Steiner (ed.), *Clusters and Regional Specialisation*, London: Pion, pp. 211–25.

Tinbergen, J. (1967), 'The hierarchy model of the size distribution of centres', *Papers of the Regional Science Association*, **20**, 65–80.

von Thünen, J.H. (1826), *Der isolierte Staat in Beziehung auf nationale Ökonomie und Landwirtschaft*, Stuttgart: Gustav Fischer.

Westlund, H. (2006), *Social Capital in the Knowledge Economy. Theory and Empirics*, Berlin: Springer Verlag.

PART ONE

AGGLOMERATION AND CLUSTER THEORY

2 Agglomeration economics
Philip McCann

1 Introduction
Agglomeration economics and the economics of industrial clustering have emerged over the last two decades as central issues of research into economic growth and performance. For both urban and regional economists and also economic geographers, the increased interest in these topics is obviously very welcome indeed. However, as the quantity and variety of research in this field has burgeoned in economics, economic geography, urban planning and even sociology, the mixing, and sometimes rather liberal use, of technical terminology, has led to a certain amount of analytical overlapping, confusion and duplication. For this reason, this chapter will consider the origins and analytical foundations of different views and hypotheses regarding the potential advantages of agglomeration, the structural assumptions underlying agglomeration and clustering, and finally the empirical challenges associated with these issues. The aim of the chapter is therefore to disentangle these various issues and to clarify the analytical foundations of agglomeration economics, as well as to outline the empirical challenges associated with these issues. In order to do this we adopt a transactions-costs framework which has been employed elsewhere. The reason is that this is the most parsimonious way of analytically disentangling these various issues from a range of different approaches and different analytical traditions. As we will see in this chapter, while analytically classifying different types of agglomeration and clusters is itself difficult, the empirical identification of these is also very difficult. As such, the observation and measurement of agglomerations and clusters is a topic which, although it initially appears to be rather straightforward, is actually a topic which requires very careful theoretical and empirical analysis.

2 The importance of clustering and agglomeration
A generally observed phenomenon is that most industrial and commercial activities tend to be clustered together in space. These clusters may take the form of industrial parks, small towns or major cities, and most countries generally exhibit a size and activity distribution of cities (Gabaix, 1999a,b), with different ranges of activities taking place in different centres. This observation, however, raises the obvious question of why it is that activities are generally grouped together geographically and what role this clustering plays in economic growth. How does such industrial clustering affect the economy; are there any dynamic aspects to this clustering; and how rapid are any such changes in the urban economic system? These are all key questions for urban and regional economists and economic geographers, yet the importance of these questions has only really become obvious to other economists over recent years.

Since the end of the 1980s and the beginning of the 1990s there has been a major change in emphasis in regional growth analysis. Prior to this, traditional neoclassical regional growth models (Borts & Stein, 1964) were developed on the basis of the original macrogrowth models of Solow (1956) and Swan (1956). These early regional models, and also their more recent subsequent manifestations (Barro & Sala-i-Martin, 1992), were essentially aspatial in construction. Geography was not explicitly modelled in this framework, with the analytical focus being primarily on the interregional factor allocation conditions. Such models incorporated geography only implicitly in their logic by assuming that, as long as markets were competitive and factors were allocated efficiently, then the factor migration process implicit in the allocation process would itself maximize both the levels of technology and also its interregional diffusion.

As such, technological diffusion across space was assumed to be both maximized and equalized simply by the existence and operation of competitive markets. Economic convergence (Barro & Sala-i-Martin, 1992) across geographical spaces was assumed to be the natural outcome of these one-sector model approaches. At the same time, even heterodox models of regional growth (Dixon & Thirlwall, 1975; McCombie & Thirlwall, 1994) which pointed rather more to divergence than convergence, also had no explicit geographical dimension to them. On the other hand, since the early 1990s, the more recent analytical and empirical approaches to regional growth have tended to be explicitly spatial in their construction, focusing on the types of characteristics of different locations which may contribute to localized growth. These more recent approaches do not assume that interregional technology flows are necessarily maximized by simple factor allocation processes; rather, they consider the conditions under which such flows may or may not occur within a competitive environment. In particular, these more modern regional growth analyses tend to emphasize the role played by agglomeration economies and industrial clustering in promoting both specifically local, as well as national, economic growth. This shift in analytical focus has come about for several reasons: one reason is analytical, the second reason is technological, and a third reason is institutional.

The first reason why cities and industrial clustering have become a central focus of research in economic growth analysis is primarily analytical. This is in response to the major theoretical contributions made by three commentators, Paul Krugman (1991), Michael Porter (1990) and Allen Scott (1988). Although their analytical approaches have differed widely, in that Scott (1988) and Porter (1998) use non-technical approaches and observation-lead approaches, whereas Krugman (1991) adopted a technical microeconomic approach, for all three commentators, the focus of analysis has been on the potential scale economy and efficiency benefits of industrial clustering. Until their work focused attention on the role played by geography, cities and clusters in the determination of national and international trade patterns and growth, most economists outside of the regional science tradition were largely unaware of the importance of these issues. Their work has subsequently opened up discussions of the role which clustering and agglomeration play in economics and business matters to a much wider academic and policy-making audience than was previously the case. In particular, following the insights of new growth theory (Romer, 1986, 1987; Lucas, 1988), the role played by local knowledge spillovers and local labour market skills is now seen to be essential in developing an understanding of local growth processes.

It can be demonstrated, however, that an unequal spatial distribution of activity is a natural outcome of a random process (Ellison & Glaeser, 1997), without any recourse to arguments about economies of scale (Gabaix, 1999a,b). It is therefore clear that other empirical evidence of the importance of locational characteristics is also required in order to provide a justification for the recent interest in cities and industrial clusters.

Fortunately, at the same time as the new theoretical agenda was being developed, there have also been two major empirical agendas developed which indicate the importance of cities and industrial clusters as sources of economic growth. The first is the agenda developed by Glaeser (Glaeser et al., 1992; Ellison & Glaeser, 1997; Gaspar & Glaeser, 1998) which has focused on the development of new ways to identify and evaluate agglomeration economies. Meanwhile, the second empirical agenda is developed on the basis of the work of Jaffe (Jaffe, 1989; Jaffe et al., 1993) and Acs and Audrestch (Audrestch & Feldman, 1996; Audretsch & Stephan, 1996; Acs, 2002), and focuses on ways of identifying empirically local knowledge spillovers using primarily patent and R&D data, and also in some cases spatial statistics (Anselin et al., 1997). These two approaches have produced a wealth of empirical evidence which suggests that economic growth processes are indeed localized in geographical space owing to the presence of agglomeration economies.

The second reason behind the increased interest in the relationship between locational characteristics and regional growth is a technological one. The primary technological development which has contributed to the renewed interest in the economic impacts of agglomeration has been the rapid improvement in information, communications and transportation technologies. These technological advances have improved the ability of corporate and government decision makers to coordinate either market or organizational activities across progressively larger geographical areas. Modern discussions about globalization (Michie, 2003) have highlighted the ability of corporate organizations to exploit resources in a more sophisticated manner across a wider geographical extent. Although the evidence on this point is rather mixed (McCann, 2004) with certain key exceptions, Glaeser (1998) argues that taking a broad view of all the empirical evidence indicates that the aggregate share of total output accounted for by transportation costs has fallen markedly over time (Glaeser & Kohlhasse, 2004). This has led to the greater geographical extending of many markets. At the same time, however, rather than reducing the importance of space and location, modern technology (Gaspar & Glaeser, 1998) is also argued to be partly responsible for the increasing dominance of particular service-oriented (Glaeser, 2005) and 'global' cities (Gordon, 2002; Buck et al., 2005) within the international financial system. This is apparently due to the increased quantity and complexity of the information generated and handled by information technology, and the resulting increased face-to-face interaction required in order to manage and act on this information. Technology has therefore given geographical proximity a renewed importance.

The third reason behind the increased interest in the relationship between locational characteristics and regional growth is an institutional one. Over the last two decades, there have been widespread institutional changes within the global and regional trade frameworks. The movements towards free-trade and integrated market areas such as the EU, NAFTA, ASEAN and MERCOSUR, have meant that the tariff structures associated with national borders may be becoming progressively less important in terms of their effects in shaping a nation's economic performance (Clement et al. 1999; Yeung et al., 1999). The role of trade barriers in determining the geographical patterns of trade is being progressively eroded while, at the same time, such institutional changes also provide for the ever-increasing two-way flows of both labour and capital across space. As such, explanations of the geography of trade patterns based on national factor proportions become progressively less realistic, while explanations based explicitly on the structure of economic geography, and in particular the urban system, become more important.

For these three analytical, technological and institutional reasons, agglomeration economics and the economics of industrial clustering have emerged over the last two decades as central issues of research. For both urban and regional economists and also economic geographers, the increased interest in these topics is obviously very welcome indeed. However, as the quantity and variety of research in this field has burgeoned, the mixing, and sometimes rather liberal use, of technical terminology, has led to a certain amount of analytical overlapping, confusion and duplication, some of which has significant problematic implications for the way we evaluate issues and design public policy. For this reason, it is necessary to consider the nature of agglomeration economics and its links with economic growth, the origins and analytical foundations of different views and hypotheses regarding the advantages of agglomeration, the structural assumptions underlying agglomeration and clustering.

3   Agglomeration, clusters and innovation

In order to account for the fact that economic activities and people are generally clustered together in space, it is necessary in part to adopt the notion that economies of scale can be place-specific. This assumption is essential, because the clustering of activities in space increases competition for land, and in turn increases in nominal local labour prices are required in order to maintain real wages. The overall resulting increases in both local land and labour prices will increase the costs and reduce the profitability of local firms, unless there are some more than compensating benefits associated with clustering. As has already been mentioned, it can be demonstrated that an unequal spatial distribution of activity is a natural outcome of a random process (Ellison & Glaeser, 1997; Gabaix, 1999a,b), without making any assumptions about the operation of economies of scale. However, in order for such uneven patterns not to disappear in response to localized factor price inflation, we still require some positive localized advantages to exist in order to sustain an equal expected growth rate in large as well as small clusterings of activity. Consequently, it is not necessary for us to assume systematically faster growth in larger cities in order to explain clustering and agglomeration, but it is necessary to accept that some clustering and agglomeration advantages must exist in order to explain why growth does not tend to slow down systematically as centres grow and rents rise.

Such location-specific economies of scale are generally known as agglomeration economies, and following Marshall's (1920) original discussion these economies are generally understood to be external economies, which are independent of a single firm, but which accrue to all of the firms located in the same area. Marshall provided three reasons why such localized economies of scale might exist, namely local knowledge spillovers, local non-traded inputs produced under scale economies, and a local skilled labour pool.

Firstly, industrial clustering allows for frequent direct informal face-to-face contact between individuals, and this may allow for tacit knowledge to be shared between firms. The advantage of spatial clustering in this case is therefore that proximity maximizes the mutual accessibility of all individuals within the cluster, thereby improving the knowledge spillovers available to all local participants. This may be particularly advantageous in market environments characterized by rapidly changing information. Secondly, industrial clustering provides for the possibility that certain specialist inputs can be provided to the local group in a more efficient manner than would be the case if all of the firms were geographically dispersed. Thirdly, the spatial grouping of firms also allows for the creation of a local specialized labour pool, thereby reducing labour hiring and search costs, and also providing a risk reduction mechanism in the face of firm-specific demand fluctuations.

Directly observing these Marshallian effects in reality can be very difficult. Therefore, in practice, urban and regional economists generally employ an Ohlin–Hoover classification (Ohlin, 1933; Hoover, 1937, 1948), which splits agglomeration economies into three types, namely internal returns to scale, localization economies, and urbanization economies. Internal returns to scale do not strictly fit with the Marshallian notion of agglomeration, which is based on externalities. However, location-specific economies of scale which are internal to a firm imply that significant stocks of both labour and capital will be spatially concentrated at one particular location. This can then contribute to the development of the other two forms of agglomeration economies, namely localization economies and urbanization economies. The difference between these two cases is that, if the agglomeration benefits accrue to activities in the same sector located at the same place these are termed 'localization economies', whereas, if the benefits accrue to a diverse range of local sectors, they are termed 'urbanization economies'. In terms of the mechanisms by which agglomeration externalities are transmitted, each of Marshall's sources of agglomeration can contribute to the development of either localization economies or urbanization economies. However, while the distinction between the Ohlin–Hoover agglomeration categories initially appears to be primarily related to the definitional boundaries of the firms and sectors in which the externality benefits accrue locally, there are also qualitative differences in the observed outcomes. In the case of localization economies, the Marshallian externalities are generally associated with the development of industrial clusters of particular sectors. On the other hand, in the case of urbanization economies, the externality benefits accrue to firms across different sectors (Jacobs, 1960) located in the same place. It is these overall urbanization economies which are normally regarded as the typical agglomeration benefits associated with large cities (Duranton & Puga, 2000), whereby the city-urbanization effects are generally assumed to comprise a range of lower-order localization economies. On the other hand, in the case of smaller cities, it may be that a small number of individual sectors will tend to dominate the city, rather than the city dominating the individual sectors (Duranton & Puga, 2000).

The notion that cities and clusters represent location-specific economies of scale, however, is still a rather static notion which is hard to relate to economic growth, unless we also introduce some dynamic elements to the activities and characteristics of cities and clusters. Although the simple Marshallian description allows for knowledge spillovers, no discussion of the types of knowledge or the role of the knowledge spillovers in local economic growth is provided; this can be achieved by incorporating notions of knowledge acquisition, learning and the evolution in knowledge within the spillovers-type framework. While modern growth theory emphasizes the role played by knowledge in the aggregate macro-growth process, modern thinking about agglomeration and clusters emphasizes the intermediate role played by cities in facilitating the process of knowledge generation, information transmission and firm creation. The analytical focus of agglomeration economics is therefore on the relationship between industrial clusters, cities and innovation, and the study of agglomeration economics has consequently emerged as something of a hybrid subject, which combines insights regarding increasing returns to scale and externalities from economics, with insights regarding processes of innovation from management studies, science and technology policy analysis, regional planning and economic geography.

The hybrid nature of the subject is also reflected in the variety of models and analytical approaches which are adopted. There are currently five families of models, plus variants thereof, which deal with the relationship between industrial clusters, agglomeration and innovation, and which are widely used in the literature. These are the growth pole model (Perroux, 1950; Boudeville, 1966), the incubator or nursery-cities model (Chinitz, 1961, 1964; Duranton & Puga, 2001), the product cycle model (Vernon, 1966, 1979; Markusen, 1985), the Porter (1990, 1998) clusters model and the new industrial areas and innovative milieux models (Scott, 1988; Saxenian, 1994; Aydalot & Keeble, 1988; Paniccia, 2002; Becattini, 2004). The first three families of models originally emerged during the 1960s, whereas the latter two families of models reflect developments during the last two decades. Not surprisingly, these various families of models tend to emphasize different aspects of the possible relationship between geography and innovation.

The growth pole model (Perroux, 1950) and its spatial manifestation (Boudeville, 1966) employed some of the ideas of Schumpeter (1934) in emphasizing the ways in which economic relationships can exhibit certain polarities regarding the particular network structures via which financial transactions are mediated. In particular, the decisions made by large 'polar' firms have major financial implications for the behaviour of other firms via the logic of buyer–supplier relationships. As such, many firms may not be independent or free to act of their own accord, and therefore the innovation behaviour of an individual firm alone may not be of significance. Rather, firm innovation behaviour may only be both possible when it is congruent with the behaviour of the key large firms linked in the same financial networks. On this argument, knowledge of these network structures and the behaviour of key large local firms will be essential for innovation, and proximity may engender such knowledge, thereby leading to significant local growth effects. At the other end of the analytical spectrum, however, is the incubator or nursery-city model of Chinitz (1961) and Duranton and Puga (2001), which argues that cities which are highly diversified and which contain a broad range of different types of industries and firm sizes will act as superior 'incubators' for the development and growth of both new and small firms, because in such environments there will be a variety of local business services available for supporting these small firms. On this argument, knowledge, the size distribution of a city or cluster is critical for innovation. Therefore, while the growth pole and the incubator hypotheses both suggest that geographical proximity is essential for innovation, the former hypothesis focuses on the key role played by large firms, whereas the latter hypothesis focuses on the importance of sectoral diversity.

The third alternative analytical approach to dealing with the relationship between industrial clusters, agglomeration and innovation is the product cycle model (Vernon, 1960; Markusen, 1985). The original product cycle argument suggested that the relationship between geography and innovation depended on the relationship between the location behaviour of firms and the structure of the urban system (Vernon, 1960). In particular, firms will tend to separate activities by location according to the stage in the life-cycle of the product. Following the subsequent work of Vernon (1966), later explicitly spatial versions of this model assume that the innovation behaviour of a geographical area is directly related to the way the location behaviour of large oligopolistic firms (Markusen, 1985) is related to the structure of the urban system. The general conclusions of this model are that, in dominant central cities, such oligopolistic firms will tend to locate information-intensive activities such as R&D and high level decision making, all of which relate to the early stages of the product life-cycle, while at the same time locating facilities producing more mature, less novel and rather standardized products in more geographically peripheral areas with lower labour costs and skills. The outcome of this behaviour is that there will tend to emerge a clear separation and qualitative distinction between activity types in central city-regions and those in more peripheral areas. In particular, only central areas will be characterized by the production of innovative activities.

Although each of these three approaches to understanding the relationship between industrial clustering, cities and innovation first emerged during the 1960s, they underpin many current lines of analysis. In addition, however, the two more recent approaches to understanding the relationship between clusters, cities and innovation have been developed. These two new models are the clusters model of Porter (1990) and the new industrial spaces model (Scott, 1988).

Porter's (1990) cluster model argues that geographical proximity facilitates mutual visibility and transparency between competitors. In others words, firms are able to observe the competitive developments of each other, and this mutual visibility and transparency itself acts as a spur to all local firms to continue to improve their own individual competitiveness. The result of this process of localized competition is that the competitiveness of the local industrial cluster as a whole is increased. This argument applies equally to both large firms and small firms, although Porter assumes that spatial clustering of firms in the same sector is particularly important for small firms which rely mainly on external sources of information and technology.

The fifth and final approach to understanding the relationship between industrial clustering, cities and innovation is provided by the literature on new industrial areas (Scott, 1988). Recent observations and anecdotal evidence suggest that the growth of regions dominated by large numbers of small firms, such as Silicon Valley and the Emilia-Romagna region of Italy (Scott, 1988), appears to be related crucially to innovation, at least in certain industrial sectors. These observations have led to suggestions from many observers that industries which are made up of spatial clusters of small firms tend to be more highly innovative than industries comprising mainly large firms (Saxenian, 1994). The reason for this is that innovation is assumed to be most likely to occur in small and medium-sized enterprises, which have neither the scale nor the risk-bearing capacity to provide all of the key inputs on their own account, and the geographical proximity of SMEs is assumed to be a key criterion for the development of mutual trust relations based on a shared experience of interaction with decision-making agents in different firms. The origin of these arguments is in the social network theory analysis of environments which reduce opportunism and promote trust between local firms. These arguments regarding what is termed 'social capital' have recently been introduced into economics (Glaeser et al., 2000, 2002) and imply that certain types of social environments provide the appropriate 'milieux' for innovations to take place (Aydalot and Keeble, 1988), primarily because firms are willing to cooperate selectively as well as compete, and individuals are willing to share information. The key development here is the integration between human capital (as defined simply in terms of skills and education) and interpersonal networking to produce 'social capital'. Currently popular twists on these arguments have also been introduced by Florida (2003) who promotes the concept of 'creativity' on the part of unorthodox 'bohemian' social groups, as a key driver of local, and particularly urban, economic development. The problem with the Florida concept of 'creativity', however, is that it is empirically indistinguishable from more general orthodox human capital arguments about the important role played by people who generate new ideas (Glaeser, 2004).

Agglomeration economies are to some extent, therefore, a 'black box', and each of these families of analytical models therefore provides a different insight and possible explanation of the workings of agglomeration economies. However, in order to identify the likely workings of a particular agglomeration or industrial cluster it is necessary to find a common system of reference, which allows us to compare and contrast these different approaches. By far the most parsimonious way to do this is to employ a transactions-costs framework in which the analytical focus is on the nature and stability of the relations between firms within an agglomeration. The original framework (Gordon & McCann, 2000) has since been used extensively in different contexts (Gordon & McCann, 2005a; McCann, 2004; McCann & Sheppard, 2003; McCann & Shefer, 2004; McCann & Mudambi, 2004, 2005; Simmie & Sennet, 1999) because it is both the simplest and also the most comprehensive organizing framework available for understanding the possible micro-foundations of industrial clusters and agglomerations.

4   Clusters, firm types and the nature of transactions

Adopting the transactions costs framework approach, we can see from the literature that there are three broad typologies of agglomerations and industrial clusters, defined in terms of the features they exhibit (Gordon & McCann, 2000). These are the *pure agglomeration*, the *industrial complex*, and the *social network*. The key feature which distinguishes each of these different ideal types of spatial industrial cluster is the nature of the relations between the firms within the cluster. The characteristics of each of the cluster types are listed in Table 2.1 and, as we see, the three ideal types of clusters are all quite different.

In the model of pure agglomeration, inter-firm relations are inherently transient. Firms are essentially atomistic, in the sense of having no market power, and they will continuously change their relations with other firms and customers in response to market arbitrage opportunities, thereby leading to intense local competition. Consequently, there is no loyalty between firms, nor are any particular relations long-term. The external benefits of clustering accrue to all local firms simply by reason of their local presence, the price of which is the local real estate market rent. There are no free-riders, access to the cluster is open, and consequently it is the growth in the local real estate rents which is the indicator of the cluster's performance. This idealized type is best represented by the pure Marshall (1920), Chinitz (1961) and Jacobs (1960) models, as well as the more recent new economic geography models (Fujita et al., 1999; Fujita & Thisse, 2002). The industrial structure represented by these models is that of monopolistic competition, and the notion of space is essentially urban space. In other words, this type of clustering only exists within individual cities. The empirical verification of this pure agglomeration phenomenon relies on evidence of localized productivity growth, associated with growth in local real estate prices, real wages and employment.

The industrial complex is characterised primarily by long-term stable and predictable relations between the firms in the cluster. This type of cluster is the type of spatial cluster typically discussed by classical (Weber, 1909) and neoclassical (Moses, 1958) location–production models, and represents a fusion of locational analysis with input–output

Table 2.1 Industrial clusters

Characteristics	Pure agglomeration	Industrial complex	Social network
Firm size	atomistic	some firms are large	variable
Characteristics of relations	non-identifiable fragmented unstable	identifiable stable trading	trust loyalty joint lobbying joint ventures non-opportunistic
Membership	open	closed	partially open
Access to cluster	rental payments location necessary	internal investment location necessary	history experience location necessary but not sufficient
Space outcomes	rent appreciation	no effect on rents	partial rental capitalization
Notion of space	urban	local but not urban	local but not urban
Example of cluster	competitive urban economy	steel or chemicals production complex	new industrial areas
Analytical approaches	models of pure agglomeration	location–production theory input–output analysis	social network theory (Granovetter)

analysis. Component firms within the spatial grouping each undertake significant long-term investments, particularly in terms of physical capital and local real estate, in order to become part of the grouping. Access to the group is therefore severely restricted by both high entry and exit costs, and the rationale for spatial clustering in these types of industries is that proximity is required primarily in order to minimize inter-firm transport transactions costs. Rental appreciation is not a feature of the cluster, because the land which has already been purchased by the firms is not for sale, nor are the informal knowledge spillovers evident in the model of pure agglomeration (McCann & Mudambi, 2004, 2005). This ideal type of cluster more closely reflects the internal returns to scale arguments of Hoover as well as aspects of the spatial growth pole model of Perroux (1950) and Boudeville (1966) and the spatial product cycle model of Markusen (1985). The literature on these types of inter-firm relations has typically focused on traditional commodities-based sectors (Isard & Kuenne, 1953) such as steel, chemical and pharmaceuticals. However, this notion of stable and well-defined inter-firm relations is equally applicable to any modern high-technology sectors running tightly-coordinated supply chains or Just-In-Time (JIT) production systems, such as aerospace, automobiles, electronics (McCann, 1997), or more standardized or lower-technology contemporary commercial sectors, such as food processing or supermarket retailing. Even some elements of the financial services industry such as retail banking and mortgage provision will fall into this grouping. The key issue here is that the industrial structure within the complex exhibits primarily oligopoly characteristics, and the notion of space in the complex model is local, but not necessarily urban. In other words, these types of local industrial clusters can exist either within, outside or beyond the limits of an individual city. The empirical verification of the industrial complex phenomenon relies on evidence of long-term and stable inter-firm transactions (McCann, 1997) and good examples of the types of possible approaches here are demonstrated by Feser and Bergman (2000), Feser and Sweeney (2000, 2002) and Feser et al. (2005).

The third type of spatial industrial cluster is the social network model. This is associated primarily with the work of Granovetter (1973, 1985), and is a response to the markets and hierarchies model of Williamson (1975). Whereas the pure agglomeration model and the industrial complex described above represent the clustered spatial equivalents of the market and the hierarchy alternative modes of coordination, the social network model argues that mutual trust relations between key decision-making agents in different organizations may be at least as important as decision-making hierarchies within individual organizations. The key feature of such trust relations is an absence of opportunism, in that individual firms will not fear reprisals after any reorganization of inter-firm relations. Inter-firm cooperative relations may therefore differ significantly from the organizational boundaries associated with individual firms, and these relations may be continually reconstituted. All of these behavioural features rely on a common culture of mutual trust, the development of which depends largely on a shared history and experience of the decision-making agents. This social network model is essentially aspatial, but, from the point of view of geography, it can be argued that spatial proximity will tend to foster such trust relations, thereby leading to a local business environment of confidence, risk taking and cooperation. Spatial proximity is necessary but not sufficient to acquire access to the network. As such, membership of the network is only partially open, in that local rental payments will not guarantee access, although they will improve the chances of access. The social network model therefore contains some elements of the Porter model (1990, 1998), but primarily it is associated with the new industrial areas model (Scott, 1988). In this model space is once again local, but not necessarily urban, and may extend across a broader definition of a city-region. These trust relations will be manifested by a variety of features, such as joint lobbying, joint ventures, informal alliances and reciprocal arrangements regarding trading relationships.

In reality, all spatial concentrations of economic activity will exhibit at least one of these cluster types, and the case of large cities will exhibit aspects of all three models. An important point here is that pure agglomerations are most definitely clusters, albeit one particular and specific type of cluster. The approach of some economic geographers which assumes that only the social network model really represents a genuine cluster is analytically nonsense, and the comparison between the different cluster concepts provides powerful insights. The reason is that all three of these industrial cluster types exhibit economies of scale which can compensate either for local factor price appreciation or for the costs involved in the overcoming of geographical space.

Following these arguments, if we assume that one of the major functions of cities, agglomerations and industrial clusters is not only to reduce the costs of spatial inter-firm transactions but also to generate new ideas and new firms, then each of these three models of agglomeration clustering can also be associated with increased levels of innovation relative to other locations. This is very important when we consider macroeconomic growth as well as regional growth. From an empirical perspective, however, the important point is to identify exactly what are the dominant transactions costs features of the agglomeration or industrial cluster in question, by assessing the stability, longevity and loyalty of inter-firm transactions and relations. Only by doing this can we clearly identify the microeconomic rationale for the existence of each agglomeration or industrial cluster.

5 Agglomeration measurement problems

Measuring agglomeration effects directly is problematic for the reasons outlined in the above section. Pure agglomeration, by definition, is an externality phenomenon and, as such, cannot be observed directly. Therefore, such effects can only be observed indirectly by observing, for example, the growth in local real estate prices and the associated growth in the local real wages and employment, as these will be the only tangible outcomes of the pure form of agglomeration. The productivity effects of agglomeration appear to be related to employment density (Ciccone & Hall, 1996). However, the local density of employment activities is not of itself sufficient evidence of agglomeration because, as we have seen, the pure agglomeration is also characterized by frequent and unstable trading relations among broadly atomistic firms. Evidence for the prevalence of these types of trading relations must also be provided. On the other hand, the empirical verification of the industrial complex phenomenon is based on evidence of long-term and stable inter-firm transactions among oligopolistic firms, along with local employment and wage growth, while the types of evidence suggestive of the existence of local social networks will be joint lobbying, joint ventures, informal alliances and reciprocal arrangements regarding trading relationships, between primarily small firms, along with employment and wage growth. Once again, in each of these cases, evidence for the prevalence of the appropriate types of trading relations or alliances must also be provided.

Unfortunately, in reality, evidence of particular types of trading relations or alliances is often very hard to find, as it requires large-scale micro-level surveys (Arita & McCann, 2000; Gordon & McCann, 2000, 2005b), and the empirical identification of the particular scale effects which contribute to specific examples of industrial clustering is therefore very difficult. As such, the actual effect of agglomeration externalities on each industrial sector, or range of sectors, is in general a priori not identifiable, and therefore ex post indirect measures are normally adopted to try to identify the effects of such externalities. In practice, observations of sectoral employment distributions in particular localities have become the most commonly used method of identifying the operation of either urbanization or localization economies. In situations of industrial clustering and employment density, indices of sectoral employment specialization and diversity are employed as proxies for various types of local agglomeration effects. In particular, indices which point to local employment specialization are treated as evidence of localization economies, while indices which point to employment diversity are treated as evidence of urbanization economies. This approach, however, is not as straightforward as might be supposed. It is a standard technique in applied regional input–output modelling to relate local employment patterns to trade patterns (Dewhurst & McCann, 1998; McCann, 2001) and this is done by treating data on the former as a proxy for the latter. However, this is a very indirect approach, the weakness of which is that it is based on the assumption of universal Leontief production and consumption technologies. In a similar vein, using measures of local employment variety as evidence of either localization or urbanization economies is also problematic, because such an approach is based on the strong new economic geography assumption that there is a direct correspondence between the variety of local production, the variety of local employment and the variety of regional trade relationships.

There are four major problems associated with using local labour or employment data in the assessment of agglomeration externalities. Firstly, using employment data to distinguish between localization economies (Marshall, 1920) and urbanization economies

(Hoover, 1948; Jacobs, 1960) is problematic from an empirical perspective, because the results of these models appear to be sensitive to the level of sectoral aggregation used (Glaeser et al., 1992; Henderson et al., 1995). Unfortunately, there is no theoretical guidance as to what is the most appropriate level of sectoral disaggregation. Moreover, the distinction between the three Ohlin–Hoover agglomeration classifications is rather arbitrary in many cases, given that mergers and acquisitions mean that firms are frequently changing ownership and sectors without necessarily changing either their locations or the nature of many of their transactions. This latter issue is particularly pertinent in the case of many service industries (Cohen, 1998).

Secondly, identifying whether industrial clustering is indeed actually due primarily to the existence of localized externalities, or rather is simply the outcome of similar location optimization behaviour by similar firms (McCann, 1995), is also empirically very difficult, and really requires additional microeconomic data on transactions and buyer–supplier relationships (Gordon & McCann, 2000, 2005b).

Thirdly, the various measures and indices of industrial specialization, based on local sectoral employment distributions which are available to us, themselves often produce quite conflicting results, with the relative rankings of different places being rather unstable, depending on which index is employed (Dewhurst & McCann, 2002).

Fourthly, the results of diversity index calculations types are very sensitive to the size of the geographical areas employed for the data aggregation (Dewhurst & McCann, 2007). It is a well-known observation that larger cities are generally more industrially diversified than smaller cities (Duranton & Puga, 2000), and this tends to suggest that urbanization economies dominate in larger cities while localization economies tend to dominate in smaller cities. However, the smaller is the area of analysis, *ceteris paribus*, the greater will be the apparent levels of specialization, while the larger is the area, the greater will be the apparent level of diversity. This endogeneity of the area size is a variation on the modifiable unit area problem (Openshaw & Taylor, 1979), and needs to be controlled for.

Moreover, even if we are able to overcome these four measurement problems, in addition, there are two other problems with empirically confirming that knowledge spillovers are a driver of localized agglomeration effects, and this concerns the evidence regarding the link between innovation and cities.

Firstly, while there is much evidence to suggest that in many cases the critical distance over which urban agglomeration externalities operate may be that of the city-metropolitan area (Gordon & McCann, 2005b), as is assumed by the pure agglomeration model. However, there is also much evidence to suggest that, for many firm-types and industries, the critical distances over which urban agglomeration externalities operate may be very much larger than that of the city-region (Arita & McCann, 2000; Caniels, 2000; Cantwell & Iammarino, 2000, 2003; Simmie, 1998; Suarez-Villa & Walrod, 1997), as is assumed by the industrial complex model and the social network model. Spatial econometrics may be able to help identify such critical distances, but this would involve re-estimating spatial models of the same overall areas for different nested subsets of regions.

Secondly, there is also much evidence to suggest that, while the link between innovation and cities can be strong in certain sectors (Acs, 2002), the evidence on these issues is not always conclusive. Cities do not always appear to be centres of innovation, nor does innovation necessarily appear to be centred on cities (Simmie, 2001; Simmie & Sennet,

1999). The reasons for these many exceptions to the simple standard hypotheses depend on how both the origins of innovation, and also the processes by which innovation emerges, relate to the different cluster concepts outlined in Table 2.1. These are complicated issues and depend on the nature of both technical and technological change. A detailed discussion of these issues can be found in Iammarino and McCann (2006).

Each of the above issues implies that identifying and measuring agglomeration economies is actually a major analytical and empirical challenge. Moreover, the balance between local specialization and diversity appears to have no effect on real wage growth (Glaeser et al., 1992) or on labour productivity (Henderson, 2003; Henderson & Thisse, 2004). This evidence implies that indices of sectoral employment diversity may not be so powerful for distinguishing between localization or urbanization economies because, in actual fact, industrial sectors may not be so relevant in explaining agglomeration economies. This largely accords with the transactions costs argument in section 3, which suggests that firm size and the nature of transactions and inter-firm relations is critical for understanding the nature of agglomeration, rather than the sectoral distributions per se. All three cluster typologies are consistent with colocated firms being either from the same sector or from a variety of different industries, although the pure agglomeration is probably more likely to be sectorally diversified than the industrial complex or the social network.

A final point concerns the issue of declining clusters. Areas such as spatially grouped industries or cities, which previously exhibited both a geographic concentration of activities and also appreciations in factor returns, but which now experience declining returns and investment, pose both an empirical and an analytical challenge to our concepts of agglomeration and clustering. In terms of our definition of clusters, such declining areas still exhibit a relatively high geographical concentration of activities, in comparison to many other localities. In this sense they are cities and clusters. However, declining factor returns implies that the congestion aspects of clustering are not compensated for by location-specific positive externalities. In this sense, these are no longer either agglomerations or clusters. Rather, such localities can be classified simply as cities or as spatially grouped industries, the characteristics of which depend on previous historical issues rather than on current productivity performance (McCann, 1995), unless the previously depressed locality is now once again exhibiting a resurgence (McCann, 1995), as is the case with the modern gentrification of many large cities which had initially emerged as industrial centres in the nineteenth century (Boddy & Parkinson 2004).

6 Conclusions

This chapter has reviewed the reasons for the dramatic increase in interest over recent decades in research concerning agglomeration economics and industrial clustering. As we have seen, this interest has arisen from a variety of sources, from a variety of analytical approaches and disciplines, and from a variety of observations from different contexts. While this burgeoning interest is very welcome indeed, it is important to consider the analytical origins and foundations of these different approaches and their associated terminology, because many of these approaches are based on different implicit assumptions. A comparison of these different analytical logics allows us to identify the specific ways in which we might be able to identify both the micro-working of particular types of agglomeration economies, and also empirical challenges that we need to overcome.

References

Acs, Z. (2002), *Innovation and the Growth of Cities*, Cheltenham, UK and Northampton, MA, US: Edward Elgar.
Anselin, L., A. Varga and Z. Acs (1997), 'Local geographical spillovers between university research and high technology innovations', *Journal of Urban Economics*, **42**, 422–48.
Arita, T. and P. McCann (2000), 'Industrial alliances and firm location behaviour: some evidence from the US semiconductor industry', *Applied Economics*, **32**, 1391–403.
Audretsch, D.B. and M.P. Feldman (1996), 'R&D spillovers and the geography of innovation and production', *American Economic Review*, **86**(3), 630–40.
Audretsch, D.B. and P.E. Stephan (1996), 'Company–scientist locational links: the case of biotechnology', *American Economic Review*, **86**, 641–52.
Aydalot, P. and D. Keeble (1988), *Milieux Innovateurs en Europe*, Paris: GREMI.
Barro, R.J. and X. Sala-i-Martin (1992), 'Convergence', *Journal of Political Economy*, **100**, 223–51.
Becattini, G. (2004), *Industrial Districts: A New Approach to Industrial Change*, Cheltenham, UK and Northampton, MA, US: Edward Elgar.
Boddy, M. and M. Parkinson (2004), *City Matters: Competitiveness, Cohesion and Governance*, Bristol: Policy Press.
Borts, G.H. and J.L. Stein (1964), *Economic Growth in a Free Market*, New York: Free Press.
Boudeville, J.R. (1966), *Problems of Regional Planning*, Edinburgh: Edinburgh University Press.
Buck, N., I.R. Gordon, A. Harding and I. Turok (eds) (2005), *Changing Cities*, London: Routledge.
Caniels, M.C.J. (2000), *Knowledge Spillovers and Economic Growth*, Cheltenham, UK and Northampton, MA, US: Edward Elgar.
Cantwell, J.A. and S. Iammarino (2000), 'Multinational corporations and the location of technological innovation in the UK regions', *Regional Studies*, **34**(4), 317–32.
Cantwell, J.A. and S. Iammarino (2003), *Multinational Corporations and European Regional Systems of Innovation*, London: Routledge.
Chinitz, B. (1961), 'Contrasts in agglomeration: New York and Pittsburgh', *American Economic Review*, **51**, 279–89.
Chinitz, B. (1964), *City and Suburb*, Englewood Cliffs, NJ: Prentice-Hall.
Ciccone, A. and R.E. Hall (1996), 'Productivity and the density of Economic activity', *American Economic Review*, **86**, 54–70.
Clement. N.C., G. del Castillo Vera, J. Gerber, W.A. Kerr, A.J. MacFadyen, S. Shedd, E. Zepeda and D. Alarcon (1999), *North American Economic Integration: Theory and Practice*, Cheltenham, UK and Northampton, MA, US: Edward Elgar.
Cohen, B. (1998), *The Geography of Money*, Ithaca, NY: Cornell University Press.
Dewhurst, J.H.L. and P. McCann (1998), 'Regional size, industrial location and input–output coefficients', *Regional Studies*, **32**(5), 435–44.
Dewhurst, J.H.L. and P. McCann (2002), 'A comparison of measures of industrial specialization for travel-to-work areas in Great Britain, 1981–1997', *Regional Studies*, **316**(5), 541–51.
Dewhurst, J.H.L. and P. McCann (2007), 'Specialisation and regional size', in B. Fingleton (ed.), *New Directions in Economic Geography*, Cheltenham, UK and Northampton, MA, US: Edward Elgar.
Dixon, R.J. and A.P. Thirlwall (1975), *Regional Growth and Unemployment in the United Kingdom*, London: Macmillan.
Duranton, G. and D. Puga (2000), 'Diversity and specialisation in cities: where and when does it matter?', *Urban Studies*, **37**(3), 533–55.
Duranton, G. and D. Puga (2001), 'Nursery cities: urban diversity, process innovation, and the life cycle of products', *American Economic Review*, **91**(5), 1454–77.
Ellison, G. and E.L. Glaeser (1997), 'Geographic concentration in US manufacturing industries: a dartboard approach', *Journal of Political Economy*, **105**, 889–927.
Feser, E.J. and E.M. Bergman (2000), 'National industry cluster templates: a framework for applied regional cluster analysis', *Regional Studies*, **34**, 1–19.
Feser, E.J. and S.H. Sweeney (2000), 'A test for the coincident economic and spatial clustering of business enterprises', *Journal of Geographical Systems*, **2**, 349–73.
Feser, E.J. and S.H. Sweeney (2002), 'Theory, methods, and a cross-metropolitan comparison of business clustering', in P. McCann (ed.), *Industrial Location Economics*, Cheltenham, UK and Northampton, MA, US: Edward Elgar, pp. 222–59.
Feser, E.J., S.H. Sweeney and H. Renski (2005), 'A descriptive analysis of discrete US industrial complexes', *Journal of Regional Science*, **45**(2), 395–415.
Florida, R. (2003), *The Rise of the Creative Class*, New York: Basic Books.
Fujita, M. and J.F. Thisse (2002), *Economics of Agglomeration*, Cambridge: Cambridge University Press.
Fujita, M., P. Krugman and A.J. Venables (1999), *The Spatial Economy: Cities, Regions and International Trade*, Cambridge, MA: MIT Press.

Gabaix, Z. (1999a), 'Zipf's law and the growth of cities', *American Economic Review: Papers and Proceedings*, **89**(2), 129–32.

Gabaix, Z. (1999b), 'Zipf's law for cities: an explanation', *Quarterly Journal of Economics*, **114**(3), 739–67.

Gaspar, J. and E.L. Glaeser (1998), 'Information technology and the future of cities', *Journal of Urban Economics*, **43**, 136–56.

Glaeser, E.L. (1998), 'Are cities dying?', *Journal of Economic Perspectives*, **12**(2), 139–60.

Glaeser, E.L. (2004), 'Book review of Richard Florida's *The Rise of the Creative Class*' (http://post.economics.harvard.edu/faculty/glaeser/papers.html).

Glaeser, E.L. (2005), 'Urban colossus: why is New York America's largest city?', *Federal Reserve Bank of New York Economic Policy Review*, **11**(2), 7–24.

Glaeser, E.L. and J. Kohlhasse (2004), 'Cities, regions and the decline of transport costs', *Papers in Regional Science*, **83**(1), 197–228.

Glaeser, E.L., D.I. Laibson and B. Sacerdote (2002), 'An economic approach to social capital', *Economic Journal*, **112**(483), 437–58.

Glaeser, E.L., D.I. Laibson, J. Scheinkman and C.L. Soutter (2000), 'Measuring trust', *Quarterly Journal of Economics*, **115**, 811–46.

Glaeser, E., H.D. Kallal, J.A. Schinkmann and A. Shleifer (1992), 'Growth in cities', *Journal of Political Economy*, **100**, 1126–52.

Gordon, I.R. (2002), 'Global cities, internationalization and urban systems', in P. McCann (ed.), *Industrial Location Economics*, Cheltenham, UK and Northampton, MA, US: Edward Elgar, pp. 187–206.

Gordon, I.R. and P. McCann (2000), 'Industrial clusters, complexes, agglomeration and/or social networks?', *Urban Studies*, **37**, 513–32.

Gordon, I.R. and P. McCann (2005a), 'Clusters, innovation and regional development: an analysis of current theories and evidence', in B. Johansson, C. Karlsson and R. Stough (eds), *Entrepreneurship, Spatial Industrial Clusters and Inter-Firm Networks*, Cheltenham, UK and Northampton, MA, US: Edward Elgar.

Gordon, I.R. and P. McCann (2005b), 'Innovation, agglomeration and regional development', *Journal of Economic Geography*, **5**(5), 523–43.

Granovetter, M. (1973), 'The strength of weak ties', *American Journal of Sociology*, **78**, 1360–89.

Granovetter, M. (1985), 'Economic action and social structure: the problem of embeddedness', *American Journal of Sociology*, **91**, 481–510.

Henderson, J.V. (2003), 'The urbanization process and economic growth: the so-what question', *Journal of Economic Growth*, **8**(1), 47–71.

Henderson, J.V. and J.F. Thisse (eds) (2004), *Handbook of Regional and Urban Economics*, vol. 4, Amsterdam: North Holland.

Henderson, J.V., A. Kuncoro and M. Turner (1995), 'Industrial development in cities', *Journal of Political Economy*, **103**, 1067–85.

Hoover, E.M. (1937), *Location Theory and the Shoe and Leather Industries*, Cambridge, MA: Harvard University Press.

Hoover, E.M. (1948), *The Location of Economic Activity*, New York: McGraw-Hill.

Iammarino, S. and P. McCann (2006), 'The structure and evolution of industrial clusters: transactions, technology and knowledge spillovers', *Research Policy*, **35**, 1018–36.

Isard, W. and R.E. Kuenne (1953), 'The impact of steel upon the greater New York–Philadelphia industrial region', *Review of Economics and Statistics*, **35**, 289–301.

Jacobs, J. (1960), *The Economy of Cities*, New York: Random House.

Jaffe, A.B. (1989), 'Real effects of academic research', *American Economic Review*, **79**, 957–70.

Jaffe, A.B., M. Trajtenberg and R. Henderson (1993), 'Geographic localization of knowledge spillovers as evidenced by patent citations', *Quarterly Journal of Economics*, **108**, 577–98.

Krugman, P. (1991), *Geography and Trade*, Cambridge, MA: MIT Press.

Lucas, R.E. (1988), 'On the mechanics of economic development', *Journal of Monetary Economics*, **22**, 3–42.

Markusen, A. (1985), *Profit Cycles, Oligopoly and Regional Development*, Cambridge, MA: MIT Press.

Marshall, A. (1920), *Principles of Economics*, 8th edn, London: Macmillan.

McCann, P. (1995), 'Rethinking the economics of location and agglomeration', *Urban Studies*, **32**(3), 563–77.

McCann, P. (1997), 'How deeply embedded is Silicon Glen? A cautionary note', *Regional Studies*, **31**(7), 695–703.

McCann, P. (2001), *Urban and Regional Economics*, Oxford: Oxford University Press.

McCann, P. (2004), 'Urban scale economies: statics and dynamics', in R. Capello and P. Nijkamp (eds), *Urban Dynamics and Growth: Advances in Urban Economics*, Amsterdam: Elsevier, pp. 31–56.

McCann, P. and R. Mudambi (2004), 'The location decision of the multinational enterprise: some theoretical and empirical issues', *Growth and Change*, **35**(4), 491–524.

McCann, P. and R. Mudambi (2005), 'Analytical Differences in the economics of geography: the case of the multinational firm', *Environment and Planning A*, **37**(10), 1857–76.

McCann, P. and D. Shefer (2004), 'Location, agglomeration and infrastructure', *Papers in Regional Science*, **83**(1), 177–96.

McCann, P. and S.C. Sheppard (2003), 'The rise, fall and rise again of industrial location theory', *Regional Studies*, **37**(6–7), 649–63.

McCombie, J.S.L. and A.J. Thirlwall (1994), *Economic Growth and the Balance of Payments Constraint*, London: St. Martin's Press.

Michie, J. (2003), *The Handbook of Globalisation*, Cheltenham, UK and Northampton, MA, US: Edward Elgar.

Moses, L. (1958), 'Location and the theory of production', *Quarterly Journal of Economics*, **78**, 259–72.

Ohlin, B. (1933), *Interregional and International Trade*, Cambridge, MA: Harvard University Press.

Openshaw, S. and P.J. Taylor (1979), 'A million or so correlation coefficients: three experiments on the modifiable area unit problem', in N. Wrigley (ed.), *Statistical Applications in the Spatial Sciences*, London: Pion, pp. 127–44.

Paniccia, I. (2002), *Industrial Districts: Evolution and Competitiveness in Italian Firms*, Cheltenham, UK and Northampton, MA, US: Edward Elgar.

Perroux, F. (1950), 'Economic space, theory and applications', *Quarterly Journal of Economics*, **64**, 89–104.

Porter, M.E. (1990), *The Competitive Advantage of Nations*, New York: Free Press.

Porter, M.E. (1998), 'Clusters and the new economics of competition', *Harvard Business Review*, **76**(6), 77–90.

Romer, P. (1986), 'Increasing returns and long-run growth', *Journal of Political Economy*, **94**, 1002–37.

Romer, P. (1987), 'Growth based on increasing specialization', *American Economic Review*, **77**(2), 56–72.

Saxenian, A. (1994), *Regional Advantage*, Cambridge, MA: Harvard University Press.

Schumpeter, J.A. (1934), *The Theory of Economic Development*, Cambridge, MA: Harvard University Press.

Scott, A.J. (1988), *New Industrial Spaces*, London: Pion.

Simmie, J. (1998), 'Reasons for the development of "Islands of innovation": evidence from Hertfordshire', *Urban Studies*, **35**(8), 1261–89.

Simmie, J. (ed.) (2001), *Innovative Cities*, London: Spon Press.

Simmie, J. and J. Sennett (1999), 'Innovative clusters: global or local linkages?', *National Institute Economic Review*, **170**, 87–98, October.

Solow, R.M. (1956), 'A contribution to the theory of economic growth', *Quarterly Journal of Economics*, **70**, 65–94.

Suarez-Villa, L. and W. Walrod (1997), 'Operational strategy, R&D and intrametropolitan clustering in a poly-centric structure: the advanced electronics industries of the Los Angeles basis', *Urban Studies*, **34**(9), 1343–80.

Swan, T. (1956), 'Economic growth and capital accumulation', *Economic Record*, **32**, 334–61.

Vernon, R. (1960), *Metropolis 1985*, Cambridge, MA: Harvard University Press.

Vernon, R. (1966), 'International investment and international trade in the product cycle', *Quarterly Journal of Economics*, **80**(2), 190–207.

Vernon, R. (1979), 'The product cycle hypothesis in a new international environment', *Oxford Bulletin of Economics and Statistics*, **41**, 255–67.

Weber, A. (1909), *Über den Standort der Industrien*, translated by C.J. Friedrich (1929), *Alfred Weber's Theory of the Location of Industries*, Chicago, IL: University of Chicago Press.

Williamson, O.E. (1975), *Markets and Hierarchies*, New York: Free Press.

Yeung, M., N. Perdikis and W. Kerr (1999), *Regional Trading Blocs in the Global Economy: The EU and Asean*, Cheltenham, UK and Northampton, MA, US: Edward Elgar.

3 The analysis of location, colocation and urbanization economies
Börje Johansson[1] and Ulla Forslund[2]

1 Introduction
Location analysis has two major perspectives. The first is concerned with where to place a given economic activity or facility, defined as an optimization problem, where the properties of the economic environment are taken as a given fact. The second perspective motivates a different question: how can the entire landscape of activity locations be understood and explained? Both approaches can be associated with an equilibrium framework. However, the second perspective also stimulates the student to think about the evolution of location patterns. How do they emerge and which are the adjustment processes?

1.1 Perspectives on location analysis
In the past, economic model-building favoured formulations, where the distance between buyer (receiving agent) and seller (delivering agent) could be ignored. In Debreu's (1959) contribution location indexing is possible, but only in an inessential way. This is manifested in the spatial impossibility theorem attributed to Starret (1978), which implies that the Arrow–Debreu model cannot be applied to a homogenous space, except in the case where transport costs are zero for any spatial competitive equilibrium. As emphasized by Fujita and Thisse (2002), this implies that regional specialization, urban regions and trade cannot be competitive equilibrium solutions.

The above problem has been avoided for a long span of time by introducing different forms of pre-located elements into location models. This is typical of the contribution of Weber (1909), in a model where input suppliers and customers all have a given location and where the single firm selects an optimal location given these facts. This approach remained in the celebrated contributions in the 1950s (Beckmann, 1952; Samuelson, 1952). Likewise, in the contribution of von Thünen (1826), the location of the city and its centre is given in advance, and this approach has dominated urban economics since then (Fujita, 1989).

The subsequent analysis draws on one fundamental idea from Weber and one from von Thünen. In the latter case a principal idea is that spatial structure is affected by the assumption that the delivery of commodities between seller and buyer is distance-sensitive, and this sensitivity varies between commodities. This is as fundamental as it is trivial. The inheritance from Weber is of the same nature, and it amounts to the recognition that a firm as well as a public service provider has to consider both the delivery of inputs and the delivery of outputs. Such an observation is clear-cut in Weber's original formulation, but becomes profound when we observe that the location of input suppliers and output customers may change in response to a sequence of individual location choices.

1.2   The colocation phenomenon

The analysis in the subsequent sections is based on the following simple assumption: The economic geography consists primarily of urban regions, some very small and others very large. Certain transactions are less costly when carried out between actors inside a region than when they take place between actors in different regions. The same applies to certain extra-market information and knowledge flows. In particular, urban regions exist because of these advantages of intraregional interaction.

The subsequent presentation attempts to outline a framework that makes it possible to understand the location decision of a firm in a context of its interaction with its input suppliers and its customers. This should form the basis for modelling colocation phenomena such as spatial clusters and urban agglomerations. A distinct message is that firms cluster together in a place because they have something in common with regard to (i) resource endowments which are available in the place, (ii) inputs suppliers that are present in the place, or (iii) customers that are accessible from the place.

These issues are central in the contribution by Ohlin (1933). He considered four factors as major causes of agglomeration economies. These are (i) internal scale economies, (ii) localization economies, (iii) urbanization economies, and (iv) inter-industry linkages (of input–output type).

According to the framework that is developed in the present chapter, only two major causes of agglomeration exist, and these are Ohlin's second and third factor. At the same time, both internal scale economies and inter-industry linkages can be essential components of a model that describes localization and urbanization economies.

Scholars that discuss localization economies frequently refer to Marshall (1920), sometimes to Hoover (1948) and very rarely to Ohlin (1933). It is as if Ohlin was disqualified because of the Heckscher–Ohlin theorem. The modern reference should definitely be Fujita and Thisse (2002). In addition, their contribution to a deeper understanding of urbanization economies is equally profound.

In a genealogy perspective, Ohlin should be recognized for having brought attention to localization and urbanization economies as two parallel agglomeration phenomena, although it is Hoover who has received the credit for doing so. With regard to urbanization economies, the definitions and explanations given by Ohlin and Hoover are quite similar and could be classified as specific to each region, with its given size and composition of a variety of industries. Ohlin and Hoover may differ somewhat in the treatment of localization economies, where Hoover stresses that localization economies are industry-specific, and this implicitly brings horizontal externalities into focus. This strong focus on the individual industry is probably unfortunate and is one reason for putting the concept of colocation to the forefront, as is done in the present study.

Colocation may imply clustering of firms that mutually benefit from being located in the proximity of each other, although they do not belong to the same industry. The mutual benefit is a place-specific increasing returns to scale (McCann, 2001). In the analysis developed stepwise in the subsequent sections, the major focus is not on horizontal but on vertical externalities. In this context, we attempt in this study to demonstrate that clustering of firms in the same industry is primarily generated by two major forms of clusters:

1.   *Cluster of input-selling firms.* In this case we observe many firms that supply differentiated and distance-sensitive products to a locally concentrated demand for

these inputs. In this general formulation inputs include both service and knowledge deliveries.

2. *Clustering of input-buying firms.* In this case we observe a spatial clustering of firms producing differentiated product varieties in a given place. These firms are attracted to stay in this particular place because this place has a concentrated supply of distant-sensitive inputs that the firms demand. Thus, the colocation force is not primarily that the clustered firms produce the same kind of outputs, but that they use similar inputs.

Obviously, these two forms of clusters may combine into a strong pattern of colocation. However, there are clear analytical advantages to be gained by treating them as two individual colocation processes. Moreover, the above approach allows the presentation to continue and depict urbanization as 'a cluster of clusters' and establish an interface with early suggestions in the works of Hall (1959), Artle (1959), Vernon (1962) and, later, Henderson (1974, 1977). The approach also opens up for a discussion of localization and urbanization economies in studies of innovation activities (e.g. Swann, Prevezer & Stout, 1998; Feldman, 1994; Steiner, 1998).

1.3   Outline of the presentation

Section 2 presents basic conditions for the location of a firm, such as distance to input suppliers and customers and accessibility to regional endowments. Another important aspect is the distinction between slow and fast adjustments. These ideas are applied in Section 3, which examines how colocation externalities make colocation processes self-reinforcing, where distance sensitivity and scale economies generate the externalities that also comprise R&D processes. Section 3 applies a simple model that is also used in Section 4. This section deals with urbanization economies, where taste for variety is emphasized with regard to both firms' demand for inputs and households' consumption demand. The same model is also applied to illustrate urbanization economies of innovation activities. Section 5 concludes that it is possible to consider a set of basic principles to describe a firm's location decisions in the context of localization and urbanization economies. This last section also identifies gaps between theoretical suggestions and empirical evidence. In view of this, a set of research problems are discussed.

2   Location of the firm

Section 2 introduces basic elements for an analysis of a firm's location decisions, such that these elements remain intact in the modelling of colocation phenomena. It is also observed that location decisions have to take into account that certain location characteristics change at a slow pace, whereas others adjust quickly. Finally, it is also stressed that a firm is involved in (i) output activities that can be analysed on a fast time scale and (ii) development activities that have to be depicted on a slower time scale.

2.1   Slow and fast location processes

A classical approach in trade and location analyses is to consider certain resources as pre-located and to examine how other resources or activities adjust their location in response to resources with a given location. For example, network infrastructure for movements of persons and products may be considered as given, whereas the location of economic

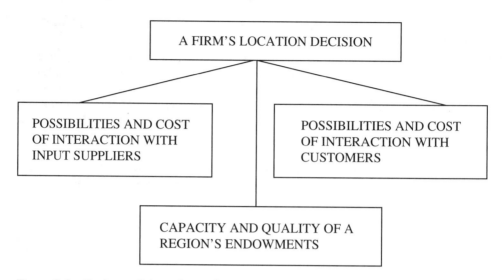

Figure 3.1   Basic conditions that influence a firm's location decision

activities adjust in response to interaction costs, which are influenced by the given infra-structure (e.g. Andersson, 1993). The factor-proportions theory provides another example, where capital and labour are given for each of two regions and cannot move between the regions, and where each region specializes by selecting production activities in concordance with its relative factor abundance.

Many resources have a given location in the short term, but they may shift location in a longer time span. These resources, like built environment and any other located endow-ments, adjust on a slow time scale. The location of firms and the intensity of different types of economic activity adjust on a faster time scale, driven by faster adjustment processes. In this sense, short-term location equilibrium is only a temporary phenomenon that applies as long as the slower location processes remain practically unchanged (Johansson, Batten & Casti, 1987).

Figure 3.1 presents three basic conditions that influence a firm's location decision, including the decision to remain in a given place. The first factor represents the costs of interacting with input suppliers, where interaction costs include the transaction costs that affect the input price (McCann and Shefer, 2004). These costs will vary across alternative locations. In an extended setting interaction also refers to R&D collaboration with input suppliers, including knowledge providers. The location pattern of input suppliers may change more slowly than the activities of the input-buying firm, but the time scales are not necessarily very different.

The second factor represents the costs of interaction with customers. In some cases these are few, and in other cases the firm has many customers that are spread over many regional markets. And such circumstances affect the size of interaction costs, which include transport and other transaction costs. Again, customer-related costs will also depend on where the firm is located. When the firm sells on many different geographi-cal markets, the pattern of customer location will adjust on a slower time scale than what applies for the selling firm itself. Gradual (and path-dependent) changes in the concentration of demand are a core element in the so-called 'new economic geography' (Fujita, Krugman & Venables, 1999; Brakman, Garretsen & Marrewijk, 2001).

The third factor in Figure 3.1 comprises the endowments of the region. Such endowments primarily consist of slowly changing features of a region, e.g. infrastructure and built environment, skills and knowledge intensity of the labour force, as well as amenities in general.

In view of the characterization in Figure 3.1, this section investigates in sequence how a firm's location can be influenced by its distance to input suppliers and customers, and by the endowments of the region where the firm is located. The presentation avoids dealing with multi-location firms, such as multinationals (Lipsey, 2003). The subsequent presentation in Section 2 primarily deals with general aspects of a firm's distance to (i) input suppliers, and (ii) customers, where distance is reflected by the firm's transaction and other interaction costs. In addition, the presentation considers the benefits the firm can have from the endowments of the functional region in which it is located.

2.2   Distance to input suppliers

A firm transforms inputs to outputs that are supplied to customers. The profit of the firm is determined by the firm's revenue minus its input costs. As inputs have to be delivered to the firm, the distance to input suppliers and resource supply points will affect input costs. In a dynamic context the inputs may be related to the firm's development activities, including search for new production routines and new product attributes. In a static setting the decision criterion is to minimize input costs.

The classical Weber problem was presented and solved in Launhardt (1882) and further analysed in Weber (1909). Following the description by Puu (2003), the problem is about the location decision of a firm that uses two different inputs to produce one output. Each input is supplied from a distinct location, which is different for each input. The demand for the output is located in still another location. Thus, everything is prelocated except the place of the producing firm. Typical prelocated input supply-points are mines, oil wells and ports.

The well-known decision criterion for the firm is to select a location such that the sum of transport costs for the two inputs and for the output is minimized. Obviously, the Weber problem can be extended to situations where a firm has several inputs and several delivery points where demand is concentrated (Beckmann & Thisse, 1986).

In Figure 3.2 the Weber problem is illustrated, where transport costs are measured per unit output. The cost of transporting input 1 and 2 to the firm's location in r is given by c_{1r} and c_{2r}, respectively, while c_{rm} represents the cost of bringing the output to the prelocated market (customer). For each location r that the firm selects, the total transport cost per unit output can be calculated as $T_r = c_{1r} + c_{2r} + c_{rm}$. By choosing the location r in an appropriate way the firm can minimize the size of T_r.

The Weber model was later extended by Moses (1958), to consider that firms will substitute inputs for each other in response to relative prices. The result of this extension is that a firm's choice of the way inputs should be optimally combined is made in conjunction with the choice of location. Thus, a firm's location problem is embedded in a more general production problem, where the firm minimizes the sum of production costs, input costs and output delivery costs (Isard, 1951, 1956).

The Weber location model illustrates for example the choice of location of a steel plant. In this case we may also permit the production to feature internal scale economies.

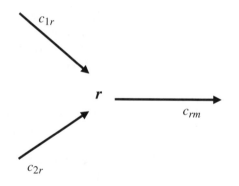

Figure 3.2   Illustration of the Weber problem

However, the model does not have much to say about agglomeration of economic activities in a specific location. In spite of this, the Weber problem remains a core model for the analysis carried out in Sections 3 and 4. In these sections we introduce the possibility that the production of input suppliers features internal scale economies, while at the same time some of these inputs are distance-sensitive. When the scenery changes in this way the landscape of solutions is altered profoundly.

The Weber model may also be seen as a basic component in analysing location in a world economy characterised by outsourcing, where the formation of economic networks generates a landscape of subcontracting component production, design and R&D, marketing activities and sales of services that accompany the sales of products (Grossman & Helpman, 2005). In this context it is vital to express transportation and other transaction costs as link-specific costs, c_{rs}, since these link costs are not proportional to geographic distance but reflect transaction arrangements and affinities between each pair of nodes. Such arrangements also include complex so-called 'supply chains' (McCann, 1998; Li and Polenske, 2003).

2.3   Distance to customers

A reversed version of the Weber problem obtains when a firm has several demand points and has to find a production or supply point that can minimize the shipment costs. Extending this formulation to include many supply and demand locations leads to models such as the transportation problem (Koopmans, 1949; Beckmann, 1952), the assignment problem (Koopmans & Beckmann, 1957) and the spatial price-equilibrium (SPE) model (Takayama & Judge, 1971). In all these formulations the demand points are prelocated as well as the locations from which supply is possible. Solving each model generates a flow pattern between supply points and locations where demand is concentrated. Thus, solutions also inform about how much is delivered from supply points and how much is purchased in demand points.

An SPE model can also be extended so that it reflects the location of production capacities, while considering capacity investments in temporal contexts (Takayama, 1994). Moreover, the problem may be formulated so that firms can make 'monopoly profits' (Johansson and Westin, 1987), although the standard approach is one of competitive equilibrium. In standard formulations the delivery networks (and the associated costs), the supply functions, and the demand functions are prelocated. Because of this, the solutions are not affected by the spatial impossibility theorem (Fujita & Thisse, 2002, pp. 30–60).

The set of models that depict location as a problem of distance or accessibility to customers can be extended to include models of spatial monopoly and oligopoly with varying price-setting rules (Beckmann and Thisse, 1986). Just like the other models mentioned in this subsection, these models are partial, temporary and constrained in various ways to make the problem formulations tractable. As will be demonstrated in Section 3, there are two major issues that are critical. The first is about the stability of each particular equilibrium solution and the presence of multiple equilibria. The second issue concerns scale economies in combination with products that are distance-sensitive – and for which the sensitivity can vary in size.

2.4   Endowments and the attractiveness of regions
Regions have different endowments in the form of climate, natural resources, infrastructure and production capital, skills of the labour force, social capital and many other things. It is a trivial conclusion that existing endowments provide regions with different opportunities or advantages as well as disadvantages. As a consequence the cost of producing a given commodity will vary across regions as a reflection of each region's endowments. The celebrated Heckscher–Ohlin theorem suggests that there is a static equilibrium solution with endogenously determined prices on production factors (endowments) and product prices. However, endowments also influence the development of each region's economy. At any moment in time, endowments are gifts from the past.

What then is a region? In a first step of making the concept precise, the present analysis adopts the view that a region is an urban-like area such that economic agents who are located inside the region have considerably lower costs when making face-to-face contacts with each other as compared with making contacts with agents who are located outside the region. Such a specification comes close to the definition of a functional urban region as elaborated by Cheshire and Gordon (1998). As a consequence, the size of a region matters and has to be considered as an endowment, because a large region has a richer set of potential contacts than a small region. Moreover, for all products that require frequent contacts between buyer and seller, the suppliers of these products have a larger market in a large region than in a small. In this sense the size of intraregional market demand constitutes a regional endowment and it can be assumed to change on a slow time scale.

The second category of endowments comprises various forms of resources that are attached to a region, such as supply of labour with different skills and knowledge, supply of capital, R&D resources and the economic milieu in general (Andersson, Anderstig & Hårsman, 1990; Florida, 2002). Such endowments in a region can be expected to change slowly over time. Moreover, they represent resources or inputs that affect a firm's development activities rather than its normal output activities. Thus, they constitute stimuli to innovations and renewal processes in general.

The endowments discussed above seem to have replaced the traditional endowments in the form of natural resources, but not entirely. With support from Glaeser and Kohlhase (2004), it can be claimed that natural resources in production are far from playing 'the first violin' any longer – if ever. However, consumption-related amenities and associated infrastructure constitute an attractor for households to locate in a functional region, and imply that amenities can support the growth of a region's local market (Cheshire & Magrini, 2005). This idea may have a long history. Here we can trace it back to Quigley (1990) and Maclennan (1990), who both suggest that the quality of housing and built environment together with attributes of the natural environment affect population growth directly and economic growth indirectly. This dynamic process has been identified as the phenomenon 'jobs follow households' (Holmberg, Johansson & Strömquist, 2003).

3   Location and colocation externalities
Section 3 investigates how colocation externalities influence individual firms to locate in a functional region. Such a region may be a small town (or a set of such neighbouring towns) or a large metropolitan region. In the presentation colocation externalities generate localization economies or, in another terminology, external economies of scale.

3.1   Distance sensitivity and scale economies
The contribution by von Thünen (1826) is recognized as a foundation for understanding the structure of an urban region and the associated land rent curve. We shall emphasize another aspect, by claiming that he detected that the delivery of products from supplier to customer is distance-sensitive and that this sensitivity varies across products. For distance-sensitive products, the geographic transaction costs increase sharply as the distance between supplier and customer increases. The importance of von Thünen's finding goes beyond urban economics, because, when it is combined with the existence of scale economies, proximity externalities arise, and these externalities bring about colocation or clustering forces.

In Johansson and Quigley (2004) it is argued that a seller and a buyer may form a transaction link that can reduce the distance sensitivity of a delivery process. However, link formation is a costly investment process, which means that proximity advantages remain for distance-sensitive products. Moreover, link formation can be assumed to be less costly when it is carried out by neighbouring firms.

Consider an individual firm, and assume that its production features internal scale economies. If in addition the output of the firm is distance-sensitive, the firm will benefit from being a short distance from its customers. This was the basic finding in Krugman (1991), where one group of products can be delivered at zero transaction costs inside the region where the firm is located and with positive costs to another region. The consequence in a two-region model is an output demand externality that can attract labour and production to concentrate in the largest of the regions. The externality depends on a combination of internal scale economies, the size of the distance-sensitive delivery costs and the mobility of production and labour, while observing that the labour generates demand inside the region where it locates. Krugman's simple example is rich in the sense that two regions will both endure, as long as there is also an industry for which the input supply is trapped in each region, whereas the output from this industry is insensitive to distance.

Let us go back to our individual firm and consider the inputs to its production. Suppose that some or all of these inputs are distance-sensitive. Each supplier of such inputs will benefit from a short distance to its customer firm. If in addition the production of these suppliers is characterized by internal scale economies, the result is an input demand externality.

Krugman (1991) discusses but does not model the input demand externality, which arises when one or several firms in a region expand the aggregate output. Such an expansion has the capacity to attract suppliers of distance-sensitive inputs to find a location in a region. When this happens, these suppliers can deliver the inputs at a lower cost and eventually higher quality. Obviously, this type of location response can stimulate the buyers of the inputs to further increase their activity, which implies that a cumulative externality is in operation. The crucial element is the degree of internal scale economies among the input suppliers, combined with distance-sensitive deliveries.

3.2 Colocation externalities via the market

In this subsection we focus on colocation externalities that are generated via the price formation in markets. These price formation processes comprise pure market exchange as well as exchange that is based on transaction links between a buying and a selling firm. The colocation phenomenon takes two forms (that may indeed coexist). The first is colocation or clustering of input suppliers that service the same customer(s). The second is colocation or clustering of firms that demand the same type of differentiated products as input in their production. In subsection 3.3, the analysis is extended to extra-market externalities.

The initial interest is now to depict a firm that services a demand, D, that is concentrated in a given region. The associated customers may be just one major firm or a set of firms that all purchase the same input(s). The demand may also arise from households in the region. The delimiting factor is that the products delivered (goods and services) are distance-sensitive.

The firm's production is depicted by the cost function

$$C(x) = vx + F, \tag{3.1}$$

where vx denotes variable costs and F fixed costs. The demand that faces the firm is modelled by the following function:

$$x = \alpha p^{-\theta} D, \tag{3.2}$$

where p denotes price, $\theta > 1$ is the price elasticity of demand, D is the demand indicator (demand budget), and α is a coefficient that reflects the market structure. Suppose that the firm is the sole supplier in the local market. Then the optimal price, $\bar{p}$, equals (e.g. Brakman, Garretsen & Marrewijk, 2001),

$$\bar{p} = v\sigma, \ \sigma = \theta/(\theta - 1). \tag{3.3}$$

This price will be viable only if the associated profit, $\pi(\bar{p}) = \bar{p}x - vx - F$, is non-negative, which requires that

$$v\alpha\bar{p}D(\sigma - 1) \geq F. \tag{3.4}$$

Equation (3.4) shows that, if D is too small relative to F, the firm cannot locate in the region – as long as its sales are limited to the regional market. The customer(s) in the regional market must then buy its distance-sensitive product from extra-regional suppliers at a price, $p^e > \bar{p}$. In such a situation, if D starts to grow, this can trigger the start of a local supplier.

In view of the single firm that we have depicted in equations (3.1)–(3.3), the condition in (3.4) can be described as an output demand externality that operates via the market. Suppose now that the customer is another firm. For this firm the condition in (3.4) is also an input-demand externality. The simple argument is that, if this customer firm can increase it sales, its demand budget, D, will grow, and when that happens it can be served by a local firm A at a reduced price. As a consequence the customer firm (B) can produce at lower costs and eventually further increase its output and thereby increase its demand for inputs. In summary, the model given by equations (3.1)–(3.4) describes a down-stream externality in view of firm A and an up-stream externality in view of firm B.

Suppose now that the demand budget refers to customers (or just one customer) with a taste for variety. This implies that firm A is just one out of a set of suppliers, indexed by j, that are involved in monopolistic competition, as described in Krugman (1980) or Brakman, Garretsen & Marrewijk (2001). If all suppliers of the differentiated varieties have the same price elasticity θ, each of them will face the following negatively sloping demand function:

$$x_j = p_j^{-\theta} P^{1-\theta} D, \; P \equiv \left[\Sigma_k p_k^{1-\theta} \right]^{1/(1-\theta)}, \tag{3.5}$$

where P is a price index for the market of differentiated products. Moreover, in this case (3.2) is transformed to (3.5) if we let $\alpha = P^{1-\theta}$.[3]

So far the analysis provides some insight into how an input-supplying firm has an incentive to locate in the proximity of an input-buying firm. Two such firms also benefit from a colocation externality as shown in Table 3.1. The input-buying firm may be a large export firm or several firms with similar input demand. In the latter case they form a cluster of input buyers.

In addition, the supply of inputs may come from many firms that deliver differentiated and distance-sensitive input products. In that case they form a cluster of input suppliers.

Table 3.1   The clustering of input-buying and input-supplying firms

Cluster of input buyers	When one or several activities in a region expand to a sufficient volume, the demand for associated, distance-sensitive inputs will be large enough to attract pertinent input suppliers (with internal scale economies) to the functional region. Such attraction can be generated by one large firm, but may also be generated by several firms in an industry, where the firms supply differentiated products. These firms would constitute an *input-buying cluster* that benefits from proximity to suppliers of distance-sensitive inputs. Such a cluster is stimulated to grow in response to better-quality inputs at prices that fall as demand for them expands
Cluster of input suppliers	When one or several activities in a region expand to a sufficient volume, the demand for associated, distance-sensitive inputs will be large enough to attract pertinent input suppliers (with internal scale economies) to the functional region. These input suppliers would constitute an *input-supplying cluster* to the extent that the input suppliers belong to the same industry and supply differentiated inputs. A major mechanism would then be a taste for variety among firms in the output industry

It should be observed that product differentiation is essential for both the cluster of input-buying and input-supplying firms. The reason is simply that internal economies of scale are assumed to be a general feature of all firms. Thus, without differentiation, there would not be many firms. Another observation that we can make in Table 3.1 is that an input-buying cluster is identified with regard to the similarity of input demand among the clustered firms.

3.3 Extra-market colocation externalities

The analysis at this point can benefit from the results in the preceding subsection, because intra-market and extra-market externalities are both influenced by proximity. Having said this, it should also be stressed that information and knowledge flows can be based on transaction principles (e.g. purchase of knowledge from a consultant), and collaboration between firms can indeed be supported by explicit and implicit contracts.

However, it is obvious that information and knowledge may be transmitted through flows that take place outside the market, such that the source of the information is not paid by those who benefit from the flow. These flows are labelled 'spillover' flows, and can be conceived as by-products of (i) pure market transactions, (ii) interaction on transaction links, and (iii) interaction in social networks in which economic actors are members.

Table 3.2 presents a simple scheme of spillover externalities. In essence, all these externalities point in a direction away from static analysis towards models of an economy that is constantly changing, although mostly at a slow pace. The reason is simple; in a static world additional information would not have any value. This is directly and indirectly confirmed in contributions such as Echeverri-Carroll (2001), Karlsson and Manduchi (2001), and de Groot, Nijkamp and Acs (2001).

Table 3.2 Spillover externalities and colocation

Form of externality	Nature of spillover flows and principle mechanisms
Vertical	*Upstream or input spillover*: as a by-product of the interaction between an input-buying firm and its input suppliers, information and knowledge can spill over and stimulate incremental adjustments as well as innovations of the buying firm. Colocation or proximity allows the interaction to be communication-intensive, and hence the occurrence of distance-sensitive spillover flows is likely to increase with proximity *Downstream or delivery spillover*: as a by-product of the interaction between an input-selling firm and its customer firm(s), information and knowledge can spill over and stimulate adjustments and innovations of the selling firm. The effects of colocation are the same as above
Horizontal	*Interaction between firms in the same industry*: owing to proximity, competing firms may imitate each other to move towards best-practice solutions and improve these solutions. Competing firms may also collaborate on R&D activities, and this can have spillover effects. The possibility of mutual spillover-benefits among competing firms is greater if the firms supply differentiated products, such that their markets are only partly overlapping

Table 3.2 reveals that upstream and downstream externalities are more tractable to analyse than are horizontal externalities, where firms producing similar products unintentionally diffuse information to each other. The major problem is that colocated firms in the same industry have a Janus relation to their competitors. They do not only gain information, they also give away information. If the latter part dominates, that provides a negative incentive for colocation.

Spillover of non-durable information among competing firms may be interpreted as a necessary part of a competitive market (general market information). The consistency problem arises when one confronts the idea of so-called 'localized' knowledge spillovers. This idea has been strongly criticized by Breschi and Lissoni (2001) for mixing knowledge diffusion, locally-constrained public knowledge and tacit knowledge in a completely inconsistent way. This problem needs much more basic research (both theoretical and empirical) and will be examined further in the following subsection.

The spillover phenomena in the table were discussed early by Marshall (1920), and the associated externalities have remained a distress for many economists (e.g. Bohm, 1987). Especially for small functional regions, these phenomena have been identified as clusters or industrial districts, defined as groups of business enterprises and other organizations for which membership within a group is an important element of each individual member firm's individual competitiveness. Enright (1996, p. 191) adds that the conditions binding the cluster together are buyer–supplier relationships, common technologies, common buyers or distribution channels, or common labour pools.

There are two problems with this idea. The first is that a cluster may influence the competitiveness (productivity) of member firms in a static sense, but it may also influence the firms' capacity to develop and renew their technology over time (Baptista, 1996, 1998). The second problem is that firms in a cluster can benefit from spillovers due to pure market externalities, network externalities based on contract agreements and social networks in which entrepreneurs and managers are members. So far, theoretical and empirical research has not managed to shed light on how these three factors combine and how they can be separated (Gordon & McCann, 2000).

3.4   Regional R&D externalities

Firms combine two activities. The first is to use established techniques or routines to produce and supply a given product or product mix. This may be thought of as the firm's basic 'supply activity'. The second area of firm activity can be labelled 'development activities', generally referred to as R&D. In this context a firm makes an innovation by developing new products and/or changing its routines. In its development efforts the firm also relies on information and knowledge flows from its environment and its R&D networks. Some of these flows are transaction-based, whereas other flows have a spillover nature.

R&D is a development activity, where the expected output is an innovation. Knowledge is an input to an innovation process, which, if successful, generates new or improved products and/or new or improved production routines. Knowledge for innovation can schematically be divided into (i) scientific knowledge in the form of basic principles, (ii) technological knowledge in the form of technical solutions, and (iii) entrepreneurial knowledge about product attributes, customer preferences and market conditions, business concepts and the like (Karlsson & Johansson, 2006). Part of such knowledge is placed inside the firm, but a vast share of all knowledge is external to the firm. In its innovation process the individual firm can make efforts to acquire additional knowledge.

Information and knowledge flows as input to a firm's innovation process may arise from market observations, purchase of knowledge from knowledge providers, and collaboration with input suppliers, customer firms, competitors in the same industry, and universities and research institutes. In all these activities additional spillover of knowledge is likely to occur. However, both transaction-based knowledge flows and knowledge spillover are frequently assumed to be distance-sensitive (e.g. Acs, 1994; Adams, 2002; Feldman & Audretsch, 1999; Verspagen & Schoenmakers, 2000). A prime argument is that knowledge that can feed R&D and innovation activities is complex and requires a high proportion of face-to-face interaction. As suggested by von Hippel (1994), the information is sticky and hence costly to transmit over longer distances. Another observation is that knowledge diffuses between firms as employees (embodying the knowledge) shift to new employers (Almeida & Kogut, 1999). This latter observation provides additional arguments to focus on local labour markets as approximations of functional urban regions.

A particular area of study is the patent production function, where the patent output often is related to firms' proximity to universities and to other firms that carry out R&D (Varga, 1997, 2002; Hendersson, Jaffe & Trajtenberg, 1995; Adams, 2002; Zucker & Darby, 2005). Studies that examine patent counts have been popular, since patents of individual firms (and of regions) are observable as register data. A recurrent question is: how is patent production affected by proximity to university research and to R&D carried out by other firms (Jaffe, Tratjenberg & Henderson, 1993; Feldman, 1994; Varga, 2001; Fischer, 2001).

Many studies that attempt to verify the importance of proximity to knowledge sources have remained imprecise about the meaning of proximity or have used ad hoc specifications of proximity. Recently, some of these deficiencies have been remedied by making use of Weibull's accessibility measure (Weibull, 1976, 1980). The approach contains two instruments. The first is information about time distances between all zones in an economy. The second is a decomposition of space into three categories: (i) local area, (ii) functional urban region, and (iii) extraregional area.

First, every R&D activity takes place in some local area, r, and time distances between zones inside such an area make it possible to calculate the local accessibility, A_r^1 to knowledge sources, K_r, inside the local area, expressed by

$$A_r^1 = \exp\left\{-\lambda^1 t_{rr}\right\} K_r,\tag{3.6a}$$

where t_{rr} is the average time distance inside the local area, and λ^1 is the time-sensitivity for local transport (5–15 minutes). Second, every local area belongs to a functional region that consists of several local areas including the region's major town or city. The accessibility from r to all other local areas, s, in the region, R, to which r belongs is given by

$$A_r^2 = \sum_{s \in R(r)} \exp\left\{-\lambda^2 t_{rs}\right\} K_s,\tag{3.6b}$$

where $R(r)$ contains all local areas in R except r itself, where t_{rs} is the time distance between r and s (15–50 minutes), λ^2 is the time sensitivity for intraregional transport (contact making), and K_s is the size of the knowledge source in location s. Third, the accessibility from r to knowledge sources in locations, $s \in E(r)$, outside region R is given by

$$A_r^3 = \sum_{s \in E(r)} \exp\left\{- \lambda^3 t_{rs}\right\} K_s, \tag{3.6c}$$

where λ^3 is the time sensitivity with regard to extraregional transport, where time distances exceed 50 minutes (Johansson, Klaesson & Olsson, 2002).

The above approach has been applied in Andersson and Karlsson (2004, 2007) and Gråsjö (2005) with data from Sweden, where innovation activities are regressed on observations of A_r^1, A_r^2 and A_r^3. In these and similar studies proximity matters. The local accessibility, A_r^1, has the strongest effect. There is also an effect from intraregional accessibility, A_r^2, whereas the influence form extraregional accessibility, A_r^3, is insignificant. Positive effects can be found for accessibility to university R&D, but if university and industry R&D are included in the same regression equations, the accessibility to industry R&D (carried out by firms) dominates completely. Having said this, there is room for a sincere reservation. It is plausible that R&D-active firms are attracted to regions with university R&D, while at the same time the size of university R&D resources adjusts to places where R&D-intensive firms are located. With this type of interdependent dynamics it matters which of the two processes adjusts fastest.

The above presentation means that a firm can improve its innovation performance by choosing a location that enhances its accessibility to knowledge-intensive labour that can participate in knowledge activities and its accessibility to knowledge sources that can generate knowledge flows that are inputs to innovation activities. In other words, locations with advantageous innovation conditions can attract firms that are innovation-intensive and also stimulate firms in such a region to intensify their innovation efforts. These suggestions are summarized in Table 3.3.

A crucial element that is not treated in the above discussion is the importance of keeping intellectual capital private. The problem is stressed when the R&D process in

Table 3.3   Location of R&D activities

Assumption	Consequence
Knowledge embodied in the labour force of a region and in the R&D organization of firms and universities is sticky	Then the knowledge assets of a region function as a regional endowment that attracts R&D active firms to the region
Knowledge flows between firms, knowledge providers and other actors influence R&D productivity of firms in a positive way	As a consequence the location of R&D activities (among firms and universities etc) is a self-reinforcing, cumulative clustering process
Multi-unit firms like multinationals employ firm-internal channels for knowledge flows. At the same time they benefit from knowledge flows inside the region where each unit is located	This can generate global R&D and innovation systems that combine network interaction over long distances and intraregional proximity-dependent knowledge flows
Successful innovation systems are based on a combination of R&D activities and entrepreneurial knowledge	Innovation activities will concentrate in regions where ordinary interaction between input-supplying and input-buying firms are colocated, where R&D actors are colocated and where entrepreneurship is present

product cycle models is examined. In such a model, firms make innovation efforts because they foresee temporary monopoly profits when new successful (and firm-specific) knowledge is created. Another aspect of the product cycle model is that the innovative firm can benefit from accessibility to diversity of demand, partly as an element of a trial-and-error interaction between the product developer and pertinent customers (Johansson and Andersson, 1998). Obviously, diverse demand spillovers have a more consistent basis than do the horizontal externalities. Information on customer preferences is transmitted not only for existing products but also for products under development. All these observations point towards the phenomenon of urbanization economies, which is the topic in the following section.

4   Agglomeration and urbanization economies
In the preceding section the focus is on colocation that brings about localization economies, which are a form of agglomeration economies. Another form is urbanization economies, and this phenomenon is based on similar mechanisms but with a focus on the role of diversity.

4.1   Agglomeration and urbanization economies
Urbanization economies arise in large functional urban regions – in particular in metropolitan regions. In such regions, of which diversity is a basic characteristic, we can observe a variety of specializations inside the region (Lucas, 2001). In a sense a metropolitan region is a self-contained universe that generates a large share of its own demand (see also Desrochers, Sautet and Hospers, in this volume). Therefore, in a large urban region, there are several location decisions to consider. Should a firm locate in a region in the first place? If the answer is affirmative, in which local area should it locate? Moreover, does it matter in which zone of a local area the firm is established? The multiplicity of alternatives in a metropolitan region makes these considerations necessary.

Urbanization and productivity   When does the selection of a particular zone matter? The general case is colocation of agents that benefit from frequent contacts, and the notion of a central business district (CBD) in the largest city of a region would be the standard case, with the financial district as the prominent CBD example. The other example is the shopping district, where shopkeepers benefit from colocation, because customers benefit from making a single multi-purpose trip to such a district rather than making many diverse trips to complete their shopping. Fujita and Thisse (2002) identify this as 'the formation of clusters of stores selling similar goods'.

An urban region has several local areas, usually with a largest central city and a set of smaller neighbouring towns. The central city is characterized by the largest diversity of certain contact-intensive activities and by having the highest land values. The local areas may have special accessibility to facilities for long-distance interaction, such as air terminals, harbour services and the like, and they have generically lower land values.

To paraphrase a statement attributed to Ernest Hemingway, metropolitan regions are different from other regions by being larger and hence capable of according more diversity. In this way they become more attractive to households, to the extent that households give priority to the diversity which large urban regions can offer. Another assumption, which goes back to Ohlin's (1933) discussion of urbanization economies, is that large urban regions are more productive. In several contributions by Henderson (1977, 1988) the suggestion is that this is verified by higher land values in large functional regions. Moreover, a recurrent conclusion in Fujita and Thisse (2002) is that productivity (or efficiency) advantages of agglomerations are ultimately collected as land value incomes in the agglomeration.

The above issue of productivity is discussed in Johansson and Quigley (2004). They separate three mechanisms that enhance productivity:

(i)   An entire industry may benefit from agglomeration, since the size of the agglomeration provides sufficient demand to allow individual firms with internal scale economies to develop differentiated products.
(ii) An individual firm may benefit from the option to buy more specialized inputs at lower transaction costs from differentiated input suppliers within the region.
(iii) An individual firm may benefit from knowledge flows outside the market (spillovers) that arise from proximity within an agglomeration.

The first two intra-market cases are symmetrical in the sense that the pertinent externalities are generated simultaneously on the supply and demand side. In the third case the externality is 'neutral' in the sense that it may affect all regional agents in the same way.

Urbanization, innovations and growth   Studies of firm and industry location frequently consider the existence of agglomeration externalities as the key force behind clustering. In this context, urban externalities involve diversity of suppliers and information spillovers about market conditions and technology. Models of dynamic externalities argue that clusters grow because they allow people to interact and learn from each other. The frequency of the interaction is facilitated by proximity. This perspective matters when the analysis is extended from studying productivity to include growth of productivity, such that income per inhabitant is augmented.

Jacobs (1969, 1984) viewed this second type of externality, which emphasizes industry diversity in a city or region, as the main factor behind regional development and national economic growth: 'People who think of cities simply as towns that have kept growing larger are believers in a *preformation* theory of city growth, an enlargement of what is essentially already there' (Jacobs, 1969: p. 126). Later work by Bairoch (1988) supports Jacobs' arguments, particularly with regard to the effects of diversity on innovation and diffusion of technologies (see also Desrochers, 2001). Jacobs' conclusions were also reiterated by Lucas (1988) in the context of *new growth economics*. Lucas argued that cities play the role of *external human capital* for economic activity and the growth of knowledge. Obviously, these considerations are compatible with how the early phase of a product cycle is described (Vernon, 1966).

Urbanization economies are those economies of agglomeration which accrue to firms across different sectors (Jacobs, 1984). People who work in sectors that feature localization economies will require legal, real estate, retail, educational, health care, and leisure services. Similarly, the firms themselves may require services such as marketing, advertising, catering, packaging, transportation, real estate and security. These various activities are not directly related to the sector experiencing internal returns to scale and localization economies. In spite of this they will still cluster in the local economy in order to provide services for the firms and employees of this sector. This clustering is a response to the large market possibilities of an urban region. However, these firms will experience increased local factor prices, which must be compensated by economies of scale if the clustering is to continue. This suggests that urbanization economies develop because many different sectors are characterized by internal scale economies. As suggested in a previous section, a metropolitan region is a 'cluster of clusters'.

However, in the literature, localization economies can appear in a small town as well as in a district of a metropolitan region. Hence, the only distinction made between localization and urbanization economies is that the latter phenomenon depends in a fundamental way on the size of an urban region, which can grow large because of urbanization economies. The subsequent analysis is an attempt to make this conclusion somewhat more precise.

4.2   Taste for input diversity

In subsection 3.2 we made use of a simple 'prototype model' to illustrate the mechanisms that generate clustering of input-buying firms and of input-selling firms. A related 'parable model' can be employed to depict one important aspect of taste for diversity among input-buying firms. To simplify, we will select a case with one input-buying firm and many suppliers of differentiated inputs. In addition, the input-buying firm produces an output under a constant-returns-to-scale regime.

The parable has the following narrative form. Firms and industries that benefit from input diversity experience an upstream externality, given that the inputs are distance-sensitive and hence can be purchased at a feasible price only if the inputs are delivered from suppliers in the proximity. The assumption is that firms (or industries) can improve their productivity by using a richer composition of input varieties. To describe this, consider a production function, which relates an output X to the input of labour resources, signified by L, and the input of producer services, Q, where the value of Q increases as the number, n, of input services increases. Letting S_i denote the amount of services of type i, this yields

$$X = L^a Q^{(1-a)}, \quad Q = \left[\sum_{i=1}^{n} S_i^\rho \right]^{1/\rho}, \tag{3.7}$$

where $0<a<1$, and $0<\rho<1$. The Cobb–Douglas production function in (3.7) implies that a given share of the returns is spent on producer services, while X expands as n increases, implying increasing returns. We assume that the service supply is characterized by monopolistic competition. In a regional equilibrium setting this means that a region that has a large output will also have a large diversity of service supply.

Let w be the given price of the L-resource, let p_i be the price of input i, and let p be a given price of the output (possibly exported). We can now see that the total service-input cost is a constant share of sales, such that $\Sigma_i p_i S_i / pX = (1-a)$, while $wL / pX = a$. This means that a given share is spent on producer services, while X expands as the number of inputs, n, increases. Thus, a large region with a rich supply of services provides a location advantage.

The externality based on (3.7) can easily be used as an argument in explaining urbanization economies. As a first alternative, suppose that there are many different industries like the one depicted in (3.7), each with a taste for input variety. Then we can just assume that each of these industries has partially overlapping patterns of demand for inputs. If, in addition, we consider that a large urban region has many such industries then the number of service varieties, S_j, will be greater in a large than in a small region, and the larger region will be more productive and diversified at the same time. A second alternative is to assume that X represents an output index for many input-buying firms, and then a large region just means a region with a large X.

The possibility of exporting the output, X, (e.g. a composite export commodity) increases as the size of the input supply, Q, increases. At the same time there is an incentive to increase Q as X increases. In this sense, X remains an exogenous demand factor that stimulates the differentiation of the distance-sensitive supply of inputs. This latter part of the circularity is a kind of downstream externality.

The above conclusion may of course be extended, given that the demand for X increases as the export price is decreased. In this case the self-reinforcing effects of the externality can be described by the sequence (i) increased diversity, (ii) increased productivity and decreased costs, (iii) reduced price and increased export sales, followed by opportunities to further increase diversity. However, a negatively sloping demand for the composite output X would change the model setting and make it more difficult to embed in an equilibrium solution.

To a large extent the discussion in this subsection reflects the ideas, already referred to, of Jacobs about the advantages that are present in a large urban region. However, Jacobs also argues that metropolitan regions are import nodes in the global economy. In this case one may observe that import activities feature both internal and external scale economies, and hence certain large regions like Los Angeles and New York have become dominating import nodes in the USA, just like Stockholm and Helsinki in the small Nordic economies (Andersson and Andersson, 2000). This would imply that imported goods are both cheaper and more diversified in large urban regions, based on a clustering of importing firms in such regions, and this would increase the diversity of inputs to the production in such large regions. In a subsequent subsection this form of import economies will be considered in relation to urbanization economies of innovation (Johansson and Westin, 1987).

4.3   Customers' taste for diversity

Customers' taste for variety generates an output-demand externality on several scales in a large urban region. The first of these scales is related to the formation of shopping districts inside an urban region. The second is related to the formation of the urban region itself and its size.

A particular form of a 'specialized shopping district' is a small spatial area in which one can find a cluster of stores selling similar goods, such as spectacles for example. The principles behind the formation of such a place are examined by Fujita and Thisse (2002) with the help of a model in which (i) consumers have a taste for variety and (ii) the sellers (shops) supply differentiated goods or services in a monopolistic competition regime with negatively sloping demand and fixed costs, similar to the assumptions in subsection 3.2. In addition the shopping activity of consumers is distance-sensitive. In view of this each firm is aware that consumers will find shopping places with much variety more attractive than those with smaller variety. As the shops cluster into a specific place, this place will be characterized by variety.

The assumption about product differentiation is essential. Differentiation together with a taste for variety implies that different shops do not have to fear the competition from the neighbouring firms, as in the competition model of Hotelling (1929). Instead, each firm can sell its variety at a price above marginal cost. As a consequence the firm will be able to compete for land in an attractive spot, i.e., a place where other similar firms also want to be. The negatively sloping demand and associated mark-up is hence essential for the formation of a shopping district.

First, we should observe that a large urban region is special in having sufficiently many consumers (and other customers) to host many different specialized shopping districts. Second, we also should observe that specialized shopping districts may cluster together into malls and other forms of centres. Indeed, colocated specialized clusters of shops in the central city of an urban region are a basic form of a shopping centre.

The preference function of customers in the above shopping-district model is a variant of the *U*-function in (3.8), where q_k denotes the amount of product variety that a typical consumer buys, and where n represents the number of varieties. The same function can also be applied to explain the role of diversity for an urban region as a whole.

$$U = \sum_{k=1}^{n} q_k^{\phi}, \, 0 < \phi < 1. \tag{3.8}$$

Consider now that each customer maximizes U for a given budget share $\hat{m}$. With a given number of customers the corresponding aggregate budget is M. The result of a customer's choice can be derived from maximizing the Lagrange function $\Lambda = \Sigma_k q_k^{\phi} + \lambda(m - \Sigma_k p_k q_k)$, where p_k denotes the price of product variety k. The solution is $p_k = \phi q_k^{\phi-1}/\lambda$. Next, consider that the number of varieties, n, is large enough to make negligible the effect that a change in any p_k may have on λ, which expresses the marginal utility of money (Dixit and Stiglitz, 2004). To the extent that this makes income effects negligible, we can introduce the variable $\theta = 1/(1-\phi) > 1$ to obtain the following demand function:

$$x_k = \alpha_k p_k^{-\theta} M, \tag{3.9}$$

which we recognize from Formula (3.2), and where the parameter θ represents the price elasticity and where $\alpha_k = \alpha$ for all products. The value of α can be thought of as a local approximation, which is constant in a temporary monopolistic-competition equilibrium. As discussed in subsection 3.2, this value of α represents a price index for the market (Fujita, Krugman & Venables, 1999).

We shall make the heroic assumption that consumers' demand in an urban region is captured by n demand functions like the one in (3.9). The major merit of the model is that it describes stringently a market in which customers have a strong taste for variety when ϕ has a low value.

Our next assumption is that the urban region hosts n suppliers, each with the cost function that is specified in (3.1), and each supplying one of the varieties included in the preference function. This means that in equilibrium each firm produces just one variety and the output satisfies $x_k = x_0 = (F/v)(\theta - 1)$ for every firm. Moreover, the number of products, n^*, and the market price, p, will be

$$n^* = M/F\theta$$
$$p = v\theta/(\theta - 1). \tag{3.10}$$

Equation (3.10) illustrates the effect that the size of fixed costs, F, has on the achievable diversity. In view of this, observe that, when an urban region grows, M will grow, and when that happens, the number of varieties n^* will also grow. As a consequence, the utility of the inhabitants in the region will increase, signalling that the region is becoming more attractive. If consumers can migrate at sufficiently low costs from other regions, a large urban region may continue to grow in a self-generating, cumulative process. One basic thing that limits such growth is that competition for space in the region will intensify and land values will increase.

One way to generalize the preference function in (3.8) is to define it as a sub-utility function, U_i, which is a component in an overall preference function,

$$U = \prod_{i=1}^{K} U_i^{\alpha_i}, \; U_i = \sum_{k=1}^{n_i} q_k^{\phi_i}. \tag{3.11}$$

With the specification in (3.11) the consumers' taste for variety is present for many categories of commodity groups, $i = 1,\ldots,K$, each with specific parameter α_i and ϕ_i as well as specific fixed costs F_i.

Consider now that equation (3.11) reflects an essential aspect of urbanization diversity. Then it is evident that the taste for variety can be better satisfied if also import flows can help to increase the variety. This suggestion is relevant for those product groups that have sufficiently low distance sensitivity. This may obtain as the result of trade network investments that make the long-haul transportation costs low. Combining this with a well-organized local import and sales organization will make it possible for importing firms to exploit customer proximity in large urban regions. In this explanation two assumptions are critical. First, large urban regions can be assumed to generate a greater demand for variety than elsewhere. Second, the described import-network solutions are based on costly investments, and these can be motivated only by a sufficiently large demand. The pertinent scale economies can be exploited best in metropolitan regions.

Associated with the outline above is a recent and vast set of contributions, which is sometimes referred to as the 'new trade theory'. One reference is the series of early contributions that are collected in Krugman (1990). Other contributions are Helpman (1981, 1984) and Brander and Spencer (1984).

4.4   Innovation and urbanization economies

Innovation is the result of a firm's development efforts. In these efforts knowledge flows from outside the firm play a crucial role. We have earlier stressed information and knowledge exchange with customers, input suppliers and specialized knowledge providers. Metropolitan regions have advantages by having a greater amount and variety of knowledge sources. This was a starting-point in Vernon (1962, 1966) and is elaborated in more recent contributions such as (Feldman and Audretsch, 1999; Acs, 1994; Jaffe, Trajtenberg and Henderson, 1993). The so-called 'Jacobs hypothesis' is that metropolitan regions are different in having both intraindustry and interindustry knowledge flows (Capello, 2001). In the subsequent analysis we emphasize that the diversity of industries in a large urban region implies an extraordinary diversity of both customers and input suppliers (including knowledge providers).

To illustrate the features of urbanization economies in the context of product development, we shall make use of the prototype model introduced in subsection 3.2. This model is altered by introducing a condition that forces the monopolistic–competition firms to carry through product innovations repetitively, because established product variants are assumed to become obsolete after a certain time on the market.

Let us consider the following framework. At any point in time, t, a monopolistic-competition market contains a set, $N(t)$, of product varieties. In a growing economy this set can be expected to expand. Each of these products has the same demand function and cost function, as specified in (3.1) and (3.2) – with one important qualification. Each product has a date of 'birth', τ, and the demand coefficient $\alpha = \alpha(t,\tau)$ is a function of its age, $t-\tau$. When the age reaches a certain level, we assume that the α-value drops, which implies that after the drop the production is no longer profitable. This will force firms to develop new products, and when a new product is ready these R&D costs amount to F.

Given the above assumptions, the demand specification takes the form

$$x(t,\tau) = \alpha(t,\tau)p(t,\tau)^{-\theta}D, \tag{3.12}$$

where D is a demand indicator (potential demand) for the entire product group, for which all different varieties are included in $N(t)$, where $\alpha(t,\tau) = \alpha$ when the product is introduced and remains at this level until it drops, and where $p(t,\tau) = v\theta/(\theta-1)$ until demand falls and the supply ends. This happens when $\Delta T = t-\tau$ has passed its critical value ΔT^*. The individual firm has to recover the fixed costs during the time period when it can sell its output at the equilibrium price given above.

In association with the demand given by (3.12) the cost function of the individual firm is given by Forslund (1998):

$$C(t,\tau) = vx(t,\tau) + F, \tag{3.13}$$

and we may consider the advantage the firm has from a location in a large urban region during a lifetime ΔT^*. We can do that by considering that the input costs of the firm has the following form:

$$v = (\beta\rho + (1-\beta)\hat{\rho})\bar{v}, \tag{3.14}$$

where ρ is the price of locally purchased input, $\hat{\rho}$ is the price of inputs bought from outside the region, where $\beta \leq 1$ is the share of local supply of inputs and $1-\beta$ is the share of inputs bought externally, and where $\bar{v}$ is a given coefficient. Assume now that $\hat{\rho} > \rho > 0$. Then the firm will benefit from being located in a large urban region, in which the size of β is large. If the production requires input diversity, large urban regions will have a larger set, N, of varieties than a smaller region.

In the setting outlined above, the individual firm has to introduce a new product variety at intervals of length ΔT^*. The associated R&D requires various kinds of knowledge (or R&D) inputs. The cost of acquiring a unit R&D input from inside the region is denoted by ω, whereas a similar input from outside the region costs $\hat{\omega}$. The share of locally supplied

R&D inputs is signified by $\delta \leq 1$ and the share of R&D inputs from outside the region is $(1-\delta)$. Then the fixed cost caused by the product development activity becomes

$$F = [\delta\omega + (1 - \delta)\hat{\omega}]\overline{F}, \tag{3.15}$$

where $\overline{F}$ is a given coefficient. Assume now that a large urban region has a greater supply of R&D inputs than other regions. Then we can expect that δ is larger in large than in small urban regions. As a consequence, there will be an R&D advantage for large urban regions, if we assume that $\omega < \hat{\omega}$ thanks to distance sensitivity of R&D deliveries.

The extremely simple model outlined here manages to suggest two advantages of large urban regions. For a given product group, both the variable and fixed cost components may be smaller. Having said this, we observe that the cost function in (3.13) excludes costs of floor space, which should be high in large urban regions because of high land values.

However, the prime observation is that, in accordance with (3.15), firms in a large urban region have lower fixed costs, as represented by F. Consider now that there are many different products that have the same elasticity θ and the same variable-cost specification as given by (3.14). Then we can say that (3.15) implies that in a large urban region firms can develop new products in product groups for which $\overline{F}$ is high, and this opportunity will not be available in smaller regions.

What conclusions can be derived from the exercise above? We can formulate three tentative conclusions that should provide incentives to future research. The first reflects on exports, the second on imports and the third on knowledge flows and intellectual property:

(i)   A firm's development of a new product variety brings about fixed costs. When fixed costs are large the intraregional market is not large enough to allow the firm to recover the fixed costs. As a consequence, a large proportion of all R&D and innovation efforts is linked to export plans. In small regions this is always the case.

(ii) The analysis above identifies the share β of local variable inputs and the share δ of local knowledge inputs. In a metropolitan region, these shares can be expected to be higher than in smaller regions. At the same time, diversified and large-scale import activities also make both the 'price' of imported current inputs, $\hat{p}$, and the 'price' of imported knowledge inputs, $\hat{\omega}$, lower than in other regions, thus providing an import-based advantage in a metropolitan region.

(iii) The variable ω is meant to reflect the cost of acquiring a unit of knowledge inputs. If many knowledge flows are not charged any price, this price variable will also be low. This brings us to the point of reflecting on the 'knowledge leakage' from the individual firm, which may be less serious in a large urban region, because the large variety in a metropolitan region could imply that, for the single firm, the benefits of inflows from a rich environment outweigh the losses of outflows that are diffused to firms that, because of diversity, are not specific competitors.

5   Is colocation dynamics the generic phenomenon?

In the previous sections a specific set of principles have been employed to depict proximity externalities that constitute one particular reason for differences in regional growth rates and location patterns. However, there is also an empirical issue, finding out to what extent one can attribute regional economic growth to urbanization economies and what role is played by localization economies.

The benefits that accrue to a firm thanks to its location can be traced in several dimensions, such as the sustainability or survival of the firm, its productivity, its innovativeness and its profitability – to mention the most basic economic indicators. Can it be empirically verified that these performance indicators are more favourable for firms located in a spatial cluster or in a large urban region, respectively? There is astonishingly little research that provides conclusive answers to this type of question.

There are indeed theoretical reasons why empirical analyses may have difficulties in verifying cumulative change based on spatial externalities. In some cases an industry cluster may grow, whereas other cases provide examples of stagnation and decline. Obviously, a cumulative change process may come to rest, and possibly satisfy equilibrium conditions. Thus, it is not sufficient with a description of how externalities can cause cumulative adjustments. Mature knowledge would include the capacity to depict the growth and decline phases as well as potential equilibria. And empirical analyses should be organized to distinguish and capture change and equilibrium aspects of localization and urbanization economies.

5.1 Clustering and localization economies

Consider colocation associated with a specific industry. In this case the following questions may be asked:

(i)   Do firms belonging to a spatial cluster have a higher survival rate than similar firms that are not colocated? When the answer is in the affirmative, it remains to find out the regional conditions that explain the observed sustainability.

(ii)   To what extent is the productivity and profitability higher for firms that are colocated compared to other firms? In addition, does the productivity rise faster for firms that are colocated?

(iii) Are firms belonging to a spatial cluster more innovative than firms that are not colocated?

At present, the above questions remain to a large extent unanswered. Widening the scope to cover both horizontal and vertical colocation may open new avenues of empirical research. Existing empirical studies do not allow for conclusions about productivity and growth differentials. However, a given industry cluster may have a past history of cumulative colocation and productivity growth (Audretsch and Feldman, 1995). If this change process has come to rest, one should expect productivity differentials to have disappeared.

In a recent study, Beaudry and Breschi (2003) ask the question: are firms in a cluster more innovative? Their answer is clear-cut. In general the firms in a spatial cluster are not more innovative. However, for specific spatial clusters, many firms are innovative and as a consequence they form a milieu from which new entrants into the cluster can benefit. This type of observation suggests that colocated activities survive through repeated product renewal and other successive innovations. Other observations in this concluding subsection tell us that longitudinal perspectives are essential. Moreover, a colocation milieu includes both social networks and policy processes.

5.2 *Urbanization economies and dynamics*

Urbanization economies are different from localization economies precisely because they rely, not on specific vertical and horizontal externalities, but on diversity of input alternatives and on customer diversity. This implies that the options of developing urbanization economies should increase as the size of an urban region grows. The empirical evidence of urbanization economies is also more clear-cut than in the case of localization economies. For a range of economic activities one can observe how productivity, wage levels and land rents are higher in large than in small urban regions (e.g. Henderson, 1988).

Recent theory is explicit in its assessment of urbanization economies. Following Fujita and Thisse (2002), these economies should give rise to productivity gains and higher wages. Moreover, given that the land market is well behaving – and hence is supporting an efficient equilibrium – the surplus from higher productivity will be accumulated in land values, which is reflected by higher floor space costs. This form of equilibrium would also wipe out profit differentials between similar firms in different regions.

The conclusions about land values are based on models depicting monopolistic competition and taste for variety. This remark also suggests an alternative view on urbanization economies, emphasizing that the benefit of the inhabitants of an urban region materializes in a greater variety. Students of R&D and innovation also argue that greater diversity in large urban regions generates distance-sensitive knowledge flows, which likewise fosters diverse innovation activities, referred to as the Jacobs hypothesis. This idea is elaborated by Capello (2002), who carries out a detailed study of the Milan region and manages to identify localization phenomena, for specific innovation-intensive activities, inside the region. Using a quite different approach, Feldman and Francis (2001) arrive at similar conclusions for a high-tech cluster in the U.S. Capitol region.

The authors of the present chapter strongly believe that models that focus on externalities that combine horizontal externalities and vertical externalities, with clustering of both input-supplying and input-buying firms can bridge the gap between the localization and urbanization routes of analysis, the prime difference being that large urban regions can more easily accord richer combinations of that type, and hence offer more novel options and be more generous in allowing failures.

Notes

1. CESIS, Centre of Excellence for Science and Innovation Studies, The Royal Institute of Technology, Stockholm and JIBS, Jönköping International Business School.
2. JIBS, Jönköping International Business School.
3. The result in (3.5) can in various ways be extended to interregional transactions (Fujita and Thisse, 2002), but at the cost of more constrained assumptions than we want to make here.

Bibliography

Acs, Z.J. (ed.) (1994), *Regional Innovation, Knowledge and Global Change*, London: Frances Pinter.
Adams, J. (2002), 'Comparative localization of academic and industrial spillovers', *Journal of Economic Geography*, **2**, 253–78.
Almeida, P. and B. Kogut (1999), 'Localization of knowledge and the mobility of engineers in regional networks', *Management Science*, **45**, 905–17.
Andersson, Å.E. (1993), 'Economic structure of the 21st century', in Å.E. Andersson, D. Batten, K. Kobayashi and K. Yoshikawa (eds), *The Cosmo-Creative Society – Logistical Networks in a Dynamic Economy*, Heidelberg: Springer Verlag.
Andersson, Å.E. and D.E. Andersson (eds) (2000), *Gateways to the Global Economy*, Cheltenham, UK and Northampton, MA, USA: Edward Elgar.

Andersson, Å.E. and B. Johansson (2000), 'The Stockholm region in the global economy', in Å.E. Andersson and D.E. Andersson (eds), *Gateways to the Global Economy*, Cheltenham, UK and Northampton, MA, USA: Edward Elgar.

Andersson, M. and C. Karlsson (2004), 'The role of accessibility for the performance of regional innovation systems', reprinted in C. Karlsson, S.-Å. Flensburg and P. Hörte (eds), *Knowledge Spillovers and Knowledge Management*, Cheltenham, UK and Northampton, MA, USA: Edward Elgar.

Andersson, M. and C. Karlsson (2007), 'Knowledge in regional economic growth – the role of knowledge accessibility', *Industry and Innovation*, **14**(2), 129–49.

Andersson, Å.E., C. Anderstig and B. Hårsman (1990), 'Knowledge and communications infrastructure', *Regional Science and Urban Economics*, **20**, 359–76.

Artle, R. (1959), 'The structure of the Stockholm economy – toward a framework for projecting metropolitan community development', Stockholm School of Economics, Stockholm.

Audretsch, D.B. and M. Feldman (1995), 'Innovative clusters and the industrial life cycle', Discussion Paper 1161, Centre for Economic Policy Research, London.

Bairoch, P. (1988), *Cities and Economic Development – From the Dawn of History to the Present*, Chicago: The University of Chicago Press.

Baptista, R. (1996), 'Industrial clusters and technological innovation', *Business Strategy Review*, **6**(96), 59–64.

Baptista, R. (1998), 'Clusters, innovation and growth: a survey of the literature', in G.M.P Swann, M. Prevezer and D. Stout (eds), *The Dynamics of Industrial Clustering: International Comparisons in Computers and Biotechnology*, Oxford: Oxford University Press.

Beaudry, C. and S. Breschi (2003), 'Are firms in clusters really more innovative? Economics of innovation and new technology', *Taylor and Francis Journals*, **12**(4), 325–42, August.

Beckmann, M.J. (1952), 'A continuous model of transportation', *Econometrica*, **20**, 643–60.

Beckmann, M.J. and J.-F. Thisse (1986), 'The location of production activities', in P. Nijkamp (ed.), *Handbook of Regional and Urban Economics – Volume 1, Regional Economics*, Amsterdam: North-Holland, pp. 21–95.

Bohm, P. (1987), 'External economies', *The Palgrave Dictionary of Economics*, London: The Macmillan Press.

Brakman, S., H. Garretsen and C. van Marrewijk (2001), *An Introduction to Geographical Economics*, Cambridge: Cambridge University Press.

Brander, J.A. and B.J. Spencer (1984), 'Tariff protection and imperfect competition', in H. Kierzkowski (ed.), *Monopolistic Competition and International Trade*, Oxford: Oxford University Press.

Breschi, S. and F. Lissoni (2001), 'Localised knowledge spillovers vs. innovative milieux: knowledge tacitness reconsidered', *Papers in Regional Science*, **80**(3), 255–73.

Capello, R. (2001), 'Urban innovation and collective learning: theory and evidence from five metropolitan cities in Europe', in M.M. Fischer and J. Fröhlich (eds), *Knowledge, Complexity and Innovation Systems*, Berlin: Springer Verlag.

Capello, R. (2002), 'Entrepreneurship and spatial externalities. Theory and measurement', *Annals of Regional Science*, **36**, 387–402.

Cheshire, P. and I. Gordon (1998), 'Territorial competition: some lessons for policy', *Annals of Regional Science*, **32**, 321–46.

Cheshire, P. and S. Magrini (2005), 'Regional demographic or economic dynamism? Different causes, different consequences', paper presented at a workshop at Jönköping International Business School, June.

Debreu, G. (1959), *Theory of Value: An Axiomatic Analysis of Economic Equilibrium*, Cowlew Commission Monograph 17, New York: John Wiley.

Desrochers, P. (2001), 'Local diversity, human creativity and technological innovation', *Growth and Change*, **32**(3), 369–94.

Dixit, A. and J.E. Stiglitz (2004), 'Monopolistic competition and optimum product diversity', in S. Brakman and B.J. Heijdra (eds), *The Monopolistic Competition Revolution in Retrospect*, Cambridge: Cambridge University Press, pp. 89–120.

Echeverri-Carroll, E. (2001), 'Knowledge spillovers in high technology agglomerations: measurement and modelling', in M.M. Fischer and J. Fröhlich (eds), *Knowledge, Complexity and Innovation Systems*, Berlin: Springer Verlag.

Enright, M.J. (1996), 'Regional clusters and economic development: a research agenda', in U.H. Staber, N.V. Schaefer and B. Sharma (eds), *Business Networks: Prospects for Regional Development*, Berlin: de Gruyter.

Feldman, M.P. (1994), *The Geography of Innovation*, Dordrecht, Boston: Kluwer.

Feldman, M.P. and D.B. Audretsch (1999), 'Innovation in cities: science-based diversity, specialisation and localised competition', *European Economic Review*, **43**, 409–29.

Feldman, M.P. and J. Francis (2001), 'The entrepreneurial spark: individual agents and the formation of innovation clusters', prepared for the conference on Complexity and Industrial Clusters – Dynamics and Models in Theory and Practice, 19 June 2001, Fondazione Comunita e Innovazione, Milan.

Fischer, M.M. (2001), 'Innovation, knowledge creation and systems of innovation', *The Annals of Regional Science*, **35**, 199–216.

Florida, R. (2002), *The Rise of the Creative Class and how it's Transforming Work, Leisure, Community and Everyday Life*, New York: Basic Books.

Forslund, U.M. (1998), 'Education intensity and interregional location dynamics', in A. Reggiani (ed.), *Accessibility, Trade and Location Behavior*, Aldershot: Ashgate, pp. 97–120.

Fujita, M. (1989), *Urban Economic Theory – Land Use and City Size*, Cambridge: Cambridge University Press.

Fujita, M. and J.-F. Thisse (2002), *Economics of Agglomeration – Cities, Industrial Location, and Regional Growth*, Cambridge: Cambridge University Press.

Fujita, M., P. Krugman and A.J. Venables (1999), *The Spatial Economy – Cities, Regions and International Trade*, Cambridge, MA: The MIT Press.

Glaeser, E.L. and J.E. Kohlhase (2004), 'Cities, regions and the decline of transport costs', *Papers in Regional Science*, **83**, 197–228.

Gordon, I.R. and P. McCann (2000), 'Industrial clusters: complexes, agglomeration and/or social networks', *Urban Studies*, **37**, 513–32.

Gråsjö, U. (2005), 'Accessibility to R&D and patent production', CESIS Working Paper Series No 37, Royal Institute of Technology, Stockholm.

Groot, de H.L.F., P. Nijkamp and Z. Acs (eds) (2001), 'Knowledge spillovers, innovation and regional development', special issue of *Papers in Regional Science*, **80**(3), 249–53.

Grossman, G.M. and E. Helpman (2005), 'Outsourcing in the global economy', *The Review of Economic Studies*, **72**, 135–59.

Hall, M. (ed.) (1959), *Made in New York*, Cambridge, MA: Harvard University Press.

Helpman, E. (1981), 'International trade in the presence of product differentiation, economies of scale and monopolistic competition: a Chamberlin–Heckscher–Ohlin approach', *Journal of International Economics*, **11**, 305–40.

Helpman, E. (1984), 'Increasing returns, imperfect markets and trade theory', in R. Jones and P. Kenan (eds), *Handbook of International Economics*, Vol. 1, Amsterdam: North-Holland, pp. 325–65.

Henderson, J.V. (1974), 'The size and types of cities', *American Economic Review*, **64**, 640–56.

Henderson, J.V. (1977), *Economic Theory and the Cities*, New York: Academic Press.

Henderson, J.V. (1988), *Urban Development Theory, Fact and Illusion*, Oxford: Oxford University Press.

Henderson, R., A.B. Jaffe and M. Trajtenberg (1995), 'Universities as a source of commercial technology: a detailed analysis of university patenting 1965–1988', NBER WP 5068, Cambridge, MA: National Bureau of Economic Research.

Hippel, E. von (1994), 'Sticky information and the locus of problem solving: implications for innovation', *Management Science*, **40**(4), 429–39.

Holmberg, I., B. Johansson and U. Strömquist (2003), 'A simultaneous model of long-term regional job and population changes', in Å.E. Andersson, B. Johansson and W.P. Anderson (eds), *The Economics of Disappearing Distance*, Aldershot: Ashgate, pp. 161–89.

Hoover, E.M. (1948), *The Location of Economic Activity*, New York: McGraw-Hill.

Hotelling, H. (1929), 'Stability in competition', *Economic Journal*, **39**, 41–57.

Isard, W. (1951), 'Distance inputs and the space economy: the locational equilibrium of the firm', *Quarterly Journal of Economics*, **65**, 373–97.

Isard, W. (1956), *Location and Space Economy*, New York: John Wiley.

Jacobs, J. (1969), *The Economy of Cities*, New York: Random House.

Jacobs, J. (1984), *Cities and the Wealth of Nations*, New York: Random House.

Jaffe, A., M. Trajtenberg and R. Henderson (1993), 'Geographical localisation of knowledge spillovers as evidenced by patent citations', *Quarterly Journal of Economics*, **108**, 577–98.

Johansson, B. and Å.E. Andersson (1998), 'A Schloss Laxenburg model of product cycle dynamics', in M. Beckmann, B. Johansson, F. Snickars and R. Thord (eds), *Knowledge and Networks in a Dynamic Economy*, Heidelberg: Springer Verlag.

Johansson, B. and J.M. Quigley (2004), 'Agglomeration and networks in spatial economies', *Papers in Regional Science*, **83**, 165–76.

Johansson, B. and L. Westin (1987), 'Technical change, location and trade', *Papers of the Regional Science Association*, **62**, 13–25.

Johansson, B., D. Batten and J. Casti (1987), 'Economic dynamics, evolution and structural adjustments', in D. Batten, J. Casti and B. Johansson (eds), *Economic Evolution and Structural Adjustment, Lecture Notes in Economics and Mathematical Systems 293*, Heidelberg: Springer Verlag.

Johansson, B., J. Klaesson and M. Olsson (2002), 'Time distances and labor market integration', *Papers in Regional Science*, **81**, 305–27.

Karlsson, C. and B. Johansson (2006), 'Towards a dynamic theory for the spatial knowledge economy', in B. Johansson, C. Karlsson and R.R. Stough (eds), *Entrepreneurship and Dynamics in the Knowledge Economy*, London & New York: Routledge.

Karlsson, C. and A. Manduchi (2001), 'Knowledge spillovers in a spatial context – a critical review and assessment', in M.M. Fischer and J. Fröhlich (eds), *Knowledge, Complexity and Innovation Systems*, Heidelberg: Springer Verlag.

Koopmans, T.C. (1949), 'Optimum utilisation of the transport system', *Econometrica*, **17**, 136–46.

Koopmans, T.C. and M. Beckmann (1957), 'Assignment problems and the location of economic activities', *Econometrica*, **25**, 53–76.

Krugman, P.R. (1980), 'Scale economies, product differentiation, and the pattern of trade', *American Economic Review*, **70**, 950–59.

Krugman, P.R. (1990), *Rethinking International Trade*, Cambridge, MA: MIT Press.

Krugman, P.R. (1991), *Geography and Trade*, Cambridge, MA: MIT Press.

Launhardt, W. (1882), 'Die Bestimmung des Zweckmässigsten Standorts einer geweblichen Anlage', *Zeitschrift des Vereins deutscher Ingenieure*, **26**, 106–15.

Li, Y. and K.R. Polenske (2003), 'Measuring dispersal economies in entrepreneurship, spatial clusters and interfirm networks', Research Report 04:01, Uddevalla Symposium, University of Trollhättan/Uddevalla, pp. 615–33.

Lipsey, R.E. (2003), 'Foreign direct investment and the operation of multinational firms: history and data', in E.K. Choi and J. Harrigan (eds), *Handbook of International Trade*, Oxford: Blackwell Publishing, pp. 287–319.

Lucas, R.E. (1988), 'On the mechanics of economic development', *Journal of Monetary Economics*, **22**(1) July, 3–42.

Lucas, R.E. (2001), 'Externalities and cities', *Review of Economic Dynamics*, **4**, 245–74.

Maclennan, D. (1990), 'Urban change through environmental investments', in *Urban Challenges*, SOU 1990:3, Stockholm, pp. 51–76.

Marshall, A. (1920), *Principles of Economics*, 8th edn, London: Macmillan.

McCann, P. (1998), *The Economics of Industrial Location – A Logistics–Costs Approach*, Berlin: Springer Verlag.

McCann, P. (2001), *Urban and Regional Economics*, Oxford: Oxford University Press.

McCann, P. and D. Shefer (2004), 'Location agglomeration and infrastructure', *Papers in Regional Science*, **83**, 177–96.

Moses, L.N. (1958), 'Location and the theory of production', *Quarterly Journal of Economics*, **78**, 259–72.

Munnel, A.H. (1990), 'Does public infrastructure affect regional economic performance?', in A.H. Munnel (ed.), *Is there a Shortfall in Public Capital Investment*, Reserve Bank of Boston, Conference Series No. 34, Boston, Mass.

Ohlin, B. (1933), *Interregional and International Trade*, Cambridge, MA: Harvard University Press.

Puu, T. (2003), *Mathematical Location and Land Use Theory – An Introduction*, Berlin: Springer Verlag.

Quigley, J.M. (1990), 'The quality of housing', in *Urban Challenges*, SOU 1990:3, Stockholm, pp. 39–50.

Samuelson, P. (1952), 'Spatial price equilibrium and linear programming', *American Economic Review*, **42**, 283–303.

Starret, D. (1978), 'Market allocations of location choice in a model with free mobility', *Journal of Economic Theory*, **17**, 21–37.

Steiner, M. (ed.) (1998), *Clusters and Regional Specialisation. On Geography, Technology and Networks*, European Research in Regional Science 8, London: Pion.

Swann, G.M.P., M. Prevezer and D. Stout (eds) (1998), *The Dynamics of Industrial Clustering: International Comparisons in Computers and Biotechnology*, Oxford: Oxford University Press.

Takayama, T. (1994), 'Thirty years with spatial and intertemporal economics', *Annals of Regional Science*, **28**, 305–22.

Takayama, T. and G.G. Judge (1971), *Spatial and Temporal Allocation Problems*, Amsterdam: North-Holland.

Thünen, J.H. von (1826 [1966]), *Der Isolierte Staat in Beziehung auf Landwirtschaft und Nationalekonomie*, Stuttgart: Gustav Fischer.

Varga, A. (1997), *University Research and Regional Innovation: A Spatial Econometric Analysis of Technology Transfers*, Boston: Kluwer Academic Publishers.

Varga, A. (2001), 'Universities and regional economic development: does agglomeration matter?', in B. Johansson, C. Karlsson and R. Stough (eds), *Theories of Endogenous Regional Growth – Lessons for Regional Policies*, Berlin: Springer Verlag, pp. 345–67.

Varga, A. (2002), 'Knowledge transfers from universities to the regional economy: a review of the literature', in A. Varga and László Szerb (eds), *Innovation, Entrepreneurship and Regional Economic Development: International Experiences and Hungarian Challenges*, Pécs: University of Pécs Press, pp. 147–71.

Vernon, R. (1962), *Metropolis 1985*, Cambridge, MA: Harvard University Press.

Vernon, R. (1966), 'International investment and international trade in the product cycle', *Quarterly Journal of Economics*, **80**, 190–207.

Verspagen, B. and W. Schoenmakers (2000), 'The spatial dimension of knowledge spillovers in Europe: evidence from firm patenting data', ECIS Working Papers 00.07, Eindhoven Centre for Innovation Studies, Eindhoven University of Technology.

Weber, A. (1909), *Über den Standorten der Industrie*, Tübingen: JCB Mohr.
Weibull, J.W. (1976), 'An axiomatic approach to the measurement of accessibility', *Regional Science and Urban Economics*, **6**, 357–79.
Weibull, J.W. (1980), 'On the numerical measurement of accessibility', *Environment and Planning A*, **12**, 53–67.
Zucker, L.G. and M.R. Darby (2005), 'Socio-economic impact of nanoscale science: initial results and NanoBank', NBER Working Paper 11181, National Bureau of Economic Research, Inc.

4 The knowledge spillover theory of entrepreneurship and spatial clusters
*David B. Audretsch and T. Taylor Aldridge**

1 Introduction

The emergence of knowledge as perhaps the key factor in shaping economic growth, employment creation and competitiveness in globally linked markets has also had an impact on the organization of economic activity. First, it has affected the spatial organization of economic activity. In particular, globalization has rendered the organization of economic activity for the spatial unit of the region more important. Just as globalization has reduced the marginal cost of transmitting information and physical capital across geographic space to virtually zero, it has also shifted the comparative advantage of a high-cost *Standort*, or location, in the developed countries from being based on capital to being based on knowledge. This shift in the relative cost of (tacit) knowledge vis-à-vis information has been identified as increasing the value of geographic proximity. To access knowledge, locational proximity is important. Thus, a paradox of globalization is that it has geographic proximity and location as being more important, not in spite of a globalizing economy, but because of it.

A very different literature has identified a second impact of globalization on the organization of economic activity, which involves the enterprise. While early analyses had predicted that large corporations were endowed with a competitive advantage in accessing, producing and commercializing knowledge, more recently studies have suggested that a very different organizational form – the entrepreneurial firm – has the competitive knowledge in the knowledge-based global economy.

The purpose of this chapter is to bring these two disparate literatures together, one focusing on the organization of economic activity for the unit of analysis of geographic space, while the other focuses on the unit of analysis of the enterprise. Integrating both the organization of economic activity in geographic space and enterprise is facilitated by the lens provided by the knowledge spillover theory of entrepreneurship (Audretsch, Keilbach & Lehmann, 2006). The knowledge spillover theory of entrepreneurship provides a focus on the generation of entrepreneurial opportunities emanating from knowledge investments by incumbent firms and public research organizations which are not fully appropriated by those incumbent enterprises. The creation of a new organization is important because it is an endogenous response to knowledge not completely and exhaustively appropriated in existing organizations. Not only does endogenous entrepreneurship serve as a conduit for knowledge spillovers, but, because such knowledge spillovers tend to be spatially localized, it results in the emergence of localized entrepreneurial clusters.

The knowledge spillover theory of entrepreneurship is explained in the following section. The spatial dimension of knowledge spillovers is analysed in the third section.

2   The knowledge spillover theory of entrepreneurship

It is a virtual consensus that entrepreneurship revolves around the recognition and pursuit of these opportunities (Shane & Eckhardt, 2003). Much of the contemporary thinking about entrepreneurship has focused on the cognitive process by which individuals reach the decision to start a new firm. According to Sarasvathy, Dew, Velamuri and Venkataraman (2003, p. 142), 'An entrepreneurial opportunity consists of a set of ideas, beliefs and actions that enable the creation of future goods and services in the absence of current markets for them.' These authors provide a typology of entrepreneurial opportunities as consisting of opportunity recognition, opportunity discovery and opportunity creation.

While much has been made of the key role played by the recognition of opportunities in the cognitive process underlying the decision to become an entrepreneur, relatively little has been written about the actual source of such entrepreneurial opportunities. The knowledge spillover theory of entrepreneurship identifies one source of entrepreneurial opportunities: new knowledge and ideas. In particular, the knowledge spillover theory of entrepreneurship posits that it is new knowledge and ideas created in one context, but left uncommercialized or not vigorously pursued by the source, actually creating those ideas, such as a research laboratory in a large corporation or research undertaken by a university, that serve as the source of knowledge generating entrepreneurial opportunities. Thus, in this view, one mechanism for recognizing new opportunities and actually implementing them by starting a new firm involves the spillover of knowledge. The source of the knowledge and ideas, and the organization actually making (at least some of) the investments to produce that knowledge is not the same as the organization actually attempting to commercialize and appropriate the value of that knowledge: the new firm. If the use of that knowledge by the entrepreneur does not involve full payment to the firm making the investment that originally produced that knowledge, such as a licence or royalty, then the entrepreneurial act of starting a new firm serves as a mechanism for knowledge spillovers.

The starting point for analysing entrepreneurship has been at the level of the individual. These studies have crossed a broad spectrum of academic disciplines, ranging from psychology to sociology and economics. Within the economics literature, the prevalent theoretical framework has been the general model of income choice, which has been at times referred to as the general model of entrepreneurial choice. The model of income or entrepreneurial choice dates back at least to Knight (1921), but was more recently extended and updated by Lucas (1978), Kihlstrom and Laffont (1979), Holmes and Schmidt (1990) and Jovanovic (2001). In its most basic rendition, individuals are confronted with a choice of earning their income either from wages earned through employment in an incumbent enterprise or else from profits accrued by starting a new firm. The essence of the income choice is made by comparing the wage an individual expects to earn through employment, W^*, with the profits that are expected to accrue from a new-firm startup, P^*, and the expected risk, R^*, of the venture. Thus, the probability of starting a new firm, $Pr(s)$, can be represented as

$$Pr(s) = f(P^* + W^* - R^*). \tag{4.1}$$

Empirical tests of the model of income or entrepreneurial choice have focused on personal characteristics with respect to labour market conditions (Parker, 2005). Both the field of management and psychology have provided insights into the decision process leading individuals to start a new firm. This research trajectory focuses on the emergence and evolution of entrepreneurial cognition. Stevenson and Jarillo (1990) assume that entrepreneurship is an orientation towards opportunity recognition. Central to this research agenda are the questions, 'How do entrepreneurs perceive opportunities and how do these opportunities manifest themselves as being credible versus being an illusion?' Krueger (2003) examines the nature of entrepreneurial thinking and the cognitive process associated with opportunity identification and the decision to undertake entrepreneurial action. The focal point of this research is on the cognitive process identifying the entrepreneurial opportunity along with the decision to start a new firm. Thus, a perceived opportunity and intent to pursue that opportunity are the necessary and sufficient conditions for entrepreneurial activity to take place. The perception of an opportunity is shaped by a sense of the anticipated rewards accruing from and costs of becoming an entrepreneur. Some of the research focuses on the role of personal attitudes and characteristics, such as self-efficacy (the individual's sense of competence), collective efficacy and social norms. Shane (2000) has identified how prior experience and the ability to apply specific skills influence the perception of future opportunities. The concept of the entrepreneurial decision resulting from the cognitive processes of opportunity recognition and ensuing action is introduced by Shane and Eckhardt (2003). They suggest that an equilibrium view of entrepreneurship stems from the assumption of perfect information. By contrast, imperfect information generates divergences in perceived opportunities across different people. The sources of heterogeneity across individuals include different access to information, as well as cognitive abilities, psychological differences and access to financial and social capital.

Why should entrepreneurship play an important role in the spillover of new knowledge and ideas? And why should new knowledge play an important role in creating entrepreneurial opportunities? In the Romer model of endogenous growth new technological knowledge is assumed to spill over automatically. Investment in new technological knowledge is automatically accessed by third-party firms and economic agents, resulting in the automatic spillover of knowledge. The assumption that knowledge automatically spills over is, of course, consistent with the important insight by Arrow (1962) that knowledge differs from the traditional factors of production – physical capital and (unskilled) labour – in that it is non-excludable and non-exhaustive. When the firm or economic agent uses the knowledge, it is not exhausted, nor can it be, in the absence of legal protection, precluded from use by third-party firms or other economic agents. Thus, in the spirit of the Romer model, drawing on the earlier insights about knowledge from Arrow, a large and vigorous literature has emerged, obsessed with the links between intellectual property protection and the incentives for firms to invest in the creation of new knowledge through R&D and investments in human capital.

However, the preoccupation with the non-excludability and non-exhaustability of knowledge first identified by Arrow and later carried forward and assumed in the Romer model, neglects another key insight in the original Arrow (1962) article. Arrow also identified another dimension by which knowledge differs from the traditional factors of production. This other dimension involves the greater degree of uncertainty, higher extent of asymmetries and greater cost of transacting new ideas. The expected value of any new idea is highly uncertain and, as Arrow pointed out, has a much greater variance than would be associated with the deployment of traditional factors of production. After all, there is relative certainty about what a standard piece of capital equipment can do, or what an (unskilled) worker can contribute to a mass-production assembly line. By contrast, Arrow emphasized that, when it comes to innovation, there is uncertainty about whether the new product can be produced, how it can be produced and whether sufficient demand for the visualized new product might actually materialize.

In addition, new ideas are typically associated with considerable asymmetries. In order to evaluate a proposed new idea concerning a new biotechnology product, the decision maker might not only need to have a PhD. in biotechnology, but also a specialization in the exact scientific area. Such divergences in education, background and experience can result in a divergence in the expected value of a new project or the variance in outcomes anticipated from pursuing that new idea, both of which can lead to divergences in the recognition and evaluation of opportunities across economic agents and decision-making hierarchies. Such divergences in the valuation of new ideas will become greater if the new idea is not consistent with the core competence and technological trajectory of the incumbent firm.

Thus, because of the conditions inherent in knowledge (high uncertainty, asymmetries and transactions cost), decision-making hierarchies can reach the decision not to pursue and try to commercialize new ideas that individual economic agents, or groups or teams of economic agents, think are potentially valuable and should be pursued. The basic conditions characterizing new knowledge, combined with a broad spectrum of institutions, rules and regulations, impose what Acs et al. (2004) term *the knowledge filter*. The knowledge filter is the gap between new knowledge and what Arrow (1962) referred to as economic knowledge or commercialized knowledge. The greater is the knowledge filter, the more pronounced is this gap between new knowledge and new economic, or commercialized, knowledge.

The knowledge filter is a consequence of the basic conditions inherent in new knowledge. Similarly, it is the knowledge filter that creates the opportunity for entrepreneurship in the knowledge spillover theory of entrepreneurship. According to this theory, opportunities for entrepreneurship are the duality of the knowledge filter. The higher is the knowledge filter, the greater are the divergences in the valuation of new ideas across economic agents and the decision-making hierarchies of incumbent firms. Entrepreneurial opportunities are generated by investments, not just in new knowledge and ideas, but in the propensity for only a distinct subset of those opportunities to be fully pursued by incumbent firms.

Thus, the knowledge theory of entrepreneurship shifts the fundamental decision-making unit of observation in the model of the knowledge production function away from exogenously assumed firms to individuals, such as scientists, engineers or other knowledge workers – agents with endowments of new economic knowledge. When the lens is shifted away from the firm to the individual as the relevant unit of observation, the appropriability issue remains, but the question becomes, *How can economic agents with a given endowment of new knowledge best appropriate the returns from that knowledge?* If the scientist or engineer can pursue the new idea within the organizational structure of the firm developing the knowledge and appropriate roughly the expected value of that knowledge, she has no reason to leave the firm. On the other hand, if she places a greater value on her ideas than do the decision-making bureaucracy of the incumbent firm, she may choose to start a new firm to appropriate the value of her knowledge.

In the knowledge spillover theory of entrepreneurship the knowledge production function is actually reversed. The knowledge is exogenous and embodied in a worker. The firm is created endogenously in the worker's effort to appropriate the value of her knowledge through innovative activity. Typically an employee from an established large corporation, often a scientist or engineer working in a research laboratory, will have an idea for an invention and ultimately for an innovation. Accompanying this potential innovation is an expected net return from the new product. The inventor would expect to be compensated for her potential innovation accordingly. If the company has a different, presumably lower, valuation of the potential innovation it may decide either not to pursue its development, or that it merits a lower level of compensation than that expected by the employee.

In either case, the employee will weigh the alternative of starting her own firm. If the gap in the expected return accruing from the potential innovation between the inventor and the corporate decision maker is sufficiently large, and if the cost of starting a new firm is sufficiently low, the employee may decide to leave the large corporation and establish a new enterprise. Since the knowledge was generated in the established corporation, the new start-up is considered to be a spin-off from the existing firm. Such start-ups typically do not have direct access to a large R&D laboratory. Rather, the entrepreneurial opportunity emanates from the knowledge and experience accrued from the R&D laboratories with their previous employers. Thus the knowledge spillover view of entrepreneurship is actually a theory of endogenous entrepreneurship, where entrepreneurship is an endogenous response to opportunities created by investments in new knowledge that are not commercialized because of the knowledge filter.

The knowledge spillover theory of entrepreneurship challenges two of the fundamental assumptions implicitly driving the results of the endogenous growth models. The first is that knowledge is automatically equated with economic knowledge. In fact, as Arrow (1962) emphasized, knowledge is inherently different from the traditional factors of production, resulting in a gap between knowledge and what he termed 'economic knowledge', or economically valuable knowledge.

The second involves the assumed spillover of knowledge. The existence of the factor of knowledge is equated with its automatic spillover, yielding endogenous growth. In the knowledge spillover theory of entrepreneurship the existence of the knowledge filter imposes a gap between new knowledge and new economic knowledge, and results in a lower level of knowledge spillovers.

Thus, as a result of the knowledge filter, entrepreneurship becomes central to generating economic growth by serving as a conduit for knowledge spillovers. The process involved in recognizing new opportunities emanating from investments in knowledge and new ideas, and attempting to commercialize those new ideas through the process of starting a new firm is the mechanism by which at least some knowledge spillovers occur. In the counterfactual situation, that is in the absence of such entrepreneurship, the new ideas would not be pursued, and the knowledge would not be commercialized. Thus, entrepreneurs serve an important mechanism in the process of economic growth. An entrepreneur is an agent of change, who recognizes an opportunity, in this case generated by the creation of knowledge not adequately pursued (in the view of the entrepreneur) by incumbent organizations, and ultimately chooses to act on that opportunity by starting a new firm.

Recognition of what Arrow (1962) termed 'the non-excludability of knowledge' inherent in spillovers has led to a focus on issues concerning the appropriability of such investments in knowledge and the need for the protection of intellectual property. However, Arrow (1962) also emphasized that knowledge is also characterized by a greater degree of uncertainty and asymmetry than are other types of economic goods. Not only will the mean expected value of any new idea vary across economic agents, but the variance will also differ across economic agents. Thus, if an incumbent firm reaches the decision that the expected economic value of a new idea is not sufficiently high to warrant the development and commercialization of that idea, other economic agents, either within or outside of the firm, may instead assign a higher expected value of the idea. Such divergences in the valuation of new knowledge can lead to the start-up of a new firm in an effort by economic agents to appropriate the value of knowledge. Since the knowledge inducing the decision to start the new firm is generated by investments made by an incumbent organization, such as in R&D by an incumbent firm or research at a university, the start-up serves as the mechanism by which knowledge spills over from the sources producing that knowledge to the (new) organizational form in which that knowledge is actually commercialized. Thus, entrepreneurship serves as a conduit, albeit not the sole conduit, by which knowledge spills over.

As investments in new knowledge increase, entrepreneurial opportunities will also increase. Contexts where new knowledge plays an important role are associated with a greater degree of uncertainty and asymmetries across economic agents evaluating the potential value of new ideas. Thus, a context involving more new knowledge will also impose a greater divergence in the evaluation of that knowledge across economic agents, resulting in a greater variance in the outcome expected from commercializing those ideas. It is this gap in the valuation of new ideas across economic agents, or between economic agents and decision-making hierarchies of incumbent enterprises, that creates the entrepreneurial opportunity

The knowledge spillover theory of entrepreneurship analogously suggests that, *ceteris paribus*, entrepreneurial activity will tend to be greater in contexts where investments in new knowledge are relatively high, since the new firm will be started from knowledge that has spilled over from the source actually producing that new knowledge. A paucity of new ideas in an impoverished knowledge context will generate only limited entrepreneurial opportunities. By contrast, in a high knowledge context, new ideas will generate entrepreneurial opportunities by exploiting (potential) spillovers of that knowledge. Thus, the knowledge spillover view of entrepreneurship provides a clear link, or prediction, that entrepreneurial activity will result from investments in new knowledge.

3   The role of geographic proximity

Why should geographic proximity influence the entrepreneurial decision presented in the previous section, particularly in terms of knowledge spillover entrepreneurship? The *endogeneous entrepreneurship hypothesis* involves the organizational interdependency between entrepreneurial start-ups and incumbent organizations investing in the creation of new knowledge (Audretsch, Keilbach & Lehmann, 2006; Audretsch, 2005). A second hypothesis emerging from the knowledge spillover theory of entrepreneurship, The *localizational hypothesis*, has to do with the location of the entrepreneurial activity and the key role that regional clusters play.

An important theoretical development is that geography may provide a relevant unit of observation within which knowledge spillovers occur. The theory of localization suggests that, because geographic proximity is needed to transmit knowledge and especially tacit knowledge, knowledge spillovers tend to be localized within a geographic region. The importance of geographic proximity for knowledge spillovers has been supported in a wave of recent empirical studies by Jaffe (1989), Jaffe, Trajtenberg and Henderson (1993), Acs, Audretsch and Feldman (1992, 1994), Audretsch and Feldman (1996) and Audretsch and Stephan (1996).

As it became apparent that the firm was not completely adequate as a unit of analysis for estimating the model of the knowledge production function, scholars began to look for externalities. In refocusing the model of the knowledge production to a spatial unit of observation, scholars confronted two challenges. The first one was theoretical. What was the theoretical basis for knowledge to spill over yet, at the same time, be spatially within some geographic unit of observation? The second challenge involved measurement. How could knowledge spillovers be measured and identified? More than a few scholars heeded Krugman's warning (1991, p. 53) that empirical measurement of knowledge spillovers would prove to be impossible because 'knowledge flows are invisible, they leave no paper trail by which they may be measured and tracked'.

In confronting the first challenge, which involved developing a theoretical basis for geographically bounded knowledge spillovers, scholars turned to the emerging literature of the new growth theory. In explaining the increased divergence in the distribution of economic activity between countries and regions, Krugman (1991) and Romer (1986) relied on models based on increasing returns to scale in production. By increasing returns, however, Krugman and Romer did not necessarily mean at the level of observation most familiar in the industrial organization literature – the plant, or at least the firm – but rather at the level of a spatially distinguishable unit. In fact, it was assumed that the externalities across firms and even industries yield convexities in production. In particular, Krugman (1991), invoking Marshall (1920), focused on convexities arising from spillovers from (1) a pooled labour market; (2) pecuniary externalities enabling the provision of non-traded inputs to an industry in a greater variety and at lower cost; and (3) information or technological spillovers.

That knowledge spills over was barely disputed. Some 30 years earlier, Arrow (1962) identified externalities associated with knowledge due to its non-exclusive and non-rival use. However, what has been contested is the geographic range of knowledge spillovers: knowledge externalities are so important and forceful that there is no reason that knowledge should stop spilling over just because of borders, such as a city limit, state line or national boundary. Krugman (1991), and others, did not question the existence or importance of such knowledge spillovers. In fact, they argue that such knowledge externalities are so important and forceful that there is no reason for a political boundary to limit the spatial extent of the spillover (Schwartz, 2006).

In applying the model of the knowledge production function to spatial units of observation, theories of why knowledge externalities are spatially bounded were needed. Thus, it took the development of localization theories explaining not only that knowledge spills over but also why spillovers decay as they move across geographic space.

Studies identifying the extent of knowledge spillovers are based on the model of the knowledge production function applied at spatial units of observation. In what is generally to be considered to be the first important study refocusing the knowledge production function, Jaffe (1989) modified the traditional approach to estimate a model specified for both spatial and product dimensions. Empirical estimations essentially shifted the knowledge production function from the unit of observation of a firm to that of a geo-graphic unit. Implicitly contained within the knowledge production function model is the assumption that innovative activity should take place in those regions where the direct knowledge-generating inputs are the greatest, and where knowledge spillovers are the most prevalent. Jaffe (1989) dealt with the measurement problem raised by Krugman (1991) by linking the patent activity in technologies located within states to knowledge inputs located within the same spatial jurisdiction.

Empirical testing for the localization of knowledge spillovers essentially shifted the model of the knowledge production function from the unit of observation of a firm to that of a geographic unit. Jaffe (1989) found empirical evidence supporting the notion that knowledge spills over for third-party use from university research laboratories as well as industry R&D laboratories. Feldman (1994) extended her model to consider other knowl-edge inputs to the commercialization of new products. The results confirmed that the knowledge production function was robust at the geographic level of analysis: the output of innovation is a function of the innovative inputs in that location.

While this literature has identified the important role that knowledge spillovers play, they provide little insight into the questions of why knowledge spills over and how it spills over. What happens within the black box of the knowledge production is vague and ambiguous at best. The exact links between knowledge sources and the resulting innova-tive output remain invisible and unknown. None of the above studies suggesting that knowledge spillovers are geographically bounded and localized within spatial proximity to the knowledge source actually identified the actual mechanisms which transmit the knowledge spillover; rather, the spillovers were implicitly assumed to exist automatically, or fall like 'Manna from heaven', but only within a geographically bounded spatial area.

One explanation was provided by the knowledge spillover theory of entrepreneurship, which suggests that the start-up of a new firm is a response to investments in knowledge and ideas by incumbent organizations that are not fully commercialized by those organi-zations. Thus, those contexts that are richer in knowledge will offer more entrepreneurial opportunities and therefore should also induce endogenously more entrepreneurial activ-ity, *ceteris paribus*. By contrast, those contexts that are impoverished in knowledge will offer only meagre entrepreneurial opportunities generated by knowledge spillovers, and therefore would induce endogenously less entrepreneurial activity.

Access to knowledge spillovers requires spatial proximity. While Jaffe (1989) and Audretsch and Feldman (1996) made it clear that spatial proximity is a prerequisite to accessing such knowledge spillovers, they provided no insight about the actual mechanism transmitting such knowledge spillovers. As for the Romer and Lucas models, investment in new knowledge automatically generates knowledge spillovers. Their only additional insight involves the spatial dimension: knowledge spills over but the spillovers are spatially bounded. Since we have just identified one such mechanism by which knowledge spillovers are transmitted (the start-up of a new firm) it follows that knowledge spillover entrepreneurship is also spatially bounded in that local access is required to access the knowledge facilitating the entrepreneurial start-up. According to the *localization hypoth-esis*, knowledge spillover entrepreneurship will tend to be spatially located within close geographic proximity to the source of knowledge actually producing that knowledge. Thus, in order to access spillovers, new firm start-ups will tend to locate close to knowl-edge sources, such as universities.

4   Entrepreneurial clusters

The fact that entrepreneurial activity varies across geographic space has long been observed. Efforts to link systematically spatial variations in entrepreneurship with locational specific characteristics showed that such spatial activity is not at all random but rather shaped by factors associated with particular regions (Reynolds, Storey & Westhead, 1994). A series of studies, dating back to at least Carlton (1983), Bartik (1985) and Reynolds, Storey and Westhead (1994), have tried to identify characteristics specific to particular regions that account for inter-spatial variations in entrepreneurship. However, while a large literature exist linking new-firm startup activity to region-specific characteristics and attributes (Fritsch, 1997; Reynolds, Storey & Westhead 1994; Carlton, 1983; Bartik, 1985; Audretsch & Fritsch, 1994), virtually none of these studies provided a theory linking knowledge spillovers to new firm start-up activity, nor did any of these studies provide a measure of knowledge spillovers.

For example, Audretsch and Fritsch (1994) examined the impact that location has on entrepreneurial activity in (West) Germany. Using a database derived from the social insurance statistics, which covers about 90 per cent of employment, they identify the birth rates of new start-ups for each of 75 distinct economic regions. These regions are distinguished on the basis of planning regions, or *Raumordungsregionen*. They find that, for the late 1980s, the birth rates of new firms are higher in regions experiencing low unemployment, which have a dense population, a high growth rate of population, a high share of skilled workers and a strong presence of small businesses.

However, none of these studies has provided a theoretical basis for the propensity for entrepreneurial activity to cluster spatially. In addition, virtually none of these studies has linked entrepreneurial activity to the knowledge context.

Systematic empirical support for both the *localization hypothesis* and the *endogeneous entrepreneurship hypothesis* is provided by Audretsch, Keilbach and Lehmann (2006), who show that the start-up of new knowledge-based and technology firms is geographically constrained within close geographic proximity to knowledge sources. Based on data from Germany in the 1990s, their evidence shows that start-up activity tends to cluster geographically around sources of new knowledge, such as R&D investments by firms and research undertaken at universities. Their findings provide compelling support for the *knowledge spillover theory of entrepreneurship*, in that entrepreneurial activity is systematically greater in locations with a greater investment in knowledge and new ideas.

5   Conclusions

That knowledge and innovative activity have become more important is not surprising. What was perhaps less anticipated is that much of the innovative activity is less associated with footloose multinational corporations and more associated with high-tech innovative regional clusters, such as Silicon Valley, the Research Triangle and Route 128. Only a few years ago the conventional wisdom predicted that globalization would bring about the demise of the region as a meaningful unit of economic analysis. According to *The Economist*, 'The death of distance as a determinant of the cost of communications will probably be the single most important economic force shaping society in the first half of the next century.' Yet the obsession of policy makers around the globe to 'create the next Silicon Valley' reveals the increased importance of geographic proximity and regional agglomerations.

Using the lens provided by the knowledge spillover theory of entrepreneurship, this chapter has explained why location is the underlying organizational context for entrepreneurship. Just as knowledge spillovers have been found to be spatially bounded, entrepreneurship has been shown to be an important conduit by which that knowledge spills over. Taken together, these two organizational units form the basis for entrepreneurial clusters.

Note

*   Audretsch is the Director of the Entrepreneurship, Growth and Public Policy division at the Max Planck Institute of Economics and a Ewing Marion Kauffman Scholar-in-Residence; Aldridge is a research fellow in the Entrepreneurship, Growth and Public Policy division at the Max Planck Institute of Economics and is a Ph.D. student in Economics at the University of Augsburg.

References

Acs, Z.J., D.B. Audretsch and M.P. Feldman (1992), 'Real effects of academic research', *American Economic Review*, **82**, 363–7.

Acs, Z.J., D.B. Audretsch and M.P. Feldman (1994), 'R&D spillovers and recipient firm size', *Review of Economics and Statistics*, **100**(1), 336–67.

Acs, Z.J., D.B. Audretsch, P. Braunerhjelm and B. Carlsson (2004), 'The missing link: the knowledge filter and entrepreneurship in endogenous growth', Discussion Paper, Centre for Economic Policy Research (CEPR).

Arrow, K.J. (1962), 'Economic welfare and the allocation of resources for invention', in R.R. Nelson (ed.), *The Rate and Direction of Inventive Activity*, Princeton, NJ: Princeton University Press, pp. 609–26.

Audretsch, D.B. (2005), 'Does the knowledge spillover theory of entrepreneurship hold for regions?', with Erik E. Lehmann, *Research Policy*, **34**(8), 1191–202.

Audretsch, D.B. and M.P. Feldman (1996), 'R&D spillovers and the geography of innovation and production', *American Economic Review*, **86**(3), 630–40.

Audretsch, D.B. and M. Fritsch (1994), 'The geography of firm births in Germany', *Regional Studies*, **28**(4), 359–65.

Audretsch, D.B. and P.E. Stephan (1996), 'Company–scientist locational links: the case of biotechnology', *American Economic Review*, **86**(3), 641–52.

Audretsch, D.B., M. Keilbach and E. Lehmann (2006), *Entrepreneurship and Economic Growth*, New York: Oxford University Press.

Bartik, T. (1985), 'Business location decisions in the US: estimates of the effects of unionization, taxes and other characteristics of states', *Journal of Business Economic Statistics*, **3**(1), 14–34.

Carlton, D.W. (1983), 'The location and employment choices of new firms: an econometric model with discrete and continuous endogenous variables', *Review of Economics and Statistics*, **65**, 440–49.

Feldman, M.P. (1994), *The Geography of Innovation*, Dordrecht, Boston: Kluwer.

Fritsch, M. (1997), 'New firms and regional employment change', *Small Business Economics*, **9**, 437–48.

Holmes, T.J. and J.A. Schmidt (1990), 'A theory of entrepreneurship and its application to the study of business transfers', *Journal of Political Economy*, **98**(2), 265–94.

Jaffe, A.B. (1989), 'Real effects of academic research', *American Economic Review*, **79**(5), 957–70.

Jaffe, A.B., M. Trajtenberg and R. Henderson (1993), 'Geographical localisation of knowledge spillovers as evidenced by patent citations', *Quarterly Journal of Economics*, **108**, 577–98.

Jovanovic, B. (2001), 'New technology and the small firm', *Small Business Economics*, **16**(1), 53–5.

Kihlstrom, R.E. and J.-J. Laffont (1979), 'A general equilibrium entrepreneurial theory of firm formation based on risk aversion', *Journal of Political Economy*, **87**(2), 719–48.

Knight, F.H. (1921), *Risk, Uncertainty, and Profit*, Boston, MA: Hart, Schaffner & Marx; Houghton Mifflin Company.

Krueger, N.F Jr. (2003), 'The cognitive psychology of entrepreneurship', in Z.J. Acs and D.B. Audretsch (eds), *Handbook of Entrepreneurship Research*, New York: Springer Verlag, pp. 105–40.

Krugman, P. (1991), *Geography and Trade*, Cambridge, MA: MIT Press.

Lucas, R.E. (1978), 'On the size distribution of business firms', *Bell Journal of Economics*, **9**, 508–23.

Marshall, A. (1920), *Principles of Economics*, 8th edn, London: Macmillan.

Parker, S. (2005), 'The economics of entrepreneurship', *Foundations and Trends in Entrepreneurship*, **1**, 1–55.

Reynolds, P., D.J. Storey and P. Westhead (1994), 'Cross-national comparisons of the variation in new firm formation rates', *Regional Studies*, **28**(4), 443–56.

Romer, P. (1986), 'Increasing returns and long-run growth', *Journal of Political Economy*, **94**(5), 1002–37.

Sarasvathy, S.D., N. Dew, S. Ramakrishna Velamuri and S. Venkataraman (2003), 'Three views of entrepreneurial opportunity', in Z.J. Acs and D.B. Audretsch (eds), *Handbook of Entrepreneurship Research*, New York: Springer Verlag, pp. 141–60.

Schwartz, D. (2006), 'The regional location of knowledge based economy activities in Israel', *Journal of Technology Transfer (JTT)*, **31**(1), 31–44.

Shane, S. (2000), 'Prior knowledge and the discovery of entrepreneurial opportunities', *Organization Science*, **11**(4), 448–69.

Shane, S. and J. Eckhardt (2003), 'The individual–opportunity nexus', in Z.J. Acs and D.B. Audretsch (eds), *Handbook of Entrepreneurship Research*, New York: Springer Verlag, pp. 161–94.

Stevenson, H.H. and J.C. Jarillo (1990), 'A paradigm of entrepreneurship: entrepreneurial management', *Strategic Management Journal*, **11**, 17–27.

5 Knowledge-based clusters: regional multiplier models and the role of 'buzz' and 'pipelines'
Harald Bathelt

1 Introduction: regional networks and growth

During the period of Fordist accumulation after World War II, many studies of economic development in industrialized countries were focused on the analysis of mass production in large, vertically-integrated firms, their input–output structure and related internationalization processes. Support policies for less industrialized, lagging regions in countries such as Germany were designed so that these regions would benefit from the investments of large Fordist firms in branch plants. Drawing on export-base models of regional development, these policies assumed that regional exports of these branch plants would trigger a regional multiplier process and stimulate growth (e.g. Klemmer, 1995).

With the Fordist crisis in the 1970s, it became clear, however, that alternative economic structures exist which can also be competitive, thanks to their capability to overcome the rigidities of the Fordist system. It was, for instance, hypothesized that tendencies toward an increasing segmentation and volatility in markets and new flexible technologies would generate new growth for small and medium-sized firms (Piore & Sabel, 1984). From this, a new interest in localized growth based on networks of small and medium-sized firms has developed. Related work has assumed that firms can improve their performance and innovativeness if they are tied to close networks with other firms in the same region. This became the basis for a new regional policy approach in the 1990s which views the support of regional networks as being crucial to strengthening regional economies. The emphasis on small-firm growth and localized networks is particularly strong in the literature on regional production systems such as industrial districts. In this literature, successful regional ensembles of firms are described which rely on intensive producer–user cooperation and market interaction between small and medium-sized, vertically-disintegrated, flexibly-specialized regional firms (Goodman et al., 1989; Pyke et al., 1990).

In a similar way, the recent literature on clusters, based on the pioneering work of Porter (1990; 2000), has argued that firms can increase their competitiveness collectively if they are located in specialized industry agglomerations and interact with other firms in these agglomerations through producer-user linkages. Focussing on clusters, this chapter will critically review the idea that regional prosperity and growth are primarily a consequence of regional networking by drawing upon a knowledge-based view of clusters (Maskell, 2001; Malmberg & Maskell, 2002; Pinch et al., 2003). The term 'cluster' will be used to refer to a local or regional concentration of industrial firms and their support infrastructure which are closely interrelated through traded and untraded interdependencies (Bathelt, 2005). A cluster approach will be presented which emphasizes both the need for close local networks and strong extra-local or global linkages. This conceptualization argues that local interaction or 'buzz' and interaction through trans-local 'pipelines' create a dynamic process of learning, knowledge production and innovation which is central to understand a cluster's success (Bathelt et al., 2004; Bathelt, 2003). The cluster approach presented can be interpreted as a knowledge-based extension of regional multiplier models. These models have been intensively discussed in regional economics since the 1960s, yet they have failed to provide a proper micro-scale explanation of regional growth processes. The buzz-and-pipeline approach suggested here aims to overcome some of the problems of these models.

This chapter is organized as follows. In the next section, it will be argued that regional input–output linkages and localized networks are in reality often less important than assumed. Empirical evidence from case studies shows that global or extraregional linkages are of major significance in understanding regional economic success, even in major industry clusters and large metropolitan regions. I will then present three partial models of regional growth which argue in different ways that combinations of internal and external linkages are the basis for economic growth as they stimulate cumulative growth processes: the export-base model, the innovative milieu approach and the super-cluster model. These partial models are the basis for the development of a new cluster approach to understanding regional innovation and growth in the knowledge-based economy building upon the reflexive relationship between local and trans-local inter-firm linkages. This will be followed by some concluding remarks.

2 Limited evidence of regional input–output linkages
Since the Fordist crisis, the literature on industry agglomerations has put particular emphasis on the role of local input–output linkages, viewing localized networks as a decisive force in the generation of dynamic regional growth processes. This relationship is, however, anything but clear. In fact, there is plenty of evidence which shows that processes of knowledge creation and innovation in clusters cannot be fully understood by simply analysing the regional divisions of labour (e.g. Oinas, 1999; Enright, 2000; Hendry et al., 2000; Bresnahan et al., 2001; Dicken, 2003; Tracey & Clark, 2003; He, 2006). Actors and markets outside the cluster are important in directing growth impulses and knowledge about new technologies into the cluster and thus require attention. Overall, empirical studies have come to question the dominance of local over non-local network relations and have identified problems which can occur owing to local over-embeddedness (Uzzi, 1997; Amin & Cohendet, 2004). This will be exemplified in the following by referring to a selection of studies on regional linkages and networks in different contexts. Although these studies may not be fully representative, they demonstrate that interregional and international interactions are often at the core of individual and collective competitiveness in industry agglomerations.

1. In a study of input–output linkages in the Philadelphia economy in 1960, Karaska (1969) found surprisingly little evidence for regional transaction networks even though the diversified regional economy had a large potential for such linkages. Only few industries had a relatively strong local supplier basis which covered most of their overall supplies.
2. Similarly, even in large specialized industry clusters like Silicon Valley, local input–output linkages were not found to be more important than non-local ties. From a survey of 60 high-technology firms in the San Francisco Bay area in 1982 by Oakey (1985), it can be concluded that local linkages were not as strong as implied in the

literature. One-third of the sample firms acquired more than half of their overall supplies outside a 30-mile radius and two-thirds sold more than half of their final products outside this radius, focusing on extra-local transaction networks.

3.   Owen-Smith and Powell (2004) concluded from their 1988–99 study of the Boston biotechnology community that access to new knowledge did not just result from local interaction but was often acquired through strategic partnerships of interregional and international reach. Even though knowledge spillovers might have been quite effective within regional networks, physical distance was not the only influence. Boston's biotechnology firms were also embedded in social networks which were not defined geographically. Decisive, non-incremental knowledge flows were often generated through close linkages with partners located in other parts of the world.

4.   A study of 70 small firms in the Sheffield metal-working cluster in the late 1990s by Watts et al. (2003) showed that face-to-face contacts with suppliers were less frequent than expected. Interestingly, such contacts were equally important in supplier relations with both local and non-local firms. Social interaction was even more intensive with non-local suppliers, indicating that supply-chain linkages had a strong external focus.

5.   In a Canadian study of 61 electronics firms in the Toronto region in 1998–99, Britton (2004) found that foreign affiliates were only weakly embedded in regional networks. Although most had entered alliances with Canadian firms, they primarily drew technologies from established inter-firm networks with other countries. Multilocational domestic firms also benefited substantially from international linkages which enabled them to extend their markets. Overall, Britton (2004) concluded that local or intraregional linkages were not more privileged than interregional or international ones.

6.   In a study of the automobile industry, Ivarsson and Alvstam (2005) investigated the supplier networks of Volvo's bus and truck operations in Brazil, China, India and Mexico, from 2001 to 2003. They found that a large proportion of Volvo's suppliers were non-local even though the nature of bus and truck production required close producer–user interaction with frequent adjustments. Although local suppliers generally benefited more from Volvo's technical support system than those further away, distance did not have an effect on supplier performance.

In accordance with Oinas (1999, 365), it can be concluded from these studies that 'it seems evident that the creation of new knowledge (learning) might be best viewed as a result of a "combination" of close and distant interactions'. The effects of local interaction and learning are obviously much stronger and durable if they constantly receive feedback and new impulses from outside. Tracey and Clark (2003, 11) rightly argue that 'geographical clusters can no longer be (if, indeed, they ever could be) thought of simply as closed local systems'. As a consequence, it will be argued in this chapter that the role of proximity in day-to-day communication between a cluster's actors is greatly supported by knowledge inputs over larger distances from outside.

3   Models of regional development and growth

Of course, it has been known for a long time that regional growth can be stimulated through interregional trade and linkages with firms located in other regions and nation states. This has also become an integral part of some models of regional development which argue that exports and interregional trade are decisive influences in triggering regional innovation, competitiveness and growth. In the following, three models of regional development and growth will be presented which acknowledge this relationship: the export-base model, the innovative milieu approach and the super-cluster model. These models explore the relationship between local and non-local linkages in different ways and incorporate external linkages in varying degrees. They are also associated with particular limitations.

(a) Regional multiplier effects in the export-base model

Regional multiplier or export-base models argue that the growth process of a region can be triggered if export activities to other regions and nations are intensified (Richardson, 1973; Lloyd & Dicken, 1977; Schätzl, 1981). These models view export activities as being decisive stimuli for regional growth. They conceptualize a regional multiplier process by distinguishing two types of regional economic activities: (i) the basic sector which exports its products to other regions and nation-states, (ii) the non-basic sector which produces for the local market. It is assumed that growing exports in the basic sector of a region will create additional income in that region over time larger than the amount of the original exports. This is viewed as a multiplier process. The rationale behind this is that exports in the basic sector will direct additional revenues to the region. Of course, not all of these will be effective locally as the basic sector may need raw materials and supplies from other regions, and thus engage in imports. It may also transfer profits to other regions if the headquarters are located elsewhere. However, the basic sector also acquires local inputs and pays additional incomes through which goods and services from the non-basic sector are bought. This will, in turn, provide additional revenues and income for this sector. Although part of this will be spent on imports, the remainder will be used again to acquire local products from the non-basic sector, thus creating further revenues and incomes, and so on. Overall, a local multiplier process is thus triggered by which further growth will occur over time through consecutive rounds of production and consumption (Figure 5.1).

The effects of this can be demonstrated in a simple multiplier model (Schätzl, 1981). In this model, it is assumed that the overall demand in region i [$Y(i)$] consists of regional consumption [$C(i)$] plus regional investments [$I(i)$] plus exports [$X(i)$] minus imports [$M(i)$]. Regional investments and regional exports are viewed as autonomous variables [$aI(i)$ and $aX(i)$, respectively]. Regional imports are viewed as being a constant proportion of the overall regional demand:

$$M(i) = m(i)\, Y(i), \text{ where } m(i) \text{ denotes the marginal import rate.}$$

The regional consumption function is a linear function of the regional demand:

$$C(i) = aC(i) + c(i)\, Y(i), \text{ where } aC(i) \text{ denotes the autonomous}$$
$$\text{consumption and } c(i) \text{ the marginal consumption rate.}$$

If we investigate the situation where regional consumption equals regional supply, the resulting equilibrium is

$$Y(i) = RM(i)\, [aC(i) + aI(i) + aX(i)], \text{ where } RM(i), \text{ the regional multiplier, is given as}$$
$$RM(i) = 1\,/\,[1 - c(i) + m(i)].$$

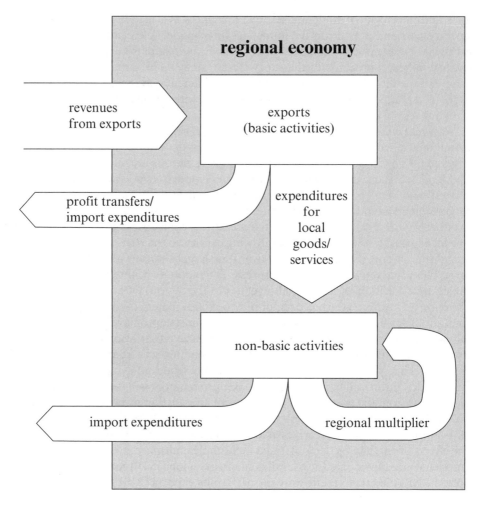

Source: Adapted from Schätzl (1981, p. 108).

Figure 5.1 Capital flows in the export-base model

If no other influences exist and the marginal consumption rate is larger than the marginal import rate, a regional multiplier results after indefinite rounds of adjustments which is larger than 1. In general, the higher the marginal consumption rate or the lower the marginal import rate the larger the regional multiplier will be. This will not change if other influences, such as direct and indirect taxes, are integrated into the model. A regional policy initiative based on this approach would focus on supporting and strengthening the basic sector of a region, as the German case illustrates (e.g., Klemmer, 1995).

Despite these important insights, regional multiplier models are, however, characterized by shortcomings which drastically limit their applicability. One problem of regional multiplier models is that they confuse regional with national boundaries by neglecting the role of the nation-state in defining and reproducing the institutional conditions for economic production and exchange. National settings constitute a basis for relatively stable linkages while it is difficult to identify regional settings with similar qualities. As a consequence, the value of the regional multiplier depends to a great extent on the size of the region defined. As such, multiplier models ignore the importance of institutions and agency. Like other neoclassical models, they do not describe the intentions and strategies of actors, the effects of their interaction and the social processes behind learning and innovation (Bathelt & Glückler, 2003). They are conceptualized as macro-scale models which try to capture the regional economy as a whole through regional aggregates of economic activities. This is problematic as such modelling ignores potentials for knowledge creation and innovation which may result from cooperative arrangements and systematic interaction between local firms. In order to become more useful, multiplier models would have to be based on an individual rather than an aggregate level. It is doubtful, however, that the required data for such modelling is readily available. Even if it was, the respective model could hardly grasp the effects of interactive learning and knowledge creation in a localized industry setting. Overall, the ability of conventional regional multiplier models to understand, explain and predict regional growth processes is rather limited.

(b)   Regional innovation in the milieu school
The critique of neoclassical modelling, such as that in regional multiplier models, has stimulated the development of alternative micro-scale approaches. These approaches focus on the analysis of economic action and the role of agency and institutions. They take the role of context seriously and investigate how particular socio-institutional conditions shape the social division of labour in a region. Among these approaches are those on industrial districts (Goodman et al., 1989; Pyke et al., 1990) and innovative milieus (Camagni, 1991a; Ratti et al., 1997). The milieu school as developed by the *Groupe de Recherche Européen sur les Milieux Innovateurs (GREMI)* focuses on the investigation of the reasons for the development of a high degree of innovativeness in selected regions (e.g. Fromhold-Eisebith, 1995; Crevoisier, 2001). Through this work it has become clear that successful innovation is not just the result of individual endeavours. Instead, innovation performance is also related to the local environment and its socio-institutional settings, referred to as 'the milieu'. Under particular circumstances, the local environment can contribute to a highly dynamic innovative milieu (Crevoisier & Maillat, 1991).

Maillat (1998) views a milieu as a territorial production system, consisting of a variety of material, labour market, technology and information linkages which develop within a particular commodity chain. Thanks to spatial proximity, firms almost automatically know about the quality and capabilities of potential partners and suppliers. This allows them to reduce transaction costs. The resulting network of social relations forms an integral component of the local socio-institutional structure. It is embedded in this structure and the way it has developed in the past. Affiliation to the same production system and its technological traditions stimulates cooperation between the actors and promotes interactive learning and collective problem solving (Bramanti & Ratti, 1997). This is because norms, routines, shared trust and a unique technology culture evolve over time which are largely accepted by the local agents, and thus create a particular order which is conducive to collective action.

By focusing on the regional agents, their socio-institutional context and the resulting network of information flows, transactions and problem-solving activities, the milieu approach overcomes some of the problems of regional multiplier models. As opposed to the latter approaches, it analyses regional innovation and growth based on the territorial division of labour and regional interdependencies between firms. In doing this, however, the milieu school has tended to overemphasize the importance of internal networks while neglecting external relationships. Although Camagni (1991b, 140) rightly emphasizes that 'the "milieu" has to open up to external energy in order to avoid "entropic death" and a decline in its own innovative capability', not much is said about the nature of social relations with agents from outside the milieu.

In recent work, the milieu school has become more aware of the importance of linkages with extra-local agents to secure access to information about global markets trends, competitors and technologies in other regions and nation states (Ratti et al., 1997; Crevoisier, 2001). Maillat (1998) has posed the questions as to what distinguishes a stagnant from a creative, innovative milieu and which forces enable a milieu to grow. To answer these, he distinguishes the internal and external relations needed to secure a milieu's success. The milieu actors need to establish systematic linkages with external information sources to maintain a flow of important information and knowledge about market trends and new technologies developed outside. The success of the actors to advance innovation processes thus relies on their capability to acquire specialized information and resources from external sources and apply them in the internal divisions of labour. This requires collective openness and 'absorptive capacity' (Cohen & Levinthal, 1990) to be able to recognize relevant external developments and to transfer the respective knowledge successfully to the internal interaction circuits. Such transfers are necessary if the milieu's actors are to reproduce their competencies and extend their competitiveness (Maillat et al., 1997).

A good example of the relation between internal and external structures is the development of the Swiss watch industry and the crises it experienced. A regional crisis which took place in the 1970s and 1980s was due to a collective underestimation of new technological trajectories (quartz and digital technologies) which had been developed in other countries and which created new market opportunities for the producers in these countries. It was due to the opening up of the Swiss production system, the integration of external partners into local networks and the development of new institutional settings that the producers were able to overcome this crisis (Maillat et al., 1997). In general, however, the milieu school has paid more attention to those processes which take place inside the milieu than to those outside.

(c)   Scott's model of super-clusters
In his work on new industrial spaces, Scott (1988) takes a different route from that of the milieu school. He relates the development of new forms of industrial agglomeration to changes in international markets and technology standards, i.e. highly volatile, segmented demand conditions and new computer-based technologies. In his view, these stimulate an increasing vertical disintegration of production and a shift from intra-firm to inter-firm transactions within particular industries and regions. Similar to the milieu school, Scott (1988) emphasises socio-economic interaction as a basis for understanding the constitution of spatial economies and their growth. Different from the approaches discussed above, however, he views shifts in the regional division of labour as always being driven by global forces in production and demand.

In his book on the role of regions in the world economy, Scott (1998) emphasizes two forces which influence the degree to which a social division of labour and clustering take place on a regional scale. These forces are (i) the level of (localized) external effects and (ii) the amount of (spatial) transaction costs. If production and innovation processes do not benefit from localized external effects, such as information spillover in innovation processes and advantages from shared socio-institutional settings, the respective producers will not locate close to one another. Industrial clusters can therefore not be established. If localized external effects do not exist, there is no incentive for firms to co-locate in any particular region. In the case of uniformly low spatial transaction costs and low levels of external effects, a quasi-random distribution of producers over space is likely to result without visible trends toward regional agglomeration, referred to as 'spatial entropy'. If transaction costs are high, small industry configurations will result, with a strong regional market focus, similar to the market areas discussed by Lösch (1962). Such configurations are classified as Lösch–Weber landscapes (Figure 5.2).

The spatial distribution of industrial firms changes when localized external effects become important. In this case, particular spatial clusters develop (Scott, 1998), the size of which depends on the extent and mix of spatial transaction costs. If transaction costs are uniformly low, inter-firm linkages are not limited to particular localities and include transactions over large distances. The resulting industrial clusters are likely to be inter-connected but remain small. In the case of uniformly high transaction costs, intraregional linkages become dominant. The resulting industrial clusters are unlikely to be systematically connected with external actors and other clusters. They remain relatively small because the internal markets are not large enough to stimulate substantial growth. The spatial configuration of production, however, changes drastically when a hybrid structure of spatial transaction costs exists. According to Scott (1998), super-clusters could then develop because external transactions transfer growth impulses to the localized production system which, in turn, disseminate through internal transaction networks and

Level of localized external effects	Level of spatial transaction costs		
	Uniformly low	Mix of high and low	Uniformly high
Low	Spatial entropy (no clusters)	Dispersal/emerging Lösch–Weber landscapes	Lösch–Weber landscapes
High	Small interconnected cluster	Super-clusters	Small unconnected clusters

Source: Adapted from Scott (1998, p. 87).

Figure 5.2   Cluster configurations according to the level of localized external effects and spatial transaction costs

stimulate regional growth (Figure 5.2). This implies that the performance of localized production systems depends on the right mix of local and non-local transactions and that strong growth can only result if external markets are linked to the production cluster.

This is an important contribution, emphasizing the need for strong interregional and international transaction networks to understand the regional division of labour and growth of large clusters. The analysis remains somewhat imprecise, however, with respect to the conceptualization of processes, such as collective learning and knowledge creation. In the end, the processes which generate regional growth in industry clusters still remain hidden. This seems due to the fact that Scott's (1998) explanation focuses on the macro level, neglecting the forces which have an impact on individual economic agents and their choices.

4   Local buzz and global pipelines: a regional model of knowledge generation

The model described in this section aims to integrate and extend some of the explanations given beforehand. In focusing on a micro perspective, the model aims to shed new light on the way regional processes of knowledge creation and growth in industry clusters are initiated and maintained through systematic external linkages. This gives rise to a broader model of industrial clustering. In recognizing that clusters are often not characterized by strong internal transactions and input–output linkages, the model shifts its focus from the explanation of production linkages toward processes of knowledge generation (Bathelt et al., 2004; Bathelt, 2003). The model recognizes knowledge creation as being the driving force behind the establishment, growth and reproduction of industry clusters (Maskell, 2001; Malmberg & Maskell, 2002; Pinch et al., 2003; Bathelt, 2005). In distinguishing information and knowledge transfers within a cluster from linkages with its global environment, structural differences in a cluster's information and communication ecology can be identified which become the basis for positive feedback loops in the production of new knowledge. In short, the combination of local interaction or 'buzz' with interaction through trans-local linkages or 'pipelines' creates a dynamic process of knowledge creation.

Local buzz refers to a thick web of information, knowledge and inspiration which circulate between the actors of a cluster. This buzz consists of specific information flows, knowledge transfers and continuous updates as well as opportunities for learning in organized and spontaneous meetings (see, particularly, Storper & Venables, 2004; Bathelt et al., 2004). What is meant by this, however, is not simply a high density of information flows. As listed below, the importance and quality of a cluster's buzz is related to a number of features which are partly overlapping and make this setting especially valuable for processes of learning and knowledge creation.

First, the co-presence of many specialized firms of a particular value chain in the same region and regular face-to-face contacts between specialists from these firms generate a specific milieu for the exchange of experiences, new information and knowledge within the cluster. This exchange is much more intense than that which could be expected in a different industry setting. Within a cluster, specific information about technologies, markets and strategies is exchanged in a variety of ways in planned and unplanned meetings. These might encompass negotiations with local suppliers, telephone conversations during the business day, lunch with colleagues or a conversation with a neighbour who works in the same industry.

Second, the agents in the cluster share similar technical traditions and views which have developed over time and which are based on similar day-to-day routines and problem-solving activities. Through this, new information and technologies are easily understood. When people of a similar technological background and realm of experience in a region converse with one another, they automatically know what others are talking about. The need to take the time to explain the background history of a given problem is thus avoided. In many clusters, the engineers and scientists also have a similar education from leading universities in the region. They sometimes even know each other from their student days and will have already become acquainted with several firms as a result of switching jobs in the area (Bathelt, 2003). As positions change hands, knowledge that would be difficult to acquire by other means is transferred between firms.

Third, the diversity of the relationships and contacts within a cluster stimulates a tight network of information flows, common problem solutions and the development of trust. Within these contact networks, agents are linked in multiple ways with each other as business partners, colleagues, peers, friends or community members. As a result, resources can be transferred from one type of relationship to another (Boissevain, 1974). Multiplex ties help firms to get access to new information, speed up the transfer of knowledge through the cluster and increase the firms' access to relevant knowledge sources (Uzzi, 1997).

Fourth, through the shared history of relationships, firms learn how to interpret the local buzz and make good use of it. As a result, communities, such as communities of practice and epistemic communities, which are characterized by a joint institutional basis, become more rooted over time (Wenger, 1998; Gertler, 2001). This helps to transfer information as well as knowledge in a precise manner, interpret new information in the context of the cluster's technological competence and extract those knowledge parts which could be valuable in future applications. Overall, active participation and membership in these communities reduce uncertainties and the degree of complexity when making decisions regarding technological shifts. This is possible because co-presence in a cluster enhances the likelihood that people will develop compatible technology outlooks and interpretive schemes. The process of building up common rules and value systems is supported by routine interaction between persons with similar expertise and experience in solving particular technological problems. Altogether, this provides a setting conducive to the development of joint institutions (Amin & Thrift, 1995).

It becomes obvious from the outset that local buzz is a complex concept which is difficult to measure. This concept does not, however, confuse aspects of co-location, face-to-face contact, information transfer, community formation and institution building. The model, rather, emphasizes that these different aspects support one another in a beneficial way under circumstances which can sometimes be found in clusters. Participation in the local buzz often does not require specific investments. The firms in the cluster do not need to search their environment for information since they are surrounded by a densely knit web of gossip, opinions, recommendations, judgments and interpretations from which they cannot escape (Gertler, 1995; Grabher, 2002).

However, it is not sufficient to rely on internal information flows and developments. Supra-regional linkages or pipelines (Owen-Smith & Powell, 2004) are important in order to find out about other markets and technologies and avoid negative lock-in. Access to trans-local pipelines, however, entails considerable uncertainties and high investments. The nature of the interaction also depends on the degree of trust that exists between the partners. Trust is not automatic, but has to be built up gradually. This takes time and money. Moreover, harmonious collaboration in innovation processes depends on a common language, a shared basic understanding and mutually compatible interpretative schemes. Obviously, this cannot be taken for granted, as is evident by the problems which can beset strategic partnerships and mergers. Of course, it may be equally or even more important for firms who do not operate in a cluster to develop strong international pipelines (Fontes, 2005). In any case, it is no simple task to establish a trans-local relationship, as the cultural and institutional contexts in which the firms operate have different roots (Gertler, 2001). If a relationship is to be successful, it is essential that the partners have a minimum amount of non-overlapping, complementary knowledge (Nooteboom, 2000). At the same time, they must be on the same 'wavelength'. The effectiveness of a firm in accessing relevant knowledge pools and finding appropriate partners depends on its absorptive capacity (Cohen & Levinthal, 1990). Because of the high uncertainties attendant on relationships in which the partners know little about each other, knowledge transfers are concentrated on precisely defined objectives and are established in a much more explicitly structured way than the communication flows within the cluster. The success of such endeavours depends on cognitive and technological affinity, as well as opportunities for face-to-face interaction in temporary settings (Amin & Cohendet, 2004; Maskell et al., 2006).

The argument made is that both local buzz and global pipelines have only limited effects if they remain separated spheres (Figure 5.3). Although the particular character of buzz and pipelines (or closure and range) may differ between industries and shift over time (He, 2006), the combination of both concepts provides new grounds for explaining the high degree of dynamism in processes of knowledge creation and innovation in some clusters (Bathelt et al., 2004; Bathelt, 2005). As argued above, local buzz in clusters has only limited effects in the absence of trans-local pipelines. The more strongly the actors in the

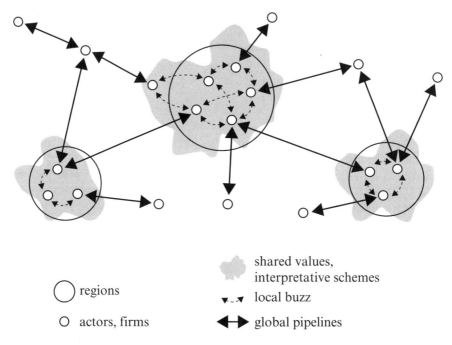

Figure 5.3   The reflexive dynamics of local buzz and global pipelines

cluster are involved in establishing and maintaining trans-local partnerships, the more information about new markets and technologies is pumped into the networks of a cluster. Without this influx of external knowledge, there is a danger that firms will pin their hopes on the wrong technology and lose their competitive edge. Pipelines which are open or 'leaky' function as sprinklers supporting the diffusion of information within the cluster (Owen-Smith & Powell, 2004). This stimulates additional buzz and serves as a basis for further product innovation and differentiation.

Without the buzz in turn, the pipelines are of little use because they predefine and, thus, restrict the way in which new knowledge is applied. The local buzz in a cluster enables firms to isolate those elements that are particularly important for the further development of technologies and to discard those with little prospect of success from the mass of external information available. This saves both time and money and speeds up innovation processes. Today's role of Stanford University in Silicon Valley is a good example in this respect. It is still quite important as a place where engineers originating from the US, India, Taiwan and other countries meet to develop a common knowledge base and industry background. This can become the basis for the establishment of networks and global pipelines between Silicon Valley and other parts of the world at later stages (Hsu & Saxenian, 2000). Intensive local buzz helps firms to recognize the significance of trans-local pipelines and acquire knowledge about the establishment of new pipelines. In other words, this cluster approach can be viewed as a fundamental reinterpretation of export-base models. The micro-scale model presented here argues that external knowledge resources enter a cluster and stimulate rounds of internal recombination through which innovation and growth impulses result. Access to external resources thus strengthens internal capabilities in a cluster.

5 Conclusions

This chapter argues that the literature on production systems since the Fordist crisis has placed too much emphasis on the analysis of local networks in enabling regional growth. As a consequence, policy programmes have been designed to support the development of such networks. Parallel to this, the decisive role of extra-local linkages has been somewhat neglected. Such linkages, however, provide access to different knowledge pools, new technologies and markets. Already traditional multiplier models have shown that it is the export sector which can particularly stimulate regional growth. Other, more recent streams in the literature on innovative milieus and super-clusters have also argued that clusters need to be open to recognize shifts in technological and market developments originating from outside. Although these approaches have provided important insights into the structure of regional economies, they do not establish a comprehensive conceptual basis for understanding the relationship between internal and external linkages in a cluster setting. This is, in part, related to limitations in these models which are due to a different focus or the dominance of a macro perspective.

The model proposed in this chapter argues that a cluster cannot unfold its growth potential in the long run if firms exclusively rely on internal markets and knowledge circulating through the local buzz. In this model, the particular combination of local buzz and trans-local pipelines is believed to generate a reflexive process of knowledge creation. The local buzz benefits from trans-local pipelines through which additional subcontracts and new knowledge are pumped into the cluster. This approach conceptualizes a regional multiplier process by including feedback loops of knowledge creation which result in increased innovativeness. The model presented goes beyond neoclassical multiplier models and other approaches as it applies an actor perspective and builds upon the social relations which are at the core of economic processes.

The model argues that spatial proximity in economic relations is neither generally more important nor more effective than other non-local networks. It is relational proximity and not spatial proximity which enables close social interaction and becomes an important source of competitiveness (Bathelt & Glückler, 2003; Atherton, 2003; Amin & Cohendet, 2004). Relational proximity is not reducible to any particular territorial setting. It can exist or develop between actors located in different parts of the world, thanks to modern technological and institutional developments that make easier both the transfer of information and the travelling of people across space. The cluster model presented here supports this conclusion. It presents (a) a relational view which overcomes the problems of export-base models, (b) a micro-scale perspective, and (c) a focus on knowledge creation in explaining economic organization in space. According to this model, network relations across space over larger distances are not only a possible option; they are, in fact, necessary to make clusters work.

Acknowledgements
I would like to thank one anonymous reviewer, Charlie Karlsson and Clare Wiseman for providing me with productive criticism and advice on a draft version of this chapter.

Bibliography
Amin, A. and P. Cohendet (2004), *Architectures of Knowledge: Firms, Capabilities, and Communities*, Oxford, New York: Oxford University Press.
Amin, A. and N. Thrift (1995), 'Living in the global', in A. Amin and N. Thrift (eds), *Globalization, Institutions, and Regional Development in Europe*, Oxford, New York: Oxford University Press, pp. 1–22.
Atherton, A. (2003), 'Examining clusters formation from the "Bottom-up": an analysis of four cases in the North of England', *Environment and Planning C: Government and Policy*, **21**, 21–35.
Bathelt, H. (2003), 'Success in the local environment – local buzz, global pipelines and the importance of clusters', *Think On*, 2/2003, 28–33.
Bathelt, H. (2005), 'Geographies of production: growth regimes in spatial perspective 2 – knowledge creation and growth in clusters', *Progress in Human Geography*, **29**, 204–16.
Bathelt, H. and J. Glückler (2003), *Wirtschaftsgeographie: Ökonomische Beziehungen in räumlicher Perspektive (Economic Geography: Economic Relations in Spatial Perspective)*, 2nd edn, Stuttgart: UTB – Ulmer.
Bathelt, H., A. Malmberg and P. Maskell (2004), 'Clusters and knowledge: local buzz, global pipelines and the process of knowledge creation', *Progress in Human Geography*, **28**, 31–56.
Boissevain, J. (1974), *Friends of Friends: Networks, Manipulators and Coalitions*, Oxford: Blackwell.
Bramanti, A. and R. Ratti (1997), 'The multi-faced dimensions of local development', in R. Ratti, A. Bramanti and R. Gordon (eds), *The Dynamics of Innovative Regions: The GREMI Approach*, Aldershot, Brookfield: Ashgate, pp. 3–44.
Bresnahan, T., A. Gambardella and A. Saxenian (2001), ' "Old economy" inputs for "new economy" outcomes: cluster formation in the new Silicon Valleys', *Industrial and Corporate Change*, **10**, 835–60.
Britton, J.N.H. (2004), 'High technology localization and extra-regional networks', *Entrepreneurship & Regional Development*, **16**, 369–90.
Camagni, R. (ed.) (1991a), *Innovation Networks: Spatial Perspectives*, London, New York: Belhaven Press.
Camagni, R. (1991b), 'Local "milieu", uncertainty and innovation networks: towards a new dynamic theory of economic space', in R. Camagni (ed.), *Innovation Networks: Spatial Perspectives*, London, New York: Belhaven Press, pp. 121–44.
Cohen, W.M. and D.A. Levinthal (1990), 'Absorptive capacity: a new perspective on learning and innovation', *Administrative Science Quarterly*, **35**, 128–52.
Crevoisier, O. (2001), 'Der Ansatz des kreativen Milieus: Bestandsaufnahme und Forschungsperspektiven am Beispiel urbaner Milieus' ('The creative milieu: state of the art, research perspectives and the case of urban milieus'), *Zeitschrift für Wirtschaftsgeographie*, **45**, 246–56.

Crevoisier, O. and D. Maillat (1991), 'Milieu, industrial organization and territorial production system: towards a new theory of spatial development', in R.Camagni (ed.), *Innovation Networks: Spatial Perspectives*, London, New York: Belhaven Press, pp. 13–34.

Dicken, P. (2003), *Global Shift: Reshaping the Global Economic Map in the 21st Century*, 4th edn, London, Thousand Oaks, CA: Sage.

Enright, M. (2000), 'The globalization of competition and the localization of competition: policies toward regional clustering', in N. Hood and S. Young (eds), *The Globalization of Multinational Enterprise Activity and Economic Development*, London: Macmillan, pp. 303–31.

Fontes, M. (2005), 'Distant networking: the knowledge acquisition strategies of "out-cluster" biotechnology firms', *European Planning Studies*, **6**, 899–920.

Fromhold-Eisebith, M. (1995), 'Das "kreative Milieu" als Motor regionalwirtschaftlicher Entwicklung: Forschungstrends und Erfassungsmöglichkeiten' ('The "creative" milieu as a motor of regional development'), *Geographische Zeitschrift*, **83**, 30–47.

Gertler, M.S. (1995), ' "Being there": proximity, organization, and culture in the development and adoption of advanced manufacturing technologies', *Economic Geography*, **71**, 1–26.

Gertler, M.S. (2001), 'Best practice? Geography, learning and the institutional limits to strong convergence', *Journal of Economic Geography*, **1**, 5–26.

Goodman, E., J. Bamford and P. Saynor (eds) (1989), *Small Firms and Industrial Districts in Italy*, London, New York: Routledge.

Grabher, G. (2002), 'Cool projects, boring institutions: temporary collaboration in social context', *Regional Studies*, **36**, 205–14.

He, S. (2006), 'Clusters, structural embeddedness, and knowledge: a structural embeddedness model of clusters', paper presented at the DRUID-DIME Winter PhD Conference, 26–28 January, Skoerping (http://www.druid.dk/conferences/winter 2006/papers/dw2006-660.pdf).

Hendry, C., J. Brown and R. DeFillippi (2000), 'Regional clustering of high technology-based firms: opto-electronics in three countries', *Regional Studies*, **34**, 129–44.

Hsu, J.-y. and A. Saxenian (2000), 'The limits to guanxi capitalism: transnational collaboration between Taiwan and the US', *Environment and Planning A*, **32**, 1991–2005.

Ivarsson, I. and C.G. Alvstam (2005), 'The effect of spatial proximity on technology transfer from TNCs to local suppliers in developing countries: the case of AB Volvo in Asia and Latin America', *Economic Geography*, **81**, 83–111.

Karaska, G.J. (1969), 'Manufacturing linkages in the Philadelphia economy: some evidence of external agglomeration forces', *Geographical Analysis*, **1**, 354–69.

Klemmer, P. (1995), 'Gemeinschaftsaufgabe "Verbesserung der regionalen Wirtschaftsstruktur" ' ('Joint program on the improvement of regional economies'), in Akademie für Raumforschung und Landesplanung (ed.), *Handwörterbuch der Raumordnung (Handbook of Spatial Planning)*, Hannover: Akademie für Raumordnung und Landesplanung, pp. 395–7.

Lloyd, P.E. and P. Dicken (1977), *Location in Space: A Theoretical Approach to Economic Geography*, 2nd edn, London, New York: Harper & Row.

Lösch, A. (1962), *Die räumliche Ordnung der Wirtschaft (The Spatial Order of the Economy)*, 3rd edn, Stuttgart: Fischer.

Maillat, D. (1998), 'Vom "industrial district" zum innovativen Milieu: Ein Beitrag zur Analyse der lokalen Produktionssysteme' ('From industrial networks to innovative milieus: towards an analysis of territorial production systems'), *Geographische Zeitschrift*, **86**, 1–15.

Maillat, D., G. Léchot, B. Lecoq and M. Pfister (1997), 'Comparative analysis of the structural development of milieux: the watch industry in the Swiss and French Jura arc', in R. Ratti, A. Bramanti and R. Gordon (eds), *The Dynamics of Innovative Regions: The GREMI Approach*, Aldershot, Brookfield: Ashgate, pp. 109–37.

Malmberg, A. and P. Maskell (2002), 'The elusive concept of localization economies: towards a knowledge-based theory of spatial clustering', *Environment and Planning A*, **34**, 429–49.

Maskell, P. (2001), 'Towards a knowledge-based theory of the geographical cluster', *Industrial and Corporate Change*, **10**, 921–43.

Maskell, P., H. Bathelt and A. Malmberg (2006), 'Building global knowledge pipelines: the role of temporary clusters', *European Planning Studies*, **14**, 997–1013.

Nooteboom, B. (2000), *Learning and Innovation in Organizations and Economies*, Oxford: Oxford University Press.

Oakey, R. (1985), 'High-technology industry and agglomeration economies', in P. Hall and A.R. Markusen (eds), *Silicon Landscapes*, Boston: Allen and Unwin, pp. 94–117.

Oinas, P. (1999), 'Activity-specificity in organizational learning: implications for analysing the role of proximity', *GeoJournal*, **49**, 363–72.

Owen-Smith, J. and W.W. Powell (2004), 'Knowledge networks as channels and conduits: the effects of spillovers in the Boston biotechnology community', *Organization Science*, **15**, 2–21.

Pinch, S., N. Henry, M. Jenkins and S. Tallman (2003), 'From "industrial districts" to "knowledge clusters": a model of knowledge dissemination and competitive advantage in industrial agglomerations', *Journal of Economic Geography*, **3**, 373–88.

Piore, M.J. and C.F. Sabel (1984), *The Second Industrial Divide*, New York: Basic Books.

Porter, M.E (1990), *The Competitive Advantage of Nations*, New York: Free Press.

Porter, M.E. (2000), 'Locations, clusters, and company strategy', in G.L. Clark, M.P. Feldman and M.S. Gertler (eds), *The Oxford Handbook of Economic Geography*, Oxford: Oxford University Press, pp. 253–74.

Pyke, F., G. Becattini and W. Sengenberger (eds) (1990), *Industrial Districts and Inter-Firm Co-operation in Italy*, Geneva: International Institute for Labour Studies.

Ratti, R., A. Bramanti and R. Gordon (eds) (1997), *The Dynamics of Innovative Regions: The GREMI Approach*, Aldershot, Brookfield: Ashgate.

Richardson, H.W. (1973), *Regional Growth Theory*, London: Macmillan; New York: Praeger.

Schätzl, L. (1981), *Wirtschaftsgeographie 1: Theorie (Economic Geography 1: Theory)*, 2nd edn, Paderborn: UTB – Schöningh.

Scott, A.J. (1988), *New Industrial Spaces: Flexible Production Organization and Regional Development in North America and Western Europe*, London: Pion.

Scott, A.J. (1998), *Regions and the World Economy: The Coming Shape of Global Production, Competition, and Political Order*, Oxford, New York: Oxford University Press.

Storper, M. and A.J. Venables (2004), 'Buzz: face-to-face contact and the urban economy', *Journal of Economic Geography*, **4**, 351–70.

Tracey, P. and G.L. Clark (2003), 'Alliances, networks and competitive strategy: rethinking clusters of innovation', *Growth and Change*, **34**, 1–16.

Uzzi, B. (1997), 'Social structure and competition in interfirm networks: the paradox of embeddedness', *Administrative Science Quarterly*, **42**, 35–67.

Watts, H.D., A.M. Wood and P. Wardle (2003), 'Making friends or making things?': interfirm transactions in the Sheffield metal-working cluster', *Urban Studies*, **40**, 615–30.

Wenger, E. (1998), *Communities of Practice: Learning, Meaning and Identity*, Cambridge: Cambridge University Press.

6 Clusters formation from the 'bottom-up': a process perspective

Andrew Atherton and Andrew Johnston

1 From 'top-down' to 'bottom-up' considerations of clusters formation

Clusters and related forms of inter-firm collaboration and networking have been a particular focus of regional, and national, policy and economic strategy over the last few decades. The identification of 'industrial districts' of innovative firms generating local wealth creation and high levels of exports in Northern Italy offered the possibility that regional prosperity was underpinned by high levels of flexible specialization (Beccatini, 1990; Brusco, 1982; Lazerson, 1995; Nadvi & Schmitz, 1994; Pyke et al., 1990). Specific cases of local economies driven by the exploitation of knowledge and invention in technology-driven firms operating within localized networks, and in particular 'success stories' such as Silicon Valley, Highway 128 and Cambridge, provided examples of the potential of clusters to contribute to economic growth and development (Castells, 1996; Cooke & Morgan, 1998; Porter, 1998; Saxenian, 1994; Segal Quince Wicksteed, 2000; Storper & Scott, 1995). Support for the notion of clusters as a means of developing economic competitiveness and growth has come from academic studies and parts of the research community (e.g. Porter, 1990, 1998; Rosenfeld, 1995). As noted by Cooke and Morgan (1998, p. 185), academic support for the notion of clusters provided a compelling rationale for the adoption and development of clusters strategies in many regions, based particularly on the work of Porter (1990).

The promise of clusters as an economic and regional development strategy has not, however, translated into successful practice and policy in many nations and regions. Indeed, there is now a growing 'crisis of faith', with many policy makers questioning the feasibility and viability of pursuing clusters development policies as a key intervention strategy (Cooke & Morgan, 1998). In countries such as the UK, regional development agencies have started to re-focus their economic strategies away from clusters towards sectoral concentrations, often as a result of less than satisfactory evaluations of their clusters development strategies and plans. Increasingly, government agencies and officials report a dichotomy between the allure and potential of the clusters concept, and the difficulties associated with applying and implementing these ideas in practice.

One reason for this may be the broad approach taken, which has tended to be 'top-down', in analytical and planning terms (Atherton, 2003), and often based on generic rather than contextually-sensitive methodologies (Enright, 2000, p. 327). Typically starting from a regional or national perspective, 'top-down' approaches tend to use administrative units, in particular regions, as the geographical basis for clusters development policies and plans. And yet, such an approach does not reflect the dynamics of clusters formation as a function of increasing collaboration between firms. A core theme in assessments of clusters emergence has been the central and essential role of businesses in driving the formation of collaborative groupings of firms (Porter, 1998). Clusters form when groups of businesses start to collaborate and through co-operation develop ties and inter-dependencies that enable them to operate with greater economies of scale and scope. The dynamics of clusters formation are emergent and iterative, in that they arise from the formation and emergence, and reinforcement of mutual understanding and trust between individuals working in and representing the organizations active in, and around, a cluster. As trust and understanding of the capacities and capabilities of clusters members is shared and developed, 'untraded inter-dependencies' emerge that reinforce the scope for collaboration (Storper & Scott, 1955), creating strong ties between firms involved in the cluster.

As Cooke and Morgan (1998, p. 191) noted: 'clusters cannot be created by political injunctions or through mere physical proximity. Clusters form as a result of a self-selection process on the part of firms which see advantages in exploiting their interdependencies for mutual benefit, a process which can be encouraged but not ordained by public agencies'. Effective clusters development policies are likely therefore to be 'bottom-up' (Atherton, 2003), in that they emerge out of sustained transactions between firms that are seeking or starting to collaborate.

2   Clusters formation as a business dynamic of relational as well as spatial proximity

The formation of clusters has not, however, received much attention within the literature (Lorenzen, 2005). The aim of this chapter is to examine the process of cluster formation in an attempt to fill this gap. Central to our approach is the argument that effective clusters are the result of a self-selection process on the part of firms, which see advantages in exploiting their interdependencies for mutual benefit; a process that can be encouraged but not ordained by public agencies. Relational proximity underpins the formation of clusters, as can be seen in definitions of clusters, including those that incorporate spatial considerations of the dynamic: [clusters are] 'geographic concentrations of interconnected companies, specialised suppliers, service providers, firms in related industries and associated institutions . . . in particular fields that compete but also cooperate' (Porter, 1998, pp. 197–8). Such considerations of clusters indicate that, although geographical proximity is important, inter-firm relationships and cooperation are also important.

The conditions within which clusters emerge are influenced and shaped therefore by relational as well as locational proximity, reflecting a focus on transaction and interaction, as well as place and space, in a globalizing and increasingly inter-connected world (e.g. Amin, 2002; Amin, 2004). The localization of competitive advantage, through clusters formation, can be characterized as symptomatic of the 'globalization of competition' (Enright, 2000). Localized collaboration as a response to and feature of increased globalization enables greater levels of local flexibility and adaptability than would be the case for a spatially dispersed group of co-operating businesses. The Marshallian logic of industrial districts, where the 'secrets are in the air' (Marshall, 1920), indicates that collaborating groups of businesses that are located close to each other benefit from the intangible advantages of knowledge spillover effects that stimulate innovation (Acs et al., 1999; Audretsch, 2003; Anselin et al., 1997; Feldman, 1999; Jaffe, 1989; Jaffe et al., 1993; Maurseth & Verspagen, 2002). Proximate location also enables greater levels of information exchange, reducing the risk of information asymmetries in inter-firm collaboration (Almeida & Kogut, 1997).

At one level, therefore, the specific dynamics of clusters formation are likely to be spatially concentrated, and localized. In many cases a cluster will be located in or around a particular city as these can be characterized as large centres of economic activity creating the opportunities for trade and collaboration (Jacobs, 1972). Economies of localization, i.e. the agglomeration effects arising from proximate location of firms in the same industries and markets, tend to occur within cities and urbanized settlements (Duranton & Puga, 2000; Rosenthal & Strange, 2003). Where they do not occur in cities and major settlements, they emerge around local sources of firm advantage, particularly infrastructure, such as airports and terminals; natural resources, such as mines and agricultural land; localized concentrations of factor inputs, such as skilled workers and staff located in and around universities, research centres and other knowledge centres.

And yet globalization means that transactions occur with firms and other entities that are located beyond the region, city or local economy. The locations of customers, suppliers and partners need not be solely within the area in which the cluster is mainly located. Indeed, the logic of the localization of competitive advantage through local clustering as a feature of increased globalization points to the likelihood that local clusters will be able to operate and trade more globally and will do so as a result of and through the internationalization of firm competition and trading patterns (Dicken, 2003; Enright, 2000). Localized cooperation, in other words, is likely to lead to enhanced scope for trading across borders, whether regional or national, as well as to greater potential locally for collaboration and innovation. Communications technologies and protocols are increasingly enabling of globalization and the ability of firms, regardless of location, to trade across regional and national borders (Castells, 1996).

Our main argument is that proximity – in terms of relationships and geography – determines the characteristics of the cluster. Overall, clusters are likely to be based on agglomeration effects through localization and urbanization, arising out of physical proximity, as well as relational proximity that is reinforced by but also transcends physical proximity. This suggests that the dynamic of clusters formation can, and should, be explored by examining (1) the localized patterns of business-to-business collaboration that allow for firm advantage through economies of localization and urbanization; and (2) the wider transactional opportunities and patterns that arise from globalization, and the use of communication technologies to enable wider scope for cooperation within spatially dispersed groups and networks of firms. The story of, and rationale behind, clusters formation is the binary relationship between greater geographical scope, because of globalization, and the geographical and relational proximity that creates local agglomeration economies leading to spillover benefits and positive externalities in particular locations. This conceptualization of clusters emergence and operation is dynamic, in that these different proximities may 'emerge, develop and disappear' (Boschma, 2004; Boschma, 2005).

3 Relational and locational dynamics of clusters emergence

The dynamics of clusters emergence indicate that there are common patterns, or paths of evolution, in their development based on the relative importance of both spatial and relational proximity. Spatial proximity refers to the physical distance between firms whereas relational proximity describes the closeness of firms in terms of culture; culture in this case referring to a number of shared institutions or rules as suggested by North (1990). These patterns in turn suggest a number of forms, or configurations, of inter-firm collaboration that describe and characterize clusters. In broad terms, three patterns in clusters emergence can be identified:

1. arising through physical proximity between firms, for example to benefit from agglomeration economies or advantages arising from particular locations: the main drivers and advantages at this stage will be the reduction of transactions costs among the interacting firms;
2. arising from transactional proximity, i.e. coming out of and resulting from intense trading and collaboration. Increasing trust between firms allows for a higher level of cooperation, as well as increasing the level of mutual interdependence;
3. arising out of relational proximity, i.e. through centres and networks of knowledge creation and dissemination that generate and transfer 'know-how' that can be exploited and that attracts as well as generates new economic activity.

Figure 6.1 outlines these three patterns of collaborative interaction graphically. At the starting point ('X') there is little spatial or relational proximity. This grouping of firms would be characterized as dispersed and unconnected, with firms operating as isolated, atomistic units. Clusters emergence can then follow several paths, as outlined in the figure. The first pattern (1) illustrates the importance of spatial proximity; the second (2) highlights the importance of both spatial and relational proximity, although the degree can vary as there are three points marked; and the third pattern highlights the importance of relational proximity (3). As the figure shows there are multiple paths and multiple outcomes in this process, the process is dynamic and a cluster may not necessarily stay static over time as the importance of spatial and relational proximity varies. Thus, cluster development may not be uniform across space. For example, one cluster may be based on spatial proximity initially, the logic of which then fades over time, for example because of changes in supply chain dynamics, to be replaced by both relational and spatial proximity. Another cluster may emerge through trading relationships which then stimulate proximate location. Figure 6.1 shows movement in all directions., signifying temporal variability in patterns and levels of collaborative interaction.

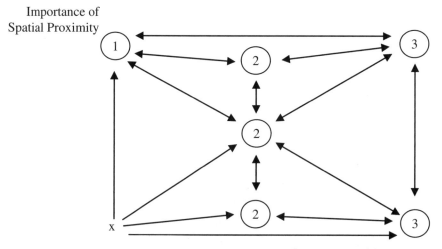

Figure 6.1   Patterns of cluster development

The first pattern of cluster development (1) relies on spatial proximity, as it is the physical proximity of the firms that generates the advantages in these clusters. Increasing advantages in terms of reduced transactions costs and agglomeration economies are generated as the number of firms in a location increases. As densities of firms increase, agglomeration effects will be greater, creating a greater incentive for firms to locate within the cluster and attracting a greater number of firms into the area. Indeed, it will only be once diseconomies of scale from congestion effects outweigh the benefits of agglomeration economies that the growth of the cluster will slow down and eventually cease.

Agglomeration economies generated through spatial proximity is one aspect of this pattern of cluster development. The second is the fact that spatial proximity facilitates face-to-face interaction. Storper and Venables (2004) suggest four important facets of face-to-face contact: it is efficient; it reduces incentive problems, permits screening of other agents, and motivates agents (p. 353). Face-to-face contact allows for a smoother transaction process between firms, reducing the costs and uncertainty associated with markets. Spatial proximity also allows the spillover of knowledge to occur; empirical evidence suggests these are bound by geography (Jaffe et al., 1993); indeed, as Glaser et al. (1992) suggest, knowledge crosses streets with greater ease than it crosses oceans.

Although spatial proximity is an important factor in the development of clusters, it is not necessarily a prerequisite. The second pattern of cluster development (2) does not exclusively rely on spatial proximity but is also predicated on relational as well as physical proximity; the formation of trust between firms, in other words, is likely to reduce the importance of physical proximity. Shared cultural values and norms are crucial to the development of trust (North, 1990: 15). As trust develops, the importance of spatial proximity declines, and relational proximity becomes the predominant logic underpinning inter-firm collaboration. Firms will not necessarily need to monitor and police collaborators actively or directly, further reducing the costs of transaction. Under these circumstances, relational proximity begins to increase in importance, enhancing shared values and stimulating a more trusting relationship between collaborating firms.

The third discernible pattern of clusters development is not reliant on spatial proximity. Instead, it is relational proximity that brings firms together. As Allen (2000) states, ' "thick" relationships may span organisational and spatial boundaries' (p. 28), and so the importance of geography recedes. This notion is similar to the concept of 'Ba' (Nonaka & Konno, 1998; Nonaka et al., 2000). 'Ba' can be a geographic entity or, alternatively, it can be a virtual knowledge-creating platform (ibid., p. 9), i.e. based on relational rather than physical proximity. Lissoni (2001) found evidence of knowledge flows within an epistemic community comprising of engineers and technicians created through trading relationships, but found no evidence that these knowledge flows were the result of geographic proximity. Morgan (2004), however, suggested that geography is still important, despite an increased interest in the relational aspects of clusters formation.

These three patterns of clustering generate different drivers for and forms of interaction and collaboration. They can also be mutually present in that they are not of themselves exclusive. For example, dense local networks of specialist firms seeking out and enjoying economies of localization may benefit from, and potentially attract, knowledge centres, which in turn may lead to greater levels of transaction between firms and the centre. Clusters that arise through physical proximity of firms will be based on agglomeration effects, through economies of localization and urbanization, i.e. on the advantages for firms when they are close to other firms, labour and consumers. Clustering arising from transactional proximity is likely to be driven less by physical location of firms and more by (1) supplier and supply relationships; and (2) location of, and proximity to, customers. This is because there may be reasons for supplier and producer location in certain places that do not necessarily coincide with market locations and concentration. Clusters around knowledge centres are likely to lead to some specialization, i.e. localization economies, but will be based on the intellectual property produced and made available from the centre itself. It is, in other words, the location of the knowledge centre, rather than proximate location, that generates potential clusters and stimulates their emergence.

4   A taxonomy of clusters emergence

For each pattern of clusters emergence, more specific dynamics can be identified (see Table 6.1):

1. Clusters emergence arising from physical proximity: (1) co-location in dedicated business spaces; (2) shared location in and around key infrastructure; (3) location to gain access to natural resources. At a broader level, firm location in cities and major settlements can also be seen as a driver of this form of agglomeration.
2. Clusters emergence through transactional proximity: (1) sectoral and market concentrations based on shared, overlapping or complementary niches and specializations ('horizontal' collaboration through forms of flexible specialization); (2) 'vertical' production and trading relationships, including buyer–supplier linkages, subcontracting, supply chains; (3) concentrations around larger firms that offer supplier and subcontracting opportunities, particularly when these lead over time to collaboration and interactions between suppliers and subcontractors.
3. Clusters around knowledge creation and distribution centres, such as universities and research centres, as well as associations and other forms of business membership organization. External facilitators and stimuli may lead to the formation of collaborating groups of firms, typically in two ways. Firstly, as can be the case for business associations and intermediary organizations like Northern Italy's technical service centres, they become a repository for and distributor of market-specific and specialist knowledge. And, secondly, they generate opportunities and scope for businesses to innovate through the sharing of knowledge and know-how.

Table 6.1   A taxonomy of cluster formation patterns

Physical proximity	Dedicated business spaces
	Key infrastructure
	Natural resources
	Cities and major settlements
Transactional proximity	'Horizontal' flexible specialization
	Vertical production and trading relationships
	Large firm 'magnets'
Knowledge centres	Universities, research institutions
	Business groups generating or codifying sectorally specific knowledge, e.g. technical institutes, trade associations

The nature, and dynamic, of clusters formation is likely to vary across these three general categories. Clusters that emerge as a result, primarily, of physical proximity will be stimulated when businesses identify and act on opportunities to collaborate with neighbouring firms. The initial stimulus therefore will be events and conditions that lead to greater levels of local interaction between firms. From a Marshallian perspective, this is likely to happen when firms are densely concentrated geographically. There are, however, indications that planning policies and related economic development strategies to encourage firm location in dedicated business spaces do not in themselves lead to inter-form collaboration (e.g. Cooke & Morgan, 1998; Massey et al., 1992). For this reason, a case can be made that clustering through proximate location is likely to occur when many businesses are located in a city or settlement, but that location per se does not drive increased collaboration in and of itself but rather increases the possibility that this may occur. Physical proximity therefore implies the possibility of clustering but does not explain how this occurs or starts. It may be for this reason that cities provide a space where the potential for clustering through agglomeration effects arises, but where clusters do not emerge without a stimulus or particular driver. Cities, in other words, are a conducive environment for clusters, but do not in themselves create anything more than the latent conditions for their emergence.

Transactional proximity, i.e. the intensity and extent of commercial ties between businesses, is fundamental to market exchange. Extensive transactional ties between businesses are, in other words, a feature of markets rather than an indication of clusters emergence and clustering between firms. Over time, however, ongoing transactional ties can lead to the formation of groups and networks of collaborating firms, and other organizations. Two changes in the nature of transactional ties are likely to presage clustering. The first is a shift from predominantly, or exclusively, binary transactional relationships to interactions that involve multiple firms. Ongoing collaboration to fulfil transactional requirements and demands is a feature of different patterns of clustering, including flexible specialization, agglomeration economies, and the development of more formalized associations and networks. In many cases, group cooperation can be informal as well as informal. Indeed, the emergence of trust within a group, and shared values and a sense of collective identity, provide a tacit sanction over non-fulfilment of agreed means of collaboration (via implicit rather than explicit contracts). It is also cumulative, in that the number and intensity of transactions and interactions build up over time. The increased knowledge of partners that this transactional familiarity generates can help to reduce transaction costs, especially via improved levels of information availability about other firms and a reduced need to 'police' agreements, formal and informal, as trust develops and is continued through successive interactions.

The second change in interactions that tends to be seen when clusters form out of transactional ties occurs when the nature and scope of exchange and partnership extends beyond the original transaction. When groups of firms develop additional and new ways of working with each other, and with other enterprises and organizations, then the scope for ongoing collaboration that leads to clusters formation increases. Network theorists have identified 'multiplex' relationships, i.e. those characterized by multiple ties and interactions, as both an indicator of and outcome from strong relationships (Boissevain, 1974). The emergence of multiplex relationships therefore increases the level of commitment between firms and individuals within them. Multiplexity also increases the prospect for more substantive collaboration, in that the transition from a single or small-scale interaction to many forms and dimensions of engagement widens the scope for identifying and agreeing upon collaborative activities. The broadening of ties, within a group rather than bilaterally, expands the scope for pursuing opportunities for cooperation.

Inter-firm collaboration, and hence the prospects for clusters formation, can also become more established through multiple interactions that 'deepen' the relationships between firms. Deepening relationships contribute to clusters formation through group collaboration in three ways. Firstly, they increase awareness of and familiarity with and between firms. Increased awareness of other firms that are active in group as well as bilateral cooperation improves understanding of and knowledge about the capacity, capabilities and activities that are available within the emerging cluster. The familiarity that grows out of greater awareness provides scope for firms to identify and seek out collaborative opportunities, such as joint tendering and flexible forms of informal subcontracting and 'putting out' (Lazerson, 1995). Granovetter (1994) noted that ongoing collaboration creates a 'cognitive hook which actors may hold onto in order to construct trust relations at a higher intensity than those outside the category'. The second way in which deeper relationships contribute to clusters formation arises out of the tendency for increased awareness and familiarity through multiple and more intense interactions to produce high levels of mutual and reciprocal trust within a group. Trust, as social capital (Lin, 2001), enables firms to reduce or remove the need to monitor or police relationships and in particular transactions where there is the possibility of moral hazard arising from information asymmetries. Trust also functions as public sanction, in that firms within an emerging grouping or potential cluster that are seen to break agreed (often implicit) norms, or that indulge in free-rider behaviour, will be identified as less trustworthy and so less desirable to cooperate with (Lyon, 2003). In extreme cases, behaviours contrary to trust-based norms within a group can lead to expulsion (ibid.).

Increased awareness and familiarity combined with trust based on multiplex, deep relationships constitute the conditions within which group collaboration can emerge. They are, as such, enablers of clusters emergence in that they allow and stimulate collaboration. As importantly, relational proximity reduces the transaction costs associated with group cooperation, in several ways. Flows of information, increased trust, and a reduced need to monitory partners, as well as informal and tacit contracts rather than formalized agreements, all reduce the costs associated with economic exchange between the collaborating firms. Collaboration therefore increases the efficiency of transactions by reducing the associated costs, and in doing so provides scope for improved competitiveness based on lower operating firms that can be enjoyed by all firms in the forming cluster.

5   The cluster formation process

Clusters form as a result of direct interactions and ongoing collaboration between businesses. These interactions create relationships, and transactional as well as relational proximity (Atherton, 2003), that in turn generate greater opportunities for substantive and ongoing cooperation. Collaboration generates economies of scope that extend beyond internal rates of return and that are available to businesses within an emergent or formed cluster. Clusters formation encompasses a transition from no collaboration between firms to cooperation and the reformulation of competitive activity around the wider economies of scale that become available to firms within an emerging cluster. The initiation of a cluster occurs when a group of firms moves from individualistic attempts to address business issues and exploit market opportunities to engagement with other firms in order to gain access to their resources and capabilities. Clusters form, therefore, when collaboration to enjoy wider economies of scope arising from cooperation underpins and becomes the basis of competitive activity and advantage for the firms involved.

Five stages in the process of clusters formation can be identified (Atherton, 2003; see Figure 6.2 below). The stages are broadly sequential, in that transition from one to the next signifies movements towards formation of a cluster and recognition by the businesses involved that this is increasingly intrinsic to their competitive advantage. Movement from stage to stage is contingent upon the emergence of greater levels of mutual commitment to cooperation, and hence to increased levels of group interaction. Clusters formation, as a result, involves the development of greater levels of collaboration between firms that both provide wider economies of scope and that create higher levels of inter-firm dependency and reciprocal trading and interdependence. Becoming a cluster entails a trade-off between agglomeration economies that can enhance individual firms as well as group competitiveness, on the one hand, and a loss of autonomy as a result of greater interdependence, on the other.

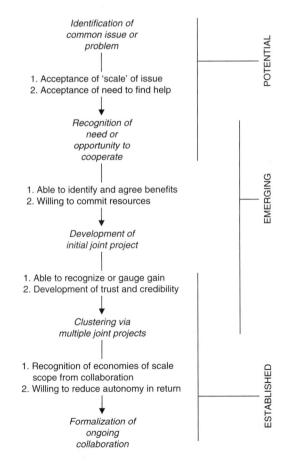

Figure 6.2   A stages model of clusters formation

Stage 1   Identification of a common issue or problem
The first step in the emergence of a group of collaborating firms, and in the formation of a cluster, is the acceptance or recognition that individual firms face issues and developmental constraints that they cannot address themselves. When an issue or problem is shared by firms, the potential for clustering exists, particularly when the combined resources and capabilities of a group of businesses provide opportunities and means to overcome a common constraint or barrier. An initial condition for clusters emergence, therefore, is that firms experience or face a shared issue that they could resolve through collaboration. At this first stage of clusters development, businesses have not agreed to work together and in most circumstances do not recognize or appreciate the potential of cooperation and group activities in helping to address shared issues or problems. The dynamics underpinning clusters formation start before actual collaboration occurs, and are predicated on the latent potential for cooperation on shared issues.

Stage 2   Recognition of a need or opportunity to cooperate
Although many firms experience similar issues and problems that constrain their development or present them with additional operating challenges and costs, this does not in itself lead to group collaboration. Clusters start to form when the potential to work together transforms into active interaction and cooperation, in order to address shared concerns. The second stage of clusters formation occurs, therefore, when firms are stimulated or pushed to collaborate with like-minded businesses. External competitive pressures, such as new market entrants and innovation leading to new business practices, can serve as a stimulus for collaboration, as can supply chain and buyer–supplier network dynamics. Regulation, and other requirements for companies with standards or agreed industrial and market norms, can also push forms towards collaboration in groups.

In all cases, clusters start to form when the pressures or need to resolve shared issues or problems becomes significant enough to drive individual firms to seek out and engage in collaboration. The critical threshold for clusters initiation, as actual collaboration between firms, is the transition from sharing a problem or issue with other firms (whether mutually recognised or not in the first instance) to agreement amongst a group of firms that there is a need or opportunity to work together on the particular issue. This transition requires a shared recognition that the issue or problem cannot be resolved without co-operation. It is also predicated on mutual recognition of the need and opportunity to collaborate to address and resolve the issue or problem. The second stage of clusters formation therefore encompasses a shift to recognition of the opportunities arising from group collaboration, and the need to do so in certain circumstances in order to enable business development and mitigate threats or constraints to firms. Recognition of the need or opportunity to co-operate moves firms closer to direct collaboration, and so involves engagement amongst the firms as well as mutual recognition that co-operation may be of benefit to all involved.

Stage 3   Development of an initial collaborative project
Once a group or network of firms that have a common issue has accepted, and then agreed, that there is scope for collaboration, the next step is to determine the form, scale and nature of cooperation. This stage of clusters formation entails a shift from exploration of the opportunities for collaboration to actual cooperation via group

engagement in shared activities. As noted by Atherton (2003), the initial form of group collaboration tends to be a joint project with an agreed and shared goal. An initial project was preferred by firms, for several reasons. Firstly, initiating group collaboration through a single, initial project reduced the risk associated with collaboration in situations where there was no history of group interaction and joint working. Trust in working relationships tends to start with lower-risk activities and accumulates over time through ongoing interactions (Lyon, 2003). Projects typically were based on agreed parameters, and means of working together, which provided explicit limits to individual firm commitment to collaboration. These limits, mostly in terms of commitment of resources and time, as well as knowledge and profile, allowed participating firms to estimate the relative risk of group collaboration on an initial project. In this way, cooperating firms were able to calculate and hence manage the potential risk arising from breakdown in relations or failure of the collaborative project. Secondly, engagement in an initial 'test' project allowed firms to learn about the partner firms that they are cooperating with, so increasing awareness of the activities and capabilities of other firms in the grouping. It also provided opportunities for the development of trust and familiarity amongst the collaborating firms. And thirdly, an initial project helped collaborating firms to develop protocols and shared 'rules' for engagement and cooperation. A 'pilot' project therefore generated the mechanisms and trust as well as explicit foundations for future cooperation.

Stage 4   Emergence of ongoing group collaboration through multiple projects
Should the initial project be successful, or provide sufficient scope for stimulating future collaboration, then the next step in clusters formation is the initiation of multiple projects. Typically, the forms and dynamics of engagement that were established in the initial project provided the basis, and many of the operational rules, for continued collaboration. Following on from an initial project, participants that can see further benefits from group collaboration explored additional opportunities to develop new projects and group activities. As multiple projects were agreed upon, and activated, participating firms became more aware of and familiar with each other, and their individual and organizational capabilities. Through ongoing collaboration via projects, the participating firms are able to develop higher levels of trust and, as a result, become more mutually dependent. Increases in mutual awareness, familiarity and trust within a group of cooperating firms in turn created increased opportunities and further scope for collaboration. In this way, ongoing collaboration through multiple projects creates the conditions for greater levels of cooperation.

The 'rules' of engagement and collaboration, both formal and tacit, that emerge in the first and initial projects inform and shape the means and nature of ongoing cooperation as the number of projects in which firms are involved expands. Typically, many of these rules were agreed and enforced informally, and tended to be based on the exchange and offer of favours that were traded and taken up by the collaborating firms. Ongoing group collaboration typically succeeded when a form of exchange currency or mechanism emerged that was recognized, agreed upon and deployed by the participating firms. In most cases, this currency or mechanism was informal, or semi-formal, and involved reciprocal exchange that generally functioned in the same or similar way as barter arrangements.

Stage 5   Formalization of the group and its collaborative activities
Engagement in multiple projects can lead to more explicit and more formalized forms of
and approaches to collaboration. The formalization of group collaboration represents a
final stage in the clusters formation process, in that the importance of cooperation and
the growth of interdependence were explicitly recognized by participating firms as the
basis for their own activities and responses to external stimuli. Via exchanges of agreements to cooperate, and contracts, collaborating firms made more explicit and more tangible the extent and importance of cooperation to their operation and future potential for
survival and growth. Over time, such agreements were likely to develop into more substantive forms of cross-investment and cross-ownership that publicly stated the extent to
which firms were collaborating. The move to formalization of previously informal ties and
interdependencies represents, therefore, a shift to more explicit investment in and commitment to the group as the basis for seeking out competitive advantage and competing
against other firms.

6   Thresholds in clusters development
Transition from one stage of clusters formation to the next is by no means an inevitable
or automatic development. In order to move from one stage of clusters development to
the next, the firms experienced, and identified, specific conditions that needed to be met,
collectively, and thresholds that needed to be overcome. The clusters formation process,
as a result, can be seen as a dynamic of navigating through and resolving constraints on
the development and emergence of initial and then ongoing collaboration between and
within a group of firms.

*From identification of a common issue or problem to recognition of the need or opportunity
to collaborate*   A first transition that firms experience is a move from individual
identification of a problem or issue that is common to a group of businesses to recognition that there is a need or opportunity to cooperate with other firms to address or resolve
the particular problem or issue. This transition, from the first to second stages in clusters
formation, represents a broadening out by the firms involved of their attempts to address
business development challenges and to exploit opportunities they would not be able to
as an individual entity. The transition, therefore, results in a shift in firm behaviour from
seeking out competitive advantage through economies of scale based on internal rates of
return to broader economies of scope through collaboration (stage two of the clusters formation process). And this occurs because firms recognize that the limits on their own
resources mean that internal rates of return cannot provide such economies, whereas collaboration presents an opportunity to secure wider economies of scale based on the collective or pooled resources of a group of cooperating firms. The initial transition in the
clusters formation dynamic therefore occurs when firms with a common issue or problem
recognize that (i) they cannot resolve it individually ('scale' of issues is beyond the individual enterprise); and (ii) they need, or there is an opportunity, to seek out assistance,
either through exploring opportunities for collaboration or other forms, to resolve or
exploit the specific issue or problem.

From opportunity to collaborate to development of an initial project   Acceptance of the
need or opportunity to cooperate does not in itself indicate or ensure that collaboration

will occur. There is a threshold between recognition of the need or opportunity to cooperate and the initiation of an initial collaborative project. Transition from recognition of to engagement in group collaboration entails: (i) identification of and agreement on the likely benefits that will arise out of a group project; and (ii) willingness by all firms involved to commit resources and effort to undertake and complete the project. A likely barrier in clusters emergence is the difficulty that firms may find in moving from agreement on the opportunities arising from group collaboration to actual commitment to a joint project. Indeed, this shift, from acceptance of the notion and benefits of collaboration to actual engagement, could be considered one of the most likely constraints on clusters emergence. It is at this point that the firms involved move from discussion and exploration of the idea and ramifications of collaboration through to commitment to a specific form of cooperation.

From initial to multiple, ongoing projects   A subsequent developmental challenge for clusters emergence occurs at the transition between development of an initial project and the undertaking of multiple collaborative projects that form the basis for ongoing clustering activity within a group of firms. Firms are likely to continue to engage in collaborative projects when (i) they recognize the gains from cooperation on the initial project; (ii) they build an initial level of mutual trust, that then reduces the perceived risks of future cooperation; and (iii) they have become aware of and more confident in each others' capabilities and ability to commit resources to collaboration, i.e. the credibility of all or most firms involved in the initial project is established within the group. There may be cases, however, where the benefits arising from the initial project are not sufficient to motivate firms to continue collaboration. In addition, participating firms may conclude that, although the initial project was of benefit, the costs and effort involved in further cooperation are either prohibitive or have an excessive opportunity cost associated with them. Under these circumstances, it is unlikely that a transition may occur from a single, 'pilot' project to multiple projects with varying scope and timescales. An alternative scenario is that some (that is, a subset) of the initial group of firms continue to collaborate via multiple projects, as a smaller group.

Should the group of firms engage in, and become committed to, cooperation on multiple projects then the final transition, or development threshold, in clusters formation is the move to formalization of ongoing collaboration. This transition is based on a recognition that cooperation offers significant benefits and opportunities for the firms involved that provides, or has the potential to provide, competitive advantage through enhanced economies of scale (and scope) that are not available to or within an individual firm. This implies a fundamental shift in the competitive stance and strategy of the firms involved; from an individualistic approach to business development and the seeking out of competitive advantage, to commitment to ongoing collaboration as a group as the basis for individual firm competitiveness and development. It signifies a shift to greater interdependence amongst the firms and to strategies that are predicated on both the collective capabilities of the firms involved and the dynamics of group collaboration as the basis for market competition. One key implication of this transition will be a loss in operating and decision-making autonomy by the firms involved as a 'trade-off' in exchange for access to opportunities for inter-firm economies of scale and scope through collaboration.

Overall, the transitions between different stages of clusters development, and in particular the ways in which each of these thresholds demands greater levels of collaboration

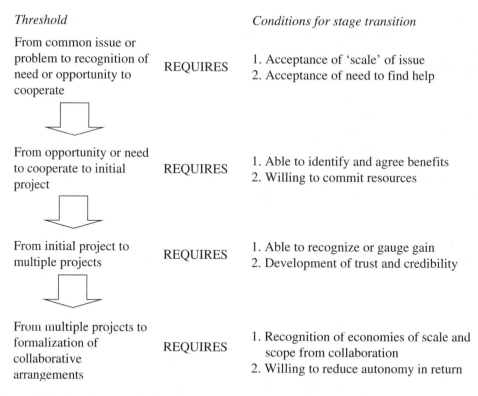

Threshold		*Conditions for stage transition*
From common issue or problem to recognition of need or opportunity to cooperate	REQUIRES	1. Acceptance of 'scale' of issue 2. Acceptance of need to find help
From opportunity or need to cooperate to initial project	REQUIRES	1. Able to identify and agree benefits 2. Willing to commit resources
From initial project to multiple projects	REQUIRES	1. Able to recognize or gauge gain 2. Development of trust and credibility
From multiple projects to formalization of collaborative arrangements	REQUIRES	1. Recognition of economies of scale and scope from collaboration 2. Willing to reduce autonomy in return

Figure 6.3   Developmental thresholds in the clusters formation process

which in turn create more interdependency, indicate that the formation of clusters is a navigated and hence unpredictable process. There is no indication that the emergence of clusters is inevitable once businesses embark on group collaboration. Movement, from one stage of clusters development to the next requires, and is predicated on, the conditions associated with the specific thresholds outlined in Figure 6.3. An inability or reluctance to accept the conditions of interdependence that underpin these thresholds will prevent or constrain the formation of clusters.

7   Phases of clusters development

The nature of the cluster, and the dynamics of collaboration and joint action within it, are likely to change during the process of its formation. In the early stages, there is greater emphasis on creating and building awareness and trust between the firms, based on and coming out of a desire to address a common issue or problem. When firmer cooperation between firms starts to emerge, the focus shifts to project collaboration, and developing tacit as well as explicit 'rules' and patterns of group interaction. As the emerging cluster becomes more conversant with group collaboration, the firms involved develop more formalized agreements and conventions that guide and provide a structure that enables ongoing cooperation within the group, in multiple forms.

Potential clusters   Clusters formation starts when there is a common issue or problem and as firms start to recognize that there may be scope for working together. Clusters have

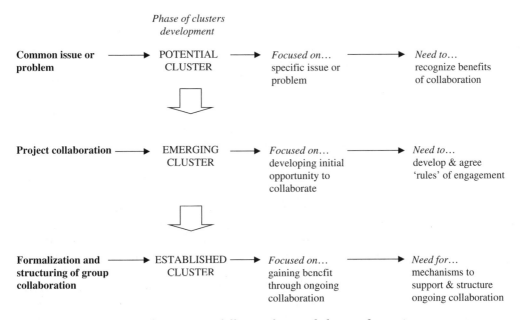

Figure 6.4 Distinctive dynamics at different phases of clusters formation

the 'potential' to form because the opportunity for collaboration exists, but has not been transformed into specific forms of interaction and group working. The latent nature of possible group cooperation at this stage of clusters formation indicates that, although there is the possibility of collaboration, there are few examples and cases of group inter-action at this point. In order to move from potential to emergence, there is a need for mutual recognition of the benefits that may arise from collaboration.

Emerging clusters As the potential for cooperation transmutes into group engagement in collaborative project work in order to address a common issue or problem, or take advantage of a shared opportunity, the grouping shifts from being a potential cluster to an emerging cluster. Emergence can be seen in and defined by the extent and level of inter-firm collaboration that forms. Emerging clusters are preoccupied, as a result, with initiat-ing and completing collaborative projects. In order to do this, there is a need to develop a common approach to organizing inter-firm collaboration, typically via the formulation and agreement, either tacitly or explicitly, of 'rules' or conventions that govern scope and nature of engagement.

Established clusters have formalized the structure and processes of group collabora-tion. The firms that are involved in such clusters have recognized and accepted the advan-tages that arise from working closely as a group of interacting and interdependent businesses. They are as a result focused on gaining benefits and greater scope for com-petitive advantage through ongoing cooperation. Typically, this results in a shift in firms' strategy to dependence on inter-firm collaboration as a key or primary source of both growth and an ability to adapt to and cope with environmental change and turbulence. Integral to this dynamic is the growth of high levels of inter-firm trust and dependency, that reduce the operational autonomy of all firms involved in the grouping.

8   Cluster gestation: the temporal dynamic of clusters formation

The emergence of a cluster, through a series of transitions from potential to emerging to established forms of inter-firm collaboration, is not an inevitable or straightforward transformation. An inability or reluctance to transcend or respond to specific thresholds in cooperation, in particular those that signify a loss of individual firm autonomy, can become insuperable barriers to clusters formation. Navigating, or overcoming, thresholds can require extensive inputs and efforts by the firms involved in the forming cluster, and often entail changes in the attitudes and perspectives of those involved. Movement from threshold to threshold, and from stage to stage, of clusters development can be time-consuming and requires effort and personal as well as organizational change in behaviours and attitudes. Acceptance of the need and opportunity to collaborate implies a related recognition that this will entail increased risk for each firm, arising from higher levels of interdependency and so increased exposure to the results of decision making in other firms. Collaboration within a cluster, in other words, provides the firms involved with greater prospects for responding to external events and dynamics, but also makes each firm more vulnerable to the actions of other firms with which they are cooperating.

Formation of a cluster, as a result, is not inevitable and, rather than being seen as a smooth process, entails significant investment and commitment by the collaborating firms. Navigation through developmental thresholds, combined with the growing interdependence that inter-firm collaboration produces, indicates that the formation process will take time and may suffer from setbacks and punctuations arising from differences in individual firm commitment to and expectations of the cluster. Clusters formation, therefore, occurs over an extended period, and will not inevitably lead to transition from the potential for a cluster to form through to its emergence and establishment.

The temporal nature of clusters formation suggests that the rate of formation, and hence the overall time required for a cluster to develop, can vary considerably, depending upon the dynamics between the firms involved, and the nature of the competitive and wider institutional framework within which they operate (Amin & Thrift, 1995; North, 2005). When acceptance of the need and opportunity to cooperate is clear, and there is commitment to seeking out inter-firm collaboration, the conditions for clusters formation are likely to be more conducive than when firms are uncertain about or sceptical of the possible gains from cooperation. The motivations and overall level of commitment of the firms involved in seeking out opportunities for cooperation will influence the rate at which a cluster is likely to form. In addition, the nature and relative strength of the drivers or stimuli that encourage, or create, the conditions for clusters formation are likely to affect the speed at which clusters form. When drivers are particularly acute, for example because of the entry of highly competitive new firms into an established market, then the rate at which firms seek out opportunities for collaboration is likely to be greater than in circumstances where competitive pressure is not high. And the perceived and experienced difficulties of overcoming thresholds during the clusters formation process will also affect the speed at which a cluster will emerge. Combined, the motivation and commitment of the firms involved, the strength of drivers for clusters formation, and the difficulty perceived and experienced in overcoming thresholds, will influence the time required for clusters formation. The gestation periods for different clusters are likely to vary considerably from case to case as a result (Figure 6.4).

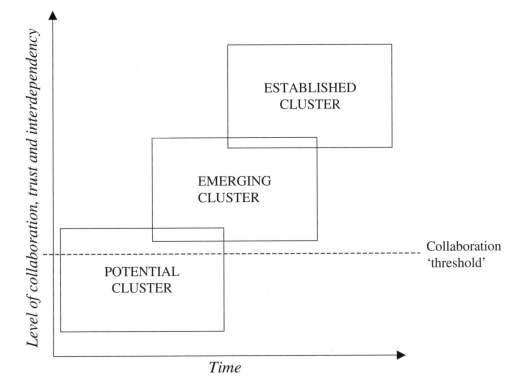

Figure 6.5   Likely variations in the gestation periods of clusters formation

9   'Bottom-up' dynamics of clusters formation: implications for public policy

This chapter argues that clusters form because of the interactions between firms that generate interdependency, trust and reciprocal 'rules' of engagement that enable and support ongoing inter-firm collaboration. Rather than conceive of clusters as industrial structures, or locationally specific agglomerations, such a view places collaborative relationships and interactions between firms at the heart of the cluster and its development. The reciprocal nature of clusters formation suggests that clusters form as a result of 'relational proximity' (Atherton, 2003) that emerges from and allows for transactional proximity, i.e. the undertaking of many interactions that lead to economies of scale and scope for the collaborating firms. As Porter (1998) noted, businesses and their interactive and interacting ties and relationships lie at the heart of and underpin clusters formation, and constitute a necessary and in many cases sufficient condition for their emergence.

A 'relational turn' (Boggs & Rantisi, 2003; Ettlinger, 2001) in conceiving of the economic geography of clusters formation provides an alternative characterization of the spatial nature of clusters. Relational proximity indicates that the strength and adaptability of collaborative relationships determines and constitutes the dynamics of clustering. Although proximate location can enable and support greater levels of relational proximity, this approach indicates that such proximity can occur and hold over longer distances should the business rationale and benefits exist and hold. Marshallian patterns of clustering, such as the flexible specialization patterns seen in Northern Italy (Brusco, 1982;

Pyke et al., 1990), present conditions where there is a high level of overlap between locational and relational proximity, as do cases of local specialization in response to increasing globalization (Enright, 2000). The confluence of close location and close relationships does not, however, suggest that the two are corresponding conditions, i.e. that both are necessary for clustering to occur. Instead, the implication is that relational proximity is enabled and supported by locational proximity in industrial districts and when firms are involved in forms of flexible specialization.

Conversely, trading and cooperative relationships that take place over distance can be underpinned and determined by relational proximity that, in turn, stimulates clusters formation. The clusters formation process outlined in this chapter indicates that inter-firm collaboration occurs when firms share a need, issue or opportunity that they can address or respond to collectively. This primary condition of clusters emergence does not, in itself, suggest a spatial dimension. Indeed, where the problem, issue or opportunity arises out of or constitutes a cross-national or non-local dynamic, then clusters are likely to form on a geographical scale that is commensurate with or relates to the spatial nature of the particular driver of clusters formation. Opportunities for global or trans-national collaboration are likely, in other words, to create conditions that might result either in localized networks of inter-firm collaboration, as indicated by Enright (2000), or in wider geographical ties that are enabled and allowed to develop because of the international nature of the common issue, problem or opportunity faced by the firms in the developing cluster. The specific spatial nature of inter-firm collaboration, in other words, is contingent upon (i) the geographic implications of a group response to a shared issue, problem or opportunity; and (ii) the locational dimensions of the responses by collaborating firms.

The spatially variable nature of clusters development, combined with its temporal variability and the central role of firm commitment to the cluster, indicate that the dynamics of clusters formation are sensitive to the specific evolutionary patterns and paths of emergence of inter-firm collaboration. Extensive comment has been made about the contextual specificity of individual cases of clustering (e.g. Amin & Thrift, 1995; Asheim, 1992; Garofoli, 1992), suggesting that each cluster is a unique combination of collaborative arrangements, transactional activities and institutional context. The 'bottom-up' approach to conceiving of clusters formation presented in this chapter suggests that the dynamics of inter-firm collaboration move through several stages of emergence that are common across different clusters. Although the individual circumstances of a cluster may be unique, therefore, the dynamics of inter-firm collaboration are observable across different cases and instances of clustering. Observable though these dynamics of cooperation may be, the complexity inherent in a stages model of clusters formation – with its spatially and temporally variable dimensions and the central role of firms in driving cooperation – indicates that analyses, descriptions and explanations of clusters are likely to require intensive and in-depth analysis and exploration.

The inherent complexity of clusters as a dynamic of inter-firm collaboration, and a source of firm advantage, presents a challenge for public policy and intervention. The thresholds that constitute transition from stage to stage in the process indicate that clusters formation is not inevitable and may suffer from barriers that are either difficult and time-consuming to navigate, or that prevent ongoing collaboration to take hold. The gestation periods that occur as a result indicate that the time required for a cluster to form will be variable, and will be difficult to predict. Indeed, a defining characteristic of a forming cluster appears to be that the time taken for inter-firm collaboration to occur and take hold cannot be predicted: by the firms involved, by observers and by entities seeking to stimulate and facilitate clustering. From this perspective, public intervention designed to enable clusters formation will not be able to determine or anticipate the gestation period, or even where the dynamics that lead to established forms of inter-firm collaboration can be mapped.

Although the process framework presented in this chapter indicates the inherent uncertainty in clusters development, it also offers a basis for selective intervention that has the potential to address the specific needs and concerns of collaborating firms. Via a focus on stages and thresholds of clusters formation, such interventions can address specific developmental constraints and challenges that need to be overcome and addressed for the cluster to develop. A focus on facilitating movement from stage to stage, through thresholds, offers scope for intervention that addresses and is tailored to the specific development needs of the collaborating firms as they arise. Intervention to encourage and facilitate clusters formation is based, from this perspective, on enabling firms to collaborate more closely and in sustainable ways. The role of public intervention, in other words, is twofold: (i) to enable the progression of firms from the initial stage in the clusters formation process (a common issue, problem or opportunity, but no recognition that there is a need or scope for collaboration); (ii) to support the development of 'rules' and protocols that enable initial and ongoing cooperation. Public intervention, in other words, is focused on movement through the stages of clusters formation and is tailored to the specific needs and opportunities for collaboration at each stage and threshold of the process.

10   Conclusion and summary

The potential for clusters to emerge occurs when firms come together to address common issues and problems or to take advantage of opportunities that would not be available or resolvable without collaboration. Through shared recognition of a need for or likely benefit from collaboration, clusters start to emerge, based on a small number of cooperative projects that firms undertake as a collective. As familiarity and trust develop between the firms, scope emerges for ongoing collaboration via multiple projects. Over time, increased familiarity, and the development of established and agreed protocols for cooperation, help to formalize ongoing collaboration within a framework of reciprocal exchange and growing interdependence.

Clusters formation, as a result, is an iterative and inherently dynamic process that engages multiple actors, cooperating in many ways, through a growing range of collaborative activities that develop closer and more intensive ties and interactions between firms. Via development of a series of collaborative 'rules', and a transactional 'exchange' currency, common and shared patterns of interaction emerge and repeat themselves across cooperative arrangements. These rules and protocols in turn develop a tacit as well as explicit dimension to collaboration, in that they are shared and agreed within the group but do not extend beyond the cluster unless other firms are involved in a collaborative project. The tacit dimension creates forms of cooperation that, through trust and familiarity, reduce the costs and risks associated with inter-firm collaboration.

The implications for understanding clusters formation are twofold. On the one hand, the dynamics of clustering and the emergence of a cluster of collaborating firms are inherently uncertain and dependent upon the adaptation and collective learning of the firms involved. On the other, the progression of groups of firms through successive stages of clusters development, and the related need to overcome specific developmental thresholds, provide the basis for inputs that can support the forming cluster. Firms will be motivated to seek out external assistance when they experience difficulty in moving from stage to stage and navigating specific thresholds, and so will be open to public intervention and inputs at these points in the clusters formation process.

References

Acs, Z., F. Fitzroy and I. Smith (1999), 'High-tech employment, wages and university R&D spillovers: evidence from US cities', *Economics of Innovation and New Technology*, **8**(1), 57–87.

Allen, J. (2000), *Regions and the World Economy*, Oxford: Oxford University Press.

Almeida, P. and B. Kogut (1997), 'The exploration of technological diversity and the geographical localization of innovation', *Small Business Economics*, **9**, 21–31.

Amin, A. (2002), 'Spatialities of globalisation', *Environment and Planning A*, **34**(3), 385–99.

Amin, A. (2004), 'Regulating economic globalization', *Transactions of the Institute of British Geographers*, **29**(2), 217–33.

Amin, A. and N. Thrift (1995), 'Globalisation, institutional "thickness" and the local economy', in P. Healey, S. Cameron, S. Davoudi, A. Graham and A. Madani-Pour (eds), *Managing Cities: The New Urban Context*, Chichester, Sussex: John Wiley.

Anselin, L., A. Varga and Z. Acs (1997), 'Local geographical spillovers between university research and high technology research', *Journal of Urban Economics*, **42**(3), 422–48.

Asheim, B. (1992), 'Flexible specialisation, industrial districts and small firms: a critical appraisal', in H. Ernste and V. Meier (eds), *Regional Development and Contemporary Industrial Response: Extending Flexible Specialisation*, London: Bellhaven Press.

Atherton, A. (2003), 'Examining clusters formation from the 'bottom-up': an analysis of four cases in the North of England', *Environment and Planning C: Government and Policy*, **21**, 21–35.

Audretsch, D. (2003), 'Agglomeration and the location of innovative activity', *Oxford Review of Economic Policy*, **14**(2), 18–29.

Beccatini, G. (1990), 'The Marshallian industrial district as socio-economic notion', in F. Pyke, G. Beccatini and P. Sengenberger (eds), *Industrial Districts and Inter-Firm Cooperation in Italy*, Geneva: International Institute for Labour Studies, International Labour Organisation.

Boggs, J. and N. Rantisi (2003), 'The relational turn in economic geography', *Journal of Economic Geography*, **3**, 109–16.

Boissevain, J. (1974), *Friend of Friends: Networks, Manipulators, Coalitions*, Oxford: Blackwell.

Boschma, R. (2004), 'Competitiveness of regions from an evolutionary perspective', *Regional Studies*, **38**(9), 1001–14.

Boschma, R. (2005), 'Proximity and innovation: a critical assessment', *Regional Studies*, **39**(1), 41–5.

Brusco, S. (1982), 'The Emilian model: productive decentralization and social integration', *Cambridge Journal of Economics*, **6**, 167–84.

Castells, M. (1996), *The Rise of the Network Society*, Oxford: Blackwell.

Cooke, P. and K. Morgan (1998), *The Associational Economy*, Oxford: Oxford University Press.

Dicken, P. (2003), *Global Shift: Reshaping the Global Economic Map in the 21st Century*, London: Sage.

Duranton, G. and D. Puga (2000), 'Diversity and specialisation in cities: why, where and when does it matter?', *Urban Studies*, **37**(3), 533–55.

Enright, M. (2000), 'The globalization of competition and the localization of competitive advantage: policies towards regional clustering', in N. Hood and S. Young (eds), *The Globalization of Multinational Enterprise Activity and Economic Development*, New York: St Martin's Press.

Ettlinger, N. (2001), 'A relational perspective in economic geography: connecting competitiveness with diversity and difference', *Antipode*, **33**, 216–27.

Feldman, M. (1999), 'The economics of innovation, spillovers and agglomeration: a review of empirical studies', *Economics of Innovation and New Technology*, **8**(1), 5–25.

Garofoli, G. (1992), *Endogenous Development and Southern Europe*, Aldershot: Avebury Press.

Glaser, E., H. Kallal, J. Scheinkman and A. Shleifer (1992), 'Growth in cities', *Journal of Political Economy*, **100**, 1126–52.

Granovetter, M. (1994), 'Business groups', in N. Smelser and R. Swedburg (eds), *The Handbook of Economic Sociology*, Princeton, NJ: Princeton University Press.

Jacobs, J. (1972), *The Economy of Cities*, London: Pelican Books.

Jaffe, A. (1989), 'Real effects of academic research', *American Economic Review*, **79**(5), 957–70.
Jaffe, A., M. Trajtenberg and R. Henderson (1993), 'Geographic localization of knowledge spillovers as evidenced by patent citations' *Quarterly Journal of Economics*, **108**(3), 577–98.
Lazerson, M. (1995), 'A new phoenix? Modern putting-out in the Modena Knitwear Industry', *Administrative Sciences Quarterly*, **40**, 34–59.
Lin, N. (2001), *Social Capital: A Theory of Social Structure and Action*, Cambridge: Cambridge University Press.
Lissoni, F. (2001), 'Knowledge codification and the geography of innovation: the case of Brescia mechanical cluster', *Research Policy*, **30**(9), 1479–500.
Lorenzen, M. (2005), 'Why do clusters change?', *European Urban and Regional Studies*, **12**(3), 203–8.
Lyon, F. (2003), 'Trader associations and urban food systems in Ghana: institutionalist approaches to understanding urban collective action', *International Journal of Urban and Regional Research*, **27**(1), 11–23.
Marshall, A. (1890/1920), *Industry and Trade*, 2nd edn, New York: Augustus M Kelley.
Massey, D., P. Quintas and D. Wield (1992), *High-Tech Fantasies: Science Parks in Society, Science and Space*, London: Routledge.
Maurseth, P. and B. Verspagen (2002), 'Knowledge spillovers in Europe: a patent citations analysis', *Scandinavian Journal of Economics*, **104**(4), 531–45.
Morgan, K. (2004), 'The exaggerated death of geography: learning, proximity and territorial innovation systems', *Journal of Economic Geography*, **4**(1), 3–21.
Nadvi, K. and H. Schmitz (1994), 'Industrial clusters in less developed countries: a review of experiences and research agenda', DP 339, Institute of Development Studies, University of Sussex, Brighton.
Nonaka, I. and N. Konno (1998), 'The concept of "Ba": building a foundation for knowledge creation', *California Management Review*, **40**(3), 40–54.
Nonaka, I., R. Toyama and N. Konno (2000), 'SECI, Ba and leadership: a unified model of dynamic knowledge creation', *Long Range Planning*, **33**, 5–34.
North, D. (1990), *Institutions, Institutional Change and Economic Performance*, Cambridge: Cambridge University Press.
North, D. (2005), *Understanding the Process of Economic Change*, Princeton, NJ: Princeton University Press.
Porter, M. (1990), *The Competitive Advantage of Nations*, New York: Free Press.
Porter, M. (1998), 'Clusters and the new economics of competition', *Harvard Business Review*, **76**(6), 77–81.
Pyke, F., G. Beccatini and W. Sengenberger (1990), 'Industrial districts and inter-firm cooperation in Italy', Institute of Labour Studies, International Labour Organisation, Geneva, Switzerland.
Rosenfeld, S. (1995), 'Industrial strength strategies: regional business clusters and public policy', Aspen Institute, Washington, DC.
Rosenthal, S. and W. Strange (2003) 'Geography, industrial organisation and agglomeration', *Review of Economics and Statistics*, **85**(2), 377–93.
Saxenian, A. (1994), *Regional Advantage: Culture and Competition in Silicon Valley and Route 123*, Cambridge, MA: Harvard University Press.
Segal Quince Wicksteed (2000), 'The Cambridge phenomenon revisited', Segal Quince Wicksteed, Cambridge.
Storper, M. and A. Scott (1995), 'The wealth of regions: market forces and policy imperatives in local and global context', *Futures*, **27**, 505–26.
Storper, M. and A. Venables (2004), 'Buzz: face-to-face contact and the urban economy', *Journal of Economic Geography*, **4**(4), 351–70.

7 Cluster life-cycles: an emerging synthesis
Edward M. Bergman

1 Introduction

Despite early and repeated predictions of a short half-life that afflicts merely fashionable ideas, regional cluster concepts continue to thrive in diverse policy theatres and benefit from the intense scrutiny of many disciplines, having already entered the provisional realm of numerous theoretical frameworks. Cluster concepts obtain their greatest traction in those fields concerned with aggregates of firms and near-market agents that self-assemble in progressively larger constellations and networks comprising whole economies, whether at regional, national or supranational levels. Clusters also offer an analytically appealing intermediate level of economic 'granularity' that accords well with parallel theoretical developments in the new economic geography, endogenous growth theory, knowledge economy, innovation systems, etc. While economic clusters still remain theoretically underdeveloped, they enjoy valuable face-validity that continues to propel policy interest, generate support and attract intellectual resources. Several other chapters of this volume develop various themes along these lines.

This chapter will focus attention on available concepts that permit better understanding of how clustered aggregations of dynamic firms come to dominate certain technologies and markets as powerful innovation and growth mechanisms, and why the same dominant aggregations may later morph successfully into novel combinations or decline into oblivion, becoming – in Wilbur Thompson's unforgettably term – 'industrial hospices'. While the policy interest in this topic is self-evident, theoretical interests might benefit from a more complete accounting of 'why' clusters may, at different life-cycle stages, be dynamically innovative, highly productive, highly concentrated, yet in the end exhibit fatal vulnerabilities. We shall also use their 'life-cycle'[1] as a selective lens by which to re-examine clusters, with the intent to reveal certain structural facets or relationships not previously considered or always made evident.

Maskell and Kebir (2005) use the terms 'existence', 'extension' and 'exhaustion' to describe specific cluster life-cycle stages; attention to these stages is essential, they argue, because certain modern cluster theory versions replaced earlier, more robust concepts with 'a one-sided model that addressed the *existence* argument in novel ways *but almost totally disregarded the extension and exhaustion arguments*' (p. 6, emphasis supplied). The present intention is therefore to help remedy such oversights by explicitly evaluating literatures that consider the full range of cluster cycle stages and by unpacking their cycle-phase implications for further consideration.[2] Accordingly, the chapter will examine principal cluster cycle concepts, including selected overview of the dynamics that propel clusters along their life-cycles and consideration of key factors seen to be relevant at various cluster cycle stages.

2 Cluster cycles and phases

Cluster cycles are usually represented either in text or diagrams as stylized 'S' curves, modelled generally after industry, technology or product cycles,[3] and often with the quite similar terms of reference. However, attention has also shifted to specific points on/stages along the curve associated with the emergence of a cluster, its early development and expansion, its ability to exploit opportunities and resist competitive replication, its attaining hypergrowth and engaging in scale-expansion, its slowing near potential inflection points, and its successful transition to a newly-launched cycle phase or perhaps the 'lock-in' and exhaustion of its final cycle phase. Changes in the cluster during its cycle phases can result from gaining new or losing old agents (mainly firms), shifts in the scale and scope of activities among stage-incumbent firms, or both.[4]

Of the many distinctions drawn to categorize types of clusters, perhaps the most important for present purposes is traded (exported) v. non-traded cluster division, which applies the classic export-base logic to clusters.[5] This distinction has increased in importance during recent periods of intense international trade and globalization, both of which further concentrate production and increase technological or industry specialization, a point remarked upon by Krugman (1991, p. 1) when he first considered the usefulness of spatial and geographic features to analyse international trade. As clusters become ever more specialized, they also exhibit stronger technological, product and industrial life-cycles that characterize their key building blocks. Clusters with the most pronounced life-cycle behaviour therefore are likely to be specialized in globally-traded goods, while regionally traded goods (cultural, territorial or tradition-intensive) are less susceptible to dynamic life-cycles due to the slowly changing quasi-oligopolistic niches they occupy.[6] Non-traded clusters of locally produced and consumed goods or services are wholly creatures of their host regions, where local firms colocate production or sales in accordance with sub-regional Hotelling (not interregional Marshallian) incentives.

The literature's focus on the dynamics of specific development stages is due in part to the relatively high frequency of stage-specific cases studied, which are necessarily positioned at the time and cycle-phase when the case was studied, or other specific cases may reflect a cyclical circumstance judged important by cluster study patrons.[7] Despite a marked preoccupation in the literature with 'lock-in' phase issues, much cluster research continues as a matter of routine to dwell on the 'existence' stage of successful, contemporary clusters, particularly among distinct research communities;[8] this leads Maskell and Kebir (2005) to observe that cluster theory remains incomplete and possibly misleading in the absence of life-cycle considerations. However, other recent research and publication reveal growing interest for a variety of reasons in examining more closely the broader question of cluster cycles and in discussing more than a single stage, a sampling of which will now be reviewed (Table 7.1).

To organize the discussion, we adopt the previously labelled phases: 1, existence, 2, expansion, and 3, exhaustion.[9] Discussion will focus on each of the principal stages separately, including additional sub-phases, drawing upon published and draft entries in Table 7.1 or from other works that have conducted research related to certain stages.

2.1 Existence phase

This initial phase includes what must happen before a cluster emerges sufficiently to be recognized as 'existing'. For Maskell and Kebir (2005), existence could be triggered by a variety of processes that lead to colocation. In reviewing various accounts of the existence phase, they refer first to the presence of tightly packed Marshallian locational economies

Table 7.1   Cluster life-cycle sources

Cluster life-cycle sources	Cycle stages identified	Featured stage(s)	Evidence supplied	Principal purpose of contribution
Tichy (1998)	creation growth maturity petrification	all	Literature review, case illustrations and policy examples	Pose relevant policy actions at various cluster cycle stages
Swann (2002)	critical mass take-off peak entry saturation	all	'Entry' firm simulations modelled for tech-intensive clusters	Framework to evaluate UK/US bio-tech and computer clusters
Fornahl and Menzel (2003)*	emerging growing sustaining stagnating	all	Literature review, concept exploration	Examine role of firm foundings at cluster life-cycle stages
Wolter (2003)*	set-up growth change adaptation	all	Literature review, model dynamics, case illustrations	Develop life-cycle theory of agglomerations
Brenner (2004)	entry exit growth	all	Population ecology modelling of clusters	Propose complete cluster theory and life-cycles
Maskell and Kebir (2005)*	existence expansion exhaustion	all	Marshall, 'Milieu' and Porter concepts	Identify key gaps in 'cluster theory'
Lorenzen (2005)	arise decline shift	all	Contributions of edited volume, editorial overview	Develop editorial framework
Hassink and Shin (2005)	positive negative	lock-ins	Contributions of edited volume, editorial overview	Develop editorial framework
Maggioni (2005)*	birth/take-off golden age maturity	all	Population ecology modelling of clusters	Relate cluster dynamics to other innovation
Bergman (2006)	formative growth maturity petrification	maturity	Literature review, cluster survey evidence, simple correlations	Sustainability factors tested

Note: * working drafts.

and spillovers[10] as the principal drivers of initial colocation, although how these first come into being as cluster factors remains undeveloped. Building on this view, colocation in existing agglomerations gradually permits the endogenous emergence in modern economies of positive externalities and generally favourable business conditions, to which additional firms are attracted and which, in certain industries, are presumably better able to exploit (and develop further) through colocation (Lorenzen, 2005).[11]

Beyond the traditional Marshallian points, Maskell and Kebir (2005) note Michael Porter's (1990) stress on the importance of local rivalry plus intra-firm and inter-firm information conduits. In marked contrast to Porterian concepts of rivalry, innovative milieu theorists place emphasis on pre-existing community values, cooperation and social capital, which 'act as an uncertainty-reducing mechanism in the innovation process' (Maskell & Kebir, 2005, citing Camagni, 1995, p. 320), thereby building trust, common work ethics, and joint economic endeavours. A clear inference is that existing community and social practices establish hospitable circumstances in which innovative agents are eventually able to prosper, a point also frequently advanced in the social capital literature, most forcefully and earliest by Putnam (1993).

Whether Marshallian or milieu-centric in nature, such accounts of cluster existence are better at establishing the necessary, although not sufficient, conditions for cluster emergence. Historical legacies and chance play important roles as well. As examples, Krugman's account of the origins of tufted rug innovations (1991, pp. 59–61) suggest how sparks of local entrepreneurial consequence can arise from simple gift-giving between friends and strangers, while Tappi's (2005, pp. 297–304) summary of accordion design-diffusion reveals the spark ignited locally by expatriates who acquired external contacts and information that enabled them to detect and organize overlooked local potentials (see also Sable, 1982, pp. 222–3). Clusters therefore usually result from some early historical initiative. Even so, policy efforts to substitute publicly-sponsored programmes of cluster stimulus for the Schumpeterian calculus of entrepreneurs are increasingly prevalent, even though conventional cluster wisdom by now firmly counsels policy support only *after* entrepreneurial activity has demonstrated cluster viability.

Among the most focused efforts to understand how clusters emerge are scholars who attempt to model theoretically and empirically the process of clusters coming into existence, drawing upon tools of population ecology, complexity analysis, agent-based modelling, etc. to characterize self-organization among cluster agents that may lead to later transitions between cycle phases. Brenner (2004) proposes that cluster emergence requires a minimal presence of industrial firms (i.e. naturally occurring presence of firms 'seeded' by externally-driven industrial cycle dynamics),[12] plus increases in exogenous demand for the products of these firms. It is then a question of whether that demand becomes sufficiently strong to trigger an expansion of firms beyond a minimal, pre-cluster stable state to a critical mass that attains a higher stable state capable of setting off endogenous ('self-augmenting') cluster growth dynamics driven by firm entry and exit.

Maggioni (2005) employs a somewhat different population ecology model to account for cluster birth and take-off, which adopts the perspective of an existing firm that might wish to locate in a potential cluster. Early locators calculate their net benefits and, if warranted (e.g., a 'critical cluster mass' has been attained), enter the cluster, thereby driving up the average profitability of this location to the next potential locator (enhanced spillovers and positive externalities), but also driving up congestion costs. Swann (2002) also focuses on critical mass as the essential 'existence' event that stimulates colocation, although the interest is less in contributing to the development of cluster cycles than in examining entry variation of firms to a cluster at points along its cycle. In this view, entry by external agents is a function of the strength of a cluster in a given industry and the strength of clusters in all other industries.

2.2   Expansion phases

Initially favourable existence conditions described above are the necessary prerequisites for a cluster's critical mass to suddenly take off, where self-organized 'swarming' of new firms, technologies and innovations, products and cluster-related activities occur rapidly and promiscuously. Perhaps this sub-phase could be distinguished and labelled as 'Exploratory expansion': it is typically concentrated before the inflection point of the typical cluster 'S' curve where rates of expansion in cluster scope activities is greatest. This phase[13] corresponds with an 'entrepreneurial technological regime', identified by Winter (1984, p. 297), 'that is favorable to innovative entry, but unfavorable to established firms'. The latter are, in Winter's term, 'routinized technological regimes' that dominate the following 'exploitative expansion' phase, during which systematic exploitation, cluster scale-economies, process technologies and efficient firm routines drive growth, often aided by the deliberate policies dedicated to the improvement and expansion of beneficial advantages. Such policies include (presumably) remedying any newly revealed scale-inhibiting bottlenecks that might limit the continued expansion of the cluster.[14]

2.2.1   Exploratory expansion

Initial stages of the familiar Marshallian,[15] 'expansion' trajectory might be described at this sub-phase as an exuberant exploration of how initial pecuniary spillovers originating in cluster-specific infrastructure, specialized worker training and education, key supplies of skilled labour, emerging specialized suppliers, and increasingly compliant institutional or regulatory practices that favour expansion and competition might be incorporated into successful business models. Maskell and Kebir (2005, citing Porter, 1998, pp. 241, 221) add that 'developing clusters also attract – and cluster participants seek out – people and ideas that reinforce the cluster. Growing clusters attract skilled people through offering greater opportunities. Entrepreneurs or individuals with ideas migrate to the cluster from other locations as well, because a growing cluster signals opportunity'.

Incumbents and (presumably) opportunistic arrivals as well benefit from a cluster's innovative milieu, which 'facilitates mutual acquaintance, collaboration, dissemination and exchange of information, just as it allows for the development of trust relations' (Maillat, 1998, p. 19, cited in Maskell and Kebir, 2005). During this intensely exploratory period of self-organization, the firms of each developing cluster may gradually and quite intuitively assemble and collectively refine a unique series of beneficial capacities, some of which may also become the 'isolating mechanisms' that help sustain growth and protect them from external regional competitors (Maskell and Malmberg, 1999, pp. 176–8).

Brenner (2004, ch.2) reviews carefully a series of distinct mechanisms that have feedback-loops and are self-augmenting, i.e. are 'growth inducing'. These include mechanisms that arise between firms (e.g., Marshallian spillovers, spin-off firms, etc.) and interactions among firms and other cluster agents (human capital, research institutions, etc.). The intensity of the expansion process from endogenous self-augmenting processes is seen by Brenner as further tempered by global (mainly industry) and local (social, cultural, governmental) factors.[16] Maggioni (2005) confirms several of these and identifies a further series of mechanisms and agent behaviours that accelerate the exploratory phase, adding to the list models of success-signalling to external agents, anchor tenant and leader–supplier dynamics, legitimating agent-forms, emerging diseconomies, and information diffusion. Swann (2002, p. 59) notes that, for innovative clusters 'in the formative (introduction and growth) stage of the life cycle, geographical proximity may be critical to tacit technology transfer – which is so essential to industry development – and hence the positive effects are large'.

The speed with which all such factors propel a cluster is, from an ecological perspective, the difference between the birth and mortality rates of the firm population, which Magionni expresses as the net rate (r) that determines a cluster's growth potential. Swann's model (2002, p. 58) is similarly based upon firm entry as the principal dynamic, where entry rates are highest in the strongest of competing clusters; the model further implies that entry-driven growth will tend to favour specialized clusters: 'if like firms convey benefits on incumbents while unlike firms do not, then if space is limited, it is better to group together with like firms'.

Bergman (2006) observed that Austrian incumbent firms of *strong regional clusters* operating where opportunities to innovate or invest were self-reported as 'excellent' also drew heavily upon universities, venture capitalists and regional firms to help generate and develop innovations, while seldom relying upon formal cluster support organizations. They behave very much as Porter might predict by deliberately positioning their products in international markets, valuing highly-demanding customers both internationally and regionally, and by monitoring supplier quality and customer feedback from regional customers.

The most successful clusters progress directly from the exploratory to the next stage where some measure of dominance is attained through scale expansion, thereby fitting the stylized 'S' curve dynamics; however, lesser (probably typical) clusters have considerable difficulty escaping their initially exuberant phase or attaining scale or industry dominance. Two examples illustrate the life-cycle interruptions faced by lesser clusters, each at different speeds.

Tappi (2005, pp. 298–304) describes a lengthy series of periodic adjustments taken by the musical instrument cluster following its emergence in Marche (Italy), early in the twentieth century. During that century, it moved from accordions to electric and electronic instruments to digital equipment and specialized digital applications as a matter of necessity during periods when demand and tastes shifted and new technologies began to penetrate its existing products, all of which transpired through a cascade of family and small firm dynamics, temporary scalar expansions, mergers, spin-offs and start-ups.

Originating as a household workshop, its entrepreneurial efforts and expanding firm population produced in the ensuing century a continuously evolving series of interrelated clusters, passing through several cluster 'half-lives', rather than becoming a single cluster that faced maturity at a single point in its life-cycle. It might be argued that the vast majority of clusters have similar histories, gradually enriching their host regions over time by exposing them to an ever-broader palette of technologies and sectors that undergird a capacity to learn and adjust over time, supportive of other clusters but never becoming dominant[17] in a specialized field, nor perhaps even dominant in their host region. However, this broader experience may also form the basis for what innovative milieu theorists envision by being 'potentially able to utilize the tensions that emerge during the process of change by guiding the localized production system towards a new state in which the territorial logic continues to manifest itself' (Maskell & Kebir, 2005, p. 12).

The Danish mobile-communications cluster emerged far more recently and has already adjusted numerous times during its relatively young life, a process accelerated by the profoundly rapid pace of innovation. Dalum et al. (2005, p. 231) focus on the role played by disruptive technologies to develop their 'analysis of sequential disruptions by using the concept of technological life-cycles, and to apply this to a single case over an extended period of time, including several (technological) cycles'. An accelerated scenario of early entrants, enabling institutions and universities, buy-outs, mergers, takeovers and exits reflect the highly unstable state of cluster development in North Jutland as repeatedly improved mobile telephone technologies shifted the attention of cluster agents swiftly from NMT to GSM to UMTS, only to be challenged again most recently by the WLAN family of technologies developed elsewhere. In comparison with the Marche musical cluster, it involves a much narrower group of technologies and sectors active over a far shorter (25 year) time frame, but this cluster too has yet to 'take off' as a scale-efficient growth cluster, and it too is probably quite representative of supporting – not dominant – technology-intensive clusters found throughout many modern regional economies. In this view, the vast majority of clusters may experience life-cycles that never pass on to the succeeding phase.

2.2.2   Exploitative expansion   Once this phase of cluster expansion has been attained, in Tichy's view (1998, p. 233), it 'appears to be the best of all worlds to participants. It is the phase, nevertheless, which may generate the first deviations [that] cause later troubles. Success is easy in this phase, so that little pressure exists to search for further development of the cluster's strengths, for other applications of its knowledge, etc. It is tempting to concentrate on the best-selling product and to produce it in ever-increasing quantity, utilizing economies of scale.

Members tend to focus less on exploring new options and more on protecting advantages that earlier arose quite spontaneously, identified by Maskell and Malmberg (1999) as regional 'isolating mechanisms', three of which are relevant to this stage:

> *isolating* mechanisms arose in innovative regions that sustain them by protecting them from external regional competitors. First, *asset mass efficiency* is the idea that historically agglomerated R&D and related innovation assets are not easily or readily duplicated in competing regions. Second, *time compression diseconomies* are the costly but necessary lags a competing region must overcome while trying to master and replicate the capacities of a superior region, which can busily continue to build upon its strengths through increasing-returns processes. Last, an externally inscrutable *interconnectedness of asset stocks* implies that simply replicating each asset stock produces no sense of how they are deployed effectively, which is another way of saying that accumulated assets develop DNA-like usage patterns not visible or apparent to outsiders or even to those who daily draw upon this embedded DNA. (Bergman, 2006)

Cluster members may complacently assume such isolating mechanisms are effectively permanent features, and perhaps also begin to rely more heavily upon membership in formally structured and managed organizations to protect initially advantaged positions. For example, Bergman (2006) found firms that self-identified membership in *relatively mature* Austrian clusters (i.e., featuring a broad range of firms and supporting institutions) indicated such membership provided access to good buyer trend information; these same firms sold relatively little of their output to demanding international customers or to non-European markets and perceived no advantages in ISO certification, thereby forfeiting opportunities to learn about global market changes and competitors. In contrast, their general orientation placed comparatively high value on *internal* member-supported R&D contacts, acquiring or developing innovative ideas principally from same-sector firms and cluster organizations, but relatively little from university and venture-capital sources. While mature cluster firms welcomed the entry of additional firms to the cluster, they saw no relative benefits of competition.

Additional forms of complacency may also begin slowly to erode initial cluster advantages during periods of consolidation and slowdown. Very significant limits to growth and overall cluster carrying capacity arise from the more rapid rise in congestion costs that offset advantages as clusters attain greater scale. Congestion costs are among the important classic factors that Maskell and Kebir (2005, p. 6) find most absent in much of the contemporary cluster literature: 'The *extension* argument of centrifugal forces was, in contrast [with contemporary views], normally based on the costs of congestion, or the bidding-up of prices for land, labor or the services of goods provided, but could be extended to include negative spillovers when different industrial logics clashed.' Escalating congestion costs of clashing industrial logics are explicitly incorporated by Swann (2002), who observes that congestion costs rise disproportionately as entrants from different clusters bid up local prices, while additional firms of each cluster add few or no Marshallian advantages to the other, therefore accelerating the loss of net benefits to potential entrants of either cluster, which probably favours initial tendencies toward single cluster specialization. Swann describes this as a pivotal situation:

> [As] the industry enters its maturity stage, the benefits of clustering start to tail off, and eventually the costs of clustering outweigh the benefits . . . At this stage the cluster is approaching its peak, but has not entered the decline phase as such. It may be growing very slowly, but it is not getting smaller. That stage starts when the *industries* located in the cluster start to decline. (2002, p. 54)

Elsewhere, Swann (2004, slide 18) summarizes the process in greater detail, deploying a matrix that indicates the effect of successive cluster entrants on various agents, until the 'final entrant', at which point no agents and only consumers benefit. In portraying the structure of congestion costs, Maggioni (2005, pp. 13–28) deploys an ecological model that draws heavily upon an elaborately conceived micro-foundation of congestion costs to examine potential rates of cluster growth, cluster carrying capacity and external challenges to mature incumbent clusters.[18]

To this point, we have focused on the processes by which a cluster matures and moves beyond its earlier innovative phases by adopting standardized, scale-efficient process technologies; perhaps firms have even spun off establishments and facilities that no longer benefit from local cluster advantages. Swann (2004, p. 54) poses rhetorical questions whose obvious answers are responsible for slowing or halting the entry of firms to incumbent clusters:

> As new industries emerge, firms in those industries may then be faced with location decisions of the following sort. Should they locate in an old cluster, where they have little commonality with incumbents, where the established infrastructure is dated and where congestion costs are still relatively high, although admittedly declining? Or do they locate in a new cluster where the incumbents, though new and small, are generating the sorts of spillovers that attract entrants and are based in more relevant industries, and where the infrastructure is better?

Brenner (2004, p. 37) sees *consolidation* across clusters, with severe life-cycle consequences for some, as the natural outcome of entry decisions by firms, particularly at later stages of industry evolution: 'At some point in time the global firm population and therefore also the supply increases faster than demand. As a consequence, competition becomes more fierce and finally leads to an increasing occurrence of shakeouts.'

It seems clear that one cannot consider the life-cycle of a cluster in the absence of its core industry life-cycle. In their broad study of industry life cycles and clustering, Audretsch and Feldman (1996, p. 271) conclude that 'what may serve as an *agglomerating influence* in triggering innovative activity to spatially cluster during the introduction and growth stages of the industry life cycle, may later result in a *congestion effect*, leading to greater dispersion in innovative activity'. Cluster growth may suddenly or gradually slow, oscillating around a stable state at some upper limit; the state of affairs obtained from this orderly and incremental development path is perceived by firms and other cluster agents in Tichy's words, 'as the best of all possible worlds . . .'.

However, a mature cluster in such a stable state may not be prepared for the unexpected disturbances it absorbed easily during its earlier exploratory rise, disturbances that now threaten its stable maturity. Maggioni (2005, p. 21) describes the following effects on established clusters:

> As long as the technology undergoes 'normal progress' (i.e. follows a technological trajectory) the interchange of knowledge within the established cluster will tend to preserve its leadership When new technologies arrive that are discontinuous with those that came before (i.e. change the technological paradigm) existing industry concentration may be of little value and the result then is that new technologies tend to be exploited in new clusters that do not suffer the diseconomies associated with an established cluster.

Events of this kind pose qualitatively different challenges to mature clusters than to clusters at earlier stages, which suddenly interrupt the slow, graceful ageing enjoyed by comfortable clusters.

2.3   Exhaustion phase
Exhaustion arises at that point in a cluster's life-cycle when maturity itself poses a clear threat to continued cluster viability.[19] Tichy describes the situation thus (p. 230):

> As the number of firms is reduced, sophisticated networks are no longer necessary, as no new information has to be transferred; nor are clusters any longer competitive, compared with vertically integrated firms, as the number of nodes has been drastically reduced. The smaller the networks, however, the less – and the less new and stimulating – information they can provide, the lower therefore the chance of the cluster inventing new products, new processes, or a new organization. The cluster has aged; the region in which the cluster is located has become a problem area, a region with little endogenous potential to find new dynamics.

What details characterize this situation and how do we understand the possibilities? First, the depletion of some vital mineral or material resource may lead to exhaustion, or the milieu deteriorates (Maskell and Kebir, 2005, p. 9, quoting Maillat, 1998, p. 15), which results when 'opportunistic behavior causes defiance or the outward openness becomes inadequate to ensure the enlargement of new cooperative relations or the replacement of technologies'. A strongly contrasting view of competitive v. cooperative behavior, perhaps addressing wholly different kinds of clusters, sees risk arising in both 'important intra-cluster forces (such as ebbing domestic rivalry, the development of internal rigidities and regulatory inflexibilities) as well as a number of externally induced influences (such as technological discontinuities, deteriorating factor conditions, and shifts in buyer's needs' (Porter, 1990, pp. 166–9; 1998, pp. 243–4, cited in Maskell and Kebir, 2005, p. 8).[20] Whatever the causes, growth and regeneration that occurred almost automatically in early phases grinds to a complete halt and the cluster pauses. At this point, either one of two different directions is possible. The pause extends and is 'locked-in' for an extended period of time, or the cluster experiences a renaissance, perhaps immediately or following a temporary period of lock-in.

2.3.1   Lock-in   A significant strand of the cluster 'lock-in' literature could be seen as framing the exhaustion phase in rich detail. Although seldom presented as a distinct life-cycle phase, lock-in describes well the inwardly-spiralled layering of events and decisions that steadily shrink 'protectively isolated' clusters, thereby progressively insulating them from external influences or internal impulses for change. Developed as territorial analogues of technological lock-in concepts advanced earlier by David (1985) and Arthur (1994), industrial district lock-ins were applied first to clusters and regions by Grabher (1993), then extended by Hassink (2005) and others. This expanded literature typically drew upon accounts of lingering malaise that afflict certain sector-dominated clusters, particularly in German iron, steel and shipbuilding regions. Grabher identifies some of the factors described at the exploitation phase as responsible for effectively locking a cluster or region into an exhausted sense of possibilities: too much inward orientation and group-think (cognitive lock-in, which becomes difficult to 'unlearn'), too tightly-tied local connections (functional lock-in among locally-oriented networks), and excessive dependence upon non-firm agents and compensatory support (political lock-ins that deny market viability issues).

   It is not merely that such factors diminish a mature cluster's viability; rather, they appear steadily to anaesthetize cluster agents, reducing their ability to recognize and make timely adjustments to fundamental changes brought on by radically altered markets, technologies and vibrant new global competitors that swarm newly formed or renascent clusters. This is the fate experienced by a vast landscape of 'old industrial area' clusters, whose former fortunes and privileged status often become irretrievably lost, although new futures might still be imagined, given a dramatic change in agents, industries and technologies. The continuing downward (and perhaps unstoppable) spiral of the US auto industry and Detroit's auto cluster is mirrored worldwide, perhaps leading many eventually to near-petrification (e.g., iron and steel of the Ruhr region). The chances, if any, of a successfully restructured innovative milieu may require considerable time: 'As milieus tend to change more slowly than industries, a sclerotic milieu can remain in a region even after the industrial structure to which it belonged has already disappeared' (Hassink and Shin, 2005, p. 573).

2.3.2   Renaissance   However, marked transitions – some quite dramatic – have been documented in former clusters of European (e.g., iron and steel in Styria, to automobile production and supply) and US regions (e.g., from tobacco and cigarettes in Durham, NC to medical-biotechnology).[21] These are quite logically seen by many as success cases and scrutinized heavily by policy analysts eager to identify the specific measures and actions responsible. One must surely acknowledge that some policies are better suited to triggering successful restructuring than others, but these often differ strongly across unique cases, thereby frustrating efforts to generalize about overall approaches that might be valuable. The identification of common cluster cycle factors at work might be a more appropriate first step, as these may then be leveraged from place to place with rather different policies.[22] The simple passage of time is surely necessary for a broad spectrum of spontaneous reactions to begin, following cluster recognition of an exhaustion crisis, not least of which is the gradual replacement (and perhaps reduction) of original agents with newcomers, the depreciation and replacement of obsolete infrastructure and institutions, the repricing of unit factor costs or capital assets, and a reactivated appreciation for external ideas, innovations and technologies. This can seldom be avoided, even though painful to absorb. It is equally painful to recognize that one's cluster is probably losing ground to competitors that meantime are rapidly establishing 'time compression diseconomies' of their own, thereby extending an insurmountable lead in stronger versions of the old cluster.[23] Painful readjustments take place in nearly all exhausted clusters, although not all recover satisfactorily and some not at all, even with lengthy passages of time.[24] There are additional assets some clusters and regions enjoy that may help speed or ensure the process of restructuring. Of these, three will be mentioned that have received attention in various literatures: agent diversity, polyvalent technology sources, and knowledge/science base.

Agent diversity
Clusters that face exhaustion and cannot self-regenerate easily have become deeply specialized along too many core dimensions, operating in extreme cases as a highly-specialized, homogenous cohort of agents captured in a self-constructed silo.[25] A mono-vintage homogeneity trap could result from extreme rates of rapid cluster development, during which nearly all agents, technologies and awareness of external environments originate over a very short span of time; this would effectively eliminate a temporally-varied portfolio of sustainable knowledge available within the cluster. Homogeneity is further enhanced in cases when congestion-cost increases favour the development of single-cluster regions; moreover, competences within a single cluster may hyperconcentrate if firms operating at the edge of a cluster are drawn inward towards its principal technological trajectory (Fornahl and Menzel, 2003, p. 5). However, single-cluster tendencies are comparatively infrequent in all but the smallest and a few larger regions, usually resource-intensive.

Cluster diversity of some type and degree is more the norm: 'London's success as a cluster also derives from its history of attracting a diverse mix of industries, and its pre-eminent success at exploiting convergence between technologies' Swann (2002, p. 63). London and similar cities reflect the so-called 'Jacobs externalities' of variety and inter-sectoral exchange that are characteristic of large metropolitan agglomeration economies.[26] At the same time, even in lesser regions, neighbouring clusters include an ensemble of different sectors, industries, technologies, business models and entrepreneurial or creative spirits that could help stimulate regeneration. While the pain of incumbents during the adjustment process is palpable, so too are opportunities and released resources made visible to *other* local cluster agents and their extended networks. Novelty and the ability to use existing resources in novel ways 'is seen more likely in networks comprising actors with different backgrounds, e.g., in extra-regional or international networks . . . [which engage] the support of selected outside specialists to help them counteract lock-in and survive' (Visser and Boschma (2004, p. 803)). Networked and even neighbouring cluster agents are likely of varying age and origin; they conduct business with different models or under varying organizational structures, and satisfy innovative needs from differing knowledge bases,[27] thereby providing new insights of considerable relevance to exhausted clusters.

Polyvalent technology sources
While an exhausted cluster may become wholly preoccupied with its deeply ingrained routines, common wisdoms, sunk costs and its technological predispositions, the surrounding region may contain overlooked technological resources and perspectives of great value. An exhausted cluster may eventually draw the attention of others to its unexploited local potentials for technological convergence: 'If industry A generates spillovers of some value to new entrants in industry B, then the cluster, while an early centre for industry/technology A, will subsequently become a center for B. This, as much as movements in relative prices, is the key to cluster revival' (Swann, 2002, p. 64). Swann further notes that chemical and ICT clusters are anything but silo-technologies: rather, they partner 'polygamously' with several sectors (ibid., p. 65). Of the 23 clusters formed by input–output relations and value-chains, 22 consisted of sectors that supplied inputs to more than a single cluster (Feser & Bergman, 2000, pp. 5–7), thereby bridging common relationships between them; the top-three ranked clusters (metalworking, vehicle manufacturing and chemicals/rubber) were each supplied by 23 to 28 specific sectors that also supplied inputs to at least one additional cluster.[28] This implies a broad palette of possibilities for tapping common supply-chain technologies that, if seized upon, could spark the regeneration or reconfiguring of an exhausted cluster.

At the same time, regeneration is likelier to succeed if the skill-set of the region's resident labour pool is capable of adapting to more than one industry or technology. Marshallian labour pooling assumptions focus upon the constellation of labour skills valued heavily by the few sectors of a single cluster, but perhaps it is more realistic to consider the key *occupations* of sectors that span several clusters. Feser (2003) reviews the literature of several skill-equivalent research studies as background to estimate empirically which combinations of over 600 specific occupations belong to 21 distinct and homogenously-defined skill clusters (including illustrations of four knowledge-intensive occupational clusters in ten important US regional economies). These skill clusters represent distinct knowledge-based labour pools within which workers are able to move between components of several industrial sectors and clusters, thereby potentially stimulating revitalization of an exhausted cluster.

Science knowledge base
How and whether technological adjustments among clusters actually take place may, in the view of many, depend upon the effectiveness of the local system of innovation available to cluster agents. Local or regional (RIS) innovation systems have received much theoretical and policy attention, particularly conceptual arguments or specific case studies of how they are structured, populated, classified and governed,[29] but empirically-based

generalizations concerning RIS potentials to reverse cluster or regional decline are notably absent. Universities and research institutes, essentially knowledge-generating and diffusing institutions, are also considered key members of a local innovation system,[30] although for Betts and Lee (2004, p. 35) 'there is a tendency in the literature to perhaps overplay the role of universities and underplay the role of the private sector', a sentiment also echoed by Laursen and Salter (2004) who argue that direct customer and supplier relationships remain far more important in terms of innovation than the 'largely indirect, subtle and complex' relation with universities. One should therefore be cautious about the prospects for stimulating exhausted clusters based solely or principally upon the local availability of an active science base.

The presence of universities and research centres near exhausted clusters represents potential access to the local science base and its academically networked global science base as well. For Betts and Lee (2004, pp. 2–3), these potentialities may be expressed in one or more of the following: 1. *trainer* (human capital formation), 2. *innovator* (direct commercialization), 3. *partner* (joint projects and research), 4. *talent magnet* (attract external knowledge-intensive workers), and 5. *facilitator* (networking), to which Goldstein and Renault (2004, p. 74) add 6. *knowledge generation and research infrastructure*, and 7. *innovation leadership*. UK universities were found to be most frequently involved at least once during 2002–3 with firms in conferences and meetings (65 per cent), as consultants or contract researchers (56 per cent) or joint research partners (45 per cent), with higher frequencies being reported in chemistry, engineering and materials sciences, which are similar to overall findings reported by Mowrey and Sampat (2004) for US survey respondents (industrial R&D managers).

Whether these potentials are well suited to existing firms now barely surviving in exhausted clusters remains in doubt: Prevezer (2002, pp. 233–4) states cluster incumbents 'do *not* absorb spillovers arising either from other sectors or from the science base', while Laursen and Salter (2004) report 'the propensity to use universities increases with the degree (percentage) of sales devoted to R&D', which affirms the importance of absorptive capacities of cluster firms at the exploratory – *not* exhaustion – phase in gaining access to scientific inputs. A study of European firms indicates that collaborations between firms and industries decrease as the share of firm sales accounted for by innovative products rise, which suggests only long-range, pre-commercial possibilities are pursued in joint university efforts (Knudsen, Dalum & Villumsen, 2001, pp. 15–16): unwelcome news to exhausted cluster firms seeking short-range remedies.

Clusters located near an accessible science base may have indeed once enjoyed and perhaps still retain remnants of a strong R&D culture and absorptive capacity, but more distant clusters will surely lack these advantages, and even locally-based clusters may have become effectively insulated through inwardly focused activities. The risk of inward orientation is great: Laursen and Salter (2004) found that university impacts accrued very narrowly to a subset of UK firms in a few sectors that have maintained capabilities in R&D *and* have adopted an 'open' – not closed – approach to innovative search.

3   Concluding comments

The weight of findings and concepts discussed here is not intended to support a novel or revised version of cluster life-cycles. Rather, relevant life-cycle concepts are seen as leading to a better understanding of detailed phases and stages, using the conventional life-cycle as a discussion template. They also help to illuminate further *other* important facets and features of clusters that may have been glossed over or perhaps draw attention to questionable generalizations concerning clusters observed at widely varying stages or phases that have been reached prematurely.

In conducting this review of concepts, several implicit assumptions embedded in the literature needed fuller explication to clarify various points, which may prove useful in future research concerning cluster life-cycles. First, at present there is no single best metric of cluster activity, nor is there an agreed-upon aggregation principle by which to create one. This means that firms, employees, capital investment, sales, output, value-added, etc. have been used in many different studies, with sometimes predictably opposing results. Second, the very idea of aggregating metrics raises the cluster to the level of a 'representative agent', somewhere between a firm and an industry. This is usually observed in research papers that imply or attribute logic, motive, incentive and action to a cluster. Third, active clusters are frequently considered to exhibit homogeneous structures, e.g., all institutional elements 'self-organize' along similar lines, including the possibility of creating support institutions to reinforce such behavior. Fourth, traded clusters alone are subject to forces and incentives that expose them to the possibilities of a full cluster cycle, particularly clusters that specialize in globally-traded products. Indeed, such clusters are truly 'trade generators' – which surely attracts policy makers so strongly to the concept – unlike locally-defined clusters that concentrate mainly to produce and distribute efficiently that output demanded within the local region. Finally, exposure to a complete life-cycle is likely only for a much smaller subset of traded clusters that at some point becomes dominant in national or global terms.

Additional points that arose within the discussion of specific cycle phases may deserve further exploration and research. Several authors try to establish the existence of a cluster with reference to the exogenous presence of an innovative product, technology or industry (PTI) available for exploitation in hospitable locales. This raises the question of whether PTI were in fact generated previously in *other* clusters that proved incapable of retaining and exploiting possibilities. Perhaps Cliometricians might wish to backtrack histories of scattered PTI families 'separated at birth' to evaluate the endogenous origins of clusters: as a counterfactual example, assume one or two of the 'Fairchildren' (Betts & Lee, 2004, p. 12) had initially exited Silicon Valley (e.g., Intel) and instead moved elsewhere to establish a new cluster. Alternative cluster origins, i.e., non-PTI, worthy of consideration are the traditional products or practices embedded in formerly untraded regional clusters that somehow gain international cachet and grow to become the traded products of concentrated clusters. One could argue that several Italian industrial districts arose through such a process; this appears to be one of the defining differences between such districts and the innovation-intensive clusters of more typical PTI origins.

Existence has also been attributed in certain clusters to chance and random events that happened in retrospect to have favoured a location, but is there not a story embedded somewhere behind *every* cluster, successful or not? Perhaps random events favour the first-mover rather than follower, amenity-rich chances may displace those in amenity-poor localities, or chance could more easily take root in SME-intense v. company-dominated localities, and so on. The contribution of economic historians could be exceedingly valuable in untangling the origin of clusters that somehow reached the existence stage.

While the expansion phase has attracted much research and conceptual examination, there may still be opportunities to explore further key differences in agent behaviour and cluster composition at what are called here the *exploratory and exploitive* sub-phases. While the expansion of a cluster is generally observable, there may be underlying shifts, for example, in the amounts, sources and uses of venture capital prior to some inflection point during the overall expansion; or perhaps major adjustments in relationships and channels through which innovative inputs are acquired help signal this point. Growth in sentiment for and progress toward establishment of cluster support institutions may trigger the shift, as might unit-price increases demanded by local factor owners who are able to valorize nearby externalities (congestion costs). Which shifts prove to be pivotal in triggering the continuing exploitative phase in clusters of various types is surely worthy of further investigation.

Equally interesting and relatively unstudied are the consequences for the much larger class of exploratory clusters that do *not progress* to an exploitive phase or eventually come to enjoy some measure of dominance, but, rather as in the Marche and North Jutland cases,[31] continue to host an ongoing series of supporting clusters, essentially providing key services or inputs for dominant clusters elsewhere until such opportunities are exhausted and then moving nimbly to the next opportunity. What may appear to be a 'failure to thrive' and become a dominant cluster may in fact be an investigation-worthy key to understanding the sustainable, slowly developing economies in many regions and communities.

How to *avoid* lock-in remains a principal lesson of life-cycle policy research and formulation, and much has been learned about its avoidance even if not always observed in practice. Far less is known about how clusters *escape* once locked in, perhaps because so few have managed it. Instead, various factors that appear to account for lock-in avoidance are proposed as potential escape measures. In addition to the timely mechanics of routine market adjustments, three measures were discussed from the perspective of offering lock-in remedies; however, surprisingly little research has been devoted to studying their effectiveness in this respect.

Exhausted, locked-in clusters accessible to diverse agents, polyvalent technologies or strong science bases have difficulty applying these and other resources to their situation. The Michigan automobile cluster, for example, is situated near to several universities, including one of the strongest public US research universities, but appears incapable of drawing upon its exceptional science base to reverse cluster fortunes. Nor apparently has Pittsburgh effectively exploited Carnegie-Mellon University's formidable scientific prowess in its transitions, although Boston has weathered the near-total loss of its ITC cluster and entered wholly new clusters, clearly drawing on the strength of its university-rich science base. More focused research might help us understand, as examples, how Boston's released ICT cluster resources were redeployed in other local fields (or relocated elsewhere), how precisely automobile cluster firms in Michigan's extreme monoculture now interact differently than before with local world-class universities, or how previously effective self-organized economic communities unravel in ways that prevent potential innovations from being recognized or deployed.

It is entirely probable that lock-ins are 'technically escapable' in many cases, i.e., innovations are available that would permit various degrees of renewal or renaissance. However, there may be failures of action or effectiveness that remain serious impediments to unlocking cluster malaise. Perhaps an exodus of expertise has depleted the cluster of key talents or it is now afflicted by an exhaustion of wilful energies and Keynesian 'animal spirits'. Forms of communal senility (Atkinson, 2000, Part 5) may have set in, seriously depleting hard-earned strengths of self-organization and reciprocal sacrifice that drove the cluster's earlier expansion. How to recognize and understand the possible reasons that underlie collective failures to act effectively surely deserves as much research attention as how these capacities were developed initially at cluster exploratory and exploitation phases. Although the literature concerning cluster life-cycles has grown rapidly and offers many useful points, it may have thus far collected only the lowest-hanging fruit.

Notes

1. Although not explicitly addressed in the literature, a cluster's cyclical dynamics should be measured by variations in aggregate outcome produced by all principal agents responsible for cluster performance. Therefore, to fully account for a 'cluster' and its position on or movement along its life-cycle, one should a. account for all agents considered significant along each cycle segment, and b. devise an aggregation principle by which agent actions are weighted and summed. Collateral work concerning identification of cluster agents is available in the diffuse research regarding cluster identification and mapping, but little of it refers to the relative significance of agents at various cycle stages or the outputs of non-firm agents. The literature appears not to have considered any aggregation principle for weighting and summing the full cluster; most studies that examine a cluster's performance or outcome rely upon a simple summation of some metric of cluster *firm* performance as its proxy. The absence of commonly collected metrics *at the cluster level* is a major stumbling block to progress along these lines, although it is unclear if all cycle-phase dynamics can be measured adequately with a *single* metric.
2. Although a considerable policy-oriented literature is available that presents widely varying and occasionally conflicting measures, it will not be systematically reviewed here to focus on the underlying conceptual issues.
3. 'In Utterback (1994), the S-curve model is used to illustrate the life cycle, where the evolution of the technology, industry or product follow an S-shaped curve over time' (Dalum, Pederson & Villumsen, 2005). See also Wolter (2003), pp. 1–2.
4. Most articles also adopt an implicit stylized version of a 'representative agent'; a full cluster is then seen to move/age homogenously through each cycle phase as a synchronized ensemble. Empirically, this usually implies that the dynamics of a single lead sector (or even one firm) proxies the central tendency of the full ensemble, even though, in fact, many firms of varying size or sectors and other agents of several kinds could be positioned at adjacent but not identical phases.
5. See discussion in Porter (2003, p. 559).
6. Regionally traded clusters can, however, be highly innovative and advanced (van den Hertog, Bergman & Charles, 2001). Regionally-traded clusters may also serve as valuable reservoirs of novelty for goods and services demanded by future customers, similar to currently growing consumption of cultural tourism. Culinary, sartorial and architectural consumer novelty now available in many regional reservoirs is also matched by locally specific capacities to manage environments (e.g., Alpine tunnelling or Israeli desalinization technologies, Japanese quake-resistant construction, Dutch seawater management) and natural resources, any of which could gain importance in future global markets.
7. Such studies are usually commissioned for emerging and growing clusters that have or are expected to become dominant. Lesser or merely aspiring clusters seldom figure prominently in life-cycle considerations, and 'we still wait for that famous case study of a cluster in *decline*' (Lorenzen, 2005, p. 207).
8. 'It is, perhaps, at this stage worth noting how later generations of mainly Anglo-Saxon scholars by deliberate decision or following the prevailing tradition in contemporary economic geography gradually turned to producing very descriptive, ideographic work [which replaced former economics-based cluster explanations with] a one-sided model that addressed the existence argument in novel ways but almost totally disregarded the extension and exhaustion arguments' (Maskell and Kebir, 2005, p. 6). Hassink and Shin (2005) indirectly supports their view, by observing that many contemporary cluster scholars 'belong to the recently coined family of territorial innovation models . . . *They increasingly turned from "economic" reasons for growth of new industrial agglomerations to "social" and "cultural" reasons* (p. 571, emphasis supplied).
9. Perhaps a fourth 'extinction' phase also applies, which in mild form simply refers to one cluster being replaced by its successor (see discussion in section 2.2.1). The utter collapse of a cluster *and* its host region is exceedingly rare, although places such as Bardou, a former 'supply region' in Jane Jacobs' view, represents the rare type of place history passed by as it became economically extinct and abandoned (Jacobs, 1984, pp. 34–5).
10. Johansson (2005) provides a thorough dissection of the various externalities and spillovers discussed in the classic literature and much of its progeny.

11.   Wolter (2003) expands this notion first by acknowledging historical accident and by explicating what she calls the 'set-up' phase, which is 'characterised by small, slowly growing numbers of companies . . . [*surviving where localization and*] agglomeration benefits and costs are weak, leaving a greater role for geographic ones in determining industry location and development' (p. 6). Although the title of Wolter's paper suggests that it examines cluster life-cycles, and strong parallels are clearly evident, the text focuses heavily on the regional 'agglomeration' context within which clusters play a major development role.

12.   An *external* industry cycle 'seeds' a new cluster in this and most modelling strategies; cluster cycle theorists assume external industries arise from an innovation, even though such innovations might endogenously *incubate initially within another parent cluster*.

13.   Swann (1998, 2004) divides the overall cluster expansion phase into 'take off' and 'peak entry' of firms.

14.   Maggioni (2005, pp. 28–30) refers to those which expand the upper size limit or carrying capacity of a cluster as 'K-policies', while those established to accelerate rates of growth during exploratory expansion are 'r-policies'.

15.   Strictly speaking, this phase could also be described as 'Schumpterian', since it usually follows some previous disturbance that stimulates entrepreneurial ambitions and willingness to explore the potentials of new technologies, markets or business models, and whose dynamics are partially responsible for Schumpterian cycles. However, the principal elements examined here and in the literature remain those of Marshall, which confirms general tendencies – as reported by Windrum (nd, p. 3) – to 'bow to Schumpeter while talking of Marshall'.

16.   In understanding processes of cluster cycles and change, Lorenzen (2005, p. 205) favours theories and models that view cluster dynamics as products of both endogenous and exogenous processes, since 'As can be seen, there is still quite some way to go before we reach a composite understanding of how exogenous and endogenous processes play together in changing clusters.'

17.   'Dominance' is a term based upon Utterback and Abernathy's (1975) concept of 'dominant designs' to signify any of the few similar clusters whose principal product(s) control large market shares and which continue to produce a stream of innovations that support continuous cluster upgrading, incessantly diffusing uncritical phases and their organizational units across the cluster landscape. Lesser clusters in far larger numbers specialize in the components, modules, inputs or niche products that support and complement dominant clusters.

18.   The discussion of firm entry and exit in this section is meant to include those movements precipitated by all possible combinations where the knitting-together/unravelling of vertical value-chains or the merger/acquisition of competitors reflects as well a blend of corporate and entrepreneurial strategies.

19.   As a cluster approaches a possible inflection point on its life-cycle curve, it could again turn upward as a revitalized, renascent cluster, or instead decline – as net location benefits plummet – more or less rapidly from an unsustainable maximum limit.

20.   Additional symptoms of how a cluster's endogenous advantage-mechanisms (Maskell and Malmberg, 1999, pp. 178–9) could disappear are summarized by Bergman (2006): 'asset erosion . . . takes place as . . . hitherto important institutions in a region are no longer reproduced at the same pace or to the same degree'. Regional lock-in can develop when initially important institutions and practices – often social and cultural in origin – focus on self-preservation or aggrandizement and become a sclerotic risk (Olson, 1982) to – rather than the life-blood of – regional progress.

21.   Toedtling and Trippl (2003).

22.   For example, Toedtling and Trippl (2005, pp. 1211–15) offer a range of policy guidelines that apply to different types of regions.

23.   Recognition of local loss and competitive external clusters is often unacceptable in politically active regions, where 'catch-up' and recovery measures are taken prematurely that work to retard the necessary readjustments and realignments.

24.   In addition to the typical resource boomtown stories, Jane Jacobs's discussion of Bardou in France (1984, pp. 32–3) illustrates the fate of highly dependent regional economies that failed historically.

25.   See Fritz et al. (1998) and Tichy (1998) for a review of risk-related issues that cluster agents and supporters should consider well before exhaustion sets in.

26.   Henderson, Kuncoro and Turner (1995, p. 1068).

27.   Hansen, Vang and Asheim (2005).

28.   Clusters ranked 4–10 also received, on average, inputs from 11 specific sectors that supplied at least one additional cluster.

29.   See Doloreux and Parto (2004) for a useful synthesis of this literature.

30.   For discussion of innovation systems and universities, see Betts and Lee (2004) and Mowrey and Sampat (2004).

31.   The fabled inability of Route 128 to become and remain a dominant computer/ICT cluster may reflect similar tendencies, although at a more advanced stage of expansion and maturity. However, the Boston region has since entered other highly successful clusters, which may prove even more beneficial than its ICT predecessor.

Bibliography

Arthur, W.B. (1994), *Increasing Returns and Path Dependency in the Economy*, Ann Arbor: The University of Michigan Press.

Atkinson, P. (2000), 'A theory of civilization' (http://www.ourcivilisation.com/index.htm).

Audretsch, D.B. and M.P. Feldman (1996), 'Innovative clusters and the industry life cycle', *Review of Industrial Organization*, **11**, 253–73.

Bergman, E.M. (2006), 'The sustainability of clusters and regions at Austria's accession edge', in Z. Bochniarz and G.B. Cohen (eds), *The Environment and Sustainable Development in the New Central Europe*, New York: Berghahn.

Bergman, E.M., P. den Hertog and D. Charles (2001), 'Creating and sustaining innovative clusters', in P. Hertog, E.M. Bergman and D. Charles (eds), *Innovative Clusters: Drivers of National Innovation Systems*, Paris: OECD.

Betts, J.R. and C.W.B. Lee (2004), 'Universities as drivers of regional and national innovation: an assessment of the linkages from universities to innovation and economic growth', presented at John Deutsch Institute Conference 'Higher Education in Canada', Queens University, 13–14 February.

Brenner, T. (2004), *Local Industry Cluster: Existence, Emergence and Evolution*, London and New York: Routledge.

Camagni, R. (1995), 'Global network and local milieu: towards a theory of economic space', in S. Conti, E. Malecki and P. Oinas (eds), *The Industrial Enterprise and its Environment: Spatial Perspectives*, Aldershot: Avebury, pp. 195–216.

Dalum, B., O.R. Pederson and G. Villumsen (2005), 'Technological life-cycles: lessons from a cluster facing disruption', *European Urban and Regional Studies*, **12**(3), 229–46.

David, P.A. (1985), 'Clio and the economics of QWERTY', *American Economic Review*, **75**, 332–7.

Doloreux, D. and S. Parto (2004), 'Regional innovation systems: a critical synthesis', United Nations University, INTECH Discussion Paper 2004-17.

D'Este, P. and P. Patel (2005), 'University–industry linkages in the UK: what are the factors determining the variety of interactions with industry?'; presented at Triple Helix5 Conference 'The Capitalization of Knowledge', Turin, 18–21 May.

Feser, E.J. (2003), 'What regions do rather than make: a proposed set of knowledge-based occupation clusters', *Urban Studies*, **40**(10), 1937–58.

Feser, E.J. and E.M. Bergman (2000), 'National industry cluster templates: a framework for applied regional cluster analysis', *Regional Studies*, **34**(1), 1–19.

Fornahl, D. and M.P. Menzel (2003), 'Co-development of firm foundings and regional clusters', conference presentation at 'Clusters, Industrial Districts and Firms: the Challenge of Globalization', Modena, Italy.

Fritz, O., H. Mahringer and M.T. Valderrama (1998), 'A risk-oriented analysis of regional clusters', in M. Steiner (ed.), *Clusters and Regional Specialization: On Geography, Technology and Networks*, London: Pion.

Goldstein, H. and C. Renault (2004), 'Quasi-experimental design approach for estimating the contribution of universities to regional economic development', *Regional Studies*, **38**(7), 733–46.

Grabher, G. (1993), 'The weakness of strong ties: the lock-in of regional development in the Ruhr area', in G. Grabher (ed.), *The Embedded Firm: On the Socioeconomics of Industrial Networks*, London: Routledge, pp. 255–77.

Hansen, H.G., J. Vang and B.T. Asheim (2005), 'The creative class and regional growth: towards a knowledge-based approach', presented at Regional Growth Agendas RSA Conference, University of Aalborg, Denmark, 28–31 May.

Hassink, R. (2005), 'How to unlock regional economies from path dependency? From learning region to learning cluster', *European Planning Studies*, **13**(4), 521–35.

Hassink, R. and D.-H. Shin (2005), 'The restructuring of old industrial areas in Europe and Asia', *Environment and Planning A*, **37**, 571–80.

Henderson, V., A. Kuncoro and M. Turner (1995), 'Industrial development in cities', *J. Pol. Econ.*, **103**(5), 1067–90.

Hertog, van den P., E. Bergman and D.R. Charles (eds) (2001), *Innovative Clusters: Drivers of National Innovation Policy*, Paris: OECD.

Jacobs, J. (1984), *Cities and the Wealth of Nations: Principles of Economic Life*, New York: Random House.

Johansson, B. (2005), 'Parsing the menagerie of agglomeration and network externalities', in C. Karlsson, B. Johansson and R.R. Stough (eds), *Industrial Clusters and Inter-Firm Networks*, Cheltenham, UK and Northampton, MA, US: Edward Elgar, pp. 107–47.

Knudsen, M.P., B. Dalum and G. Villumsen (2001), 'Two faces of absorptive capacity creation: access and utilisation of knowledge', presented at Nelson and Winter/DRUID Conference, Aalborg.

Krugman, P.R. (1991), *Geography and Trade*, Cambridge, MA: MIT Press.

Laursen, K. and A. Salter (2004), 'Searching high and low: what types of firms use universities as a source of innovation?', *Research Policy*, **33**(8), 1201–15.

Lorenzen, M. (2005), 'Why do clusters change?', *European Urban and Regional Studies*, **12**(3), 203–8.

Maggioni, M.A. (2005), 'The rise and fall of industrial clusters: technology and the life cycle of region', Institut d'Economia de Barcelona, Espai de Recerca en Economia, Facultat de Ciències Econòmiques i Empresarials, Universitat de Barcelona.

Maillat, D. (1998), 'From the industrial district to the innovative milieu: contribution to an analysis of territorialised productive organisations', *Recherches Economiques de Louvain*, **64**, 111–29.

Maskell, P. and L. Kebir (2005), 'What qualifies as a cluster theory?', DRUID Working Paper No 05–09, Department of Industrial Economics and Strategy, Copenhagen Business School.

Maskell, P. and A. Malmberg (1999), 'Localized learning and industrial competitiveness', *Cambridge Journal of Economics*, **23**, 167–85.

Mowrey, D.C. and B.N. Sampat (2004), 'Universities in national innovation systems', Chapter 8 in J. Fagerberg, D.C. Mowery and R.R. Nelson (eds), *The Oxford Handbook of Innovation*, Oxford: Oxford University Press.

Olson, M. (1982), *The Rise and Decline of Nations*, New Haven: Yale University Press.

Porter, M.E (1990), *The Competitive Advantage of Nations*, New York: Free Press.

Porter, M.E. (1998), *On Competition*, Boston: Harvard Business School Publishing.

Porter, M.E. (2003), 'The economic performance of regions', *Regional Studies*, **37**(6&7), 549–78.

Prevezer, M. (2002), 'Comparison and interaction between computing and biotechnology', in G.M.P. Swann, D.K. Stout and M. Prevezer (eds), *The Dynamics of Industrial Clustering: International Comparisons in Computing and Biotechnology*, Oxford: Oxford University Press, pp. 225–56.

Putnam, R.D. (1993), *Making Democracy Work: Civic Traditions in Modern Italy*, Princeton: Princeton University Press.

Sable, C. (1982), *Work and Politics: The Division of Labor in Industry*, Cambridge: Cambridge University Press.

Swann, G.M.P. (1998), 'Towards a model of clustering in high technology industries', in G.M.P. Swann, M. Prevezer and D. Stout (eds), *The Dynamics of Industrial Clustering: International Comparisons in Computing and Biotechnology*, Oxford: Oxford University Press, pp. 52–76.

Swann, G.M.P. (2002), 'Towards a model of clustering in high-technology industries', in G.M.P. Swann, M. Prevezer and D. Stout (eds), *The Dynamics of Industrial Clustering*, Oxford: Oxford University Press.

Swann, G.M.P. (2004), 'Cluster theory: opportunities and problems', presented at ESRC Conference 'Regions in Context', Durham, slide 18, 17 November.

Tappi, D. (2005), 'Clusters, adaptation and extroversion: a cognitive and entrepreneurial analysis of the Marche music cluster', *European Urban and Regional Studies*, **12**(3), 289–307.

Tichy, G. (1998), 'Clusters: less dispensible and more risky than ever', in M. Steiner (ed.), *Clusters and Regional Specialization: On Geography, Technology and Networks*, London: Pion.

Toedtling, F. and M. Trippl (2003), 'Like Phoenix from the ashes? The renewal of clusters in old industrial areas', *Urban Studies*, **41**(5/6), 1175–95.

Toedtling, F. and M. Trippl (2005), 'One size fits all? Towards a differentiated regional innovation policy approach', *Research Policy*, **34**(8), 1203–19.

Utterback J.M. and W.J. Abernathy (1975), 'A dynamic model of process and product innovation', *Omega*, **3**(6), 639–56.

Visser, E.-J. and R.A. Boschma (2004), 'Learning in districts: novelty and lock-in in a regional context', *European Planning Studies*, **12**(6), 793–808.

Windrom, P. (1999), 'Unlocking a lock-in: towards a model of technological succession', MERIT, University of Maastricht, The Netherlands.

Winter, S. (1984), 'Schumpeterian competition in alternative technological regimes', *Journal of Economic Behaviour and Organisation*, **5**, 287–320.

Wolter, K. (2003), 'Life cycle for clusters? The dynamics governing regional agglomerations', Conference presentation, 'Clusters, Industrial Districts and Firms: The Challenge of Globalization', Modena, Italy.

8 Clustering in space versus dispersing over space[1]
Karen R. Polenske

8.1 Introduction

In a previous study (Polenske, 2001b), I have maintained that assets should form the base of a regional economic-development strategy, where assets include both tangible (e.g., physical infrastructure) and intangible (e.g., skills and knowledge) ones. I laid out the underlying institutional, economic and physical factors needed to have successful development. In this chapter, I analyse regional economic development from a different, but related, perspective to examine the role played by economies of scale and innovation in making regions competitive and to help make regional economic development sustainable.

I hypothesize that two types of economies of scale may enhance regional economic growth. The first type is the well known 'agglomeration economies'. The second type is 'dispersion economies', a concept that I first introduced in an earlier paper (Polenske, 2001a). Other analysts either have dealt with this concept only indirectly in their discussions of the grouping and dispersing of economic activities, or they have used it in a different sense than I use the term here. Storper (1997, pp. 299–300), for example, briefly discusses how agglomeration economies may be more regional than local or may operate at a 'system-of-city level'.

Also, in an earlier book, Storper and Walker (1989, pp. 70–71) discuss dispersing as one of four types of locational patterns of industries, calling it 'deagglomeration'. Analysts explain this process of growth, they say, using either neoclassical or product-life cycle theories. Of the five variants of their theories of growth, the third one (p. 83) comes closest to my dispersion economy perspective. They state that 'industry . . . has dispersed rapidly in the twentieth century thanks to the flexibility and speed of truck traffic'. They cite various factors as causes of deagglomeration, such as deindustrialization processes (p. 97), core–periphery relations (p. 180), and deskilling of labour (p. 181), but they do not think in terms of regional and global supply-chains.

Dispersion economies/diseconomies, as I define them, may occur if cost savings/cost increases result when firms disperse their activities away from the home office, often along regional or global supply-chains. One typical cost-saving method is the potential reduction in inventories when suppliers and customers of a firm are distributed along a supply chain. The new information and communication technologies (ICTs) certainly play an important role in promoting the dispersion of firms over space, partly because they may allow firms to reduce costs, details of which I discuss later.

In contrast, cost savings/increases that occur when firms locate in one geographical location may create agglomeration economies/diseconomies. If firms belonging to the same sector locate in one area, they may take advantage, on the one hand, of the same training facilities, reaping a saving for all firms of a given sector (locational economies) or for firms from all sectors in a given region (urbanization economies). On the other hand, by locating close to other firms producing similar goods, they may create so much traffic that the

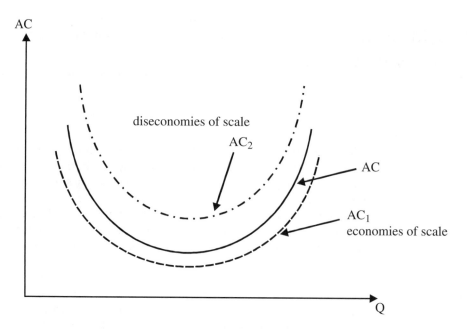

*Figure 8.1   Agglomeration and dispersion economies and diseconomies of scale, AC =
average cost, Q = quantity*

congestion increases the time to ship inputs and outputs (locational/urbanization diseconomies). Following Hoover (1937, pp. 90–91), in his now classic location study of the shoe and leather industries, I distinguish two types of agglomeration economies: locational and urbanization economies. I use locational economies for the agglomeration economies accruing when similar firms locate in one area and take advantage of the various facilities in the region (trade associations, training institutes, etc.) and urbanization economies for the agglomeration economies accruing to a firm from the many different suppliers and producers locating in a particular area, each of whom takes advantage of the presence of banks, universities, labour, etc. that service diverse industries.

Thus, the factors leading to agglomeration and dispersion economies differ. Such a distinction should help policy planners realize that they need not follow a clustering strategy in order to have increased regional growth. Rather, for some situations, analysts should consider dispersing activities to reap cost-savings and other benefits.

An analyst can use the same theoretical structure, shifts in the average cost curve of the firm/industry, to measure both of these concepts. In other words, Figure 3.1 represents both agglomeration and dispersion economies/diseconomies. A dispersion economy/diseconomy, for example, is external to the firm; thus, it moves the entire cost curve of the firm down (up) at all output levels, although the old and the new cost curves do not have to be parallel at different scales of output. An agglomeration economy/diseconomy has the same effect on the cost curve. I stress, however, that the causes of the shifts from agglomeration economies usually differ from those for dispersion economies.

I explore factors creating the agglomeration and dispersion economies and the formation of world-class information and communication technologies and practices, regardless of size and type of industry, by examining (1) industrial clusters, industrial complexes, industrial districts, growth poles and inter-firm networks; (2) learning regions, (3) innovations; and (4) supply chains.

8.2   Industrial clusters, growth poles, industrial complexes, industrial districts and inter-firm networks

Location theories are partially distinguished by the type of agglomeration economy emphasized, partly by whether they can account for both initial firm location and firm mobility, and partly by the focus on one or more of five major spatial concepts: (1) industrial clusters, (2) industrial complexes, (3) industrial districts, (4) growth centres/poles, and (5) inter-firm networks. Many analysts seem to have gravitated to the use of the word 'cluster'. Martin and Sunley (2003, p. 2) effectively deconstruct the cluster concept to show the 'many fundamental conceptual, theoretical and empirical questions', indicating that their concerns 'relate to the definition of the cluster concept, its theorization, its empirics, the claims made for its benefits and advantages, and its use in policy-making'. I would go even further than they have, because I believe that there is a strong similarity among the first four concepts I list above, including clusters, in the way in which they are used to define a spatial boundary.

The 'industrial-complex' and 'industrial-district' concepts are very similar, in that both focus mainly on *localization economies/diseconomies*. Isard et al. (1959) and Isard and Vietorisz (1955), for example, use an input–output table to identify an 'industrial complex' of interrelated Puerto Rican firms that have strong interindustrial linkages. To achieve high rates of economic growth, countries (regions) are advised to concentrate investments in firms located within the boundaries of this industrial complex in order to achieve agglomeration economies (Isard & Schooler, 1959; Isard et al., 1959). This type of industrial concentration is very similar to the 'industrial districts', such as the Third Italy and Silicon Valley (Sabel, 1989; Saxenian, 1994), which became the centre of economic activity for certain types of industries, such as textiles, tiles, microcomputers and electronics. One important difference between the two concepts is that most industrial-complex analysts use quantitative methods to group firms and conduct regional development analyses, while industrial-district analysts most frequently use qualitative methods (e.g., case studies and firm surveys) to make and analyse the groupings.

Storper and Walker (1989), Porter (1985, 1990, 2000, 2001) and Markusen et al. (1999), for example, use the 'industrial cluster' concept, which is based upon the 'innovation cluster' concept of Schumpeter (1939, pp. 100–101). These two concepts are closely related to the 'growth-pole (growth-centre)' concept (Perroux, 1951) in that both are based upon the need for *urbanization economies*. Using an input–output table, growth-pole analysts select the key sector(s), not necessarily just one, and determine which ones have the highest backward linkages with suppliers and forward linkages with customers or consumers (Hirschman, 1958) and hence create the largest multiplier effects.

Analysts who discuss an industrial cluster generally include firms from a number of sectors, whereas, when they discuss an industrial complex, they refer to industries that form a single set of interrelated sectors (e.g., petrochemicals in the case of the Isard et al. (1959) study of Puerto Rico). For the remainder of this chapter, I will use the terms 'industrial cluster' and 'growth poles' interchangeably and the terms 'industrial districts' and 'industrial complexes' interchangeably. All four concepts help analysts define spatial economic boundaries around industrial activities. In terms of the focus of this chapter, I stress that all four concepts relate to agglomeration economies, so that I will later show that analysts conducting regional analyses tend to overlook the possibilities of regional growth occurring because of dispersion economies.

What about inter-firm networks? The inter-firm network concept is sometimes the same as and sometimes different from other industrial group notions. Inter-firm networks, industrial clusters and growth-poles all deal with the economic effects of spatial agglomeration of innovations with a given set of interorganizational (network) relationships (DeBresson & Amesse, 1991, p. 364; Karlsson, 1997). Markusen et al. (1999) maintain that inter-firm networking occurs more within than across district boundaries. Their perspective of an inter-firm network is therefore almost identical to an industrial cluster (district) or growth pole. Locke (1995), however, shows that more and more inter-firm networking is occurring across industrial districts and national boundaries.

Inter-firm networks, however, can be very different from an industrial cluster or growth pole. Locke (1995), for example, defines three ideal-types of inter-firm networks: (1) hierarchical, (2) polarized and (3) polycentric, which differ in regard to the structure of inter-group relations, patterns of association, and linkages of central policy makers. To participate in an inter-firm network, industry managers do not necessarily need the same spatial location. Firms can network across geographic, social and political boundaries (Messner, 1997; Podolny & Page, 1997). Thus, the information-economy revolution is allowing firms to develop national or global networks, which, at times, can assist and, at other times, hamper firm mobility and regional economic development (Castells & Hall, 1994; Glaeser & Ellison, 1997). Considerably more research is required concerning networks to determine (1) whether industrial clusters, industrial districts or inter-firm networks operate most efficiently in terms of agglomeration economies, especially in terms of reducing the average cost to the individual firm; (2) the relationship among distance, regional boundaries and clusters/districts/networks for different types of interchange; and (3) the role of networking in helping clusters and districts to function effectively.

In Table 8.1, under Old Concepts, I show the relationship between these four grouping concepts and one or more of four types of agglomeration economies (diseconomies): (1) *scale*, (2) *localization*, (3) *urbanization*, and (4) *spatial juxtaposition* (the latter hereafter called *social*).[2] Then, under New Concepts, I list some of the many types of chains that are discussed in the literature. Analysts should find the distinction among the four types of agglomeration economies and the four types of dispersion economies useful for developing new location theories, extending existing ones, testing the theories with empirical data, and providing appropriate industrial and regional-development advice to policy makers.

Because there is so much similarity among these industrial-concentration concepts, I discuss three major questions around which analysts can conduct systematic tests of the interaction between industrial concentration and innovation. First, do industrial concentration and innovation lead to new business growth, as posed by increasing returns and some other location theorists?

DiPasquale and Wheaton (1996, pp. 170–72) conducted a test in 11 states, specifically to refute Krugman (1991). They used the 1987 share of national jobs for a given industry in each state and concentration ratios, i.e., the percentage of total jobs accounted for by a particular SIC (standard industrial classification) industry. They conclude that, for

Table 8.1   Agglomeration and dispersion economies/diseconomies

Agglomeration	Dispersion concept type of agglomeration/dispersion Economies/diseconomies and networks
Old Concepts[a]	
Industrial cluster	Internal, urbanization, scope
Industrial complex	Internal, localization, social, scope
Industrial district	Internal, localization, social, scope
Industrial growth pole/centre	Internal, urbanization, scope
New Concepts	
Chain (consumer-driven)	Dispersion, Scope, Horizontal Networks
Chain (producer-driven)	Dispersion, Internal, Vertical Networks
Chain (supply)	Dispersion, Internal, Vertical Networks
Inter-firm Network	Dispersion, Scope

[a]   Alfred Marshall (1890) is the first analyst to use the actual terms 'internal economies' and 'external economies'. Alfred Weber (1929), the father of location economics, used these terms to help explain the concentration of small workshops in Germany.

aggregate industries, concentration theory does not seem to hold, 'but if done for four-digit SIC industries, it may hold' (p. 172). Even so, DiPasquale and Wheaton did not conduct a definitive test, partly because they were unable to control for industrial and sub-regional mixes. Also, their quantitative tests may not appropriately account for social and other agglomeration economies/diseconomies in the economy. Firms may cluster, for example, to take advantage of both physical and financial infrastructure support (Kaufman et al., 1994; Scott & Bergman, 1995) and of external support organizations, such as trade and industrial associations, educational and training facilities, and research and development laboratories (Rosenfeld, 1995; Sabel, 1989; Saxenian, 1994).

Concentration of firms may enhance the localization, social and urbanization economies in the region. Over the last 70 years, for example, the Tooling and Manufacturing Association, to which many of Chicago's metalworking firms belong, helped to maintain the network of those firms as it went through various phases of a life cycle, enhancing its localization economies (McCormick, 1996). Support systems, however, are sometimes inadequate. If industries are not making profits, for instance, the trade and industrial association formed by them will have a hard time to survive. Analysts testing statistically for concentration tendencies need to account for quantitative measures, such as profits, and other more qualitative measures, such as social networking.

Second, what other factors than transportation costs help firms determine whether or not to locate in a particular location? Labour costs usually represent a much larger cost to the firm than transport costs. In the United States in 1987, for example, transportation direct costs averaged less than 3 per cent of total costs for all except one of 79 sectors, whereas labour direct costs were over 15 per cent for most sectors (U.S. Department of Commerce, 1994, pp. 64–71). Location theorists can also improve their theories by analysing not only transportation and labour costs, but also the relevance of various transportation characteristics. Supply chain and other analysts (e.g., Pereira, 1996; Polenske et al., 1996) show that, for a significant number of firms, speed and reliability of shipments are of as much, or even more, concern than transport costs to both the shipping and receiving firm, with other attributes, such as accessibility, flexibility in delivery times, safety and tracing of the shipments usually ranking high as well. These studies indicate that, although Glaeser and Ellison (1997) say that transportation cost is easy to model, it may not be the most critical location factor for most firms today.

Third, are dispersion economies benefiting regional development and, if so, how? Some evidence is surfacing that strong agglomeration tendencies seem to be counterbalanced by equally strong dispersion tendencies. Analysts, for example, find that industrial concentration in one region creates competitive disadvantages at given points of the business cycle and for large urban centres, especially if it is excessive. When technological change is rapid, the industrial complex of firms may be at a competitive disadvantage because firms resist, or do not have access to, information outside the complex (Glasmeier, 1987; Glasmeier & Sugiura, 1991). This resistance may also lead these firms to be less innovative than they otherwise would be (Harrison, 1994, chap. 4). These findings suggest that an agglomeration diseconomy may lead to firms moving to other locations in order to reap dispersion economies.

In addition, in countries as different as Brazil, Japan, the Republic of Korea and the United States, concentration of firms seems to create adverse economic impacts on urban size and income distribution among regions (Markusen et al., 1999). In some countries, the government may disperse industries from the core to the periphery, trading agglomeration economies for lower location costs and, if income distribution improves, helping to assure social and political stability. Industries may also disperse of their own accord. Another consideration is that excessive urbanization in New York and Pittsburgh was found to hinder the intergenerational transfer of entrepreneurial skills (Chinitz, 1961).

Finally, firms usually concentrate in a region under distinct circumstances (Harrison et al., 1995, 1996). If the economic activity does not already exist in a region, economic specialization in that activity is difficult to foster. An example is the lack of regional development in Appalachia (Hansen, 1966). Analysts can devise ways to test for at least some of these agglomeration-dispersion tendencies.

In order to look at these concentration/dispersal tendencies in more detail, I first discuss analysts who have examined 'learning regions', which may be a leading example of an innovative concentration of firms taking advantage of agglomeration economies. I then contrast these agglomeration tendencies of the learning region with the dispersion tendency of regional and global supply chains, which are prime examples of some of the many ways firms are dispersing innovation across regions and the globe.

8.3   Learning regions
I define regions to include communities, cities, provinces and countries. Regardless of how analysts define a geographic region, in the learning region, the community/city/province/country combines with academic institutions, firms and government in the 'region' in collective-learning environments (Keeble & Wilkinson, 1999). What is the purpose of a learning region? Do learning regions/communities initiate and sustain the development of ICTs? If so, how? How do they affect these technologies? What type(s) of assets (human, physical, and/or natural) help them to achieve sustainable development? To answer these questions, at least partially, I briefly review some of the extensive literature on learning regions/communities. Underlying my discussion are ideas obtained from Lundvall and Johnson's (1994) and Lundvall's (1996) classic articles on learning economies,

supplemented by the extensive writing on learning regions by Asheim (1996, 1998, 1999, 2001a, 2001b), including two of his latest joint articles (Asheim & Herstad, 2002; Asheim & Isaksen, 2002).

For the firms, the learning may be based on intra-firm, inter-firm, and/or regional coalitions. Analysts emphasize the importance of knowledge and learning and the need to increase the rate of change of learning. In this respect, ICTs play an important role. As Lundvall (1996, p. 4) states, however, 'The learning economy is affected by the increasing use of information technology, but it is not synonymous with what is often called "the information society"'.

A learning region is one in which industry, community, government and educational centres in a region all work together to help the region develop (Polenske, 2004). It is characterized by a set of horizontal relationships among the actors, who exchange and compare knowledge and experiences, so that problems are solved by 'extracting the best out of a broad range of experiences and ideas' (Asheim, 2001b, p. 9). Networks and organizations in the region share the knowledge interactively (Lundvall, 1996, p. 2); thus, knowledge becomes one of the intangible collective assets of the region (Polenske, 2001b).

Although the term 'learning region' is relatively new, it has important roots in the flexible production, flexible-specialization literature (Plummer & Taylor, 2001), and even in writings of Alfred Marshall (Asheim, 2000). Valuable discussions of the concept are included in many articles, including those by Asheim (2001a, 2001b), Asheim and Dunford (1997), Boekema et al. (2000), Florida (1995), Lundvall (1996), Lundvall and Johnson (1994) and Morgan (1997), to name just a few. One view is that the idea of a learning region modified the interpretation of industrial districts by incorporating social relations, competitiveness, networks, learning, knowledge and innovations. By locating in industrial districts, Piore and Sabel (1984) indicated firms were able to achieve the multiplier effects and agglomeration economies of growth poles. Another perspective of the learning region is that it modified the way in which policy makers use 'flexible specialization' at a regional level. Thus, analysts, such as Sabel (1989), Hirst and Zeitlin (1992) and Best (1990), use the term 'flexible specialization' to show policy makers that small and medium-size firms, research and development institutes, and contractual relations are important elements of the way firms can share distribution, production inputs, information and technologies.

Porter (1998, p. 78) represents another perspective. He defines clusters as 'geographic concentrations of interconnected companies and institutions in a particular field. Clusters encompass an array of linked industries and other entities important to competition'. According to Porter's definition, all learning regions are clusters. Even so, usually, not all clusters are learning regions. Ennals and Gustavsen (1999) define a different type of learning region, namely, development coalitions, indicating that these coalitions may range all the way from small and medium workplaces to regions and larger networks of firms to entire nations. According to Ennals and Gustavsen's definition, not all learning regions are clusters, which counters Porter's definition.

Asheim (1996, 2001a), Lundvall and Johnson (1994) and other European analysts indicate that regional policy makers need to establish learning regions in order to achieve community revitalization. Authors such as Lundvall (1996) emphasize the need to build social capital and to create educational initiatives. Lundvall (1996, p. ii) maintains, that in the learning economy, 'the capacity to learn increasingly determines the relative position of individuals, firms, and national systems'. For a learning region to be sustainable, policy makers in the region must emphasize the distribution of capabilities to learn; otherwise the labour markets will become increasingly polarized. Concerning the learning, Lundvall and Johnson (1994) distinguish four types of knowledge: (1) *know-what* (knowledge of facts, which is easy to codify), (2) *know-why* (knowledge of principles that exist in nature, the human mind and the society, some of which is relatively easy to codify), (3) *know-how* (knowledge of skills, capabilities and other knowledge that in today's world creates incentives for firms to develop networks to exchange this know-how. Only some of this knowledge can be codified), (4) *know-who* (socially embedded knowledge, learned from customers, contractual arrangements, etc., that is difficult to transfer because it is tacit knowledge). The know-how and know-who forms of knowledge are playing increasingly important roles in society. Asheim (2001b, p. 10) maintains that, in a learning economy that is being globalized, there is a 'transition from an internal knowledge base in specific industries (i.e., high-tech sectors) to a globally distributed knowledge base of firms, caused by the general increased knowledge intensity in post-Fordist learning economies'.[3]

As the reader can see, these analysts are creating some confusion by calling the same notion by a different name, most with the word 'learning' attached. For example, Asheim uses the terms 'learning organizations', 'learning regions', 'learning systems' and 'development coalitions', but so far he has not clearly identified the differences, if any, among these concepts. He only says that a development coalition is one type of learning organization, which are organizations that are 'fluid, transnational, continuously reshaping themselves to meet new challenges' (Asheim, 2001b, p. 9).

What do these authors say about the effect of learning regions on the development of ICTs and vice versa? Lundvall (1996, p. ii) maintains that 'the relationship between codified and tacit knowledge is symbiotic and that . . . tacit knowledge and the learning of skills will be fundamental for the economic success of agents.' I leave the remainder of the answer to this question to the next section, because innovation is an important component of the ICT sector.

8.4   Innovation

The British government has called for an intensive investigation of the role that innovation is playing in regions in Britain and has provided a considerable amount of funding for studies of innovation and entrepreneurship in what is called CMI (an alliance between Cambridge University in England and the Massachusetts Institute of Technology in the United States). Fingleton et al. (2002, p. 1) state that high-technology production is increasing in economic importance for the biotechnology, telecommunications, electronics and computer services sectors. As a result, the British government has declared knowledge to be the most important 'driver' of economic growth for economies that are trying to achieve an overall competitive advantage. This growth, they maintain, leads to geographically concentrated economic activity, that some economic analysts call 'high-technology cluster'.

Innovation is important to the survival of most firms, but the type of innovation that occurs differs from firm to firm and depends partially on the size of the firm (Keeble, 1997).[4] Some innovations seem to occur when firms locate in one region, while other types of innovation need firms to be dispersed.

One example of differences even when firms are clustered is the innovative, cooperative, collaborative aspects of firms in the Silicon Valley versus the hierarchical, centralized decision making of the firms along Route 128 (Saxenian, 1994). Firms in both regions started producing electronics: semiconductors (1960s) and chips (1970s) in the Silicon Valley and transistors and other solid-state devices (1960s) and microcomputers (late 1970s) along Route 128. According to Saxenian, however, Silicon Valley firms soon dominated the semiconductor field and also took a lead with small workstations and personal computers. Although firms in both regions were relatively clustered, Saxenian maintains that it was the type of decision making, not the clustering, that helped one type to succeed better than the other.

Instead of looking at the success of a cluster of innovative industries in a particular region, Gertler (1993) looks at the restructuring of particular innovative sectors, such as advanced technology machinery producers. Gertler (1995) has an intriguing way of looking at the successful relationships between the producers and users of this machinery, showing that they are enhanced by three types of 'closeness': (1) physical (geographical) distance, (2) organizational (interaction, collaboration, shared workplace practices and training) distance, and (3) cultural (common language, modes of communication, customs, conventions and social norms) distance.

Gertler (1995, 1996) articulates his approach clearly. Each type of distance, he claims, has a strong influence on whether or not new technology will be adopted and, if it will, on the ease with which it is adopted. Through an extensive postal survey of 400 so-called 'technology-implementation experiences' in 170 plants, combined with personal interviews in 20 plants, he finds that implementation difficulties are persistent and significant (1996, p. 20). The greatest difficulties were experienced by small plants, by firms using foreign (especially overseas) technology, and by firms using technology that had one or more of the three 'distance' attributes. Physical distance did affect implementation for all firms, but especially for small firms. This finding would imply that dispersion economies differ for large and small firms. Gertler also found that, when the 'workplace culture' between the producer and the user of the technology is distinctly different (cultural distance), implementation is very difficult. Such differences may be related to physical distance, but more often are associated with social diseconomies. In addition, he determined that institutions and regulatory systems that assist firms in maintaining long-term relations with their employees are important factors that shorten the organizational distance and lead to effective implementation on a timely basis.

In summary, Gertler found that long and extended interactions between producers and users are very important for small enterprises and those that are domestically owned, single-plant establishments and that large distances (in any of the three meanings) reduced the effectiveness of the implementation. Even large enterprises feel the need for closeness, not only in terms of distance, but also organizationally and culturally. He would maintain, I assume, that distance does create extra costs for innovators.

Block (1990) presents a treatise that tends to destroy the traditional concepts of capital. Based upon Block's conceptions, Gertler discusses some of the qualitative changes that are occurring in process technologies, such as the use of microprocessors and electronic controls in industrial machinery.[5] The results of these changes include lower machine prices and smaller size of plant (both of which lead to capital savings), lower capital/output ratios, and machines that are capable of producing a large number of products. At the same time, Gertler maintains that the plant size is being reduced (again creating cost savings) owing to changes in the internal and inter-firm organization of production, such as fewer inventories and fewer machines. He does not indicate, however, whether the decline in machinery costs is greater than the decline in plant costs.

If all of this is indeed occurring, physical accounts for the firm will show that fewer machines and less floor space are needed than before such change occurred, and the value accounts of the firm will show a decline in the dollar value of investment. However, the productive capacity of a region where the firm is located will be greater than before. These and other dilemmas attached to accurate measurement have led some analysts, influenced by new growth theorists, to study only the machinery and equipment portion of annual investment, believing that technology and investment are closely linked, but their approach is still aggregate. Gertler favours examining the adoption of each new process technology individually, as he did in his survey discussed above, indicating that a socially constructed model of technology aids an understanding of the sectors and regions in which investment occurs and its relationship to the process of technological change.

Lam (1998a) has conducted an extensive study of an advanced information technology Japanese and British firm who wish to collaborate to acquire skills and knowledge from each other. She finds that the socially embedded nature of knowledge can impede cross-national collaborative work and knowledge sharing. This is knowledge that 'is not migratory, because it is embedded in complex social interactions and team relationships within organizations' (p. 10). In fact, the two firms have completely different methods of organizing work, with the Japanese having an 'organizational' method of structuring high-level work that relies on worker interaction and minimum hierarchy, thus relying on tacit knowledge that can mainly be obtained through experience. The British have a 'professional' method in which workers rely on formulas, manuals and blueprints. Considerable friction developed when the teams from each firm tried to work together, until finally, they divided most work between the two firms, rather than collaborating on it (Lam, 1998a, 1998b).

Her study is captivating because it lends yet one more example to the debate concerning whether tacit knowledge, as originally defined by Polanyi (1966), can be codified. Her example seems to say that it cannot be when the social differences are as great as those between Japan and Britain. She states that the 'differences are deeply embedded in the contrasting national systems of skills formation, labour markets and occupational structures', concluding that 'there is no evidence in the present study that the two partner firms, despite their long years of close collaboration, have become more alike in their organizational forms or knowledge bases. On the contrary, the two firms appear to have become more divergent in their distinctive and complementary capabilities' (Lam, 1998a, p. 36). Lam's findings are supported by her later study (Lam, 1998b) and are partially based on the extensive study of these factors by Nonaka (1994) and Nonaka and Takeuchi (1995). Nonaka calls the Japanese type of factor 'knowledge of experience', which is tacit knowledge learned within a particular context.

The Japanese style of management is one factor that analysts are examining. Gertler's research of German and Canadian firms tends to support Nonaka's findings in that German workers seem able to fix problems as they arise on the job, whereas, for many problems, Canadian workers need to call in someone to fix the problem. Thus, whereas location theorists stress the need for geographic proximity among firms, Gertler, Nonaka

Lam and others stress organizational and cultural proximity as well. Fine et al. (1995, p. 5) add electronic proximity, which refers 'to the form and intensity of electronic communication between economic agents'. They indicate (1995, p. 11) that 'electronic proximity may act as a substitute or either physical or organization proximity, or both'.

Lundvall (1996, p. 11) is less optimistic, indicating that firms introducing new automation and information technology in Denmark initially elicit a significant slowing of productivity growth for at least four years, compared with firms that do not use the new technology. This slowing is caused, he says, by many factors, but especially by firm workers needing to accept substantial organizational change in order to learn the new technologies. For those firms that introduce simultaneously the new technology and new forms of organization, the learning costs are significantly reduced.

Leamer and Storper (2001) are more upbeat in their discussion of the economic geography associated with the Internet. Some scholars (e.g., DeBresson & Amesse, 1991, p. 388) argue that a network of innovators is needed to ensure success. This network supposedly could be dispersed across space. Scholars maintain that a network can help reduce transaction costs, foster collective learning, link the innovation to the market, overcome failures in market creation for technological services, establish social norms and standards for the new market and generate trust (Sabel, 1992; Teubel et al., 1991). Continuous innovation, timeliness and rapid product development, in turn, require cooperation and trust among firms (Saxenian, 1994). According to Schmitz (1996), the basis of trust between firm owners, workers and others changes over time and evolves from an 'ascribed' trust among those in the same social group within a region to 'earned' trust among outsiders in the global market.

Cooperation allows firms to share research and development costs, access to credit, training, etc. (Sabel, 1992). This sharing reduces the production costs of each small firm, which otherwise would not have low-cost access to such services.[6] Firms in the Silicon Valley, for example, form a regional network where there is collective learning, dense social networks and open labour markets, with considerable horizontal communication among firm divisions and with outside suppliers, trade associations and universities (Saxenian, 1994). The Silicon Valley firms thus form a learning region. An important finding, if true, from the Silicon Valley case is that the firms were able to capture the economies of scale and scope simultaneously at the level of the district, not the individual firm.

Also, Porter (1998, pp. 85–6) maintains that, 'In fact, there is no such thing as a low-tech industry. There are only low-tech companies – that is, companies that fail to use world-class technology and practices to enhance productivity and innovation.' If this is so, technological and biological firms are not the only ones that can be competitive, productive and innovative in the new global arena. Rather, most firms with the right set of tangible and intangible assets can succeed.

So far, I have dealt with dispersion economies only briefly, yet I maintain that they are playing an increasingly important role in today's global economy, and I examine them through the concept of 'supply chains'.

8.5 Supply chains

Earlier, in Table 8.1, I listed supply chains and then two specific types of supply chains, producer-driven and consumer-driven. In addition to reducing costs, managers of consumer-driven supply chains have, as one of the primary goals, helping to create improvements in customer service. Either type of supply chain can be internal to a firm/region or extend beyond the boundaries of the firm/region to the nation or globally. In an earlier paper (Polenske, 2001a), I examined some of the factors affecting both the internal and external types of supply chains. Most analysts discuss producer supply chains, or discuss supply chains without differentiating them. I note that the supply-chain terms used by regional scientists and economists often differ from those used by management and transportation analysts. As an example, a customer-driven chain is often called a 'pull' system, while a producer-driven chain is called a 'push' system.

In this chapter, I concentrate on the global supply chain, although many dispersion economies/diseconomies affect regional or internal supply chains as well. Most global supply-chain analysts focus on the producer-driven supply chain, in which the producer is looking for ways to reduce costs, reduce the time it takes to get the product to market and expand the market for the product(s).

In a different study (Polenske, 2004), I differentiate three types of analysts who wrote about restructuring, namely: (1) Italian model, (2) Japanese model, and (3) global model. I call those who study the success of multinational corporations in the post-Fordist period the 'global-model analysts', which include Amin and Robbins (1990), Gereffi and Korzeniewicz (1994), Harrison (1992, 1994), MacDuffie and Helper (1999), Martinelli and Schoenberger (1991) and Scott (1993). These global analysts disagree with those who emphasize the role of small firms in the restructuring of production, although they agree that restructuring is occurring and that flexibility is being incorporated into the production and distribution processes. Castells and Hall (1994) assert that networks among all sizes of firms are critical to allow flexible specialization to thrive.

The global firms are adopting supply-chain management techniques, enabling them to push risks and costs along the supply chain by just-in-time (JIT) production. Specifically, rather than having to absorb the cost of warehousing or of having extra supplies on hand at the production site, the global analysts indicate that the suppliers and the customers are now having to cover these costs. Five chief characteristics are associated with these firms: (1) an increased internationalization of capital, (2) more effective corporate integration, (3) increased control over markets and finance, (4) pushing of risks and costs along the supply chain onto small suppliers, and (5) the need for support from both the public and private sectors.

An important forerunner to the global perspective and supply chains is the work by Chandler (1977) on the rise of large firms. The managers of these firms created the hierarchically organized firm to achieve their dominant competitive position. They used producer-driven supply chains, where managers oversaw the entire supply chain from the raw-material supplier to the ultimate consumer. As a result, they were able to use these attributes and scientific-management procedures to reap 'economies of time'. Such an organizational structure seems to stand in sharp contrast to that proposed by the horizontal structure of the learning-region advocates.

Why is the large firm adopting more flexible production techniques and flourishing? Harrison (1994, pp. 9–10) argued as follows. First, they are downsizing both the number of activities and number of employees, thus reducing costs. Second, the directors of the large firms develop a core–periphery labour relationship. They segment the employees into a core group, who are kept at the headquarters, are paid high salaries and collabo-rate in the production decisions, and a periphery group, who are dispersed to other loca-tions or hired in locations distant from the plant, some of which may be overseas. I argue that this is one of several ways in which firms can reap dispersion economies. Third, they network both within their own corporation and with other corporations, through respec-tive intra-firm and inter-firm networks. Finally, managers are using computers increas-ingly both for manufacturing and management information systems to help coordinate and monitor their activities and employees and to increase the flexibility of production and marketing. Thus, firms are working not only to reduce costs, but also to disperse them along the supply chain.

As is the case of Harrison, many of these global analysts deal with regions in terms of the way the corporations develop a network of supplier firms across space and allocate core workers to the urban centres and peripheral workers to the suburbs or elsewhere. By incorporating the regional dimension, these analysts can determine the way the organi-zational boundary of the firm changes and the way costs are dispersed across regions. Ettlinger (1992) investigates the specific way in which large corporate organizations affect the regional geography. The Gereffi and Korzeniewicz (1994) research on global com-modity chains supports my contention that dispersion economies are helping to maintain a viable supply chain. They develop a global commodity-chain framework to study different segments of the chain, from the core region, where the innovating firms locate, to the peripheral regions, where the low-cost firms locate and employ low-skill workers. Rather than look at networks of firms in a region, they study the network of large transna-tional firms and their customers across political boundaries.

Because large transnational producers control the supply chain, they disperse globally and control the way the costs are dispersed along the chain. Thus, they control many of the small firms. As I have stated in another paper (Polenske, 2004), these large multina-tionals do inter-firm networking within the large corporation, among other large firms, and between the large and the small firms, mostly through supply chains, with the spatial boundary being extended globally. The organizational boundary extends along the pro-ducer supply chain, with the large producer controlling the market.

8.6   Conclusions

I began this chapter by hypothesizing that two types of economies are affecting regional economic growth, namely, agglomeration economies/diseconomies and dispersion econo-mies/diseconomies. A number of analysts reviewed above show that this may be so. More empirical tests, however, still need to be made. No analyst has tested the hypothesis I put forth, partly perhaps because the concept of dispersion economies is only five years old (introduced in 2003). I created the concept on the basis of a belief that the economies from dispersing economic activity is an important factor affecting regional development, but regional analysts have not yet systematically examined the effects.

I think that the increasing number of global and regional supply-chain analyses may be a good place to start with the empirical tests. In fact, my own research staff and I have several case studies in the United States and the People's Republic of China that may provide sources for such tests. We had a different objective for our work on supply chains for the Chicago metalworking sector (Polenske et al., 1996), but the plant surveys we con-ducted may provide some information we could use.

Likewise, I could glean some empirical data from our six-year environmental and energy study of the coke-making sector in the People's Republic of China in which we are conducting surveys of coke-making township and village enterprises (TVEs) and state-owned enterprises (SOEs). I can use these data to help determine whether or not dispersal of plants leads to cost savings – at least for the metalworking and coke making sectors.

I did not expect to find studies of dispersion economies, but I think it is important to measure empirically the cost-savings of the agglomeration/dispersion of firms. Fingleton et al. (2002) recently conducted some tests of cluster intensity. They are looking at a different question from mine, but they found that their econometric estimates 'support the hypothesis that cluster intensity is a cause of employment growth, although there are important differences of scale at which this effect operates for the two sectors [computing services and research and development] considered' (Fingleton et al., 2002, p. 1).

Many analyses are needed to provide sufficient empirical evidence that will support or not support my hypothesis that both agglomeration and dispersion economies are important for regional economic development. The analyses should be both quantitative and qualitative. There is obviously considerable need for such studies. The results should be fascinating and will help policy makers as they implement industrial policies.

Acknowledgements

I thank Natalia Sizov for technical assistance, and the two reviewers and Yu Li for insightful comments. For additional discussion of some of the restructuring literature, the reader is encouraged to refer to my paper on cooperation, collaboration and competition (Polenske, 2004).

Notes

1. This article has previously been published in B. Johansson, C. Karlsson and R. Stough (eds) (2006), *The Emerging Digital Economy: Entrepreneurship, Clusters, and Policy*, Series: Advances in Spatial Science, 352 p. 36 illus., ISBN: 978-3-540-34487-2, Springer Verlag, pp. 35–54.
2. Spatial-juxtaposition economies/diseconomies, a distinction originated by Isard et al. (1959), are scale-economy (other than size) factors, such as quality control, training and social-welfare economies that result when an industrial complex is located at only one site.
3. If this type of diffusion is occurring, then learning regions may be helped by dispersion economies, although my main argument in this section is that learning regions are prime examples of agglomeration economies.
4. Schumpeter (1939) differentiates between innovations and entrepreneurship.
5. Block supports his position with studies of the metalworking industries where productivity gains from these qualitative improvements range from 200 to 300 per cent (Block, 1990, pp. 142–3).
6. A similar concept of sharing is behind the creation of the manufacturing centres in the United States that have been set up by the U.S. National Institute of Science and Technology (Sabel, 1996).

References

Amin, A. and K. Robbins (1990), 'The re-emergence of regional economies? The mythical geography of flexible accumulation', *Environment and Planning: Society and Space*, **8**, 7–34.
Asheim, B.T. (1996), 'Industrial districts as "learning regions": a condition for prosperity?', *European Planning Studies*, **4**, 379–400.
Asheim, B.T. (1998), 'Learning regions as development coalitions: partnership as governance in European workfare states?', paper presented at the Second European Urban and Regional Studies Conference on 'Culture, Place and Space in Contemporary Europe', University of Durham, Durham, September 17–20.
Asheim, B.T. (1999), 'Interactive learning and localised knowledge in globalising learning economies', *Geography Journal*, **49**, 345–52.
Asheim, B.T. (2000), 'Industrial districts: the contributions of Marshall and beyond', in G.L. Clark, M. Feldman and M. Gertler (eds), *The Oxford handbook of economic geography*, Oxford: Oxford University Press, pp. 413–31.

Asheim, B.T. (2001a), 'Learning regions as development coalitions: partnership as governance in European workfare states? Concepts and transformation', *International Journal of Action Research and Organizational Renewal*, **6**, 73–101.

Asheim, B.T. (2001b), 'Project organisation and globally distributed knowledge bases', Centre for Technology, Innovation and Culture Working Paper, University of Oslo.

Asheim, B.T. and M. Dunford (1997), 'Regional futures', *Regional Studies*, **31**, 445–55.

Asheim B.T. and S. Herstad (2002), 'Regional clusters under international duress: between local institutions and global corporations', in B.T. Asheim and Å. Mariussen (eds), 'Innovations, regions and projects: studies in new forms of knowledge governance', NORDREGIO report R2003: 3, NORDREGIO, Stockholm, pp. 203–39.

Asheim, B.T. and A. Isaksen (2002), 'Regional innovation systems: the integration of local "sticky" and global "ubiquitous" knowledge', *Journal of Technology Transfer*, **27**, 77–86.

Best, M. (1990), *The new competition: institutions of industrial restructuring*, Cambridge, MA: Harvard University Press.

Block, F.L. (1990), 'Postindustrial possibilities: a critique of economic discourse', Berkeley, CA: University of California Press.

Boekema, F.K., M.S. Bakkers and R. Rutten (2000), 'Knowledge, innovation and economic growth: the theory and practice of learning regions', Cheltenham, UK and Northampton, MA, USA: Edward Elgar.

Castells, M. and P. Hall (1994), 'Technopoles of the world: the making of 21st century industrial complexes', London: Routledge.

Chandler, A.D. Jr (1977), *The visible hand*, Cambridge, MA: Harvard University Press.

Chinitz, B. (1961), 'Contrasts in agglomeration: New York and Pittsburgh', *American Economic Review*, **51**, 279–89.

DeBresson, C. and F. Amesse (1991), 'Networks of innovators: a review and introduction to the issue', *Research Policy*, **20**: 363–79.

DiPasquale, D. and W.C. Wheaton (1996), *Urban economics and real estate markets*, Englewood Cliffs, NJ: Prentice-Hall.

Ennals, R. and B. Gustavsen (1999), *Work organisation and Europe as a development coalition*, Amsterdam: John Benjamin.

Ettlinger, N. (1992), 'Modes of corporate organization and the geography of development', papers in Regional Science, **71**, 107–26.

Fine, C., G. Gilboy, K. Oye and G. Parker (1995), 'Technology supply chains: an introductory essay', Working Draft by the International Motor Vehicle Program at MIT Sloan School of Management, Cambridge, MA (available at http://imvp.mit.edu/papers/95/Fine/fine2.pdf).

Fingleton, B., D.C. Igliori and B. Moore (2002), 'Employment growth of small high-technology firms and the role of horizontal clusters: evidence from computing services and R&D in Great Britain 1991–2000', paper presented at the 'High-Technology, Small Firms One-Day Clusters' Conference, Manchester Business School, Small Business Service, Manchester, 18 April.

Florida, R. (1995), 'Toward the learning region', *Futures*, **27**, 527–36.

Gereffi, G. and M. Korzeniewicz (eds) (1994), *Commodity chains and global capitalism*, Westport, CT: Praeger.

Gertler, M.S. (1993), 'Implementing advanced manufacturing technologies in mature industrial regions: towards a social model of technology production', *Regional Studies*, **27**, 665–80.

Gertler, M.S. (1995), ' "Being there": proximity, organization, and culture in the development and adoption of advanced manufacturing technologies', *Economic Geography*, **71**, 1–26.

Gertler, M.S. (1996), 'Worlds apart: the changing market geography of the German machinery industry', *Small Business Economics*, **8**, 87–106.

Glaeser, E. and G. Ellison (1997), 'Geographic concentration in U.S. manufacturing industries: a dartboard approach', *Journal of Political Economy*, **105**, 889–927.

Glasmeier, A. (1987), 'Factors governing the development of high technology clusters: a tale of three cities', *Regional Studies*, **22**, 287–301.

Glasmeier, A. and N. Sugiura (1991), 'Japan's manufacturing system: small business, subcontracting, and regional complex formation', *International Journal of Urban and Regional Research*, **15**, 395–414.

Hansen, N. (1966), 'Some neglected factors in American regional development policy: the case of Appalachia', *Land Economics*, **62**, 1–9.

Harrison, B. (1992), 'Industrial districts: old wine in new bottles?', *Regional Studies*, **26**, 469–83.

Harrison, B. (1994), *Lean and mean: the changing landscape of corporate power in the age of flexibility*, New York: Basic Books.

Harrison, B., A.K. Glasmeier and K.R. Polenske (1995), 'National, regional, and local economic development policy: new thinking about old ideas' (report prepared for the Economic Development Administration, U.S. Department of Commerce).

Harrison, B., M. Kelley and J. Gant (1996), 'Innovative firm behavior and local milieu: exploring the intersection of agglomeration, firm effects, and technological change', *Economic Geography*, **72**, 233–58.

Hirschman, A.O. (1958), *The strategy of economic development*, New Haven, CT: Yale University Press.
Hirst, P. and J. Zeitlin (1992), 'Flexible specialization versus post-Fordism: theory, evidence, and policy implication', in M. Storper and A.J. Scott (eds), *Pathways to industrialization and regional development*, London: Routledge, pp. 70–115.
Hoover, E.M. (1937), 'Spatial price discrimination', *Review Economic Studies*, **4**, 182–91.
Isard, W. and E.W. Schooler (1959), 'Industrial complex analysis, agglomeration economies, and regional development', *Journal of Regional Science*, **1**, 19–33.
Isard, W. and T. Vietorisz (1955), 'Industrial complex analysis and regional development, with particular reference to Puerto Rico', *Papers and Proceedings of the Regional Science Association*, **1**, 227–56.
Isard, W., E.W. Schooler and T. Vietorisz (1959), *Industrial complex analysis and regional development*, New York: John Wiley.
Karlsson, C. (1997), 'Product development, innovation networks, infrastructure and agglomeration economies', *The Annals of Regional Science*, **31**, 235–58.
Kaufman, A., R. Gittell, M. Merenda, W. Naumes and C. Wood (1994), 'Porter's model for geographic competitive advantage: the case of New Hampshire', *Economic Development Quarterly*, **8**, 43–66.
Keeble, D. (1997), 'Small firms, innovation and regional development in Britain in the 1990s', *Regional Studies*, **31**, 281–93.
Keeble, D. and F. Wilkinson (1999), 'Collective learning in knowledge development in the evolution of regional clusters of high technology SMEs in Europe', *Regional Studies*, **33**, 295–303.
Krugman, P. (1991), *Geography and trade*, Cambridge, MA: MIT Press.
Lam, A. (1998a), 'The social embeddedness of knowledge: problems of knowledge sharing and organisation learning in international high-technology ventures', DRUID Working Paper No. 98–7, Danish Research Unit for Industrial Dynamics, Aalborg Copenhagen.
Lam, A. (1998b), 'Tacit knowledge, organisational learning and innovation: a societal perspective', Danish Research Unit for Industrial Dynamics (DRUID) Working Paper No. 98– 22, Danish Research Unit for Industrial Dynamics, Aalborg Copenhagen.
Leamer, E. and M. Storper (2001), 'The economic geography of the Internet age', National Bureau of Economic Research (NBER) Working Paper 8450, National Bureau of Economic Research, Washington, DC.
Locke, R.M. (1995), *Remaking the Italian economy*, Ithaca, NY: Cornell University Press.
Lundvall, B.Å. (1996), 'The social dimension of the learning economy', Danish Research Unit for Industrial Dynamics (DRUID) Working Paper No. 96–1, Danish Research Unit for Industrial Dynamics, Aalborg Copenhagen.
Lundvall, B.Å. and B. Johnson (1994), 'The learning economy', *Journal of Industry Studies*, **1**, 23–42.
MacDuffie, J.P. and S. Helper (1997), 'Creating lean suppliers: diffusing lean production throughout the supply chain', in J. Liker, P. Adler and M. Friun (eds), *Remade in America: transplanting and transforming Japanese production systems*, New York: Oxford University Press, pp. 154–200.
Markusen, A.R., Y.S. Lee and S. DiGiovanna (eds) (1999), *Second-tier cities: rapid growth beyond the metropolis*, Minneapolis, MN: University of Minnesota Press.
Marshall, A. (1890), *Principles of economics*, London: Macmillan.
Martin, R. and P. Sunley (2003), 'Deconstructing clusters: chaotic concept or policy panacea?', *Journal of Economic Geography*, **3**, 5–35.
Martinell, F. and E. Schoenberger (1991), 'Oligopoly is alive and well: notes for a broader discussion of flexible accumulation', in G. Benko and M. Dunford (eds), *Industrial change and regional development: the transformation of new industrial spaces*, London/New York: Belhaven Press/Pinter, pp. 117–33.
McCormick, L.E. (1996), 'The rise and fall of network production in twentieth century Chicago manufacturing', PhD thesis, Massachusetts Institute of Technology, Cambridge, MA.
Messner, D. (1997), 'The network society: economic development and international competitiveness as problems of social governance', GDI Book Series No. 10, Great Britain.
Morgan, K. (1997), 'The learning region: institutions, innovation and regional renewal', *Regional Studies*, **31**, 491–503.
Nonaka, I. (1994), 'A dynamic theory of organizational knowledge creation', *Organization Science* **5**, 14–37.
Nonaka, I. and H. Takeuchi (1995), *The knowledge creating company*, New York: Oxford University Press.
Pereira, A.E. (1996), 'Implications for transportation planning of changing production and distribution processes', PhD thesis, Massachusetts Institute of Technology, Cambridge, MA.
Perroux, F. (1951), *The economy of the 20th century* (in French), Paris: Presses Universitaires de France.
Piore, M.J. and C.F. Sabel (1984), *The second industrial divide: possibilities for prosperity*, New York: Basic Books.
Plummer, P. and M. Taylor (2001), 'Theories of local economic growth (part 1): concepts, models, and measurement', *Environment and Planning A*, **33**, 219–36.
Podolny, J.M. and K. Page (1997), 'Network forms of organization', *Annual Review of Sociology*, **24**, 57–76.
Polanyi, M. (1966), *The tacit dimension*, New York: Anchor Day Books.

Polenske, K.R. (2001a), 'Competitive advantage of regional internal and external supply chains', in M. Lahr and R.E. Miller (eds), *Essays in honor of Benjamin H. Stevens*, Amsterdam: Elsevier Publishers, pp. 259–84.

Polenske, K.R. (2001b), 'Taking advantage of a region's competitive assets: an asset-based regional economic-development strategy', in *Entrepreneurship, firm growth, and regional development in the new economic geography*, Uddevalla Symposium 2000, 15–17 June, Trollhättan, Sweden, pp .527–44.

Polenske, K.R. (2004), 'Competition, collaboration, cooperation: an uneasy triangle in networks of firms and regions', *Regional Studies*, **38**, 1029–43.

Polenske, K.R., L.E. McCormick, A.E. Perreira and N.O. Rockler (1996), 'Industrial restructuring, infrastructure investment, and transportation in the Midwest', Report to the Joyce Foundation, Chicago Manufacturing Center, and National Institute for Science and Technology, Chicago.

Porter, M.E. (1985), *Competitive advantage: creating and sustaining superior performance*, New York: Free Press.

Porter, M.E. (1990), *The competitive advantage of nations*, New York: Free Press.

Porter, M.E. (1998), 'Clusters and the new economics of competitiveness', *Harvard Business Review*, **76**, 77–90.

Porter, M.E. (2000), 'Location, competition, and economic development: local clusters in a global economy', *Economic Development Quarterly*, **12**, 15–42.

Porter, M.E. (2001), 'Regions and the new economics of competition', in A.J. Scott (ed.), *Global city-regions*, New York: Oxford University Press, pp. 139–57.

Rosenfeld, S. (1995), 'Industrial strength strategies: regional business clusters and public policy', The Aspen Institute Rural Economic Policy Program, Washington, D.C.

Sabel, C.F. (1989), 'Flexible specialization and the re-emergence of regional economics', in P. Hirst and J. Zeitlin (eds), *Reversing industrial decline*, Oxford: Berg, pp. 17–70.

Sabel, C.F. (1992), 'Studied trust: building new forms of co-operation in a volatile economy', in F. Pyke and W. Sengenberger (eds), 'Industrial districts and local economic regeneration', International Institute for Labour Studies, Geneva, pp. 215–50.

Sabel, C.F. (1996), 'A measure of federalism: assessing manufacturing technology centers', *Research Policy*, **25**, 281–307.

Saxenian, A.L. (1994), *Regional advantage: culture and competition in Silicon Valley and Route 128*, Cambridge, MA: Harvard University Press.

Schmitz, H. (1996), 'From ascribed to earned trust in exporting clusters', Institute of Development Studies, University of Sussex, Brighton.

Schumpeter, J.A. (1939), *Business cycles*, New York: McGraw-Hill.

Scott, A.J. (1993), *Technopolis: high-technology industry and regional development in Southern California*, Berkeley, CA: University of California Press.

Scott, A.J. and D. Bergman, (1995), 'The industrial resurgence of southern California? Advanced ground transportation equipment manufacturing and local economic development', *Environmental Planning C* (Government and Policy) **13**, 97–124.

Storper, M. (1997), *The regional world: territorial development in a global economy*, New York: Guilford Press.

Storper, M. and R. Walker (1989), *The capitalist imperative: territory, technology, and industrial growth*, Oxford: Basil Blackwell.

Teubal, M., T. Yinnon and E. Zuscovitch (1991), 'Networks and market creation', *Regional Policy*, **20**, 381–92.

U.S. Department of Commerce (1994), 'The input–output structure of the U.S. economy, 1987', U.S. Department of Commerce, Bureau of Economic Analysis, Washington, D.C., pp. 64–71.

Weber, A. (1929), *Theory of the location of industries* (English edn), Chicago, IL: University of Chicago Press.

PART TWO

CLUSTER RESEARCH METHODS

9 Industrial clusters in the input–output economic system

Michael Sonis, Geoffrey J.D. Hewings and Dong Guo

1 Introduction

This chapter returns to the issue of cluster identification using a set of inter-industry accounts; in this sense, it is rooted more in the legacy of industrial cluster and complex analysis associated with the early work of Czamanksi (1971, 1974, 1976) and Czamanski and Ablas (1979) and deepens the now more involved cluster-based development strategies described in detail by Bergman and Feser (2000) and the methods linking clusters and innovation presented in Bröcker et al. (2003). It does not focus on the more extensive cluster-based approaches popularized by Porter (1990) since the objective is to explore the industrial interdependencies in more detail. However, it does share with Dridi and Hewings (2002) the need to make more imaginative use of the structures present in inter-industry tables to draw out more information about the structure of the economy being evaluated.

The major purpose of this chapter is to propose a new method of identification of the more important industrial (sectoral) backward and forward linkages clusters in input–output systems in a way that avoids the rigidities of some of the earlier approaches (that identified mutually exclusive clusters). Our attention is directed to the application and further elaboration of the ideas of combinatorial topology to the analysis of economic structure of input–output systems in the form of structural Q-analysis originally proposed by Atkin (1974, 1981) for the analysis of the structure of human interactions. Our central concern is the *complication* of regional or interregional structure that results from the deepening of economic complexity in the form of hierarchies of interacting economic subsystems. Industrial clusters are thus seen as important examples of such subsystems. Their structural changes will require new tools for illustration, interpretation and visualization. We will start from the presentation and the interpretation of the procedure of structural Q-analysis based on the *slicing* procedure of the ordered set of the elements of the Leontief inverse. Further, the chains of structural complication and rank-size ordering procedure will be introduced and interpreted as backward and forward industrial linkages clusters.

An important component of the modern process of industrialization is the change in the nature of interdependence in production characterized by the essential interdependence found in input–output and social accounting tables. Analysis of the *evolution* of inter-industry relations has now become, once more, a major point of interest for economic analysts. The traditional approach, proposed by Chenery in the 1950s (Chenery, 1953; Chenery & Watanabe, 1958; Chenery & Clark, 1959) was extended further in various subsequent studies (see Carter, 1970; Long, Jr., 1970; Ohkawa & Rosovsky, 1973; Song, 1977; Matthews et al., 1982; Harrigan et al., 1980; Deutsch & Syrquin, 1989, among others). As indicated, the main purpose of this chapter is to illustrate some new approaches using Q-analysis to enhance the understanding of the economic structural changes caused by simultaneous technological changes reflected in a set of input–output tables. With this methodology, alternative slicing procedures can be adopted to reveal the finer structure of an economy. In addition, the methodology may be seen to have important relationships with popular notions of backward and forward linkages.

In the next section, the methodology will be described; section 3 develops the slicing procedure that is derived from the decomposition algorithm. This section also provides an illustration with reference to the Chicago metropolitan region for the year 2000. Section 4 presents the industrial clusters and their augmentation. The chapter concludes with some summary comments and potential links to some recent work proposing the notion of fragmentation of production systems.

2   Methodology of structural Q-analysis
The following methodological description of the procedure of Q-analysis is taken from the Atkin studies (Atkin, 1974, 1981; see also, Sonis, 1988; Sonis & Hewings, 1998, 2000; Sonis et al., 1994).

2.1   Slicing procedure
Consider the Leontief inverse matrix $B = \|b_{ij}\|$ of some Input–Output system and let (i_1, j_1), $(i_2, j_2), \ldots, (i_m, j_m)$ be a fixed set of pairs of economic sectors entering the input–output system. Let $b_{i_1 j_1}, b_{i_2 j_2}, \ldots, b_{i_m j_m}$ be the corresponding components of the matrix B. The *slicing procedure* results in the construction of a new matrix B_s whose only non-zero components are $b_{i_1 j_1}, b_{i_2 j_2}, \ldots, b_{i_m j_m}$ while all other components are zeroes. This slicing procedure referred to as a variable *filter* approach is the basic element of minimal flow analysis (see Holub & Schnabl, 1985; Holub et al., 1985; Schnabl & Holub, 1979; Schnabl, 1993).

The matrix I_S with the unit entries on the place of non-zero components of the matrix B_s is called the *incidence matrix* associated with the slicing procedure. Obviously, 2^{n^2} different slicing procedures exist for each $n \times n$ matrix B. The simplest slicing procedure consists of the choice of the slicing parameter μ, and the exclusion from the matrix B of all components b_{ij} such that $b_{ij} < \mu$. The choice of a definite slicing parameter depends on the investigator's preferences about the economic structure of the interaction matrix.

2.2   Simplicial families for backward linkages
We will consider the procedure of the Q-analysis of backward linkages (forward linkages can be considered analogously). Consider a slicing procedure defined with the help of the set of components, $b_{i_1 j_1}, b_{i_2 j_2}, \ldots, b_{i_m j_m}$. This procedure defines the sliced matrix B_s and the corresponding incidence matrix I_S. The set $j_1, j_2, \ldots, j_m$ of the corresponding economic sectors serves as a set of vertices of a many-dimensional polyhedron generating the *partial backward linkages backcloth*.

The procedure for the construction and partition of this polyhedron into a set of simplexes can be defined in the following way: for each fixed economic sector, i_k, $k = 1, 2, \ldots, m$, consider the set of all different economic sectors $j_{r_0}, j_{r_1}, \ldots, j_{r_{qk}}$ corresponding to the non-zero $b_{i_k j_{r_0}}, b_{i_k j_{r_1}}, \ldots, b_{i_k j_{r_{qk}}}$ associated with the inputs into the sector i_k from the economic sectors $j_{r_0}, j_{r_1}, \ldots j_{r_{qk}}$. The *simplex*, $S^b_{qk}(i_k) = S_{i_k}$ associated with the sector i_k, is a minimal convex polyhedron in q_k-dimensional space with $q + 1$ vertices $j_{r_0}, j_{r_1}, \ldots j_{r_{qk}}$.

Figure 9.1 provides an example of an incidence matrix from a 10×10 input–output table; sales (rows) are shown as $S(i)$ entries and purchases (columns) as $P(j)$ entries; interaction between sectors is signified by a value '1' while a '0' indicates no interaction. From this matrix, the simplex associated with S1 (5-simplex) and P10 (4-simplex) are shown as illustrations.

The set of simplexes ,$S^b_{q_1}(i_1), S^b_{q_2}(i_2), \ldots, S^b_{q_m}(i_m)$ associated with all economic sectors i_k, $k = 1, 2, \ldots, m$, is called *the backward linkages simplicial family*, generating the polyhedron with vertices $j_1, j_2, \ldots, j_m$, and its partition – *the simplicial complex K(S)*.

2.3 Q-nearness and q-connectedness

Two simplices $S(i_k)$ and $S(i_s)$ are *q-near* in the simplicial family *iff* they share at least $q + 1$ vertices. Thus, two sectors i_k and i_s are *q-near iff* there are at least $q + 1$ economic sectors with the inputs into the sectors i_k and i_s. If all vertices of a simplex $S(i_s)$ are the vertices of

–	P1	P2	P3	P4	P5	P6	P7	P8	P9	P10
S1	1	0	1	0	0	1	0	1	1	1
S2	1	1	0	0	0	0	1	1	0	0
S3	0	1	1	1	1	0	0	1	0	1
S4	1	0	1	0	0	0	0	0	0	0
S5	0	1	0	0	0	1	0	0	1	1
S6	0	1	0	0	0	0	0	1	0	0
S7	0	0	1	0	0	1	0	0	0	0
S8	0	1	0	0	1	0	0	1	0	1
S9	1	0	1	0	0	1	0	0	0	0
S10	0	1	1	0	0	0	1	1	1	0

Shared faces are indicated by cells with a dotted box

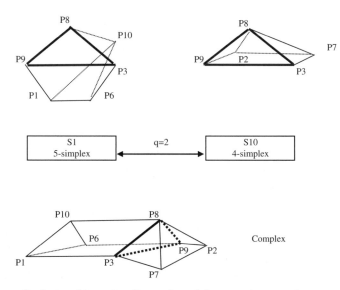

Figure 9.1 Structure of relationships: simplices, shared faces and a complex

a simplex $S(i_k)$ then the simplex $S(i_s)$ is a face of the simplex $S(i_k)$. In Figure 9.1, the shared face is between the simplexes in highlighted (P3, P8 and P9); from this the complex whereby these sets of activities are linked (through the shared face) is also shown.

Two simplices $S(i_k)$ and $S(i_s)$ are *q-connected* by a chain of simplices of length r *iff* there is a sequence of r pair-wise *q-near* simplices $S(i_k), S(i_p), \ldots, S(i_q), S(i_s)$. The relationship of *q-connectedness* generates the partition of the simplicial family $K(S)$ into *q-connected* components.

The enumeration of all *q-connected* components for each dimension $q \geq 0$ is the essence of the Q-analysis of the simplicial family. In Figure 9.1, two simplices are connected by a shared face (P3, P8 and P9) generating a complex.

2.4   Procedure and meaning of the backward linkages Q-analysis
Following Atkin (1974, 1981) the operational basis for Q-analysis is given by a shared face matrix SF of the form:

$$SF = I_S I_S^T - U, \tag{9.1}$$

where I_S is the incidence matrix corresponding to the chosen slicing procedure, I_S^T is its transpose and U is the matrix with unit entries. The components of the matrix SF provide the amounts of mutual vertices for each pair of sectors $i_k, i_s, k, s = 1, 2, \ldots, m$. In other words, the components of the shared face matrix SF are the dimensions of the maximal mutual faces for each pair of simplices, $S(i_k)$ and $S(i_s)$.

The Atkin operational algorithm for Q-analysis includes the following iterative steps for each dimension $q, q = 0,1, \ldots, N$, where N is the maximal dimension of simplices from the simplicial complex:

Identify the economic sectors and their corresponding simplices whose dimensions are equal to or larger than q; these dimensions are on the main diagonal of the shared face matrix SF.

Identify all distinct *q-connected* components (*q-chains*) of the set of simplices constructed in the previous step: two *q-dimensional* simplices $S_q(i_k)$ and $S_q(i_s)$ belong to the same *q-chain* if the corresponding rows i_k and i_s of the shared face matrix SF include at least one column with entries larger than or equal to q; the number of distinct *q-chains* is denoted as Q_q. The vector

$$Q = \{Q_N, Q_{N-1}, \ldots, Q_0\} \tag{9.2}$$

is called the *structural vector* of the simplicial complex $K(S)$ and the maximal q-value N is a dimension of this complex.

2.5   Chains of structural complication of simplicial families and the rank-size ordering
Consider two slicing procedures S_1 and S_2 and their corresponding simplicial families associated with the simplicial complexes $K(S_1)$ and $K(S_2)$. The simplicial complex $K(S_2)$ is called the *structural complication* of the simplicial complex $K(S_1)$ and noted $K(S_1) < K(S_2)$ if each simplex $S'_p(i_k)$ from $K(S_1)$ is a face of some simplex $S''_q(i_k)$ from $K(S_2)$. This means that the incidence matrix I_{S_2} includes all non-zero (unit) components from the incidence matrix I_{S_1}. The set of m simplicial complexes $K(S_1), K(S_2), \ldots, K(S_m)$ is called *the chain*

of structural complication if for each pair of complexes $K(S_s)$ and $K(S_r)$, one of them is the structural complication of the other. Obviously, the chain of structural complication is defined with the help of the set of corresponding incidence matrices such that, for each pair of incidence matrices, one of them includes all the units from the other. This means also that the chain of structural complication is generated by the sequence of extending sets of the components of the interaction matrix B.

One of the important methods of the generation of the chains of structural complication will now be illustrated, namely, the *rank-size ordering method*. The rank-size ordering method is based on the construction of the sequence of all components of the interaction matrix $B = \|b_{ij}\|$ ordered by size in such a way that the largest components are at the top of the decreasing-by-size sequence of components. Thus, it is possible to consider only the qualitative rank-size sequence in place of the absolute value of each component. Consider the sequence of slicing procedures and the corresponding set of sliced matrices, the first of which includes only the largest components of the interaction matrix B, while the second matrix includes the two largest components, the third matrix includes the three largest components, and so forth. In such a way, one obtains the chain of structural complication associated with the relative size on the matrix components. The Q-analysis of each element of the chain of structural complication reveals some hidden features of the intersectoral interactions.

3   Slicing procedure based on decomposition method: links between Q-analysis and the superposition principle[1]

The main operational tool of Q-analysis is the slicing procedure, i.e. a procedure for the choice of unit non-zero components in the matrix of structural incidence. Simultaneously, the algorithmic procedure of the superposition principle (see Sonis & Hewings, 1988, 1998, 2000) generates the decomposition of the flow matrix A into the weighted sum:

$$A = p_1 A_1 + p_2 A_2 + \ldots + p_k A_k \tag{9.3}$$

where the components $p_i A_i$, $i = 1, 2, \ldots, k$, represent the hierarchy of spatioeconomic substructures within the input–output or social accounting system. Since each matrix A_i is the optimal solution of some linear programming optimization problem, usually it includes many zero components. We can use the decomposition (9.3) for derivation of the set of incidence matrices for Q-analysis of the flow matrix A in the following way. First consider the first tendency $p_1 A_1$ and construct the first incidence matrix I_S^1, whose unit non-zero components are located in the place of non-zero components of matrix $p_1 A_1$. The first incidence matrix I_S^1, represents the first slicing for the matrix A. The second slicing will be associated with the incident matrix I_S^2 including the unit non-zero components located in the place of non-zero components of the matrix, $p_1 A_1 + p_2 A_2$. In the same way the incident matrix, I_S^r, will be generated with the help of non-zero components of the matrix $p_1 A_1 + p_2 A_2 + \ldots + p_r A_r$; $r = 1, 2, \ldots, k$.

Next, for the description of the structural complication of the flow, A, we can apply the procedure of Q-analysis to each incidence matrix from the sequence of incident matrices $I_S^1, I_S^2, \ldots, I_S^k$. The corresponding sequence of the structural vectors

$$Q^r = \{Q_N^r, Q_{N-1}^r, \ldots, Q_0^r\}, r = 1, 2, \ldots, k \tag{9.4}$$

will present the topological structural complication of the matrix of flows A. The component, Q_N^r, will be interpreted further as the main backward linkages industrial cluster.

3.1 Example

For better demonstration of the slicing procedure of the construction of incidence matrix corresponding to the extreme tendencies $p_1A_1 + p_2A_2 + \ldots + p_rA_r; r = 1, 2, \ldots, k$, we consider the case of the analysis of the main backward linkages industrial clusters of the Chicago metropolitan economy in 2000. Table 9.1 describes the aggregated sectors used in the analysis of the Chicago economy; the input–output tables are extracted from the region's econometric input–output model (see Israilevich et al., 1997, for details) while the flows are shown in Table 9.2.

Table 9.1 Sector definitions in the Chicago input–output table

Sector	Name	Content
1	RES	Resources
2	CNS	Construction
3	MNF	Non-durable and durable goods
4	TTF	Transportation, trade, FIRE
5	SRV	Services
6	GOV	Government

Table 9.2 Total flows for the Chicago region, 2000

	RES	CNS	MNF	TTF	SRV	GOV	Total
RES	29	25	640	183	76	6	959
CNS	277	816	2892	5096	4152	574	13806
MNF	453	4668	17534	9338	13640	474	46106
TTF	431	2578	10697	12041	9284	475	35506
SRV	210	2255	6452	8153	6860	229	24159
GOV	15	49	566	617	344	41	1633
Total	1416	10391	38781	35428	34356	1800	122171

Note: RES (resources), CNS (construction), MNF (manufacturing), TTF (trade, transportation), SRV (services), GOV (government).

Table 9.3 The coefficient table and largest entries (by column)

	1	2	3	4	5	6
1	0.020662	0.002402	0.016503	0.005169	0.002202	0.00358
2	0.195747	0.078485	0.074577	0.143844	0.120843	0.318719
3	0.319912	0.449218	0.452127	0.263576	0.397018	0.263391
4	0.304647	0.248104	0.275841	0.339856	0.270234	0.263987
5	0.14828	0.217044	0.166361	0.230131	0.19968	0.12735
6	0.010752	0.004746	0.014591	0.017424	0.010023	0.022973

Table 9.3 defines the first extreme tendency acting within the framework of the backward linkages. The first incident matrix, corresponding to this first extreme tendency, has a form

$$p_1 A_1 = 0.319 \begin{pmatrix} 0 & 0 & 0 & 0 & 0 & 0 \\ 0 & 0 & 0 & 0 & 0 & 0 \\ 0 & 0 & 0 & 0 & 0 & 1 \\ 1 & 1 & 1 & 0 & 1 & 0 \\ 0 & 0 & 0 & 1 & 0 & 0 \\ 0 & 0 & 0 & 0 & 0 & 0 \end{pmatrix}.$$

This implies that the first incidence matrix is as follows:

$$\Lambda^1 = I_S^1 = \begin{pmatrix} 0 & 0 & 0 & 0 & 0 & 0 \\ 0 & 0 & 0 & 0 & 0 & 1 \\ 1 & 1 & 1 & 0 & 1 & 0 \\ 0 & 0 & 0 & 1 & 0 & 0 \\ 0 & 0 & 0 & 0 & 0 & 0 \\ 0 & 0 & 0 & 0 & 0 & 0 \end{pmatrix}.$$

The second slicing will have a form

$$p_1 A_1 + p_2 A_2 = 0.319 \begin{pmatrix} 0 & 0 & 0 & 0 & 0 & 0 \\ 0 & 0 & 0 & 0 & 0 & 1 \\ 1 & 1 & 1 & 0 & 1 & 0 \\ 0 & 0 & 0 & 1 & 0 & 0 \\ 0 & 0 & 0 & 0 & 0 & 0 \\ 0 & 0 & 0 & 0 & 0 & 0 \end{pmatrix} + 0.248 \begin{pmatrix} 0 & 0 & 0 & 0 & 0 & 0 \\ 0 & 0 & 0 & 0 & 0 & 0 \\ 0 & 0 & 0 & 1 & 0 & 0 \\ 1 & 1 & 1 & 0 & 1 & 1 \\ 0 & 0 & 0 & 0 & 0 & 0 \\ 0 & 0 & 0 & 0 & 0 & 0 \end{pmatrix}$$

This generates the second cumulative incidence matrix. This cumulative incidence matrix includes units in the place they appeared in one of the matrices A_1, A_2:

$$\Lambda^2 = I_S^2 = \begin{pmatrix} 0 & 0 & 0 & 0 & 0 & 0 \\ 0 & 0 & 0 & 0 & 0 & 1 \\ 1 & 1 & 1 & 1 & 1 & 0 \\ 1 & 1 & 1 & 1 & 1 & 1 \\ 0 & 0 & 0 & 0 & 0 & 0 \\ 0 & 0 & 0 & 0 & 0 & 0 \end{pmatrix}$$

The next incidence matrices can be constructed in the same manner:

$p_1A_1 + p_2A_2 + p_3A_3 =$

$$
= 0.319
\begin{pmatrix}
0 & 0 & 0 & 0 & 0 & 0 \\
0 & 0 & 0 & 0 & 0 & 1 \\
1 & 1 & 1 & 0 & 1 & 0 \\
0 & 0 & 0 & 1 & 0 & 0 \\
0 & 0 & 0 & 0 & 0 & 0 \\
0 & 0 & 0 & 0 & 0 & 0
\end{pmatrix}
+ 0.248
\begin{pmatrix}
0 & 0 & 0 & 0 & 0 & 0 \\
0 & 0 & 0 & 0 & 0 & 0 \\
0 & 0 & 0 & 1 & 0 & 0 \\
1 & 1 & 1 & 0 & 1 & 1 \\
0 & 0 & 0 & 0 & 0 & 0 \\
0 & 0 & 0 & 0 & 0 & 0
\end{pmatrix}
$$

$$
+ 0.166
\begin{pmatrix}
0 & 0 & 0 & 0 & 0 & 0 \\
1 & 0 & 0 & 0 & 0 & 0 \\
0 & 0 & 0 & 0 & 0 & 1 \\
0 & 0 & 0 & 0 & 0 & 0 \\
0 & 1 & 1 & 1 & 1 & 0 \\
0 & 0 & 0 & 0 & 0 & 0
\end{pmatrix},
$$

with cumulative incidence matrix generating from matrices A_1, A_2, A_3:

$$
\Lambda^3 = I_S^3 =
\begin{pmatrix}
0 & 0 & 0 & 0 & 0 & 0 \\
1 & 0 & 0 & 0 & 0 & 1 \\
1 & 1 & 1 & 1 & 1 & 1 \\
1 & 1 & 1 & 1 & 1 & 1 \\
0 & 1 & 1 & 1 & 1 & 0 \\
0 & 0 & 0 & 0 & 0 & 0
\end{pmatrix}
$$

and

$p_1A_1 + p_2A_2 + p_3A_3 + p_4A_4 =$

$$
= 0.319
\begin{pmatrix}
0 & 0 & 0 & 0 & 0 & 0 \\
0 & 0 & 0 & 0 & 0 & 1 \\
1 & 1 & 1 & 0 & 1 & 0 \\
0 & 0 & 0 & 1 & 0 & 0 \\
0 & 0 & 0 & 0 & 0 & 0 \\
0 & 0 & 0 & 0 & 0 & 0
\end{pmatrix}
+ 0.248
\begin{pmatrix}
0 & 0 & 0 & 0 & 0 & 0 \\
0 & 0 & 0 & 0 & 0 & 0 \\
0 & 0 & 0 & 1 & 0 & 0 \\
1 & 1 & 1 & 0 & 1 & 1 \\
0 & 0 & 0 & 0 & 0 & 0 \\
0 & 0 & 0 & 0 & 0 & 0
\end{pmatrix}
$$

$$
+ 0.166
\begin{pmatrix}
0 & 0 & 0 & 0 & 0 & 0 \\
1 & 0 & 0 & 0 & 0 & 0 \\
0 & 0 & 0 & 0 & 0 & 1 \\
0 & 0 & 0 & 0 & 0 & 0 \\
0 & 1 & 1 & 1 & 1 & 0 \\
0 & 0 & 0 & 0 & 0 & 0
\end{pmatrix}
+ 0.103
\begin{pmatrix}
0 & 0 & 0 & 0 & 0 & 0 \\
0 & 0 & 0 & 1 & 1 & 0 \\
0 & 1 & 1 & 0 & 0 & 0 \\
0 & 0 & 0 & 0 & 0 & 0 \\
1 & 0 & 0 & 0 & 0 & 1 \\
0 & 0 & 0 & 0 & 0 & 0
\end{pmatrix},
$$

with

$$\Lambda^4 = I_S^4 = \begin{pmatrix} 0 & 0 & 0 & 0 & 0 & 0 \\ 1 & 0 & 0 & 1 & 1 & 1 \\ 1 & 1 & 1 & 1 & 1 & 1 \\ 1 & 1 & 1 & 1 & 1 & 1 \\ 1 & 1 & 1 & 1 & 1 & 1 \\ 0 & 0 & 0 & 0 & 0 & 0 \end{pmatrix}.$$

3.2 Structure of the simplices of backward linkages for each industry

The augmentation of structure of the simplices of backward linkages for each industry can be extracted from the location of units in the set of columns of matrices $\Lambda^1, \Lambda^2, \Lambda^3, \Lambda^4$ corresponding to the given industry (see Table 9.4).

Table 9.4 The augmentation of the simplices of backward linkages for each industry

$S_0^b(RES)$	$S_1^b(RES)$	$S_2^b(RES)$	$S_3^b(RES)$	$S_0^b(CNS)$	$S_1^b(CNS)$	$S_2^b(CNS)$	$S_3^b(CNS)$
		CNS	CNS				
MNF	MNF	MNF	MNF	MNF	MNF	MNF	MNF
	TTF	TTF	TTF		TTF	TTF	TTF
			SRV			SRV	SRV
$S_0^b(MNF)$	$S_1^b(MNF)$	$S_2^b(MNF)$	$S_3^b(MNF)$	$S_0^b(TTF)$	$S_1^b(TTF)$	$S_2^b(TTF)$	$S_3^b(TTF)$
							CNS
MNF	MNF	MNF	MNF			MNF	MNF
	TTF	TTF	TTF	TTF	TTF	TTF	TTF
		SRV	SRV			SRV	SRV
$S_0^b(SRV)$	$S_1^b(SRV)$	$S_2^b(SRV)$	$S_3^b(SRV)$	$S_0^b(GOV)$	$S_1^b(GOV)$	$S_2^b(GOV)$	$S_3^b(GOV)$
		CNS	CNS	CNS	CNS	CNS	CNS
MNF	MNF	MNF	MNF				MNF
	TTF	TTF	TTF		TTF	TTF	TTF
			SRV				SRV

3.3 Analysis of the shared face matrices for cumulative incidence matrices

The numerical procedure of structural Q-analysis yields the following shared face matrices, SF^1, SF^2, SF^3, SF^4, that correspond to the sequence of the incidence matrices Λ^1, Λ^2, Λ^3, Λ^4:

$$SF^1 = \begin{pmatrix} -1 & -1 & -1 & -1 & -1 & -1 \\ -1 & 0 & -1 & -1 & -1 & -1 \\ -1 & -1 & 3 & -1 & -1 & -1 \\ -1 & -1 & -1 & 0 & -1 & -1 \\ -1 & -1 & -1 & -1 & -1 & -1 \\ -1 & -1 & -1 & -1 & -1 & -1 \end{pmatrix},$$

with q-chain

$$Q^1_q = \begin{cases} q = 4: \{MNF\} \\ q = 3: \{MNF\} \\ q = 2: \{MNF\} \\ q = 1: \{MNF\} \\ q = 0: \{MNF\}, \{TTF\} \end{cases}$$

(9.5)

and the structural vector $Q^1 = \begin{Bmatrix} 4 & & & & 0 \\ 1 & 1 & 1 & 1 & 2 \end{Bmatrix}$;

$$SF^2 = \begin{pmatrix} -1 & -1 & -1 & -1 & -1 & -1 \\ -1 & 0 & -1 & 0 & -1 & -1 \\ -1 & -1 & 4 & 4 & -1 & -1 \\ -1 & 0 & 4 & 5 & -1 & -1 \\ -1 & -1 & -1 & -1 & -1 & -1 \\ -1 & -1 & -1 & -1 & -1 & -1 \end{pmatrix},$$

with the structural chain:

$$Q^2_q = \begin{cases} q = 5: \{TTF\} \\ q = 4: \{MNF, TTF\} \\ q = 3: \{MNF, TTF\} \\ q = 2: \{MNF, TTF\} \\ q = 1: \{MNF, TTF\} \\ q = 0: \{MNF, TTF, CNS\} \end{cases}$$

(9.6)

and the structural vector $Q^2 = \begin{Bmatrix} 5 & & & & & 0 \\ 1 & 1 & 1 & 1 & 1 & 1 \end{Bmatrix}$;

Further,

$$SF^3 = \begin{pmatrix} -1 & -1 & -1 & -1 & -1 & -1 \\ -1 & 1 & 1 & 1 & -1 & -1 \\ -1 & 1 & 5 & 5 & 3 & -1 \\ -1 & 1 & 5 & 5 & 3 & -1 \\ -1 & -1 & 3 & 3 & 3 & -1 \\ -1 & -1 & -1 & -1 & -1 & -1 \end{pmatrix} 1,$$

with the structural chain:

$$Q_q^3 = \begin{cases} q = 5: \{MNF, TTF\} \\ q = 4; \{MNF, TTF\} \\ q = 3; \{MNF, TTF, SRV\} \\ q = 2; \{MNF, TTF, SRV\} \\ q = 1; \{MNF, TTF, SRV, CNF\} \\ q = 0; \{MNF, TTF, SRV\} \end{cases} \tag{9.7}$$

and the structural vector $Q^3 = \begin{Bmatrix} 5 & & & & & 0 \\ 1 & 1 & 1 & 1 & 1 & 1 \end{Bmatrix}$;

Next

$$SF^4 = \begin{pmatrix} -1 & -1 & -1 & -1 & -1 & -1 \\ -1 & 3 & 3 & 3 & 3 & -1 \\ -1 & 3 & 5 & 5 & 5 & -1 \\ -1 & 3 & 5 & 5 & 5 & -1 \\ -1 & 3 & 5 & 5 & 5 & -1 \\ -1 & -1 & -1 & -1 & -1 & -1 \end{pmatrix},$$

with structural chain

$$Q_q^4 = \begin{cases} q = 5: \{MNF, TTF, SRV\} \\ q = 4; \{MNF, TTF, SRV\} \\ q = 3; \{MNF, TTF, SRV, CNS\} \\ q = 2; \{MNF, TTF, SRV, CNS\} \\ q = 1; \{MNF, TTF, SRV, CNS\} \\ q = 0; \{MNF, TTF, SRV, CNS\} \end{cases} \tag{9.8}$$

and the structural vector $Q^4 = \begin{Bmatrix} 5 & & & & & 0 \\ 1 & 1 & 1 & 1 & 1 & 1 \end{Bmatrix}$.

4 Industrial clusters and their augmentation

The consideration of the first incidence matrix Λ^1 and its structural vector (see equation 9.6) will generate the appearance of the main industrial cluster in the first decomposition tendency. The chain of the highest dimension $q = 3: \{MNF\}$ presents the main industrial cluster existing in the first tendency of the decomposition of the matrix of backward linkages. The structure of this cluster can be derived from the cumulative incidence matrix corresponding to the first tendency:

$$\Lambda^1 = \begin{pmatrix} 0 & 0 & 0 & 0 & 0 & 0 \\ 0 & 0 & 0 & 0 & 0 & 1 \\ 1 & 1 & 1 & 0 & 1 & 0 \\ 0 & 0 & 0 & 1 & 0 & 0 \\ 0 & 0 & 0 & 0 & 0 & 0 \\ 0 & 0 & 0 & 0 & 0 & 0 \end{pmatrix} \overset{\text{Cluster}}{\underset{\downarrow}{\rightarrow}} \{MNF\} = \boxed{\begin{array}{|c|c|c|c|c|} \hline RES & CNS & MNF & SRV & \\ \hline \end{array}} \}$$

The appearance of the next industrial cluster of the highest dimension $q=5:\{TTF\}$ can be derived from the second incidence matrix (see equation 9.7):

$$\Lambda^2 = \begin{pmatrix} 0 & 0 & 0 & 0 & 0 & 0 \\ 0 & 0 & 0 & 0 & 0 & 1 \\ 1 & 1 & 1 & 1 & 1 & 0 \\ 1 & 1 & 1 & 1 & 1 & 1 \\ 0 & 0 & 0 & 0 & 0 & 0 \\ 0 & 0 & 0 & 0 & 0 & 0 \end{pmatrix} \begin{matrix} Cluster \\ \downarrow \\ \rightarrow \{TTF\} = \\ \\ \\ \end{matrix} \quad \{\boxed{RES | CNS | MNF | TTF | SRV | GOV}\}$$

The merger of previous two clusters into the industrial cluster of dimension $q=4:\{MNF, TTF\}$ has a form:

$$\Lambda^2 = \begin{pmatrix} 0 & 0 & 0 & 0 & 0 & 0 \\ 0 & 0 & 0 & 0 & 0 & 1 \\ 1 & 1 & 1 & 1 & 1 & 0 \\ 1 & 1 & 1 & 1 & 1 & 1 \\ 0 & 0 & 0 & 0 & 0 & 0 \\ 0 & 0 & 0 & 0 & 0 & 0 \end{pmatrix} \begin{matrix} Cluster \\ \downarrow \\ \rightarrow \{MNF\} = \\ \rightarrow \{TTF\ \} = \\ \\ \end{matrix} \quad \begin{matrix} \{\boxed{RES | CNS | MNF | TTF | SRV |}\} \\ \{\boxed{RES | CNS | MNF | TTF | SRV | GOV}\} \end{matrix}$$

This cluster appears as main cluster in the next cumulative incidence matrix (see equation 9.7). Its structure has the highest dimension $q=5:\{MNF, TTF\}$:

$$\Lambda^3 = \begin{pmatrix} 0 & 0 & 0 & 0 & 0 & 0 \\ 1 & 0 & 0 & 0 & 0 & 1 \\ 1 & 1 & 1 & 1 & 1 & 0 \\ 1 & 1 & 1 & 1 & 1 & 1 \\ 0 & 1 & 1 & 1 & 1 & 0 \\ 0 & 0 & 0 & 0 & 0 & 0 \end{pmatrix} \begin{matrix} Cluster \\ \downarrow \\ \rightarrow \{MNF\} = \\ \rightarrow \{TTF\ \} = \\ \\ \end{matrix} \quad \begin{matrix} \{\boxed{RES | CNS | MNF | TTF | SRV |}\} \\ \{\boxed{RES | CNS | MNF | TTF | SRV | GOV}\} \end{matrix}$$

The augmentation of this cluster has the following form:

$$\Lambda^3 = \begin{pmatrix} 0 & 0 & 0 & 0 & 0 & 0 \\ 1 & 0 & 0 & 0 & 0 & 1 \\ 1 & 1 & 1 & 1 & 1 & 0 \\ 1 & 1 & 1 & 1 & 1 & 1 \\ 0 & 1 & 1 & 1 & 1 & 0 \\ 0 & 0 & 0 & 0 & 0 & 0 \end{pmatrix} \begin{matrix} Cluster \\ \downarrow \\ \rightarrow \{MNF\} = \\ \rightarrow \{TTF\ \} = \\ \rightarrow \{SRV\ \} = \\ \end{matrix} \quad \begin{matrix} \{\boxed{RES | CNS | MNF | TTF | SRV |}\} \\ \{\boxed{RES | CNS | MNF | TTF | SRV | GOV}\} \\ \{\boxed{ | CNS | MNF | TTF | SRV |}\} \end{matrix}$$

The final augmentation of industrial clusters has the following form: $q=5:\{MNF, TTF, SRV\}$ (see equation 9.8) and

$$\Lambda^4 = \begin{pmatrix} 0 & 0 & 0 & 0 & 0 & 0 \\ 1 & 0 & 0 & 1 & 1 & 1 \\ 1 & 1 & 1 & 1 & 1 & 1 \\ 1 & 1 & 1 & 1 & 1 & 1 \\ 1 & 1 & 1 & 1 & 1 & 1 \\ 0 & 0 & 0 & 0 & 0 & 0 \end{pmatrix} \begin{array}{l} \textit{Cluster} \\ \downarrow \\ \rightarrow \{MNF\} = \\ \rightarrow \{TTF\} = \\ \rightarrow \{SRV\} = \end{array} \begin{array}{l} \\ \\ \boxed{RES}\,\boxed{CNS}\,\boxed{MNF}\,\boxed{TTF}\,\boxed{SRV}\,\boxed{GOV} \\ \boxed{RES}\,\boxed{CNS}\,\boxed{MNF}\,\boxed{TTF}\,\boxed{SRV}\,\boxed{GOV} \\ \boxed{RES}\,\boxed{CNS}\,\boxed{MNF}\,\boxed{TTF}\,\boxed{SRV}\,\boxed{GOV} \end{array}$$

The consecutive stages of the augmentation of industrial clusters can be presented in the form of deepening of complexity (complication) of the sectors of Chicago economy. These results imply the following complication diagram of backward Chenery–Watanabe linkages in Chicago economy in 2000:

31.5%	MNF
57.6%	MNF,TTF
73.3%	MNF,TTF,SRV
83.6%	MNF,TTF,SRV,CNS

This complication diagram of backward linkages (on the aggregation level of six economic sectors) is characteristic of Chicago economy during all periods, 1975–2000 (see Guo et al., 2005).

The analogous Q-analysis of forward linkage sector structure is presented in Table 9.5. In the first two decomposed levels, the number of sectors obtaining the inputs from MNF for inputs have decreased since 1980; in 1980, all the six sectors obtain MNF's input ($q=5$), but, by 1985, the number decreases to four ($q=4$) and, since 1990, only four sectors obtain MNF's input inside the Chicago regional economy. On the other hand, the service sector (SRV) has been sending inputs to more and more sectors, increasing from only one sector in 1980 to two in 1985 and three after 1990.

In analogous fashion, the complication diagram for the Chenery–Watanabe backward linkages for 2000 has a form:

33.7%	TTF
62.1%	TTF,MNF
81.2%	TTF,MNF,SRV
87.1%	TTF,MNF,SRV,CNS

This complication diagram is also characteristic of the complication of backward linkages during the period 1980–2000. It is important to note the main key sector for forward linkages is MNF, which is replaced by TTF for backward linkages.

5 Conclusion

While earlier analysis of the production structure in Chicago's economy suggested that the economy was becoming simpler (see Hewings et al., 1998) in the sense that the degree of intraregional intermediation was declining, the analysis of sectoral structure explored a more detailed picture of the changes, showing the relationships of the sectoral structure in different levels of the transaction flows. For about 50 per cent of the total transaction

Table 9.5   *Forward linkages, sectoral structure*

q	1980	1985	1990	1995	2000
q=3	{TTF}	{TTF}	{TTF}	{TTF}	{TTF}
q=2	{TTF}	{TTF}	{TTF}	{TTF}	{TTF}
q=1	{TTF}; {MNF}	{TTF}; {MNF}	{TTF}; {MNF}	{TTF}; {MNF}	{TTF}; {MNF}
q=0	{TTF}; {MNF}	{TTF}; {MNF}	{TTF}; {MNF}	{TTF}; {MNF}	{TTF}; {MNF}
CP1	0.329	0.332	0.332	0.335	0.337
q=5	{MNF}				
q=4	{MNF}	{MNF}			
q=3	{MNF, TTF}	{MNF}; {TTF}	{MNF}; {TTF}	{MNF}; {TTF}	{MNF}; {TTF}
q=2	{MNF, TTF}	{MNF, TTF}	{MNF}; {TTF}; {SRV}	{MNF}; {TTF}; {SRV}	{MNF}; {TTF}; {SRV}
q=1	{MNF, TTF}	{MNF, TTF}; {SRV}	{MNF, TTF, SRV}	{MNF, TTF, SRV}	{MNF, TTF, SRV}
q=0	{MNF, TTF, SRV}	{MNF, TTF, SRV}	{MNF, TTF}; {SRV}	{MNF, TTF, SRV}	{MNF, TTF, SRV}
CP2	0.587	0.607	0.615	0.619	0.621
q=5	{MNF, TTF}	{MNF, TTF}	{MNF, TTF}	{MNF, TTF}	{MNF, TTF}
q=4	{MNF, TTF, SRV}	{MNF, TTF, SRV}	{MNF, TTF, SRV}	{MNF, TTF, SRV}	{MNF, TTF, SRV}
q=3	{MNF, TTF, SRV}	{MNF, TTF, SRV}	{MNF, TTF, SRV}	{MNF, TTF, SRV}	{MNF, TTF, SRV}
q=2	{MNF, TTF, SRV}	{MNF, TTF, SRV}	{MNF, TTF, SRV}	{MNF, TTF, SRV}	{MNF, TTF, SRV}
q=1	{MNF, TTF, SRV}	{MNF, TTF, SRV}	{MNF, TTF, SRV}	{MNF, TTF, SRV}	{MNF, TTF, SRV}
q=0	{MNF, TTF, SRV}	{MNF, TTF, SRV}	{MNF, TTF, SRV}	{MNF, TTF, SRV}	{MNF, TTF, SRV}
CP3	0.770	0.794	0.801	0.808	0.812
q=5	{MNF, TTF}	{MNF, TTF}	{MNF, TTF}	{MNF, TTF, SRV}	{MNF, TTF, SRV}
q=4	{MNF, TTF, SRV}	{MNF, TTF, SRV}	{MNF, TTF, SRV}	{MNF, TTF, SRV}	{MNF, TTF, SRV}
q=3	{MNF, TTF, SRV}	{CNS, MNF, TTF, SRV}	{MNF, TTF, SRV}	{MNF, TTF, SRV}	{CNS, MNF, TTF, SRV}
q=2	{CNS, MNF, TTF, SRV}	{CNS, MNF, TTF, SRV}	{CNS, MNF, TTF, SRV}	{CNS, MNF, TTF, SRV}	{CNS, MNF, TTF, SRV}
q=1	{CNS, MNF, TTF, SRV}	{CNS, MNF, TTF, SRV}	{CNS, MNF, TTF, SRV}	{CNS, MNF, TTF, SRV}	{CNS, MNF, TTF, SRV}
q=0	{CNS, MNF, TTF, SRV}	{CNS, MNF, TTF, SRV}	{CNS, MNF, TTF, SRV}	{CNS, MNF, TTF, SRV}	{CNS, MNF, TTF, SRV}
CP4	0.836	0.849	0.858	0.866	0.871

166

flows, the manufacturing and service sectors have the most noticeable changing features in that manufacturing has fewer and fewer connections with other sectors, while the service sectors, on the other hand, expanded their connections with other sectors inside the economy, further indicating their growing importance in the region.

The analysis reveals some features of the structure of Chicago's economy in the last two decades that can be summarized as follows. The results indicate that the production process in Chicago is increasingly becoming more dependent in a backward and forward sense on regions outside the Chicago economy. This result is especially true for manufacturing: the fragmentation of production has been facilitated by the fast growth of the service sectors, especially transportation and communications, that have made it possible to source inputs from distant sources and to serve markets that are more geographically diverse. This kind of production process has been observed internationally (see Jones and Kierzkowski, 1990, 2001a, 2001b). Even though fragmentation of production may happen domestically and internationally, the process has not been documented at the regional level.

The process of cluster development and its evolution remain a challenge; fragmentation may essentially result in a declustering process whereby major parts of the value chain of production may be spatially scattered rather than geographically concentrated. Q-analysis offers a methodology that provides a simple way to explore these structural changes. Obviously, the aggregated sectors employed here do not reveal the richness that can be explored; further, with interregional tables, the possibility exists to evaluate the way in which structural changes have manifested themselves in the exchange of intraregional for interregional interactions, thereby generating complication chains that extend far beyond the bounds of traditionally conceived geographically concentrated clusters.

Note
1. This section draws on Guo et al. (2005).

References

Atkin, R.H. (1974), *Mathematical Structures in Human Affairs*, London: Heineman Educational.
Atkin, R.H. (1981), *Multidimensional Man*, Harmondsworth, UK: Penguin.
Bergman, E.M., and E.J. Feser (2000), 'Industrial and regional clusters: concepts and applications', Morgantown, WV, Regional Research Institute, Web Book of Regional Science (www.rri.wvu/WebBook/Bergman-Feser/contents.htm).
Bröcker, J., D. Dohse and R. Soltwedel (eds) (2003), *Innovation Clusters and Interregional Competition*, Heidelberg: Springer Verlag.
Carter, A.P. (1970), *Structural Change in American Economy*, Cambridge, MA: Harvard University Press.
Chenery, H.B. (1953), 'Regional analysis', in H.B. Chenery, P.G. Clark and V. Cao-Pinna (eds), *The Structure and Growth of the Italian Economy*, US Mutual Security Agency.
Chenery, H.B. and P.B. Clark (1959), *Interindustry Economics*, New York: Wiley.
Chenery, H.B. and T. Watanabe (1958), 'International comparisons of the structure of production', *Econometrica*, **26**, 487–521.
Czamanski, S. (1971), 'Some empirical evidence of the strengths of linkages between groups of industries in urban regional complexes', *Papers of the Regional Science Association*, **27**, 137–50.
Czamanski, S. (1974), *Study of Clustering of Industries*, Halifax, Nova Scotia: Institute of Public Affairs.
Czamanski, S. (1976), *Study of Spatial Industrial Complexes*, Halifax, Nova Scotia: Institute of Public Affairs.
Czamanski, S. and L.A. de Ablas (1979), 'Identification of industrial clusters and complexes: a comparison of methods and findings', *Urban Studies*, **16**, 61–80.
Deutsch J. and M. Syrquin (1989), 'Economic development and the structure of production', *Economic Systems Research*, **1**, 447–64.

Dridi, C. and G.J.D. Hewings (2002), 'An investigation of industry associations, association loops and economic complexity: application to Canada and the United States', *Economic Systems Research*, **14**, 275–96.

Guo, D., G.J.D. Hewings and M. Sonis (2005), 'Integrating decomposition approaches for the analysis of temporal changes in economic structure: an application to Chicago's economy from 1980 to 2000', *Economic Systems Research*, **17**, 297–315.

Harrigan, F., J.W. McGilvay and I. McNicoll (1980), 'A comparison of regional and national technical structures', *Economic Journal*, **90**, 795–810.

Hewings, G.J.D., M. Sonis, J. Guo, P.R. Israilevich and G.R. Schindler (1998), 'The hollowing out process in the Chicago economy, 1975–2015', *Geographical Analysis*, **30**, 217–33.

Holub, H.W. and H. Schnabl (1985), 'Qualitative input–output analysis and structural information', *Economic Modeling*, **2**, 67–73.

Holub, H.W., H. Schnabl and G. Tappeiner (1985), 'Qualitative input–output analysis with variable filter', *Zeitschrift für die gesamte Staatswwissenschaft*, **141**, 282–300.

Israilevich, P.R., G.J.D. Hewings, M. Sonis and G.R. Schindler (1997), 'Forecasting structural change with a regional econometric input–output model', *Journal of Regional Science*, **37**, 565–90.

Jones, R.W. and H. Kierzkowski (1990), 'The role of services in production and international trade: a theoretical framework', in R.W. Jones and A. Krueger (eds), *The Political Economy of International Trade*, Oxford: Basil Blackwell.

Jones, R.W. and H. Kierzkowski (2001a), 'A framework for fragmentation', in S.W. Arndt and H. Kierzkowski (eds), *Fragmentation: New Production Patterns in the World Economy*, Oxford: Oxford University Press, pp. 17–34.

Jones, R.W. and H. Kierzkowski (2001b), 'Horizontal aspects of vertical fragmentation', in L.K. Cheng and H. Kierzkowski (eds), *Global Production and Trade in East Asia*, Norwell, MA: Kluwer Academic Publishers, pp. 33–51.

Long, N.B. Jr (1970), 'An input–output comparison of the economic structure of the US and the USSR', *Review of Economics and Statistics*, **52**, 434–41.

Matthews, R.C.O., C. Feinstein and C. Odling-Smee (1982), *British Economic Growth*, Oxford: Oxford University Press.

Ohkawa, K. and H. Rosovsky (1973), *Japanese Economic Growth: Trend Acceleration in the Twentieth Century*, Stanford: Stanford University Press.

Porter, M.E. (1990), *The Competitive Advantage of Nations*, New York: Free Press.

Schnabl, H. (1993), 'The evolution of production structures – analyzed by a multi-layer procedure', paper presented to the 10th International Conference on Input–Output Techniques, Seville, Spain.

Schnabl, H. and H.W. Holub (1979), 'Qualitative und quantitative aspekte der input–output analyse', *Zeitschrift für die gesamte Staatswissenschaft*, **135**, 657–78.

Song, B.N. (1977), 'The production structure of the Korean economy: international and historical comparisons', *Econometrica*, **45**, 147–62.

Sonis, M. (1988), 'Q-analysis of migration streams: spatio-temporal invariability and relative logistic dynamics', paper presented at the 35th North American Meeting of the Regional Science Association, Toronto, Canada.

Sonis, M. and G.J.D. Hewings (1988), 'Superposition and decomposition principles in hierarchical social accounting and input–output analysis', in F.J. Harrigan and P.G. McGregor (eds), *Recent Advances in Regional Economic Modelling*, London: Pion, pp. 46–65.

Sonis, M. and G.J.D. Hewings (1998), 'Theoretical and applied input–output analysis: a new synthesis. Part I: structure and structural changes in input–output systems', *Studies in Regional Science*, **27**, 233–56.

Sonis, M. and G.J.D. Hewings (2000), 'Introduction to input–output structural Q-analysis', discussion paper 00-T-1, Regional Economic Applications Laboratory, University of Illinois (http://www.real.uiuc.edu).

Sonis, M., G.J.D. Hewings and A. Bronstein (1994), 'Structure of fields of influence of economic changes: a case study of changes in the Israeli economy', *discussion paper* 94-T-10, Regional Economic Applications Laboratory, University of Illinois, (http://www.real.uiuc.edu).

10 Clustering using wavelet transformation
Abdullah Almasri and Ghazi Shukur

This chapter introduces and describes an alternative clustering approach based on the Discrete Wavelet Transform (DWT) which satisfies requirements that other clustering methods, like discriminative-based clustering and model-based clustering approaches, do not satisfy.

The clustering method has been constructed using wavelet analysis that has the ability of decomposing a data set into different scales. Wavelet algorithm is then used to specify the number of the clusters and quality of the clustering results at each scale. The same algorithm can be generalized for more than one-dimensional data. Some examples about how to use this approach are presented in this chapter, using different sample sizes, and where different kinds of noises are imposed on simulated data. These examples show the successfulness and efficiency of this kind of methodology in detecting clusters under different situations.

1 Introduction

Cluster analysis (originally used by Tryon, 1939) combines a number of different classification algorithms that are usually done to join cases or a set of data objects into groups or clusters when the group membership is not known a priori. Hence, it is a technique for linking individuals or objects into unknown groups or clusters such that those within each group or cluster are more closely related to one another than those assigned to other clusters. An observation or object can be explained by a number of measurements or by its relation to other observations or objects. Clustering, generally, is an unsupervised classification where no predefined classes are given. It can be used as a tool to gain insight into data, or as a pre-processing step for other algorithms. Cluster analysis is used in several areas, e.g. in pattern recognition, spatial data analysis, image processing and economic science (especially, market research, labour market and regional economics).

In the last few decades a variety of methods has been proposed for ways to conduct cluster analysis. In general, there are two main categories into which existing clustering approaches can be classified, namely, discriminative and model-based approaches.

In the discriminative based approaches one measures the distance or similarity/dissimilarity between two individual observations, and then join similar samples together into clusters. The most commonly used distance measures are Euclidean or standardized Euclidean distance and Mahalanobis distance. These approaches include hierarchical agglomerative clustering using various between-cluster dissimilarity measures, such as smallest dissimilarity (single linkage, also called the nearest-neighbour technique, that takes the inter-group dissimilarity to be that of the closest or least dissimilar pair); maximum dissimilarity (complete linkage, also called furthest-neighbour technique, takes the inter-group dissimilarity to be that of the furthest or most dissimilar pair); average dissimilarity (average linkage uses the average dissimilarity between the groups); or the k-means algorithm (MacQueen, 1967); and Self-Organizing Maps (Kohonen, 2001). These methods are relatively easy to apply and often give good results in simple cases. At this stage, it is crucial to mention that these methods are highly empirical, and that, in more complex cases, different methods can lead to different clustering, regarding both the number of clusters and the content. This might be due to the facts that these methods are sensitive for outliers; they do not involve statistical tools for choosing the number of clusters and do not pay attention to measurement error in the dissimilarities or to clustering uncertainties.

Parametric model-based approaches, on the other hand, try to find generative models from the data, with each model corresponding to one particular cluster. Note that the type of model here is often specified a priori, e.g. Gaussian or hidden Markov models, and can be processed in both single and multi-level perspectives. In other words, model-based clustering is a framework for putting cluster analysis on a principle statistical footing; for reviews and more discussions, see Fraley and Raftery (2002). It is based on probability models in which objects are assumed to follow a finite mixture of probability distributions such that each component distribution represents a cluster. One of the most important advantages of the model-based clustering over the discriminative based clustering is that the model-based clustering objects and estimates component parameters simultaneously. Processing in this manner leads to avoiding biases that might exist when the clustering and the estimation are done separately. Another advantage is the ability to use statistical model selection methods when specifying the number of components and their probability distributions. Moreover, model-based clustering provides clustering uncertainties, which is important especially for objects close to cluster boundaries. On the other hand, model-based clustering requires object coordinates rather than dissimilarities between objects (as in the discriminative based clustering) as an input. This means that model-based clustering is only applicable when object coordinates are available, and not when dissimilarities are provided.

More recently, Oh and Raftery (2003) developed a model-based clustering method for dissimilarity data. They assume that an observed dissimilarity measure is equal to the Euclidean distance between the objects plus a normal measurement error. They model the unobserved object configuration as a realization of a mixture of multivariate normal distributions, each one of which corresponds to a different cluster. The authors then carried out Bayesian inference for the resulting hierarchical model using Markov Chain Monte Carlo (MCMC). The resulting method combines multidimensional scaling and model-based clustering in a coherent framework.

Note that these and several other methods for clustering are not easy to apply when dealing with large and/or multidimensional data sets. In our opinion, we consider a clustering approach to be good if it is efficient, it detects clusters of arbitrary shape and it is insensitive to the noise (outliers).

In this chapter we introduce another clustering approach based on Discrete Wavelet Transform (DWT) which satisfies all the above requirements. The wavelet methods have been shown to be very useful in different areas of research, such as signal processing, image analysis, geophysics and atmospheric sciences. Recently, the wavelet methods have also been introduced to the subject of economics and, in particular, time series econometrics (see, e.g. Almasri & Shukur, 2003; Percival & Walden, 2000; Ramsey and Lampart, 1998). However, using the multi-resolution property of wavelet transform, we can effectively identify arbitrarily shaped clusters in different degrees of detail. Since the wavelet transform is a very natural tool to detect spatial scales and clusters in an image, the technique can even be applied to spatial patterns. The main advantages of this technique over other methods of spatial analysis are its ability to preserve and display hierarchical information while allowing for pattern decomposition; see Chave and Levin (2003). The wavelet transform can be used in many applications such as Geographic Information Systems (GIS), segmentation of airborne laser scanner data, image database exploration, seismology, etc. It can also be used in economics and other social sciences in a GIS framework which increase the understanding of many sorts of social processes, including patterns of employment and unemployment, crime, economic growth and population change; see, e.g. Morehart et al. (1999) and Vu and Tokunaga (2001). In the two-dimensional cases one can apply our methodology to study real-life data such as the relationship between firms of different sizes and their natural resource bases. Here, the centre of geographically referenced bins/blocks can be considered as the first dimension and the second dimension as the variable of interest.

Since clustering analysis is a vast area of statistical methodology, we previously confined ourselves to a brief description of some of the available methods, and further details are found in standard textbooks and cited references. We will, however, discuss more thoroughly the clustering associated with the wavelet methodology, since this topic is not mentioned in standard textbooks.

The chapter is arranged as follows: in the next section we present the wavelet methodology as an alternative clustering approach. In Section 3, we demonstrate a number of artificial examples, while, in Section 4, we give some concluding remarks.

2   Methodology

In this section we define the wavelet filter and DWT in one and two dimensions. The basic idea of wavelet analysis is to imitate the Fourier analysis, but with functions (wavelets) that are better suited to capture the local behaviour of data sets. The wavelet transform utilizes a basic function (called the mother wavelet), then dilates and translates it to capture features that are local in time and local in frequency. The wavelet function, say $\psi(.)$, should satisfy the following two basic properties:

- The integral of the real-valued function $\psi(.)$ is zero:

$$\int_{-\infty}^{\infty} \psi(u) du = 0. \tag{10.1}$$

- The square of $\psi(.)$ integrates to unity:

$$\int_{-\infty}^{\infty} \psi^2(u) du = 1. \tag{10.2}$$

The oldest and simplest wavelet which satisfies (10.1) and (10.2) is called the Haar wavelet, and is given by

$$\psi^H(u) \equiv \begin{cases} \dfrac{-1}{\sqrt{2}}, & -1 < u \leq 0 \\ \dfrac{1}{\sqrt{2}}, & 0 < u \leq 1 \\ 0, & \text{otherwise.} \end{cases}$$

This function is a basis for other wavelets by means of two operations, dyadic dilation and integer translation, producing an orthonormal basis for $L_2(R)$:

$$\psi_{j,k}^H(u) = 2^{j/2}\psi(2^j u - k), \ j,k \in Z = \{0, \pm 1, \pm 2,...\},$$

where j denotes the dilation index and k represents the translation index. In this section we describe the Haar wavelet and other wavelets in discrete terms.

Daubechies (1992) derives a class of wavelets defined by two filters of positive integer width L:

- The high-pass filter (wavelet filter): $\{h_l\}=\{h_0,\ldots,h_{L-1}\}$.
- The low-pass filter (scaling filter): $\{g_l\}=\{g_0,\ldots,g_{L-1}\}$ which is defined via the quadrature mirror relationship $\{h_l=(-1)^l g_{L-1-l}; l=0,\ldots,L-1\}$.

Fundamental properties of the continuous wavelet functions, such as integration to zero and unit energy in (10.1) and (10.2), respectively, have discrete counterparts. A discrete wavelet filter must satisfy the following three properties:

$$\sum_{l=0}^{L-1} h_l = 0;$$

$$\sum_{l=0}^{L-1} h_l^2 = 1;$$

and

$$\sum_{l=0}^{L-1} h_l h_{l+2n} = \sum_{l=-\infty}^{\infty} h_l h_{l+2n} = 0,$$

for all nonzero integers n, and where we define $h_l=0$ for $l<0$ and $l\geq L$ so that $\{h_l\}$ is an infinite sequence with at most L nonzero values. This means that a wavelet filter must sum to zero, must have unit energy and must be orthogonal to its even shifts.

The transfer functions for $\{h_l\}$ and $\{g_l\}$ are given by

$$H(f) \equiv \sum_{l=0}^{L-1} h_l e^{-i2\pi fl} \tag{10.3}$$

and

$$G(f) \equiv \sum_{l=0}^{L-1} g_l e^{-i2\pi fl}, \tag{10.4}$$

where f is the Fourier frequencies. Further, useful functions are the squared gain function for $\{h_l\}$ and $\{g_l\}$:

$$\mathcal{H}(f) \equiv |H(f)|^2 \text{ and } \mathcal{G}(f) \equiv |G(f)|^2.$$

The Daubechies wavelets are most easily defined through the squared gain function of their scaling filter:

$$\mathcal{G}^{(D)}(f) \equiv 2\cos^L(\pi f)\sum_{l=0}^{\frac{L}{2}-1}\binom{\frac{L}{2}-1+l}{l}\sin^{2l}(\pi f),$$

where L is a positive even integer. By using the relationship $\mathcal{H}^{(D)}(f) = \mathcal{G}^{(D)}(f+\frac{1}{2})$, we find that the corresponding Daubechies wavelet filters have squared gain function satisfying

$$\mathcal{H}^{(D)}(f) \equiv 2\sin^L(\pi f)\sum_{l=0}^{\frac{L}{2}-1}\binom{\frac{L}{2}-1+l}{l}\cos^{2l}(\pi f).$$

Daubechies (1992) introduces two types of wavelets, the extremal phase $D(L)$ and the least asymmetric $LA(L)$. The difference between them lies only in their phase functions, i.e., $\theta^{(G)}(.)$ in the polar representation

$$G(f) = [\mathcal{G}^{(D)}(f)]^{1/2}e^{i\theta^{(G)}}(f).$$

The Haar wavelet or $D(2)$, is a filter of width $L = 2$, that can be defined through its wavelet filter,

$$h_0 = \frac{1}{\sqrt{2}} \text{ and } h_1 = \frac{-1}{\sqrt{2}},$$

or, equivalently, through its scaling filter,

$$g_0 = g_1 = \frac{1}{\sqrt{2}}.$$

The wavelet filter coefficients for the $D(4)$ wavelet, at unit scale, are defined by

$$h_0 = \frac{1-\sqrt{3}}{4\sqrt{2}}, h_1 = \frac{-3+\sqrt{3}}{4\sqrt{2}}, h_2 = \frac{3+\sqrt{3}}{4\sqrt{2}} \text{ and } h_3 = \frac{-1-\sqrt{3}}{4\sqrt{2}}.$$

The scaling coefficients for the $LA(8)$ and other Daubechies wavelets are given in Daubechies (1992). The wavelet filter $\{h_l\}$ approximates an ideal high-pass filter, and the scaling filter $\{g_l\}$ approximates an ideal low-pass filter. The accuracy of the approximation increases as L increases, so that the squared gain functions for $\{h_l\}$ and $\{g_l\}$ converge to the squared functions for an ideal high-pass and an ideal low-pass, respectively.

2.1 The discrete wavelet transform

The key idea of the discrete wavelet transform (DWT) is to decompose a data set orthogonally into different new data sets. In this section we are going to introduce the one-dimensional DWT (1D DWT) and two-dimensional DWT (2D DWT).

2.1.1   The 1D DWT   Let $\mathbf{X}=(X_0, \ldots ,X_{N-1})$ be a data vector of length N, where we assume that N is an integer divisible by 2^J, where J is a positive integer. The wavelet and scaling filters are used in parallel to define the DWT, i.e., we have two types of coefficients in the DWT based on these two types of filter:

- The scaling coefficients which represent the smoothed version of the original data. These coefficients can help us in detecting the number of clusters.
- The wavelet coefficients.

The 1D DWT is calculated using Mallat's algorithm, introduced by Mallat (1989), which uses linear filtering operations. The transform coefficients, $V_{j,k}$ and $W_{j,k}$, at different scales, are calculated using the following convolution-like expressions. There are $J - 1$ subsequent stages of the pyramid algorithm. The scaling coefficients for level j ($j, \ldots , J$) are given by

$$V_{j,k} = \sum_{l=0}^{L-1} g_l V_{j-1, 2k+1-l \bmod N_{j-1}} \text{ for } k = 0,\ldots,N_j - 1, \tag{10.5}$$

and the wavelet coefficients for level j are given by

$$W_{j,k} = \sum_{l=0}^{L-1} h_l V_{j-1, 2k+1-l \bmod N_{j-1}} \text{ for } k = 0,\ldots,N_j - 1, \tag{10.6}$$

where $\mathbf{V}_0 \equiv \mathbf{X}$ and $N_j \equiv N2-j$. The modulus operator in (10.5) and (10.6) is required in order to deal with the boundary of a finite length vector of observations. This operator circularly filters the data, by using a fast filtering algorithm of order $O(N)$. We see from (10.5) and (10.6) that at each step we filter the previous level scaling coefficients using either the scaling or wavelet filter, and then subsample the resulting sequence. The DWT can be defined also by matrix calculation. Let $\mathbf{W}_j \equiv [W_{j,0}, W_{j,1}, \ldots , W_{j,N_{j-1}}]^T, j = 1, 2, \ldots ,$ J and $\mathbf{V}_J \equiv [V_{J,0}, V_{J,1}, \ldots , V_{J,N_{J-1}}]^T$. The elements of the subvectors $\mathbf{W}_j$ correspond to those in (10.6) and the subvector $\mathbf{V}_j$ correspond to those in (10.5). We then have the analysis equation $\mathbf{W} = \mathcal{W}\mathbf{X}$, where $\mathbf{W}$ contains the DWT coefficients, i.e.,

$$\mathbf{W} = \begin{pmatrix} W_1 \\ W_2 \\ \vdots \\ W_j \\ \vdots \\ W_J \\ V_J \end{pmatrix}, \tag{10.7}$$

and $\mathcal{W}$ is an orthonormal $N \times N$ real-valued matrix whose rows depend on the wavelet filter h_l, i.e., $\mathcal{W}^{-1} = \mathcal{W}^T$, so $\mathcal{W}^T\mathcal{W} = \mathcal{W}\mathcal{W}^T = \mathbf{I}_N$ (Percival & Walden, 2000, Ch. 4). A partial DWT will be obtained by stopping the algorithm after $j_0 < J$ repetitions. The partial DWTs are more commonly used in practice than the full DWT, owing to the flexibility they offer in specifying a scale beyond which a wavelet analysis into individual large scales is no longer of real interest.

2.1.2   The 2D DWT   Similarly, the 2D DWT is computed using 2D filtering and down-sampling operations. Let $\mathbf{Y}_{x,z}$ be an image with two dimension. The image will be transformed through the two stages of analysis filters h and g and subsampled by two. Analogous to the 1D DWT, the 2D DWT is decomposed into a sum of fine to coarse resolution detail coefficients and sum of coarse resolution smooth coefficients. The coefficients for the first scale are given by the following formulas:

$$W^{(d)}_{z,x,1} = \sum_{k=0}^{L-1}\sum_{l=0}^{L-1} h^0 Y_{2z+1-k \bmod M, 2x+1-l \bmod N} \tag{10.8}$$

$$W^{(v)}_{z,x,1} = \sum_{k=0}^{L-1}\sum_{l=0}^{L-1} h^1 Y_{2z+1-k \bmod M, 2x+1-l \bmod N} \tag{10.9}$$

$$W^{(h)}_{z,x,1} = \sum_{k=0}^{L-1}\sum_{l=0}^{L-1} h^2 Y_{2z+1-k \bmod M, 2x+1-l \bmod N} \tag{10.10}$$

$$V_{z,x,1} = \sum_{k=0}^{L-1}\sum_{l=0}^{L-1} h^3 Y_{2z+1-k \bmod M, 2x+1-l \bmod N}, \tag{10.11}$$

where the filters h^0, h^1, h^2 and h^3 are formed by vector outer products of the quadrature mirror filters h and g.

$$h^0 = h.h^T, \; h^1 = h.g^T, \; h^2 = g.h^T, \; h^3 = g.g^T \tag{10.12}$$

where $W^{(d)}_{z,x,1}$, $W^{(v)}_{z,x,1}$, $W^{(v)}_{z,x,1}$ and $V_{z,x,1}$ are coefficients from the diagonal, vertical, horizontal and scaling.

We can obtain the second scale of coefficients by replacing $Y_{2z,2x}$ with $V_{z,x,1}$ in (10.8)–(10.11). In summary, the 2D DWT consist of four sub images:

- $W^{(h)}_{z,x,1}$ is associated with horizontal features in the image.
- $W^{(v)}_{z,x,1}$ is associated with vertical features in the image.
- $W^{(d)}_{z,x,1}$ is associated with diagonal features in the image.
- $V_{z,x,1}$ is the smoothed version of the original image.

More details can be found in Mallat (1989). A major goal in this chapter is to study the smoothed version of the original image to get an idea about the number of clusters.

2.2   Maximal overlap DWT (MODWT)

An alternative wavelet estimation is achieved by using the maximal overlap DWT (MODWT): see Percival and Walden (2000). The MODWT is also called the undecimated or translation invariant or shift invariant DWT: see Nason and Silverman (1995). The MODWT either for one dimensional or two dimensional data is computed by the same filtering steps as the ordinary 1D DWT or 2D DWT, respectively, but without subsampling the filtered output. The MODWT gives up orthogonality in order to gain features which the DWT does not possess.

2.3   Multi-resolution analysis

The concept of multi-resolution analysis (MRA) was first introduced by Mallat (1989). The multi-resolution analysis of the data leads to a better understanding of wavelets. The idea behind multi-resolution analysis is to express the right-hand side of (10.7) as the sum of several new data sets, each of which is related to variations in the data at a certain scale. Now, since the matrix is orthonormal, we can reconstruct our data sets from the wavelet coefficients $\mathbf{W}$ by using $\mathbf{X} = \mathcal{W}^T \mathbf{W}$.

We partition the columns of $\mathbf{W}$ commensurate with the partitioning of $\mathcal{W}$ to obtain

$$\mathcal{W}^T = [\mathcal{W}_1 \mathcal{W}_2 \dots \mathcal{W}_j \dots \mathcal{W}_J \mathcal{V}_J],$$

where $\mathcal{W}_j$ is an $N \times N/2^j$ matrix and $\mathcal{V}_J$ is an $N \times N/2^J$ matrix. Thus, we can define the multi-resolution analysis of a data set by expressing $\mathcal{W}^T \mathbf{W}$ as a sum of several new data sets, each of which is related to variations in X at a certain scale:

$$\mathbf{X} = \mathcal{W}^T \mathbf{W} = \sum_{j=1}^{J} \mathcal{W}_j \mathbf{W}_j + \mathcal{V}_J \mathbf{V}_J = \sum_{j=1}^{J} D_j + S_J. \qquad (10.13)$$

The terms in (10.13) constitute a decomposition of X into orthogonal data sets components D_j (detail) and S_J (smooth) at different scales and the length of D_j and S_J coincides with the length of $\mathbf{X}$ ($N \times$ vector). Because the terms at different scales represent components of $\mathbf{X}$ at different resolutions the approximation is called 'multi-resolution decomposition' (Percival and Walden, 2000). The smooth scale S_J gives a smooth approximation to $\mathbf{X}$. Adding the detail scale, D_J, yields S_{J-1}, a scale 2^{J-1} approximation to $\mathbf{X}$. The S_{J-1} approximation is a refinement of the S_J approximation. Similarly, we can refine further to obtain the scale 2^{J-1} approximations. The collection S_J, S_{J-1} and S_1 provides a set of multi-resolution approximations of X. Analogous to kernel smoothing, which has a parameter called bandwidth or smoothing parameter, the index J is called a wavelet smoothing parameter. Increasing the smoothing parameter J allows less detail in the smooth approximation of $\mathbf{X}$, while a small J allows additional detail in the smooth approximation of $\mathbf{X}$ (see Ogden, 1997). The principle of the one-dimensional MRA can be extended to two or several dimensional MRA.

2.4   Wavelet algorithm

The DWT decomposes the data into two parts, the high frequency part and the low frequency part. The high frequency part consists of the detail coefficients and represents the boundaries of clusters, where the low frequency part consists of the smooth coefficients and represents the clusters. The goal of DWT-based clustering (DWTBC) is to detect different smooth versions of the data at different scales by removing the background noise in the wavelet coefficients. By reconstructing the DWTBC at different scales, we get a multi-resolution approximation of our data set that represents the original data set at different levels of smoothing. We can summarize the wavelet clustering algorithm as follows:

- Apply the DWT of the data by starting with $j = 1$.
- Increase the value of j until getting a clear picture of the number of clusters.
- Reconstruct the smooth coefficients at suitable j.

The same algorithm can also be used by applying MODWT instead of the DWT. The same algorithm could be generalized for two-dimensional data.

3 Examples

In this section we give some examples about using the DWTBC and the multi-resolution approximation-based clustering (MRABC). Figure 10.1a shows two simulated normal distributed clusters with means equal to 3 and 5, and with standard deviations equal to 0.40 and 0.40, respectively; and with sample size equal to 1024 observations each. Figure 10.1b shows the two clusters with additive normal noise with mean equal to 4 and standard deviation equal to 2. We apply the D(2) wavelet in our wavelet algorithm to the simulated data sets in order to detect the number and quality of existing clusters. Figures 10.1c–10.1h show the first, second and third level of the DWT and MRA. These results show a clear recovery of the two clusters.

In Figure 10.2 we present the last example with larger sample size (4096 observations). We increase the number of clusters from two to four to check the ability of DWT-based

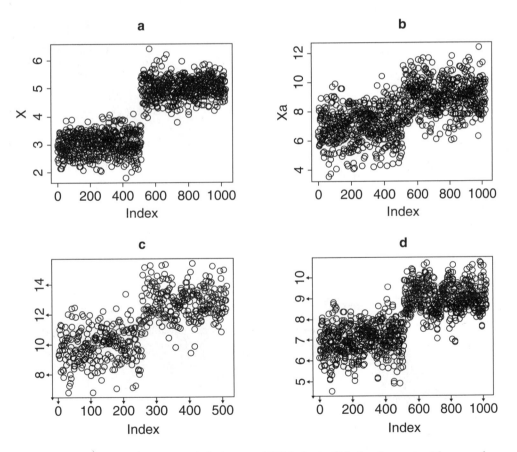

Figure 10.1a–d   (a) data set with 2 clusters (1024 obs.), (b) the data set with normal noise, (c) first scale DWTBC, (d) first scale MRABC

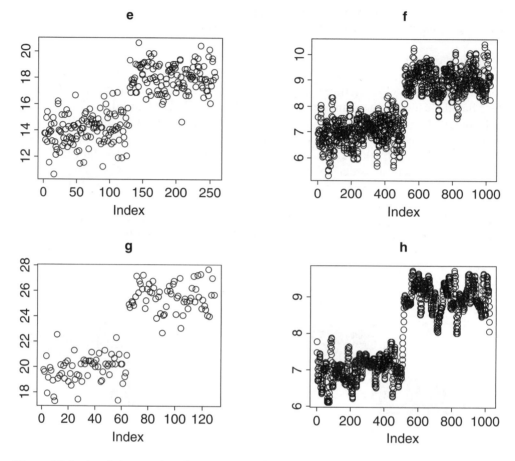

Figure 10.1e–h   *(e) second scale DWTBC, (f) second scale MRABC, (g) third scale DWTBC, (h) third scale MRABC*

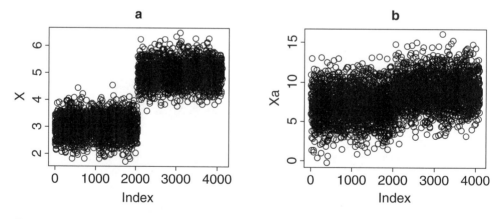

Figure 10.2a–b   *(a) data set with 2 clusters (4096 obs.), (b) the data set with normal noise*

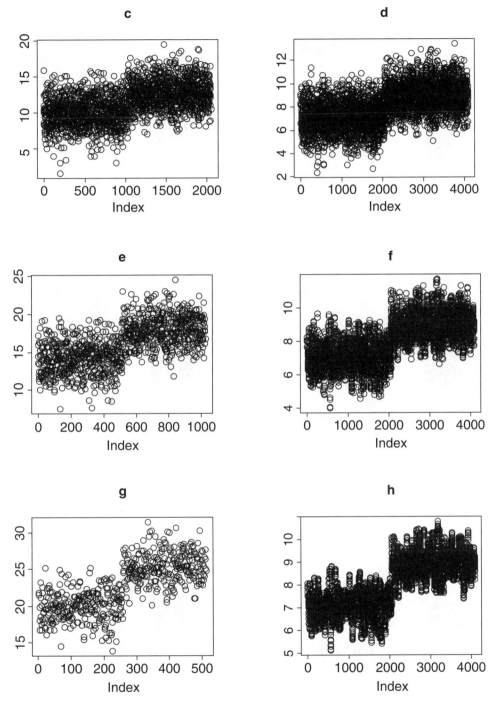

Figure 10.2c–h   (c) first scale DWTBC, (d) first scale MRABC (e) second scale DWTBC, (f) second scale MRABC, (g) third scale DWTBC, (h) third scale MRABC

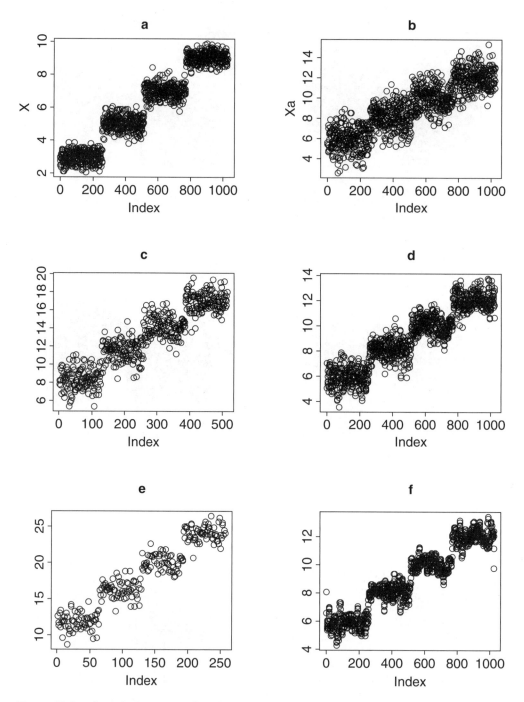

Figure 10.3a–f   *(a) data set with 4 clusters (1024 obs.), (b) the data set with normal noise, (c) first scale DWTBC, (d) first scale MRABC, (e) second scale DWTBC, (f) second scale MRABC*

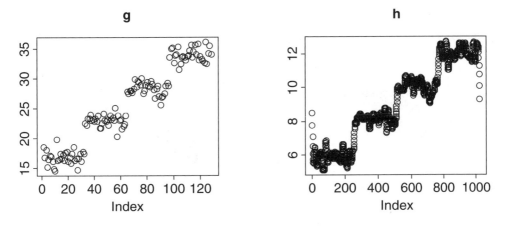

Figure 10.3g–h   (g) third scale DWTBC, (h) third scale MRABC

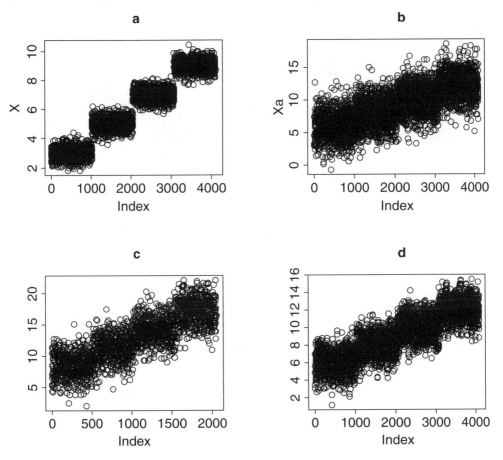

Figure 10.4a–d   (a) data set with 4 clusters (4096 obs.), (b) the data set with normal noise, (c) first scale DWTBC, (d) first scale MRABC

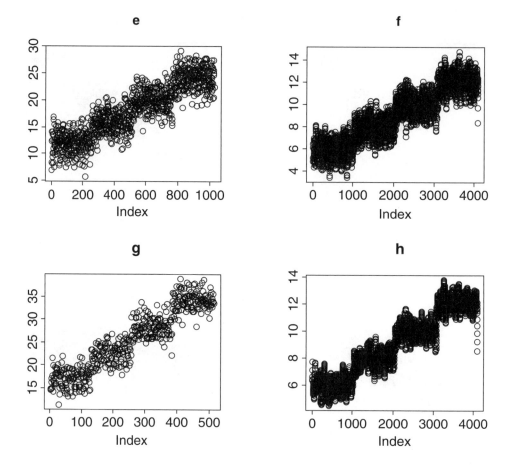

*Figure 10.4e–h   (e) second scale DWTBC, (f) second scale MRABC, (g) third scale
DWTBC, (h) third scale MRABC*

clustering in detecting them. Figures 10.3 and 10.4 show the data and the results for
sample sizes equal to 1024 and 4096 observations, respectively.

In addition to the normal noise, we also imposed a poisson and lognormal noises to check
the robustness of the clustering process. The poisson noise is with mean equal to 6 and the
lognormal noise whose logarithm has mean equal to 0 and standard deviation equal to 1.
The DWT clustering results at scale three for these two noises (added to the data sets in
Figure 10.1a) are shown in Figure 10.5. In the poisson noise case, the results have been
shown to be very similar to the normal noise. In the lognormal case, however, we might need
some handling like using wavelet shrinkage method: see Donoho and Johnstone (1994).

Moreover, we apply the same algorithm to two-dimensional data by using two-
dimensional DWT and MRA. This example consists of two dimensional images (1024 ×
2) that have two columns; each column has two clusters, and they have the normal distribution. The image has two clusters which can be shown in Figure 10.6a. In Figure 10.6b

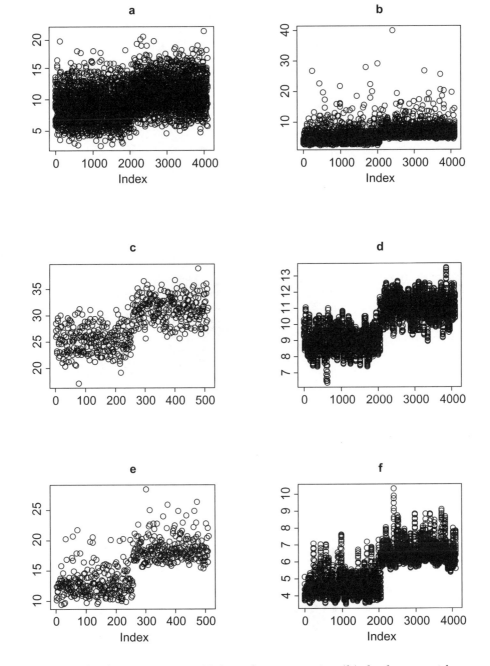

Figure 10.5   *(a) the data set in Figure 10.1a with poisson noise, (b) the data set with lognormal noise, (c) third scale DWTBC of a, (d) third scale MRABC of a, (e) third scale DWTBC of b, (f) third scale MRABC of b*

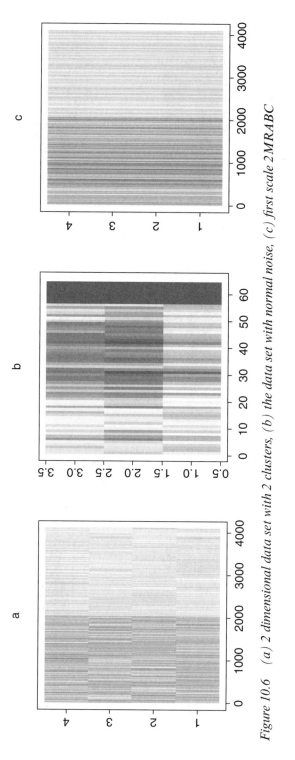

Figure 10.6   (a) 2 dimensional data set with 2 clusters, (b) the data set with normal noise, (c) first scale 2MRABC

we have the original image with additive normal noise with means (3, 5); and with standard deviations (0.40, 0.40), respectively. From Figure 10.6c, we can see that the wavelet algorithm can easily detect the two clusters in this two-dimensional data set.

From our results, we can conclude that the wavelet algorithm can successfully and effectively reveal the clusters in the data both in the case of one-dimensional data sets (with different sample sizes, different numbers of clusters and different noises) and the two-dimensional data sets.

4   Concluding remarks

The goal of cluster analysis is to partition the observations into clusters so that the pairwise dissimilarities between those observations assigned to the same cluster tend to be smaller than those in different clusters. Discriminative and model-based clustering are two main categories into which clustering approaches can be classified. Each has its own advantages and disadvantages regarding, e.g., detecting the correct number of clusters, measurement error in the dissimilarities and sensitivity to outliners, requiring the number of clusters before the analysis.

In this chapter we introduce another clustering approach based on the discrete wavelet transform (DWT) which satisfies the requirements that other clustering methods do not satisfy and is more efficient and easy to apply using standard statistical computer packages like R and S+. Moreover, the approach can easily be applied to large data sets and it can also be generalized to be applicable to higher dimension data. Under these conditions other clustering methods are either inapplicable or inefficient.

The wavelet methodology has previously been used in many fields, such as signal processing, image analysis, geophysics, atmospheric sciences, geology, climatology and time series econometrics.

To demonstrate our approach, a number of artificial examples have been conducted under different situations where the sample size, the noise imposed on the data and the number of clusters have been varied. These examples have shown the effectiveness of the DWT clustering approach in detecting the correct number of clusters.

References

Almasri, A. and G. Shukur (2003), 'An illustration of the causality relation between government spending and revenue using wavelets analysis on Finnish Data', *Journal of Applied Statistics*, **30**, 571–84.

Chave, J. and S. Levin (2003), 'Scale and scaling in ecological and economic systems', *Environmental and Resource Economics*, **26**, 527–57.

Daubechies, I. (1992), *Ten Lectures on Wavelets*, Philadelphia, PA: SIAM.

Donoho, D.L. and I.M. Johnstone (1994), 'Ideal spatial adaption via wavelet shrinkage', *Biometrika*, **81**, 425–55.

Fraley, C. and A.E. Raftery (2002), 'Model based clustering, discriminant analysis, and density estimation', *Journal of the American Statistical Association*, **97**(458), 611–31.

Kohonen, T. (2001), *Self Organising Maps*, Heidelberg: Springer Verlag.

MacQueen, J. (1967), 'Some methods for classification and analysis of multivariate observations', in L.M.L. Cam and J. Neyman (eds), *Proceedings of the 5th Berkeley Symposium on Mathematical Statistics and Probability*, Vol. 1, Berkeley, CA: University of California Press, pp. 281–97.

Mallat, S. (1989), 'A theory for multiresolution signal decomposition: the wavelet representation', *IEEE Transactions on Pattern Analysis and Machine Intelligence*, **11**, 674–93.

Morehart, M., F. Murtagh and J. Starck (1999), 'Multiresolution spatial analysis', *Proceedings GeoComp 99*, (http://www.geovista.psu.edu/sites/geocomp99/Gc99/088/gc_088.htm).

Nason, G.P. and B.W. Silverman (1995), 'The stationary wavelet transform and some statistical applications', in A. Antoniadis and G. Oppenheim (eds), *Lecture Notes in Statistics*, 103, New York: Springer Verlag, pp. 281–300.

Ogden, R.T. (1997), *Essential Wavelets for Statistical Applications and Data Analysis'*, Boston, MA: Birkhuser.

Oh, M-S. and A.E. Raftery (2003), 'Model based clustering with dissimilarities: a Bayesian approach', *Technical Report*, no. 441, Department of Statistics, University of Washington.

Percival, D.B. and A.T. Walden (2000), *Wavelet Methods for Time Series Analysis*, Cambridge, UK: Cambridge University Press.

Ramsey, J.B. and C. Lampart (1998), 'Decomposition of economic relationships by timescale using wavelets, money and income', *Macroeconomic Dynamics*, **2**, 49–71.

Tryon, R. (1939), *Cluster Analysis*, Ann Arbor, MI: Edwards Brothers.

Vu, T.T. and M. Tokunaga (2001), 'Wavelet and scale–space theory in segmentation of airborne laser scanner data', *Proceedings of the 22nd Asian Conference on Remote Sensing*, 176–80, November, Singapore.

PART THREE

CLUSTERS IN DIFFERENT
SPATIAL CONTEXTS

11 Industrial districts: theoretical and empirical insights
Giulio Cainelli

1 Introduction

Since the 1980s, Italian industrial districts (IDs) have received increasing attention from both academic research and policy makers. Following the pioneering contributions of Becattini (1989, 1990, 1998), Brusco (1982), Brusco et al. (1996), Brusco and Paba (1997), Bellandi (1982) and Dei Ottati (1994, 1996), a great number of studies have focused on this topic (Bagella & Becchetti, 2000; Belussi & Gottardi, 2000; Belussi et al., 2003; Cainelli & Zoboli, 2004; Guerrieri et al., 2001; Paniccia, 1998, 2002; Rabellotti, 1995, 1998; Quadrio Curzio & Fortis, 2002; Viesti, 2000). Also Italian institutions such as the National Statistical Institute (ISTAT) and the Bank of Italy have conducted in-depth investigations of various aspects of these production structures (ISTAT, 1995; Bank of Italy, 1999; Signorini, 2000).

Significant efforts, at the different levels of government, have been undertaken to define and implement specific industrial policies for IDs in Italy. The most important of these resulted in national law no. 317 of 1991; the most recent examples are the norms introduced in the 2005 Budget Law. Although the feasibility of legally defining IDs based on statistical criteria developed by ISTAT[1] has been widely debated – and on which the above-mentioned law which institutionalized IDs has had little impact – the policy process is indicative of the importance of IDs for the Italian economy. In our view, there are two reasons for this increasing interest in IDs in Italy. Initially, and particularly during the 1970s, the interest in IDs was mainly stimulated by attempts to define the model as an 'alternative' form of industrial organization to Fordism-Taylorism. Research by international scholars (Piore & Sabel, 1984; Storper, 1989; Best, 1990; van Dijk, 1995), focused on IDs as a specific 'model of capitalism' based on strong spatial interaction between three different dimensions: (i) the productive dimension, as represented by the local system of small and medium-sized enterprises (SMEs) or micro-firms; (ii) the social dimension, as represented by the 'local community' with its specific 'identity' based on cultural, historical and social values; and (iii) the institutional dimension, as represented by local authorities and by a wide range of 'intermediate' (private and public) institutions (Arrighetti & Seravalli, 1999). Therefore, IDs became a model of local capitalism in which knowledge spillovers and intangible assets, such as trust and, a sense of belonging, which became a kind of 'social capital', played a fundamental role in fostering socio-economic development at the local level.

Later, in the 1980s up to the mid-1990s, interest was mainly motivated by the features of IDs, based on which helped to explain some of the 'anomalies' that characterized patterns of industrial development and international competitiveness in the Italian economy. The attempt to explain why Italian manufacturing industry was able to achieve significant growth performance, despite the dominance of SMEs in those industries classified as 'traditional' which were allegedly poor innovators, found some resonances in the peculiarities of IDs. Potential explanations, although at times exaggerated and unduly idealized, focused on the merits of 'small size', the roles of incremental innovations and tacit knowledge and the role of historical and social specificities in determining the competitive advantage of IDs.

One of the results of this lengthy process, and the accompanying debate at the academic and policy-making levels, was the crystallization of the 'district paradigm' based on an organizational model with a significant abstract component. In other words, a picture that is 'realistic' for only a small number of Italian IDs: for instance, the extensively-studied case of Prato's textile ID (Signorini, 2000). Within this idealized conception of IDs, research interest has been on analysis of the organizational structure of IDs and examination of the nature of the relationships between district firms within a generally static framework.

The shortcomings of this idealized concept in accounting for the actual working and evolution of IDs has become obvious and, from the second half of the 1990s, the debate on the 'nature' and the dynamics of this form of industrial organization has been reopened. Research that departs from the 'canonical' view of IDs includes Carbonara (2002), Ferrucci and Varaldo (1993, 2004), Balloni and Iacobucci (1997, 2004), Brioschi et al. (2002, 2004), Iacobucci (2004) and Cainelli et al. (2006) among many others. Central to these contributions is the focus on the necessity, using different methodological approaches, to study the actual process of change that is occurring in Italian IDs and compare it to the traditional model. According to this strand of literature, attention is placed, not on the ID as a static organizational form, but on the process of change and adaptation that occurs within it, with particular emphasis on firms and their strategic behaviour. Although firms in IDs can benefit from the 'systematic' positive influences of the ID itself ('Marshallian' externalities, knowledge spillovers, interaction with social and local cultural values, etc.) these studies assume that the key role is their ability to adapt, respond to and guide the change process. In other words, the role of and the strategic choices made by firms in IDs is acknowledged.

In line with this 'new' approach, this contribution aims to assess whether the so-called 'traditional model' of an ID is still a valid theoretical framework for interpreting the changes, and the evolution that have recently occurred in Italian IDs. The notion of IDs generally employed in the traditional Italian literature highlights three aspects of this form of production organization: (i) high degree of (informal) coordination with little (if any) ownership integration; (ii) low level of innovativeness; and (iii) prevalence of system effects over the strategic decisions made by individual firms. Recent contributions on corporate groupings and technological innovation have questioned these characteristics of Italian IDs, thus reopening the debate about the 'nature' of and the mechanisms behind the functioning of these productive structures. In other words, these studies have questioned the ability of the traditional ID model to account for the evolution that occurred in these forms of production organizations during the 1990s.

The purpose of this chapter is to review and discuss these recent contributions, comparing their results with those from the traditional model. We examine two different aspects of this research stream in particular. The first concerns the widely analysed phenomenon of corporate grouping within IDs. Analyses of the presence and characteristics of business groups within IDs have opened up the question of how corporate grouping processes actually change the structure and the internal organization of IDs. According to this line of research, the presence of business groups, defined as sets of firms that are legally distinct but are owned and controlled by the same owner(s),[2] can change the internal organization and the governance structure of IDs through its effects on degree of industrial concentration and 'hierarchization' of these local production systems. The second aspect we are interested in involves the relationships between technological innovation and IDs. We review some recent analyses of the nature and characteristics of the innovative processes within IDs, with particular emphasis on product innovations. It should be noted that we do not analyse the 'direct' connection between these two dimensions of an ID, which, despite its relevance, has been rather neglected in the literature on IDs.

The chapter is organized as follows. In the second section we describe the main characteristics of the so-called 'traditional' ID model. The third section analyses the recent literature on the presence and the characteristics of business groups in IDs and how they affect the structure and the governance of these production structures. The fourth section investigates the relationships between technological innovation and IDs.

2 The 'traditional' ID model

The concept of ID dates back to Marshall's (1920) work. In the late 1970s and the 1980s, Becattini (1989) and Brusco (1982) 'revisited' the original Marshallian concept, in an effort to explain the anomalous socioeconomic development in the Third Italy.[3] Although there is no universally accepted notion of an ID, a definition of the 'canonical' Italian ID model that would be acceptable to most scholars is 'a territorial agglomeration of small firms, normally specialized in one product or phase of production, held together by interpersonal relationships, by the common social culture of workers, entrepreneurs and politicians surrounded by an industrial atmosphere which facilitates the diffusion of innovation, generating, in this way, important flows of external economies that are still internal to the local productive systems' (Bianchi, 1994, p. 14).

According to this definition, the basic features characterizing an Italian ID can be summarized as (i) firms that generally are quite small, specialized in 'traditional' manufacturing industries such as food, textiles and clothing and localized in bounded geographic areas; (ii) firms that 'compete' or 'cooperate' with other production units in the district: more specifically, 'competition' occurs between firms active in the same stage of the production process, while 'cooperation' tends to take place between firms active in different stages of the production process;[4] (iii) spatial proximity among firms, which tends to stimulate the diffusion of information, (tacit) knowledge, and ideas, the latter two being related to the movement of skilled workers from one district firm to another; and (iv) regional and local institutions and intermediate organizations such as entrepreneurial, artisan and worker associations, etc., all of which play a role. These institutions not only provide real services to firms, they also help broker compromises between the actors operating in the local system.

Accompanying these features of the ID's 'productive' structure, traditional scholars have suggested that these local systems are characterized by an additional dimension: that is, the social. This social dimension emerges from the active presence of both a community of people and a population of firms which share the same social, cultural and political value systems. This value sharing tends to increase the degree of social cohesion between the agents operating in this production system. The effect of this is to lower transaction costs, which fosters cooperation and trust between firms and individuals operating in the district.

Two aspects of the 'traditional' definition of IDs need to be stressed. The first is that this definition differs slightly from that commonly attributed to the tradition based on Marshall (1920). This term, as applied to the Italian case, describes, as we have seen, a somewhat different type of organizational structure. In particular, it indicates 'a higher degree of cooperative coordination than would be present in a Marshallian ID. Product differentiation rather than price is the dominant competitive characteristic. Tacit idiosyncratic knowledge is central to firm performance and competition is limited to certain spheres of activity in which firms might be expected to develop distinctive competencies' (Langlois & Robertson, 1995, p. 125)

Moreover, relations within the ID are deemed not only to be informal, but also to be based on equal rights, thus precluding the possibility of hierarchical relations. Coordination of the activities of different district firms is achieved through market transactions, but nevertheless interactions (including social interactions), based on trust, reputation and cooperation, play a major role (Dei Ottati, 1994). In such a theoretical framework, the ID appears as a production arrangement characterized by a high degree of coordination and little (if any) ownership integration. This model, therefore, rules out any form of ownership integration and thus of hierarchization of the production structure within an ID.

The second aspect, and related strictly to the first, concerns the fact that, according to this traditional 'view', the growth of these local systems takes place as a simple organizational replication of already existing production units, prevailing over the 'system effect' on the strategic choices made by firms. According to this perspective, the internal organization of IDs tends to assume a typical horizontal structure, within which leader firms do not have a role.[5]

3   Business groups and IDs
In this section we analyse two different aspects of the empirical literature on 'district groupification'. The first concerns the presence and the organizational characteristics of business groups within IDs. The second looks at the impact of these processes on the structure and internal organization of these local systems.

3.1   The presence and the characteristics of business groups within IDs
Analysis of the presence and characteristics of business groups in IDs is not new in the ID literature and has been the subject of pioneering works by Dei Ottati (1996), Brusco et al. (1996) and Cainelli and Nuti (1996). Dei Ottati (1996), in her analysis of the main Tuscan IDs, shows that district firms tend to organize themselves into business groups. She identified this tendency as emerging in the early 1970s, though it was not until the 1980s, she maintains, that district firms essentially began to grow 'by the creation of new units . . . and by the acquisition of new companies which were already operational but possibly found themselves in financial difficulties, owing to a lack of orders because of changes in demand' (Dei Ottati, 1996, p. 52). In their analysis of 13 IDs in the Emilia Romagna region, Brusco et al. (1996) suggest that there is a strong tendency in that area for industrial concentration. These authors show, in particular, that this process has been advanced through the creation of business group linkages rather than through mergers

and acquisitions. Finally, Cainelli and Nuti (1996), suggested that these production systems reorganize themselves in hierarchies because predictable relationships between partners can be an effective weapon against unpredictable market relationships, 'prevailing voice over exit' (Whitford, 2001, p. 48).

These contributions shed some light on these phenomena. Unfortunately, none of them was able to 'measure' the extent of business grouping within IDs. Some early attempts in this direction were provided in studies by Balloni and Iacobucci (1997), Bianchi et al. (2001), Brioschi and Cainelli (2001), Brioschi et al. (2002, 2004), which estimated the presence of business groups within some Italian IDs. Discussing the findings of a survey of groups of small firms in the leading IDs of the Marche Region, Balloni and Iacobucci (1997) highlight several interesting features of the group organizational form within IDs: (i) close relationship between the activities of the group firms and those of the 'originator' firm; (ii) growth of groups through formation of new firms engaged in activities similar (especially in the 1970s) or complementary (especially in the 1980s) to those of the originator firm; and (iii) a low degree of separation between ownership and control: the equity held by shareholders outside the controlling core (typically, the family of the founder or the originator) is unlikely to reach 20 per cent. Focusing on IDs in the Emilia Romagna region, Bianchi et al. (2001) and Brioschi and Cainelli (2001) show that 'at least for some industries, the phenomenon of IDs can be traced back not only to the sort of informal links among firms largely highlighted in the literature but also to the presence of formal, equity arrangements' (Bianchi et al., 2001, p. 281, our translation). More specifically, Bianchi et al. (2001), Brioschi and Cainelli (2001) and Brioschi et al. (2002, 2004) analyse the presence and the characteristics of business groups in the main IDs of Emilia Romagna.

As in the other studies referred to above, their work focuses on specific areas, although they express explicit interest in analysing the characteristics of business groups, their role within the district and their evolution over time. In particular, Brioschi et al. (2002, 2004) hypothesize that the presence and characteristics of business groups are influenced by their belonging to an ID. Using an extensive field survey, they identify a specific organizational form of an ID business group: that is, the 'district group'. This group form is composed of a set of firms located within the district area and operating in the district reference industry. This organizational architecture has become pre-eminent in some IDs, for example in Reggio Emilia (agricultural machinery), San Mauro Pascoli (footwear), Parma (food processing), Mirandola (biomedical products) and Carpi (textiles, clothing). Of the 211 groups identified in the field survey, 112 were district groups: that is, business groups comprising manufacturing firms operating in the district reference industry and located within the geographic boundaries of the ID. The interviews that Brioschi et al. (2002) carried out during their field survey revealed the 'specific' motives and thus the factors underlying 'district group' formation. As a result of their deep familiarity with other firms in the district (competitors, suppliers and customers) district entrepreneurs were able to acquire businesses with confidence, secure in their knowledge of their characteristics, with no need for the intermediation of an investment bank. In other words, the mutual familiarity of firms within each district, and the relationships of trust built up between businessmen – which the literature (correctly) considers to be the fundamental element in the very formation and development of an ID (Lazerson & Lorenzoni, 1999) – were decisive factors in many of the corporate finance undertakings of district firms.

However, this stream of empirical research on IDs also has some shortcomings. As already noted, it generally refers to specific IDs in a small number of regions: typically, Marche, Tuscany and Emilia Romagna. For this reason, it is difficult to assess to what extent the results of these studies can be generalized to other Italian IDs. An attempt in this direction was recently undertaken by Cainelli et al. (2006). Taking advantage of a new and large data set on Italian business groups developed by ISTAT, the authors generalize the results of earlier studies to the Italian case, confirming that business groups are generally more widespread in IDs than in non-district areas. Moreover, they show that business groups located in IDs are less diversified and, in some cases, more spatially concentrated than groups outside IDs, thus partially confirming Brioschi and colleague's (2002) hypothesis of the prevalence in IDs of specific types of business groups, which, as already mentioned, they define as 'district groups'.

Consideration of the results developed in this recent empirical literature on Italian IDs suggests that, on the one hand, the agglomerative forces operating in IDs foster the formation of business groups within these production systems, while, on the other hand, they significantly affect their organizational structures. In particular, the high incidence of business groups within Italian IDs can be explained on the basis of the costs to district firms of acquiring information on the characteristics of competitors and/or suppliers. These costs are lower in IDs than in non-district areas, thus favouring acquisitions. Spatial proximity and face-to-face interaction, enabling more rapid circulation and sharing of information among district firms, tend to reduce the cost of acquiring information within these production structures.

The evidence on the organizational specificity of district groups is also interesting and suggests that agglomeration forces operating in IDs are sector-specific, thus confirming the idea that in these production structures knowledge spillovers are of the intra-industry type (Glaeser et al., 1992).

3.2   The impact of business groups on the structure and the governance of IDs

The empirical identification of the 'district group' as a key form of business organization in Italian IDs raises some interesting issues about the (potential) impact of these phenomena on the structure, the (internal) organization, and the governance of these production systems. In fact, as some authors (Brusco et al., 1996; Balloni & Iacobucci, 1997; Brioschi et al., 2002) have shown, the presence of 'district groups' directly affects the internal organization and the governance structure of an ID since it affects the degree of industrial concentration and of hierarchization in these forms of industrial organizations. The prevalence of one or other of these effects on the structure and the governance of IDs depends (according to this empirical evidence) on the type of growth strategy adopted by 'district groups': that is, vertical integration or horizontal diversification. In particular, these writers suggest that, within 'traditional' IDs such as textile-clothing in Carpi or footwear in San Mauro Pascoli seem to result in vertical integration strategies that enable district firms to acquire control over early and/or final stages of the supply chain. This type of strategy is generally adopted by the leader firms in these 'traditional' districts to improve the quality of their products and thus to position them in higher market segments. In this case, 'groupification' produces an increase in the degree of hierarchization of the district via the substitution of the traditional long-run cooperative relationships between subcontractors and final firms – aptly described in the literature on IDs (Brusco, 1982) – with ownership relationships which are, by definition, more hier-archical.

By contrast, in the IDs of Bologna (packaging machinery) and Modena-Reggio Emilia (farm machinery), where groups mainly adopt a strategy of horizontal diversification, dis-trict firms belonging to a group aim to differentiate their business, completing the product range and exploiting the synergies between different business areas. In this case, the overall outcome of 'groupification' seems to be an increase in the level of industrial concen-tration. Thus, district group growth takes place through the processes of horizontal differentiation and/or vertical integration, which affect both the degree of industrial con-centration and the hierarchization of the district. It should be noted that it is not easy to quantify empirically the impact of these processes on the structure, the internal organ-ization and the evolution of these local production systems, for two reasons. The first is that comparisons with the past are quite difficult since information on these phenomena are not generally available for previous years; and second, there is currently no theoreti-cal underpinning for these phenomena.

4   Technological innovation and IDs

A common criticism in the debate over Italian IDs is their low level of innovativeness. The assumption is that, since Italian district firms are generally specialized in 'traditional' industries such as textiles, footwear, food, etc., their innovative performance, measured in terms of input and/or output indicators, is generally modest. Since the mid-1980s, a number of important contributions (Bellandi, 1989, 1996; Pontarollo & Martini, 1990) has challenged this view; that is, the limited ability of IDS to produce innovations, by stressing the extensive role of formal and informal processes of innovation associated with Marshallian and agglomeration economies, and the importance of learning by doing and by using, all of which can be said to explain the otherwise perplexing good perfor-mance of these local systems. For example, Bellandi (1989, 1996) shows how spatial agglomeration of district firms producing the same products tends to generate rapid diffusion of innovation, through mehcanisms of learning by using and by doing. Along similar lines, Pontarollo and Martini (1990) stress the relevance in IDs of the innovative push, intended as a continuous evolutionary process generated by the accumulation of knowledge and accompanied by the continuous upgrading of the machinery utilized in the production process.

In the second half of the 1990s, innovation activity in IDs received renewed interest, generally coinciding with the growing attention to the geographic dimension of innova-tion and its spatial determinants. This strand of literature includes studies of the possible interactions between innovative activity and spatial agglomeration of production (see Maillat et al., (1994); Maillat et al., (1995); Maillat (1996); Baptista and Swann (1998); Beaudry and Breschi (2000); Oerlemans et al. (2001); Cooke (2001, 2004); Smith et al. (2002). These works, using different (theoretical and empirical) approaches, have shown that firms located in IDs (or clusters), show a greater propensity for innovation than firms located outside these production systems. In particular, based on a sample of 248 British firms, Baptista and Swann (1998) showed that innovative activities, measured by the numbers of innovations achieved between 1975 and 1982, are significantly greater for firms located within clusters. Similar, albeit not completely convergent, results were achieved by Beaudry and Breschi (2000), who analysed a large sample of Italian and

British firms in the period 1988 to 1998. More recently, Cainelli et al. (2001) and Cainelli and De Liso (2005), using a sample of Italian manufacturing firms operating in 'traditional' industries, showed that belonging to an ID has a generally positive effect on innovative performance and thus on productivity growth. More specifically, Cainelli and De Liso (2005), using a panel of 1218 district and non-district firms in traditional industries, over the period 1992–95, show that Italian manufacturing firms belonging to Marshallian industrial districts engaged in much greater innovative effort than is generally acknowledged. Their estimates make it possible to identify empirically three different determinants of firms' productivity: (i) intentional innovative activity; (ii) the 'district effect'; and (iii) the joint district and innovation effect. Cainelli and De Liso's results show that firms' membership in an industrial district, their product innovations and their interaction are key factors explaining the productivity of firms in Italy's traditional sectors. Cainelli (2003) confirms these results. Using a sample of 2821 firms operating in the Italian manufacturing industry during the same period (1992–95) and adopting the same empirical framework,[6] he found that membership in IDs and product innovations were key factors in explaining firms' productivity growth. Moreover, he found that product innovations were more frequent in IDs.

All these studies suggest the specific role of product innovation within the innovative process of IDs. In order to interpret these findings, and particularly the relationship between IDs and product innovations, and following the most recent contributions in this field, it is useful to analyse these phenomena by distinguishing between 'supply' and 'demand' factors in IDs (Baptista & Swann, 1998).[7]

We start with the 'supply' factors. In contrast to what is generally assumed by the traditional literature on IDs, the crucial ID supply-side factor is the competitive rather than the cooperative element. This has also been termed the 'rivalry factor' among district firms. Indeed, Malmberg and Power (2003, p. 6) note:

> rivalry between similar firms in a local milieu will be more intensive, almost emotional, and this will create a pressure to innovate in order to outsmart the local rival. In part, this is related to the fact that co-located firms are more visible to each other, and thus that observation, monitoring and benchmarking is thereby easier and more efficient. Therefore, firms with nearby rivals will be more innovative than firms who have their main competitors located elsewhere.[8]

In addition, as suggested by Malmberg and Maskell (2002, p. 11),

> spatial proximity brings with it the special feature of spontaneous, automatic observation. Just as people in a residential area simply cannot help noticing what their nearest neighbours do (regrettably, many would say), business firms often have remarkably good knowledge of the undertakings of nearby firms even if they do not make any dedicated efforts in systematic monitoring. If these neighbouring firms are in the similar business, it is the more likely that the observing firms will understand, and learn from, what it sees.

For these reasons, in these production systems, relationships among firms are characterized by strong rivalries: because firms know their rivals, they constantly monitor each other's activities (including innovative activities). This rivalry leads, as recent contributions (Porter, 1998; Boari et al., 2003) have suggested, to a greater innovative effort, thereby producing efficiency. The easy observation of rival firms, thanks to physical proximity and familiarity with them, tends to favour imitation processes and spillovers of the most visible components of innovative activity in the district firms: that is, improvements to existing products and/or the introduction of new products. Rivalry is therefore (in our opinion) at the root of the phenomena identified by this new strand of empirical literature on IDs. However, it must be noted that, even if the emphasis of these contributions is on local rivalry, the role of cooperation in enhancing a district firm's performance must not be ruled out. In fact, as already mentioned, while competition, and thus local rivalry, take place between firms operating at the same stage in the production process (the so-called 'horizontal dimension' of the ID), cooperation occurs between production units operating in different stages of the production process (or the so-called 'vertical dimension' of the district). In other words, in this production arrangement, the role of vertical relationships between firms – that is, the role of cooperation – continues to be crucial in determining the techno-economic performance of individual firms and thus of the whole production system.[9]

In terms of the 'demand' side, the crucial element here seems to be market segmentation, and the need for district firms – most of which are specialized in traditional or in specialized supplier industries – to position themselves upmarket in order to avoid competition from foreign producers which could benefit from lower labour costs. This process, which can have a significant impact on performance, is implemented by firms through the adoption of innovative strategies based on product innovations. Improvements in quality, design, appearance and so forth are a strategic option of fundamental importance for district firms. These improvements allow them to differentiate themselves from rival firms and thus gain market share. At this point, the diffusion/imitation mechanisms (local rivalry) and the vertical relationships between firms (cooperation) operating on the supply side tend to diffuse into the ID those products that are most successful on the market.

5 Conclusions

In this chapter we have reviewed and discussed some recent studies in the recent empirical literature on Italian IDs. Particular emphasis was given to two aspects of this debate that we believe to be relevant to an understanding of the recent evolution in Italian IDs: that is, the role and the characteristics of district groups, and the nature and the characteristics of technological innovation within these production structures. With regard to the first issue, we discussed recent findings which show that business groups are generally more widespread in district than in non-district areas and they are generally characterized by a specific organizational form: namely, the district group. These phenomena are generally acknowledged as being relevant since they directly affect the structure, the internal organization and the governance of Italian IDs, thus producing hierarchization and industrial concentration. The second issue concerns the nature of technological innovation within IDs. We debated the role of product innovation within these production structures. In fact, some features of IDs, such as spatial proximity, local rivalry and easy observation of rival firms, tend to favour imitation processes and spillovers of the more visible components of the innovative activities of district firms: that is, the upgrading of existing products and/or the introduction of new products. Finally, it should be noted that it is quite likely that there is a strong connection between these two phenomena in IDs: (i) presence and characteristics of business groups and (ii) technological innovation. In fact, 'indirect' evidence seems to suggest that belonging to a group tends to enhance a firm's innovative performance. Further analysis of these phenomena should await evidence from direct investigations.

To sum up, these results have some interesting theoretical implications for the international debate on Italian IDs. The first concerns the concept of ID. We showed that the notion of ID employed in the 'traditional' Italian literature is slightly different from that commonly attributed to Marshall (1920). Within the traditional view, the ID is a production arrangement characterized by a high degree of coordination and little (if any) ownership integration. The emergence of organizational forms based on ownership linkages is altering these traditional arrangements, which are at the basis of the traditional model, gradually replacing the old mechanisms of competition and cooperation with others based on more formal and stable relations.

A second implication, strictly related to the first, relates the debate on the prevalence of the systemic nature of the district or of the centrality of the single firm as the unit of analysis. In the Italian ID literature two different approaches have been developed: a system-centred view and a firm-centred view.[10] Behind the first approach is the idea that the district works as a complex evolutionary system, in which integration between firms is mainly achieved by means of a mix of automatic mechanisms based on market competition between firms involved in the same stage of the production process and cooperative behaviours between firms belonging to different stages of the *filière*. In this perspective, mainly developed by Becattini and Brusco, little room is left for the strategic behaviour of firms. Recently, Ferrucci and Varaldo (1993, 2004) proposed an alternative approach to analysing the pattern of evolution of IDs. They suggest that the appropriate unit of analysis of a district is the district firm and that the strategic behaviour of district firms is the key variable in an analysis of an industrial district and its pattern of evolution. The recent literature on IDs, reviewed here, which emphasizes the role of business strategies and hence the strategic behaviour of 'district groups' in the process of evolution and transformation of an ID, seems to support this second approach. This does not mean that the ID as a system does not matter. On the contrary, the ID promotes a favourable environment stimulating the formation and development of 'district groups'.

The third point concerns the role of product innovations. The problem here is that a unifying theory capable of explaining the conditions under which an ID can be innovative and the kind of innovations that may be engendered by the action of agglomerative forces, does not exist. Thus, identification of a strong empirical link between product innovations and clustering and, more generally, spatial agglomeration, needs further theoretical and empirical investigation.

We conclude by highlighting some implications for policy from these new research perspectives on IDs. With regard to corporate grouping, it would be useful to start from the actual experience of industrial policy in an Italian region such as Emilia Romagna. It is well known that regional policy makers generally have the ID as the reference organizational model when designing industrial policy.[11] The findings in this chapter show that the small legal size of individual firms in these IDs is only one of the variables that must be considered in the design of industrial policy programmes. The high level of corporate grouping certainly suggests that firm ownership is concentrated in a small number of controlling owners. One possible implication of this is that the fragmentation of organically unified enterprises into a large number of legally independent firms may result in the concentration of policy benefits on a smaller number of beneficiaries. In addition, as legal size is often an essential factor in determining eligibility for a given benefit, the 'district group' form may allow circumvention of size ceilings. That is, corporate grouping within IDs could distort the allocation of public resources within a district to the disadvantage of small independent firms.

In terms of innovation policies, in Italy they have in the past been largely based on the idea that the innovativeness of IDs was attributable to informal phenomena such as 'unintentional' knowledge spillovers and 'simple' imitation. The results of this new strand of empirical literature indicate that policies aimed at stimulating IDs should also take into account the role played by intentional product innovation, which, in our opinion, is what would make industrial policy much more effective.

Acknowledgements
I thank three anonymous referees for comments and suggestions on a previous version of this chapter, which substantially improved the work. I also want to thank Professor Karlsson for giving me the opportunity to contribute to this Handbook, and Ulla Forslund Johansson for her patience and courtesy.

Notes
1. ISTAT's statistical definition of IDs is based on what is known as the Sforzi-ISTAT methodology (ISTAT, 1997). Within this definition 156 Italian IDs can be identified based on information on commuting taken from the 2001 Population Census. This statistical procedure comprises two steps. First, the national territory is divided into 686 Local Labour Systems (LLS) which are made up of groups of contiguous municipalities characterized by a high degree of commuting to work. Second, it defines IDs as those LLS that satisfy the following requirements: (i) percentage of manufacturing employees compared to total non-agricultural workers higher than the national average; (ii) specialization in one particular manufacturing industry; (iii) percentage of employees in firms employing fewer than 250 employees is higher than the national average (ISTAT, 1997). This results in 156 IDs. These 156 'official' IDs include 212, 410 production units, and 1.9 m. manufacturing employees. It is estimated that some 43 per cent of total Italian exports come from IDs – mainly specialized in food (7 IDs), textiles and clothing (45 IDs), leather and footwear (20 IDs), furniture (32 IDs), mechanics (38 IDs) and other industries (14 IDs).
2. It is worth noting that this is not the only definition of a business group. The main differences lie in the 'nature' of the relationships between the units comprising the group, the most important distinctions being between ownership and non-ownership links. In the case of ownership, belonging to a group is determined by a majority share – or a stake large enough to secure control – in the hands of one owner. In the case of non-ownership links, the literature proposes several forms of stable connections through which a business group can be identified: subcontracting, franchising, alliances, etc. In general, the economics literature stresses ownership ties, while the sociological literature emphasizes the importance of non-ownership ties also (Granovetter, 1994). Besides the notion of business groups, the literature also refers to 'interfirm networks'. Although the two terms are often used interchangeably, they differ in an important way. When talking about ownership ties, the commonly used term is 'business groups'; when referring to non-ownership links, the term generally used is 'interfirm network'.
3. The first contribution to the empirical literature on Italian IDs was the IRPET (1969) study entitled '*Lo Sviluppo Economico della Toscana. Un'ipotesi di Lavoro*'. In this study, the notion of ID was extensively used to investigate empirically the characteristics and determinants of economic development in the Tuscany region.
4. These two mechanisms, underlining the relationships between district firms, identify what has generally been defined as the competitive–cooperative 'nature' of the ID.
5. Some contributions have defined this 'traditional' notion of ID as Mark I (Amin, 2000; Brusco, 1992). These authors describe a typology of ID as a form of production organization 'in which the small firms have come to be surrounded by more formalized institutional support, as well as increased capacity for technological innovation among some firms . . . Innovative firms include so-called network leader firms within the districts, usually medium-sized companies, which have emerged in technology or research-intensive industries with high levels of customized demand (e.g. agromachinery, biomedical instruments). They subcontract products and tasks to other much smaller specialized firms, but provide the managerial, commercial and technological expertise that takes the district forward into international markets driven by advancement in science and technology. Thus, Mark II industrial districts are less dependent on informal

Marshallian traditions and craft institutions' (Amin, 2000, p. 159). In other words, this typology of ID (Mark II) is characterized by more technological innovation and change with respect to the traditional 'static' model (Mark I). See also, on this topic, Garafoli (1991) and Asheim (1995).

6. An 'augmented' Cobb–Douglas production function to account for the impact of innovative activity and agglomeration effects on firms' productivity growth.
7. It must be underlined that, generally, the literature on IDs has suggested that, typically, in these production structures technological change takes the form of 'incremental' rather than 'radical' innovations. In our opinion, it is not easy in the case of product innovations to distinguish between these two. In most cases, the distinction between the upgrading of existing products and the introduction of completely new products is difficult to detect. For this reason, we do not adopt this perspective in our analysis.
8. Also Porter (1998, p. 83) suggests that 'local rivalry is highly motivating. Peer pressure amplifies competitive pressure within a cluster, even among non-competing or indirectly competing companies. . . . Clusters also often make it easier to measure and compare performances because local rivals share general circumstances – for example, labour costs and local market access – and they perform similar activities. Companies within clusters typically have intimate knowledge of their suppliers' costs. Managers are able to compare costs and employees' performance with other local companies'.
9. Besides cooperation, the role of external linkages in enhancing technological innovations within IDs must be considered. In fact, some studies have shown that, in some IDs, leading firms absorb external knowledge and have demonstrated how this process affects their innovative activities: see, for example, Boschma and ter Wal (2006) and Morrison (2004).
10. See Whitford (2001) for an extensive description of the two approaches.
11. Consider, for instance, the ERVET system centres, conceived from the outset as centres to support small businesses with the provision of real services (Bellini et al., 1990; Mazzonis, 1996)

References

Amin, A. (2000), 'Industrial districts', in E. Sheppard and T.J. Barnes (eds), *A Companion to Economic Geography*, Oxford: Blackwell Publishing.

Arrighetti, A. and G. Seravalli (eds) (1999), *Istituzioni Intermedie e Sviluppo Locale*, Rome: Donzelli Editore.

Asheim, B. (1995), 'Industrial districts as "learning regions". A condition for prosperity?', *STEP report, R-03*, Oslo.

Bagella, M. and L. Becchetti (eds) (2000), *The Competitive Advantage of Industrial Districts. Theoretical and empirical analysis*, Heidelberg: Physica-Verlag.

Balloni, V. and D. Iacobucci (1997), 'Cambiamenti in atto nell'organizzazione dell'industria Marchigiana', *Economia Marche*, vol.16, n.1.

Balloni, V. and D. Iacobucci (2004), 'The role of medium-sized and large firms in the evolution of industrial districts. The case of Marche', in G. Cainelli and R. Zoboli (eds), *The Evolution of Industrial Districts. Changing Governance, Innovation and Internationalisation of Local Capitalism in Italy*, Heidelberg: Physica-Verlag.

Bank of Italy (1999), *Considerazioni Finali*, Assemblea Generale Ordinaria dei Partecipanti, 31 May 1998, Rome.

Baptista, R. and P. Swann (1998), 'Do firms in clusters innovate more?', *Research Policy*, **27**(5), 525–40.

Beaudry, C. and S. Breschi (2000), 'Does clustering really help firms' innovative activities?', *Working Paper 111*, CESPRI, Bocconi University, Milan.

Becattini, G. (1989), 'Sectors and/or districts: some remarks on the conceptual foundation of industrial economics', in E. Goodman and J. Bamford (eds), *Small Firms and Industrial Districts in Italy*, London: Routledge.

Becattini, G. (1990), 'The Marshallian industrial district as a socio-economic notion', in F. Pyke, G. Becattini and W. Sengenberger (eds), *Industrial Districts and Inter-firm Co-operation in Italy*, Geneva: International Labour Office (ILO).

Becattini, G. (1998), *Distretti Industriali e Made in Italy: Le Basi Socioculturali del Nostro Sviluppo Economico*, Turin: Bollati Boringhieri.

Bellandi, M. (1982), 'Il distretto industriale in Alfred Marshall', *L'industria*, **3**, 355–75.

Bellandi, M. (1989), 'Capacità innovativa diffusa e sistemi locali di imprese', in G. Becattini (ed.), *Modelli Locali di Sviluppo*, Bologna: Il Mulino.

Bellandi, M. (1996), 'Innovation and change in the Marshallian industrial districts', *European Planning Studies*, **4**(3), 357–68.

Bellini, N., M.G. Giordani and F. Pasquini (1990), 'The industrial Policy of Emilia Romagna: the business service centres', in R. Leopardi and R.Y. Nanetti (eds), *The Regions and European Integration*, London: Frances Pinter.

Belussi, F. and G. Gottardi (eds) (2000), *Evolutionary Patterns of Local Industrial Systems. Towards a Cognitive Approach to the Industrial District*, Aldershot: Ashgate.

Belussi, F., G. Gottardi and E. Rullani (eds) (2003), *The Technological Evolution of Industrial Districts*, Boston: Kluwer Academic Publisher.

Best, M. (1990), *The New Competition: Institutions and Industrial Restructuring*, Cambridge: Harvard University Press.

Bianchi, G. (1994), 'Tre e più Italie: Sistemi Territoriali di Piccola Impresa e Transizione Post-Industriale', in F. Bortolotti (ed.), *Il Mosaico e il Progetto: Lavoro, Imprese, Regolazione nei Distretti Industriali della Toscana*, Milan: Franco Angeli.

Bianchi, R., M.S. Brioschi and G. Cainelli (2001), 'Gruppi di Imprese e Distretti Industriali in Emilia Romagna', in V. Balloni (ed.), *Piccole e Grandi Imprese Nell'attuale Contesto Competitivo*, Turin: Giappichelli Editore.

Boari, C., V. Odorici and M. Zamarian (2003), 'Clusters and rivalry: does localisation really matter?', *Scandinavian Journal of Management*, **19**(4), 467–89.

Boschma, R.A. and L.J. ter Wal (2006), 'Knowledge network and innovative performance in an industrial district. The case of a footwear district in the South of Italy', *Industry and Innovation*, **14**(2), 177–99.

Brioschi, F. and G. Cainelli (eds) (2001), *Diffusione e Caratteristiche dei Gruppi di Piccole e Medie Imprese nelle Aree Distrettuali*, Milan: Giuffrè Editore.

Brioschi, F., M.S. Brioschi and G. Cainelli (2002), 'From the industrial district to the district group. An insight into the evolution of local capitalism in Italy', *Regional Studies*, **36**(9), 1037–52.

Brioschi, F., M.S. Brioschi and G. Cainelli (2004), 'Ownership linkages and business groups in industrial districts. The case of Emilia Romagna', in G. Cainelli and R. Zoboli (eds), *The Evolution of Industrial Districts. Changing Governance, Innovation and Internationalisation of Local Capitalism in Italy*, Heidelberg: Physica-Verlag.

Brusco, S. (1982), 'The Emilian model: production decentralisation and social integration', *Cambridge Journal of Economics*, **2**(6), 167–84.

Brusco, S. (1992), 'Small firms and the provision of real services', in F. Pyke and W. Sengenberger (eds), *Industrial Districts and Local Economic Regeneration*, Geneva: International Labour Office (ILO).

Brusco, S. and S. Paba (1997), 'Per una Storia dei Distretti Industriali Italiani dal Secondo Dopoguerra agli Anni Novanta', in F. Barca (ed.), *Storia del Capitalismo Italiano dal Dopoguerra ad Oggi*, Rome: Donzelli.

Brusco, S., G. Cainelli, F. Forni, M. Franchi, A. Malusardi and R. Righetti (1996), 'The evolution of industrial districts in Emilia Romagna', in F. Cossentino, F. Pyke and W. Sengenberger (eds), *Local and Regional Response to Global Pressure. The Case of Italy and its Industrial Districts*, Geneva: International Labour Office (ILO).

Cainelli, G. (2003), 'Agglomeration, technological innovations, and productivity. Evidence from the Italian industrial districts', *Dynamis-Quaderni IDSE*, 2/03, Milan.

Cainelli, G. and F. Nuti (1996), 'Directions of change in Italy's manufacturing industrial districts. The case of the Emilian footwear districts of Fusignano and San Mauro Pascoli', *Journal of Industry Studies*, **3**(2), 105–18.

Cainelli, G.and R. Zoboli (eds) (2004), *The Evolution of Industrial Districts. Changing Governance, Innovation and Internationalisation of Local Capitalism in Italy*, Heidelberg: Physica-Verlag.

Cainelli, G. and N. De Liso (2005), 'Innovation in industrial districts: evidence from Italy', *Industry and Innovation*, **12**(3), 383–98.

Cainelli, G., D. Iacobucci and E. Morganti (2006), 'Spatial agglomeration and business groups: new evidence from Italian industrial districts', *Regional Studies*, **40**(5), 507–18.

Cainelli, G., N. De Liso, G. Perani and R. Monducci (2001), 'Technological innovation and firm performance in Italian traditional manufacturing sectors', *Innovation and Enterprise Creation: Statistics and Indicators*, Sophia Antipolis: Eurostat.

Carbonara, N. (2002), 'New models of inter-firm network within industrial districts', *Entrepreneurship and Regional Development*, **14**, 229–46.

Cooke, P. (2001), 'Regional innovation systems, clusters, and the knowledge economy', *Industrial and Corporate Change*, **10**, 945–74.

Cooke, P. (2004), 'Regional innovation systems. An evolutionary approach', in P. Cooke, M. Heidenreich and H. Braczyk (eds), *Regional Innovation Systems. The Role of Governance in a Globalized World*, 2nd edn, London: Routledge.

Dei Ottati, G. (1994), 'Trust, interlinking transactions and credit in the industrial district', *Cambridge Journal of Economics*, **18**(6), 529–46.

Dei Ottati, G. (1996), 'The remarkable resilience of the industrial districts of Tuscany', in F. Cossentino, F. Pyke and E. Sengenberger (eds), *Local and Regional Response to Global Pressure. The Case of Italy and its Industrial Districts*, Geneva: International Labour Office (ILO).

Ferrucci, L. and R. Varaldo (1993), 'La Natura e la Dinamica dell'Impresa Distrettuale', *Economia e Politica Industriale*, **80**, 25–48.

Ferrucci, L. and R. Varaldo (2004), 'Institutional innovations in industrial districts', in G. Cainelli and R. Zoboli (eds), *The Evolution of Industrial Districts. Changing Governance, Innovation and Internationalisation of Local Capitalism in Italy*, Heidelberg: Physica-Verlag.

Garofoli, G. (1991), *Modelli Locali di Sviluppo*, Milan: Franco Angeli.

Glaeser, E., H. Kallal, J. Scheinkaman and A. Schleifer (1992), 'Growth in cities', *Journal of Political Economy*, **100**(6), 1126–52.

Granovetter, M. (1994), 'Business groups', in N.J. Smelser and R. Swedberg (eds), *The Handbook of Economic Sociology*, Princeton: Princeton University Press.

Guerrieri, P., S. Iammarino and C. Pietrobelli (2001), *The Global Challange to Industrial Districts. Small and Medium-sized Enterprises in Italy and Taiwan*, Cheltenham, UK and Northampton, MA, US: Edward Elgar.

Iacobucci, D. (2004), 'Groups of small and medium-sized firms in industrial districts in Italy', in G. Cainelli and R. Zoboli (eds), *The Evolution of Industrial Districts. Changing Governance, Innovation and Internationalisation of Local Capitalism in Italy*, Heidelberg: Physica-Verlag.

IRPET (1969), 'Lo Sviluppo Economico della Toscana. Un'Ipotesi di Lavoro', *Il Ponte*, 11/12.

ISTAT (1995), *Rapporto Annuale. La Situazione del Paese nel 1994*, Rome: Istituto Poligrafico e Zecca dello Stato.

ISTAT (1997), *I Sistemi Locali del Lavoro 1991*, Rome: Istituto Poligrafico e Zecca dello Stato.

Langlois, R.and P.L. Robertson (1995), *Firms, Markets, and Economic Change. A Dynamic Theory of Business Institutions*, London: Routledge.

Lazerson, M. and G. Lorenzoni (1999), 'The firms that feed industrial districts: a return to the Italian source', *Industrial and Corporate Change*, **8**, 235–66.

Maillat, D. (1996), 'From the industrial district to the innovative milieu: contribution to an analysis of territorialized productive organizations', *Working Paper 9606b*, IRER, University of Neuchatel.

Maillat, D., O. Crevoisier and B. Lecoq (1994), 'Innovation networks and territorial dynamics: a tentative typology', in B. Johansson, C. Karlsson and L. Westin (eds), *Patterns of a Network Economy*, Berlin: Springer Verlag.

Maillat, D., B. Lecoq, F. Nemeti and M. Pfister (1995), 'Technology district and innovation: the case of the Swiss Jura arc', *Regional Studies*, **29**(3), 251–63.

Malmberg, A. and P. Maskell (2002), 'The elusive concept of localization economies. Towards a knowledge-based theory of spatial clustering', *Environment and Planning A*, **34**(5), 429–49.

Malmberg, A. and D. Power (2003), '(How) do clusters create knowledge?', DRUID Summer Conference on 'Creating, Sharing And Transferring Knowledge – The Role of Geography, Institutions and Organizations', Copenhagen, Denmark, 12–14 June.

Marshall, A. (1920), *Principles of Economics*, 8th edn, London: Macmillan.

Mazzonis, D. (1996), 'The changing role of Ervet in Emilia Romagna', in F. Cossentino, F. Pyke and E. Sengenberger (eds), *Local and Regional Response to Global Pressure. The Case of Italy and its Industrial Districts*, Geneva: International Labour Office (ILO).

Morrison, A. (2004), 'Gatekeepers of knowledge within industrial districts: who they are, how they interact', *Working Paper 163*, CESPRI, Bocconi University, Milan.

Oerlemans, L., M. Meeus and F. Boekema (2001), 'Firm clustering and innovation: determinants and effects', *Papers in Regional Science*, **80**(3), 337–56.

Paniccia, I. (1998), 'One, a hundred, thousands of industrial districts: organizational variety in local network of small and medium-sized enterprises, *Organization Studies*, **4**(19), 667–99.

Paniccia, I. (2002), *Industrial Districts: Evolution and Competitiveness in Italian Firms*, Cheltenham, UK and Northampton, MA, US: Edward Elgar.

Piore, M.J. and C. Sabel (1984), *The Second Industrial Divide*, New York: Basic Books.

Pontarollo, E. and G. Martini (1990), 'Distretti Industriali e Tessuti Economici Circostanti: il Caso di Como', in F. Gobbo (ed.), *Distretti e Sistemi Produttivi alla Soglia degli Anni '90*, Milan: Franco Angeli.

Porter, M.E. (1998), 'Clusters and the new economics of competition', *Harvard Business Review*, **76**(6), 77–90.

Quadrio Curzio, A. and M. Fortis (eds) (2002), *Complessità e Distretti Industriali. Dinamiche, Modelli e Casi Reali*, Fondazione Montedison 'Comunità e Innovazione', Bologna: Il Mulino.

Rabellotti, R. (1995), 'Is there an "industrial district model"? Footwear districts in Italy and Mexico Compared', *World Development*, **23**(1), 29–41.

Rabellotti, R. (1998), 'Collective effects in Italian and Mexican footwear industrial clusters', *Small Business Economics*, **10**(3), 243–62.

Signorini, L.F. (ed.) (2000), *Lo Sviluppo Locale. Un'Indagine della Banca d'Italia sui Distretti Industriali*, Rome: Donzelli Editore.

Smith, V., A. Broberg and J. Overgaard (2002), 'Does location matter for firms' R&D behaviour? Empirical evidence for Danish firms', *Regional Studies*, **36**(8), 825–32.

Storper, M. (1989), 'The transition to flexible specialization in the US firm industry', *Cambridge Journal of Economics*, **13**(1), 17–32.

van Dijk, M.P. (1995), 'Flexible specialisation, the new competition and industrial districts', *Small Business Economics*, **7**(1), 15–27.

Viesti, G. (2000), *Come Nascono i Distretti Industriali*, Rome-Bari: Editori Laterza.

Whitford, J. (2001), 'The decline of a model? Challenge and response in the Italian industrial districts', *Economy and Society*, **30**(1), 38–65.

12 Cluster renewal in old industrial regions: continuity or radical change?
Michaela Trippl and Franz Tödtling

The aim of this chapter is to explore conceptually the role of clusters for the economic recovery of old industrial regions. We will identify three types of cluster-based renewal, distinguishing between an innovation-oriented adjustment of mature clusters (incremental change), the emergence of new agglomerations in established industries (diversification) and the rise of knowledge-intensive and high-technology activities (radical change). It will be shown that each of these development scenarios for old industrial areas requires different firm strategies, and presupposes varying degrees of changes in the region's knowledge infrastructure, its relational assets and institutional fabric, and its policy environment.

1 Introduction
The aim of this chapter is to deal with the cluster approach in the spatial context of old industrial areas. Clusters are defined here as geographic concentrations of firms specialized in a particular field and horizontally and vertically related companies. While not ignoring the legacy of clusters in mature industries, it will be shown that it has the potential to be a useful concept for the renewal of these regions. We intend to examine critically different kinds of approaches in this respect.

In the past years clusters have become a subject of major interest for scholars in regional studies and in related fields. Much of the ever-growing literature on this topic emphasizes that the spatial concentration of similar or related firms is a key source of competitiveness encouraging innovation and learning on local and regional scales (Porter, 1998; Feldman, 2000; Keeble & Wilkinson, 2000; Cooke, 2002). This one-sided view on the benefits of clusters has recently been criticized by several authors (Martin & Sunley, 2003; Trippl, 2004; Chapman, 2005; Hassink, 2005; Hassink & Shin, 2005) who stress that more attention should be devoted to the possible risk, fallacies and harmful effects of geographically concentrated industries.

Old industrial regions can, in fact, be regarded as a prime example of the negative side of clustering, uncovering the 'failure modes' (Enright, 2003) of a strong spatial concentration of industries in particular regions. Clusters are a main reason why these formerly dynamic and prospering regions have experienced an economic downturn (Cooke, 1995a; Boschma & Lambooy, 1999; Tichy, 2001; Tödtling & Trippl, 2004), challenging the prevailing view that clusters are always and overwhelmingly favourable for regional economic development.

Although we do not neglect this critique, we will argue here that clusters can play a key role for the renewal and recovery of old industrial regions. These areas face the challenge to reposition their economies by promoting a transition towards more knowledge-intensive forms of development. To scrutinize the relationship between clusters and regional renewal constitutes the core theme to be addressed in the following. The principal questions to be dealt with include (a) which types of a cluster-based renewal in old industrialized regions can be distinguished and observed? and (b) what are the preconditions, supporting factors and key mechanisms for each type of regional change?

The remainder of this chapter is organized as follows: Section 2 establishes a theoretical basis for analysing these questions by identifying clusters as a main building block of regional innovation systems. Section 3 provides an overview of the key challenges of old industrial regions, exposing its main socioeconomic problems as a fundamental innovation dilemma. This is followed by an examination of the prospects and conditions for a cluster-based renewal of old industrialized areas, in Section 4. Finally, in Section 5, the key arguments are summarized and conclusions are drawn.

2   Clusters and regional innovation
In order to analyse the problems of old industrial regions and to examine the conditions and critical factors for a recovery of these areas we propose a theoretical framework that highlights the embeddedness of clusters in the innovation setting of the region. From this perspective, clusters are regarded as an integral part of regional innovation systems (RIS). The RIS approach (Autio, 1998; Doloreux, 2002; Cooke et al., 2004) provides a useful conceptual basis for the purpose of this chapter. Figure 12.1 depicts the architecture of a RIS, revealing that clusters represent the key structures of the knowledge application and exploitation subsystem as it includes the industrial companies, their clients, suppliers and

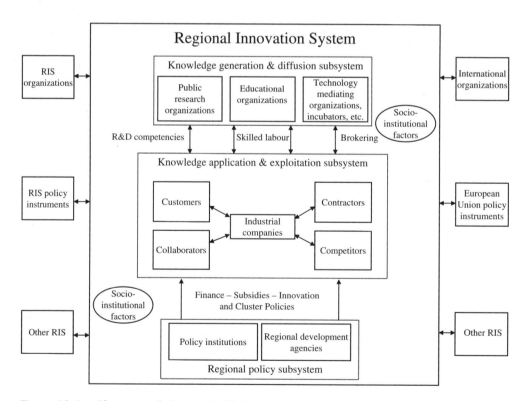

Figure 12.1   Clusters and their embeddedness in regional innovation systems

competitors, as well as their cooperation partners. These firms and clusters are surrounded by a variety of organizations that are specialized in the production of knowledge and skills and in their diffusion and transfer to the business system. The main players here are public research institutes, technology mediating organizations (technology licensing offices, innovation centres, etc.) and educational bodies (universities, polytechnics, vocational training organizations, etc.). These actors constitute the knowledge generation and diffusion subsystem (i.e. the region's knowledge infrastructure). The development of clusters and regions is also influenced by the regional policy system and its innovation and cluster promotion activities. These three subsystems of a RIS are embedded in a common socioinstitutional and cultural setting that is specific for the region. Of key importance in this respect are factors such as dominating patterns of behaviour, values and routines, the prevailing culture of cooperation, or also attitudes towards innovation and technology. Finally, it is important to note that a RIS has various links to national and international actors and innovation systems. These include both the extralocal contacts of regional firms that provide access to ideas, knowledge and technologies, which are not generated within the limited context of the region (Camagni, 1991; Oinas & Malecki, 1999, 2002; Bunnel & Coe, 2001) and policy measures and actions undertaken at the national and European levels that shape the region's development and dynamics (Cooke et al., 2000).

What follows from this perspective is that the development problems of old industrial regions can only be fully understood if the analysis is not confined to the business sector. The activities and orientation within the subsystem of knowledge generation and diffusion, the role of regional policy agencies and the prevailing mode of state intervention as well as the extent and nature of linkages of these subsystems to the business sector and the socio-institutional fabric have also to be taken into consideration.

Linking the analysis of the evolution of clusters and regions to the conceptual framework of RIS also enables us to identify critical conditions for the recovery of old industrial areas. The restructuring of the business sector (i.e. the knowledge application and exploitation subsystem) is only one aspect of such revitalization processes. The key idea that will be proposed below is that a cluster-based renewal of old industrial regions is critically dependent on changes in the other RIS subsystems and the relational and institutional fabric of the region. Consequently, the capacity of the region to transform the whole RIS turns out to be the decisive factor for renewal processes.

3   The innovation dilemma of old industrial areas

After almost three decades of research there exists a vast range of literature on the evolution of old industrial areas, documenting their rise, fall and, occasionally, revitalization in recent years (see, for example, Hamm & Wienert, 1990; Häußermann, 1992; Cooke, 1995a; Chapman et al., 2004; Cooke et al., 2004; Hilbert et al., 2004; Sadler, 2004; Hudson, 2005). As we have argued elsewhere (Tödtling & Trippl, 2005) the development problems of old industrialized regions are strongly related to the fact that these areas suffer from a fundamental innovation dilemma that becomes manifest in a lack of radical innovation. Indeed, many studies have shown that innovation activities in old industrial areas often follow mature technological trajectories and are frequently of an incremental character. Process innovation dominates over systematic efforts to introduce (radically) new products into the market (Tödtling, 1992; Cooke, 1995a; Cooke et al., 2000; Tichy, 2001). We suggest that this diagnosis has to be interpreted against the background of particular deficiencies of the regional innovation system prevailing in these areas (see also Tödtling & Trippl, 2005). The failures of the regional innovation system of old industrial areas have three main sources, including (a) a narrowly specialized and declining industrial base, (b) an overspecialized knowledge infrastructure, and (c) various forms of lock-in.

Several authors have argued that clusters have to be considered as a key reason for the downturn of old industrial areas (Grabher, 1993; Steiner, 1998; Tichy, 1998, 2001; Tödtling & Trippl, 2004; Trippl, 2004). This explanation rests on reflections on the danger of economic monostructures, suggesting that a narrow and specialized economic base could imply that the fate of the whole region is intrinsically tied to that of the cluster. Indeed, there is ample evidence that old industrial regions exhibit a too narrow specialization in mature clusters experiencing decline.

However, it is not only the subsystem of knowledge application and exploitation that hampers regional innovation and learning in old industrial regions. The poor innovation capabilities of these areas are reinforced by some specific characteristics of the knowledge generation and diffusion subsystem. The key point in this context is that this subsystem is often too strongly oriented on the traditional industries and technology fields of the region (Cooke et al., 2000; Kaufmann & Tödtling, 2000). Moreover, in many cases a supply-oriented approach of technology transfer can be identified which reaches traditional and larger firms better than the smaller and young ones (Kaufmann & Tödtling, 2000; Asheim et al., 2003). This holds particularly true for old industrial areas based on heavy industries. The demand of small companies and young firms is often not met adequately and interactive learning is rarely achieved (Asheim et al., 2003).

Finally, there seems to be a widespread agreement in the literature that old industrialized regions are characterized by the existence of different types of lock-ins (Grabher, 1993; Hassink, 2005; Hassink & Shin, 2005). Thus, the focus is on deficiencies of the relational and institutional fabric of regional innovation systems and clusters. Grabher's (1993) often cited elaboration of the concept of lock-in is based on a distinction between functional lock-ins (too strong inter-firm networks), cognitive lock-ins (homogenization of world views) and political lock-ins (strong, symbiotic relationships between public and private key actors hampering industrial restructuring). The lock-in concept has proved to be a sound theoretical basis for investigating these factors and their relations to low levels of adaptability, learning and innovation in old industrialized areas (Morgan & Nauwelaers, 1999; Wößmann, 2001; Isaksen, 2003; Hassink & Shin, 2005).

4 Challenges and prospects for a cluster-based renewal of old industrial areas

As old industrial regions suffer from an overspecialization in mature, declining industries they face the key challenge to revitalize these clusters and to build up new ones. In this section we are going to deal with the prospects for a restructuring and recovery of old clusters and for the emergence of new clusters. The aim is to identify specific conditions and critical factors for such a cluster-based renewal of old industrialized areas. This will be illustrated with examples of various old industrial regions in Europe and North America. The following types of renewal can be distinguished (see Figure 12.2): (a) old clusters experiencing innovation-based adjustment processes, (b) diversification into established industries that are new for the region, and (c) new clusters based on knowledge-intensive industries.

The differentiation between these types of clusters is important because they reflect varying degrees of regional renewal. An adjustment process of old clusters represents only

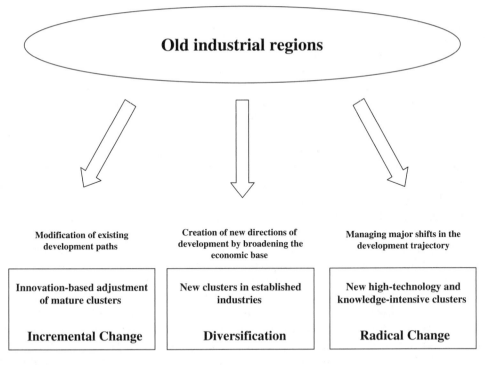

Figure 12.2   Types of cluster-based renewal of old industrial areas

an incremental change. The development of new clusters in traditional industries is a bigger step. The most fundamental change is brought about by the emergence of a really new cluster, i.e. the breeding of high-tech or knowledge-intensive industries such as environmental technology or information and communication technologies.

It is important to note that these types of cluster-based renewal are not mutually excluding phenomena. On the contrary, in many old industrial regions we might find a coexistence of traditional and modern clusters, indicating an overlapping of various development trajectories.

4.1   Incremental change: innovation-based adjustment of old clusters

The revitalization of traditional clusters can be associated with an incremental, modest change in old industrial regions, modifying their existing development trajectory rather than altering it. At the core of such a transformation is a reconquering of competitiveness in the ancestral branches brought about by a 'creative recycling' and further development of the existing regional knowledge base. An innovation-based restructuring of old clusters could embrace different forms, ranging from a shift from mass products towards specialities and higher value products as has been observed in the Styrian metal cluster (see Tödtling & Trippl, 2004; Trippl, 2004) to the introduction of new technologies and organizational practices as was seen, for example, in the Swiss watch making industry (Maillat et al., 1997) and the automotive cluster in Ontario (Gertler & Wolfe, 2004).

The capacity of a cluster to escape from lock-in and to regain its competitive position is critically dependent on the nature of the restructuring strategies followed by the large, endogenous firms (Trippl, 2004; Schamp, 2005). In most cases a simple cost reduction response to a severe crisis is not a viable way, whereas a search for market niches and an orientation towards innovation promises better results (Cooke, 1995a; Maillat et al., 1997; Chapman et al., 2004). If the firms succeed in enhancing their competencies to operate innovatively within their existing markets and to move to the upstream end of their industries, the accumulated knowledge and skills are redeployed in a creative way. To take the innovation path, however, often presupposes a major reorganization of the large dominating companies. Organizational innovations and changes such as a decentralization (Maillat & Kebir, 2001) – and in some cases a privatization – of these firms and an enforcement of innovation related functions (such as R&D) and management tasks might be regarded as crucial factors in this context (see the case of the metal cluster in the region of Styria, as described by Tödtling & Trippl, 2004). It would be too simplistic, however, to assume that an innovation-oriented restructuring of leading firms could always be equated with the rejuvenation of traditional clusters. This is only the case if the core activities of the firms stay within the region and are not relocated abroad. In the latter case we might see a successfully restructured firm but a decline of the respective region.

The strong focus proposed here on the restructuring, reorganization and modernization of large endogenous firms dominating the cluster does not imply that exogenous impulses are negligible. On the contrary, subsidiaries of foreign companies can also be an engine of change within old clusters. Provided that they do not remain 'cathedrals in the desert' but become embedded in the local industry, such companies can be an important source of new knowledge. Gertler and Wolfe (2004), for example, report that transplant firms have contributed significantly to the enhancement of the innovation capacity of the automotive cluster in Ontario by diffusing best practices in the fields of quality control, simultaneous engineering, inventory management and worker participation in design and production. Similar processes have been observed in Detroit, where Japanese firms have played a crucial role in the revitalization of the automotive cluster by transferring new management practices and production technologies to the region (Florida, 1995).

To take into consideration firm strategies, however, is not enough to capture the complexity of cluster adjustment in old industrialized areas. The activities of research organizations, educational institutions and technology transfer agencies can be vital to the restructuring process of mature industries, pointing to the importance of the region's knowledge infrastructure. Compared to the other development paths discussed later, an innovation-oriented revitalization of traditional clusters in most cases does not presuppose a far-reaching transformation of the knowledge generation and diffusion subsystem. The changes required are more modest in nature, being largely about an adaptation of existing structures. This has at least two dimensions: on the one hand, there is a need for research and educational organizations that support firms to introduce new technologies and to move towards an upgrading and improvement of their products by providing specialized knowledge and highly qualified labour. Thus, to adapt the knowledge infrastructure can have an essential impact on the recovery of old industrial areas, leading to the application of new technologies in traditional sectors. The metal cluster in the region of Styria (introduction of laser techniques and new compound materials) and the watch industry in the Swiss Jura arc (introduction of microelectronics) demonstrate the significance of rejuvenating by building bridges to new technologies (see Maillat et al., 1997; Tödtling & Trippl, 2004). In such cases new technological trajectories may be opened up for traditional industries. On the other hand, in many cases a stronger orientation of knowledge providers to the requirements of smaller firms is also crucial. As outlined in Chapter 3, old industrial areas hosting heavy industries are often characterized by a supply-driven approach of technology transfer which reaches larger firms better than the smaller ones. A cluster-wide adjustment can only be realized if restructuring and innovation are not confined to the larger companies. Smaller firms must also be enabled to improve their innovation capabilities. This underscores the importance of improving the existing technology transfer system by placing more emphasis on the needs of smaller companies.

Finally, as already outlined above, changes in the socio-cultural fabric and the relational assets of the cluster and its hosting region are also necessary. Breaking out of lock-ins and overcoming various forms of rigidities are a key precondition for the recovery of mature clusters (Morgan, 1997; Lagendijk, 2000). Getting rid of the institutional legacy of the past and of ossified networks, however, might be the most difficult aspect in the process of cluster regeneration. Drawing on evidence from the North East of England, Hudson (2005), for example, has shown convincingly that traditions and old patterns of behaviour and thought can be long-lived, indicating the negative impact of institutional persistency on regional adaptation and change. Institutional unlearning encompasses several dimensions. First, there is the need of a renewal of business networks by forging a substitution of hierarchical inter-firm linkages by more innovation-oriented interactions leading to regional collective learning and innovation processes. This is not an easy task, given the low level of trust in old industrial regions. Nevertheless, several authors have suggested that promoting the emergence of social capital in such areas is not an impossible endeavour (Sabel, 1992; Morgan, 1997; Storper, 2002). Second, a substantial amount of policy learning is crucial for mature clusters to follow an innovation-oriented development path. To break up petrified policy networks and to unlearn old patterns of intervention such as the provision of subsidies for declining industries in favour of new growth coalitions and modern approaches of governance are crucial in this respect. To refer once again to the experiences of the region of Styria such changes are clearly visible. We have seen a withdrawal of the state from the cluster as an owner of the large companies and permanent source of industrial subsidies and its re-emergence as promoter of research–industry interfaces, thus facilitating networking and collective learning activities (Tödtling & Trippl, 2004).

4.2   Diversification: new clusters in traditional industries

Diversification as a mechanism of the renewal of old industrial regions involves a more significant change than the regeneration of mature clusters. It opens up new directions of development, broadening the economic base of the regional economy. Diversification is defined here as the emergence of clusters in established industries, that are, however, new for the region. Examples include the automotive cluster in the region of Styria (Tödtling & Trippl, 2004; Trippl, 2004) or the automobile and electronic industries in Wales (Cooke & Morgan, 1998; Cooke, 2004). The rise of new clusters in such industries can take different routes.

There is the way of exogenously driven development where diversification occurs through inward investment. The potential role of foreign companies as key agents of change is highly contingent on the specific nature of their activities. Classical branch plants of multinational companies seldom serve to encourage the birth and growth of innovative clusters in established sectors. Foreign companies, in contrast, that feature high value-added functions and embed themselves in the local economy by forming long-term linkages to regional suppliers and partners can give an important impetus to the emergence of a new complex. Processes like these have been observed in Wales, where the arrival of global transplant firms and their subsequent embedding in the local economy has fuelled the creation of clusters in the automotive and electronic industries (Cooke & Morgan, 1998; Lagendijk & Charles, 1999; Cooke, 2004). The attraction of foreign direct investment has been combined with various measures aiming at establishing an endogenous supplier base with strong innovation capabilities and the promotion of networks and vertical supply chain links between foreign firms and the indigenously developed supplier companies. Thus, the critical factors for successfully constructing an innovative cluster around the operations of foreign companies are the nature of their activities and the type of their interactions with local firms. An exogenous-led cluster building is, however, not without danger. The case of the region of Wales is instructive in demonstrating that the withdrawal of foreign companies from the cluster often has negative impacts for the region (Cooke, 2004).

It would be misleading, however, to argue that diversification is only driven by foreign direct investment. This type of cluster-based renewal can also have endogenous sources. In this case the emergence of a new cluster is based upon sectoral diversification activities of home-grown firms that are capable of moving into new sectors by redeploying existing assets and capabilities. It goes without saying that a new cluster can only be built up if such diversification strategies are regionally based. This is not always the case. The case of the Ruhr area underscores the importance of the geographical focus. Several steel groups diversified into the mechanical engineering industry, plant construction and supply to the motor industry and ship-building, whereby many of these activities are located outside the region (see Rehfeld, 1999; Hilbert et al., 2004).

The emergence of new clusters in traditional industries could also be the outcome of a combination of endogenous and exogenous factors. This is clearly demonstrated by the case of the automotive industry in the region of Styria where an interplay of the attraction of foreign owned companies, diversification strategies of home grown firms and the existence of some traditional roots and competencies in automotive sector has resulted in the establishment of a new growing cluster (see Tödtling & Trippl, 2004; Trippl, 2004).

The formation of new agglomerations in established industries can be heavily supported by an accompanying reconfiguration of the knowledge generation and diffusion setting of the regional innovation system. The changes required in this field are twofold. On the one hand, there is the need of a reorientation of those research and educational organizations that are too strongly oriented to the old industrial specialization pattern. On the other hand, it appears to be significant that new institutions are established to support the rise of new clusters in old industrial areas. The Styrian automotive cluster provides a good illustration for the relevance of spurring such a process of institution building in order to encourage the growth of new complexes. The establishment of a technical college for automotive engineering and the creation of various cooperative research centres between universities and firms had a positive effect, enhancing the learning and innovation capabilities of the regional automotive industry (Tödtling & Trippl, 2004).

A regeneration of old industrial regions by diversifying their industrial base is closely connected to the creation of networks in the newly emerging cluster. This highlights the necessity for changes in the relational and institutional structures of the region. The key challenge in this context is to avoid the traditional arm's length and hierarchical ties prevailing in the region being replicated in the new cluster. To establish more cooperative and innovation-relevant interactions is a far more advantageous strategy. This, however, often presupposes changes in the prevalent pattern of behaviour that are directed to trust building and interactive learning (Morgan, 1997; Lagendijk, 2000). To break up institutional inertia and to initiate such a socio-cultural shift towards more cooperative attitudes in order to build up an innovation enhancing stock of relational assets is one of the key tasks of policy makers and regional development agencies. A policy strategy that is concentrated on the attraction of foreign direct investment or on supporting the diversification efforts of endogenous firms alone is clearly not enough. The emergence of new clusters in established industries can only be effectively supported, if the key agents in the political system promote the reconfiguration of the region's knowledge infrastructure and if they redefine their role and learn to act as interlocutors and facilitators of innovation networks (Cooke & Morgan, 1998). This is exactly what has been observed in the regions of Wales and Styria, where policy makers have essentially contributed to the rise of new clusters in the automobile and electronics industries (see Morgan, 1997; Tödtling & Trippl, 2004).

4.3   Towards a radical change: the rise of high-tech clusters
The most radical form of change in old industrialized areas is certainly brought about by the emergence and growth of knowledge-intensive and high-technology industries (Hospers, 2004), implying a major shift in the development trajectories of these regions. What are the prospects for old industrial areas that aim at introducing new growth sectors? The conventional wisdom in the literature appears to be that new industries eschew old industrial regions (Hall, 1985; Storper & Walker, 1989; Castells & Hall, 1994) because of economic, social and institutional rigidities prevailing in these areas. Also Cooke (1995b) concluded from a comparative analysis of old industrialized regions in Europe and North America that leapfrogging into high-tech industries is not a viable way. These assessments may have been too pessimistic. Several old industrial regions have done the unthinkable as they have opened up new trajectories of development by breeding new high-technology clusters. Examples include the IT cluster in the Finnish region of Tampere (O'Gorman & Kautonen, 2004; Schienstock et al., 2004), the emergence of medical technology activities in Styria, the environment protection industry in the Ruhr area, the software and IT-service branch in the city of Dortmund (Hilbert et al., 2004), the rise of biotechnology in Scotland (Leibovitz, 2004) or the ICT cluster in the Canadian region of Ontario (Gertler & Wolfe, 2004).

Such high-tech clusters could not be built from scratch or by fiat. More specifically, a regional renewal of a radical nature requires the existence of specific assets, resources or competencies rooted in the area. Otherwise the efforts result in what Enright (2003) has referred to as 'wishful thinking cluster' as they lack specialized competencies or resources on which the industry can grow. These could include, amongst other factors, an excellent scientific base or the availability of a highly skilled labour force. The development of a new high-tech agglomeration might also be the result of a strong local demand.

The emergence of such knowledge-intensive clusters hinges less on incumbent firms but more on the establishment of completely new companies. This constitutes a demanding challenge for old industrial regions specialized in heavy sectors, as they are often characterized by low rates of new firm formation, which is mainly due to the dominance of large enterprises and trade unions. To emphasize the importance of new firm creation does not mean that existing endogenous firms or foreign direct investment cannot play a powerful role in 'seeding' a new high-tech complex. The rise of the software industry in Ireland, for example, has been spurred on essentially by the attraction of foreign companies (O'Malley & O'Gorman, 2001) and the IT industry in the Finnish region of Tampere exemplifies the importance of large home-grown firms such as Nokia that stimulate the growth of the local cluster by acting as sophisticated customers (O'Gorman & Kautonen, 2004). The environment protection industry in the Ruhr area is another good example in this context. It has its origins in the old mining and steel complex (Hilbert et al., 2004). The leading firms of this cluster and their suppliers were forced by legal restraints and other political measures to reduce pollution and contamination caused by their traditional business by developing internal solutions to the environmental problems. What is essential here is that they managed to transfer these competencies and skills situated within the old cluster into new markets, giving rise to the new environment protection industry. Nevertheless, compared to the two other development scenarios of cluster-based renewal discussed here, new firm formation is a crucial element for the emergence of high-technology industries (Audretsch, 1995; Feldman et al., 2005).

The formation and growth of high-technology clusters in old industrial regions presupposes a major transformation in the knowledge generation and diffusion dimension of the regional innovation system. Taking the high-tech road is strongly linked to intensive processes of institution building and institutional change. Creating or further developing a relevant scientific knowledge base, upgrading the education and training system, and establishing specialized support structures are key factors that contribute to developing and sustaining new knowledge-intensive clusters. The presence of excellent research organizations, higher education institutes and supporting agents such as science parks, academic spin-off centres, incubators, technology licensing offices or innovation centres that are specialized in promoting young high-tech companies can have an important impact on the emergence of high-technology agglomerations.

New firm formation and the creation of a variety of new knowledge organizations and supporting institutions has to be complemented by the development of strong connections and linkages within the emerging cluster, leading to regional collective learning and innovation. Furthermore, the relevance of knowledge and resources from outside the region ought not to be neglected. This holds true in particular for those regions that lack expertise and resources necessary for promoting high-technology industries (Leibovitz, 2004; Rees, 2005), a condition that is often given in old industrial areas. Consequently, extra-local networks emerge as a key factor supporting the rise of new high-tech clusters in this type of regions.

Policy makers can play an important role in encouraging the development of new high-technology clusters in old industrialized regions. Stimulating new industries can not be achieved with old policy recipes and traditional instruments such as subsidies, tax incentives or low-cost labour (Audretsch, 2003; Feldman & Francis, 2004; Trippl et al., 2006). It requires a new mode of state engagement, covering aspects such as investments in the knowledge infrastructure, securing the availability of risk capital and other measures to promote entrepreneurship, and assisting the formation of innovation links to encourage a steady flow of knowledge. Furthermore, to pick up aborning future topics and projects with uncertain outcomes (see, for example, the case of fuel cells in North Rhine-Westphalia: Institut Arbeit und Technik et al., 2003) might also be an important step towards opening up new development trajectories. This requires a long-term perspective and willingness to take risks within the political system. Consequently, in old industrial regions a substantial amount of policy learning is necessary as the key agents of the political system have good knowledge and experience of how to support traditional sectors, but often lack a profound understanding of the needs of high-tech industries. If this learning challenge is met, then policy makers can play a critical role in encouraging new agglomerations of high-technology activities. There is evidence from several old industrial areas indicating that policy interventions had a favourable impact on the emergence of the knowledge-intensive clusters (see, for example, the case of the region of Tampere, as described by O'Gorman & Kautonen, 2004; Schienstock et al., 2004).

5   Summary and conclusions

In most of the literature on clusters there is a strong focus on explaining the advantages of specialized agglomerations of economic activity. What is often ignored is the fact that clusters can be a blessing and a curse for regional development as the experiences of old industrial regions show. These areas face the challenge to reinvent themselves by rejuvenating their economy. We have argued that the cluster approach might be a useful concept in this respect, distinguishing between (a) an innovation-based adjustment of mature clusters, (b) a diversification into established industries, and (c) the development of clusters based on knowledge intensive-industries.

These three different types of clusters reflect various degrees of regional renewal. An innovation-oriented transformation of old and declining clusters could be equated with continuity in the economic evolution of the region, as it implies a maintaining of the status quo in sectoral terms. In comparison, the rise of new clusters in established industries constitutes a more significant transformation. Finally, the emergence of agglomerations based on knowledge-intensive activities represents the most radical form of change.

Departing from a theoretical framework that conceives clusters as an integral part of regional innovation systems, we have identified four dimensions that are of key relevance for analysing cluster-based renewal processes in old industrial areas:

- the subsystem of knowledge application and exploitation (firm dimension);
- the subsystem of knowledge generation and diffusion (knowledge infrastructure dimension);
- the relational assets and institutional fabric of the region (network and institutional dimension); and
- the political system (policy dimension).

Each mode of cluster-based renewal discussed here has specific preconditions and hinges on various critical factors. Table 12.1 provides an overview of our key findings in this respect, revealing considerable differences between the three development strategies for the regeneration of old industrial areas.

Table 12.1   Critical factors of different types of cluster-based renewal in old industrial regions

	Incremental change innovation-based adjustment within mature clusters	Diversification new clusters in established industries	Radical change new knowledge-intensive clusters
Firm dimension (RIS subsystem of knowledge application and exploitation)	• regionally based innovation-oriented restructuring, modernization and reorganization of large, endogenous firms • foreign companies as providers of new knowledge	• innovative 'embedded' foreign firms as catalysts of new directions of development • diversification of endogenous firms	• newly founded small firms as key agents of change • supportive role of larger endogenous and exogenous firms
Knowledge infrastructure dimension (RIS subsystem of knowledge generation and diffusion)	• focus on modernization of traditional industries and on building bridges to new technologies • orientation to needs of smaller firms	• break-up overspecialization in old industrial / technological pattern • focusing on requirements of new industries	• emphasis on basic research in new fields • orientation on higher education institutes, science parks, academic spin-off centres
Network and institutional dimension	• breaking up petrified ties • reconfiguration and renewal of existing relations	• creation of supplier networks • formation of innovation linkages	• creation of local knowledge links, university–industry linkages • insertion into extra-local networks
Policy dimension	• support of restructuring of large endogenous firms • support adaptation of knowledge infrastructure • new growth coalitions	• attract and 'embed' foreign direct investment • support reconfiguration of knowledge infrastructure • promotion of innovative networks	• promotion of (academic) entrepreneurship • support transformation of knowledge infrastructure • fostering of local and international knowledge links

- *Firm dimension:* Each mode of cluster-based renewal requires specific firm strategies. Not every type of firm is able to be a key agent of change for all kinds of regional renewal. Large endogenous firms usually play a key role in the rejuvenation of old industries, provided that they follow an innovation-oriented restructuring strategy that is regionally based. Also foreign companies that become embedded in the region may trigger processes of change within mature and declining clusters by transferring new management practices and production technologies to the region. Foreign direct investment can also give a decisive impetus to the rise of new clusters in established industries, if they feature high value added functions and are anchored to the region by forming innovative relations with local firms. But also regionally based diversification strategies of home-grown firms can pave the way for this type of cluster-based renewal. The development of high-technology and knowledge-intensive clusters, in contrast, depends much more on newly founded small firms that act as crucial innovation agents in the new field.
- *Knowledge infrastructure dimension:* It has been argued that the institutional infrastructure that generates knowledge and promotes innovation and learning is a crucial element of cluster-based approaches to regional renewal. The degree of changes necessary in this setting varies markedly between the scenarios of development discussed here. An innovation-oriented restructuring of mature clusters in many cases implies only an adaptation of the knowledge infrastructure that allows building bridges to new technologies. Taking the diversification path, in contrast, presupposes bigger steps such as the creation of a variety of specialized research and educational institutes focused on the new clusters, leading to a reconfiguration of the subsystem of knowledge generation and diffusion. The emergence of new high-technology agglomerations is linked to a fundamental transformation of the knowledge infrastructure brought about by the 'introduction' of a range of new elements, including excellent research organizations and higher education institutes, academic spin-off centres, science parks and technology licensing offices.
- *Network and institutional dimension:* Transformations in the relational and institutional fabric have been identified as another key factor contributing to the regeneration of old industrial areas. Again, the nature of these changes can only be specified in dependence on the route that is followed. An innovation-oriented restructuring of old clusters is critically dependent on overcoming institutional inertia. A breaking up of petrified ties and a reconfiguration of existing relations are of key importance in this respect. For new clusters in established industries to grow, the emergence of trust based cooperation and interactive learning plays a crucial role, highlighting the challenge of creating social capital in old industrial regions. The development prospects of high-technology clusters are largely influenced by the formation of local and international knowledge-intensive networks.
- *Policy dimension:* The three types of cluster-based renewal require different degrees of policy learning. To escape from political lock-in by replacing old policy networks with new growth coalitions appears to be an essential ingredient for fostering an adjustment of traditional clusters and for supporting diversification. Also new modes of state intervention such as the promotion of innovation networks might be essential for effectively supporting the regeneration of old clusters and the rise

of new ones in established industries. Wholly new high-technology agglomerations, in contrast, can only be 'seeded' if additional steps are taken, reflecting a more substantial policy learning process. Policy makers face the challenge of acquiring knowledge about the needs of knowledge-intensive industries, creating a variety of new institutions in order to transform the region's knowledge infrastructure, and developing new financial and support structures that encourage the emergence of a culture of entrepreneurship.

A key conclusion that can be drawn from these considerations is that processes of cluster-based renewal are a complicated and challenging endeavour, resting on a complex interplay of firm strategies, changes in the knowledge infrastructure, institutional innovations and policy learning processes.

The question remains of how to support an innovation-oriented restructuring of old clusters and to build up new ones while avoiding the pitfalls of specialized concentrations of economic activity. To prevent a repeat of history is indeed a key challenge for every strategy of cluster-based renewal in old industrial regions. What seems to be of utmost importance in this context is a more or less regular search for and support of new clusters and new applications of existing competences to elude the risk of a too narrow regional specialization (see also Tichy, 1998). To work against a 'closure' of business and policy networks (Messner, 1997) that underpins lock-in effect might be another crucial factor. To keep networks open for new members and to 'inject' new ideas and knowledge into existing ties could be sound precautions that ensure that clusters do not turn into obstacles for regional development.

References

Asheim, B., A. Isaksen, C. Nauwelaers and F. Tödtling (eds) (2003), *Regional Innovation Policy for Small-Medium Enterprises*, Cheltenham, UK and Northampton, MA, US: Edward Elgar.
Audretsch, D. (1995), *Innovation and Industry Evolution*, Cambridge, MA: MIT Press.
Audretsch, D. (2003), 'The role of small firms in US biotechnology clusters', in G. Fuchs (ed.), *Biotechnology in Comparative Perspective*, London and New York: Routledge, pp. 14–32.
Autio, E. (1998), 'Evaluation of RTD in regional systems of innovation', *European Planning Studies*, **6**, 131–40.
Boschma, R. and J. Lambooy (1999), 'The prospects of an adjustment policy based on collective learning in old industrial regions', *Geojournal*, **49**, 391–9.
Bunnel, T. and N. Coe (2001), 'Spaces and scales of innovation', *Progress in Human Geography*, **25**, 569–89.
Camagni, R. (1991), 'Local "milieu", uncertainty and innovation networks: towards a new dynamic theory of economic space', in R. Camagni (ed.), *Innovation Networks: Spatial Perspectives*, London: Belhaven Press, pp. 121–44.
Castells, M. and P. Hall (1994), *Technopoles of the World: The Making of the 21st Century Industrial Complexes*, London: Routledge.
Chapman, K. (2005), 'From "growth centre" to "cluster": restructuring, regional development, and the Teesside Chemical Industry', *Environment and Planning A*, **37**, 597–615.
Chapman, K., D. MacKinnon and A. Cumbers (2004), 'Adjustment or renewal in regional clusters? A study of diversification amongst SMEs in the Aberdeen Oil Complex', *Transactions of the Institute of British Geographers*, **29**, 382–96.
Cooke, P. (ed.) (1995a), *The Rise of the Rustbelt*, London: UCL Press.
Cooke, P. (1995b), 'Introduction', in P. Cooke (ed.), *The Rise of the Rustbelt*, London: UCL Press, pp. 1–19.
Cooke, P. (2002), *Knowledge Economies. Clusters, Learning and Cooperative Advantage*, London: Routledge.
Cooke, P. (2004), 'The regional innovation system in Wales: evolution or eclipse?', in P. Cooke, M. Heidenreich and H-J. Braczyk (eds), *Regional Innovation Systems*, 2nd edn, London and New York: Routledge, pp. 214–33.
Cooke, P. and K. Morgan (1998), *The Associational Economy*, New York: Oxford University Press.
Cooke, P., P. Boekholt and F. Tödtling (2000), *The Governance of Innovation in Europe*, London: Pinter.
Cooke, P., M. Heidenreich and H-J. Braczyk (eds) (2004), *Regional Innovation Systems*, 2nd edn, London and New York: Routledge.

Doloreux, D. (2002), 'What we should know about regional systems of innovation', *Technology in Society*, **24**, 243–63.

Enright, M. (2003), 'Regional clusters: what we know and what we should know', in J. Bröcker, D. Dohse and R. Soltwedel (eds), *Innovation Clusters and Interregional Competition*, Berlin: Springer Verlag, pp. 99–129.

Feldman, M. (2000), 'Location and innovation: the New Economic Geography of innovation, spillovers, and agglomeration', in G. Clark, M. Feldman and M. Gertler (eds), *The Oxford Handbook of Economic Geography*, Oxford: Oxford University Press, pp. 373–94.

Feldman, M. and J. Francis (2004), 'Home-grown solutions: fostering cluster formation through entrepreneurship', *Economic Development Quarterly*, **18**, 127–37.

Feldman, M., J. Francis and J. Bercovitz (2005), 'Creating a cluster while building a firm: entrepreneurs and the formation of industrial clusters', *Regional Studies*, **39**, 129–41.

Florida, R. (1995), 'The industrial transformation of the Great Lakes region', in P. Cooke (ed.), *The Rise of the Rustbelt*, London: UCL Press, pp. 162–76.

Gertler, M. and D. Wolfe (2004), 'Ontario's regional innovation system. The evolution of knowledge-based institutional assets', in P. Cooke, M. Heidenreich and H-J. Braczyk (eds), *Regional innovation systems*, 2nd edn, London and New York: Routledge, pp. 91–124.

Grabher, G. (1993), 'The weakness of strong ties: the lock-in of regional development in the Ruhr area', in G. Grabher (ed.), *The Embedded Firm: On the Socioeconomics of Industrial Networks*, London: T.J. Press, pp. 255–78.

Hall, P. (1985), 'The geography of the fifth Kondratieff', in P. Hall and A. Markusen (eds), *Silicon Landscapes*, London: Allen & Unwin.

Hamm, R. and H. Wienert (1990), *Strukturelle Anpassung altindustrieller Regionen im internationalen Vergleich*, Schriftenreihe des Rheinisch-Westfälischen Institutes für Wirtschaftsforschung, Neue Folge Heft 48, Berlin: Duncker & Humblot.

Hassink, R. (2005), 'Geography, networks and renewal of old industrial areas?', paper prepared for the Fourth European Meeting on Applied Evolutionary Economics (EMAEE), Utrecht, The Netherlands, 19–21 May.

Hassink, R. and D.-O. Shin (2005), 'Guest editorial: the restructuring of old industrial areas in Europe and Asia', *Environment and Planning A*, **37**, 571–80.

Häußermann, H. (ed.) (1992), *Ökonomie und Politik in alten Industrieregionen Europas*, Basel, Boston, Berlin: Birkhäuser.

Hilbert, J., J. Nordhause-Janz, D. Rehfeld and R. Heinze (2004), 'Industrial clusters and the governance of change: lessons from North Rhine-Westphalia', in P. Cooke, M. Heidenreich and H-J. Braczyk (eds), *Regional Innovation Systems*, 2nd edn, London and New York: Routledge, pp. 234–58.

Hospers, G.J. (2004), 'Innovationspolitik: auf der Suche nach neuen Kombinationen von Trends und Tradition', *Wirtschaftsdienst: Zeitschrift für Wirtschaftspolitik*, **83**, 450–53.

Hudson, R. (2005), 'Rethinking change in old industrial regions: reflecting on the experiences of North East England', *Environment and Planning A*, **37**, 581–96.

Institut Arbeit und Technik, Österreichisches Institut für Raumplanung, European Policy Research Centre (2003), Halbzeitbewertung des Ziel 2-Programms 2000-2006 des Landes Nordrhein-Westfalen – Materialband, Gutachten im Auftrag des Landes Nordrhein-Westfalen, Gelsenkirchen, Wien und Strathclyde.

Isaksen, A. (2003), '"Lock-in" of regional clusters: the case of offshore engineering in the Oslo region', in D. Fornahl and T. Brenner (eds), *Cooperation, Networks and Institutions in Regional Innovation Systems*, Cheltenham, UK and Northampton, MA, US: Edward Elgar, pp. 247–73.

Kaufmann, A. and F. Tödtling, (2000), 'Systems of innovation in traditional industrial regions: the case of Styria in a comparative perspective', *Regional Studies*, **34**, 29–40.

Keeble, D. and F. Wilkinson (eds) (2000), *High-Technology Clusters, Networking and Collective Learning in Europe*, Aldershot: Ashgate.

Lagendijk, A. (2000), 'Learning in non-core regions: towards "intelligent clusters"; Addressing Business and Regional Needs', in F. Boekema, K. Morgan, S. Bakkers and R. Rutten (eds), *Knowledge, Innovation and Economic Growth*, Cheltenham, UK and Northampton, MA, US: Edward Elgar, pp. 165–91.

Lagendijk, A. and D. Charles (1999), 'Clustering as a new growth strategy for regional economies? A discussion of new forms of regional industrial policy in the United Kingdom', in OECD (ed.), *Boosting Innovation. The Cluster Approach*, Paris: OECD, pp. 127–53.

Leibovitz, J. (2004), '"Embryonic" knowledge-based clusters and cities: the case of biotechnology in Scotland', *Urban Studies*, **41**, 1133–55.

Maillat, D. and L. Kebir (2001), 'The learning region and territorial production systems', in B. Johannson, C. Karlsson and R. Stough (eds), *Theories of Endogenous Regional Growth. Lessons for Regional Policies*, Berlin: Springer Verlag, pp. 255–77.

Maillat, D., G. Léchot, B. Lecoq and M. Pfister (1997), 'Comparative analysis of the structural development of milieux: the watch industry in the Swiss and French Jura arc', in R. Ratti, A. Bramanti and R. Gordon (eds), *The Dynamics of Innovative Regions: The GREMI Approach*, Aldershot, Brookfield: Ashgate, pp. 109–37.

Martin, R. and P. Sunley (2003), 'Deconstructing clusters: chaotic concept or policy panacea?', *Journal of Economic Geography*, **3**, 5–35.

Messner, D. (1997), *The Network Society. Economic Development and International Competitiveness as Problems of Social Governance*, London: Frank Cass.

Morgan, K. (1997), 'The learning region: institutions, innovation and regional renewal', *Regional Studies*, **31**, 491–503.

Morgan, K. and C. Nauwelaers (1999), 'A regional perspective on innovation: from theory to strategy', in K. Morgan and C. Nauwelaers (eds), *Regional Innovation Strategies. The Challenge for Less-Favoured Regions*, London: The Stationery Office and Regional Studies Association, pp. 1–18.

O'Gorman, C. and M. Kautonen (2004), 'Policies to promote new knowledge-intensive industrial agglomerations', *Entrepreneurship & Regional Development*, **16**, 459–79.

Oinas, P. and E. Malecki (1999), 'Spatial innovation systems', in E. Malecki and P. Oinas (eds), *Making Connections*, Aldershot: Ashgate, pp. 7–33.

Oinas, P. and E. Malecki (2002), 'The evolution of technologies in time and space: from national and regional to spatial innovation systems', *International Regional Science Review*, **25**, 102–31.

O'Malley, E. and C. O'Gorman (2001), 'Competitive advantage in the Irish indigenous software industry and the role of inward foreign direct investment', *European Planning Studies*, **9**, 303–21.

Porter, M. (1998), *On Competition*, Boston: Harvard Business School Press.

Rees, K. (2005), 'Collaboration, innovation and regional networks: evidence from the medical biotechnology industry of Greater Vancouver', in A. Lagendijk and P. Oinas (eds), *Proximity Distance and Diversity. Issues on Economic Interaction and Local Development*, Aldershot: Ashgate, pp. 191–215.

Rehfeld, D. (1999), *Produktionscluster. Konzeption, Analysen und Strategien für eine Neuorientierung der regionalen Strukturpolitik*, München und Mehring: Reiner Hampp Verlag.

Sabel, C. (1992), 'Studied trust: building new forms of co-operation in a volatile economy', in F. Pyke and W. Sengenberger (eds), *Industrial Districts and Local Economic Regeneration*, Geneva: International Institute for Labour Studies, pp. 215–50.

Sadler, D. (2004), 'Cluster evolution, the transformation of old industrial regions and the steel industry supply chain in North East England', *Regional Studies*, **38**, 55–66.

Schamp, E. (2005), 'Decline of the district, renewal of firms: an evolutionary approach to footwear production in the Pirmasens Area, Germany', *Environment and Planning A*, **37**, 617–34.

Schienstock, G., M. Kautonen and P. Koski (2004), 'Escaping path dependency. The case of Tampere, Finland', in P. Cooke, M. Heidenreich and H-J. Braczyk (eds), *Regional Innovation Systems*, 2nd edn, London and New York: Routledge, pp. 127–53.

Steiner, M. (ed.) (1998), *Clusters and Regional Specialisation*, London: Pion.

Storper, M. (2002), 'Institutions of the learning economy', in M. Gertler and D. Wolfe (eds), *Innovation and Social Learning. Institutional Adaption in an Era of Technological Chance*, Basingstoke: Palgrave, pp. 135–58.

Storper, M. and R. Walker (1989), *The Capitalist Imperative: Territory, Technology and Industrial Growth*, Cambridge, MA: Basil Blackwell.

Tichy, G. (1998), 'Clusters: less dispensable and more risky than ever', in M. Steiner (ed.), *Clusters and Regional Specialisation*, London: Pinter, pp. 226–37.

Tichy, G. (2001), 'Regionale Kompetenzzyklen – Zur Bedeutung von Produktlebenszyklus- und Clusteransätzen im regionalen Kontext', *Zeitschrift für Wirtschaftsgeographie*, **45**, 181–201.

Tödtling, F. (1992), 'Technological change at the regional level: the role of location, firm structure, and strategy', *Environment and Planning*, **24**, 1565–84.

Tödtling, F. and M. Trippl (2004), 'Like Phoenix from the ashes? The renewal of clusters in old industrial areas', *Urban Studies*, **41**, 1175–95.

Tödtling, F. and M. Trippl (2005), 'One size fits all? Towards a differentiated regional innovation policy approach', *Research Policy*, **34**, 1203–19.

Trippl, M. (2004), *Innovative Cluster in alten Industriegebieten*, Vienna: LIT.

Trippl, M., J. von Gabain and F. Tödtling (2006), 'The role of public policy in promoting knowledge links in the biotechnology sector', SRE Discussion Paper 2006–02, Vienna: Department of Regional Development and Environment, Vienna University of Economics.

Wößmann, L. (2001), 'Der Aufstieg und Niedergang von Regionen: Die dynamische Markttheorie von Heuß in räumlicher Sicht', *Jahrbuch für Regionalwissenschaft*, **21**, 65–89.

13 The reciprocal relationship between transnationals and clusters: a literature review
Filip De Beule, Daniël Van Den Bulcke and Haiyan Zhang

1 Introduction

The central question which is dealt with in this chapter is the reciprocal relationship and impact of transnational corporations (TNCs) and clusters. Both foreign direct investment (FDI) and industry clusters have received considerable and growing worldwide attention from academics and policy decision makers in many countries. Both TNCs and clusters are broadly thought to affect the host economy positively through technology, production and trade linkages, human capital, the facilitation of knowledge and, last but not least, innovation. While FDI and clusters have most often been studied separately, they have recently been regarded as rightly being linked.

There are indications that the globalization of tangible and especially intangible assets across borders is being constrained by the fact that the location of the creative activities and use of these assets is becoming increasingly influenced by immobile clusters of complementary value-added activities. Silicon Valley (Scott & Angel, 1987; Saxenian, 1990; Scott, 2002) and Hollywood (Christopherson & Storper, 1986) may be the world's best-known clusters, but other examples of such initiatives abound in every international, national, regional, state and even metropolitan economy, especially in the more advanced nations (Paniccia, 1998; Porter, 1998). A number of developing countries in South America and the Caribbean, as well as China and India, have also taken cluster formation to heart. Thus, while globalization suggests that the location and ownership of production is becoming geographically more dispersed, other economic forces are stimulating a more pronounced geographical concentration of economic activity within particular regions and countries (Dunning, 1998a).

As the impact of TNCs and clusters derives from the more general impact of TNCs on host countries, the chapter will first give an overview of the generic impact of TNCs on host economies, before discussing the new economic geography of clusters. Next, the specific reciprocal relationship of TNCs and local clusters, in particular the role of foreign subsidiaries, will be discussed. The chapter will end by drawing some concluding remarks.

2 Theoretical and empirical literature

2.1 Impact on host countries

Over the years, one of the persistent aims of the analysis of the activities of TNCs has been to identify the nature and value of their impact on host countries (Dunning, 1994; Ozawa, 1992). FDI comprises a bundle of tangible and intangible assets. The proprietary or ownership advantages give multinational enterprises an edge over local firms and allow them to overcome the costs of operating across national boundaries and to compensate the so-called 'liability of foreignness'. These oligopolistic advantages mean that TNCs can provide assets to host countries that other firms can not. Dicken (1992, 1998) distinguishes five major areas where TNCs affect the host economy. More specifically, TNCs may assist developing countries through the provision of capital, through the inflow of technology, through trade and linkages, through the inflow and upgrade of human resources and, finally, through their impact on the creation of efficient markets. All these effects derive essentially from the fact that TNCs provide resources that would not otherwise be sufficiently available or even lacking in host countries (Blomström, 1991; Blomström & Kokko, 1996).

While transnational companies are generally regarded as a source of substantial net benefits to developed economies, there has always been a lingering fear about the loss of control over the domestic economy brought about by the removal and centralization of decision-making authority to TNCs' parent companies in the home countries. Substantial concerns have also been voiced over the branch plant syndrome (Hood & Young, 1976), where a large proportion of the employees work in firms whose head office lies outside the region or country. Also host economies are concerned about the extent of backward linkages into the local economy in terms of sourcing of services and material inputs, about overemphasis on suppliers from the home country or other parts of the multinational network, about the use of the low value-added screwdriver plants, about insufficient exports and about the lack of local R&D activity particularly in relation to the development of new and improved products: questions that to-date are still as relevant as ever, especially in developing countries.

Many important issues concerning the costs and benefits of FDI with respect to linkages, technology, skills and competitiveness revolve around the static or dynamic nature of their activities (Lall, 1993). TNCs are often considered as highly efficient vehicles for the transfer of technologies and skills suited to existing or static factor endowments in host economies. They are able to adapt a particular technology to very different levels of scale and complexity in different locations, depending on market orientation and size, labour skills, technical capabilities and supplier networks (OECD, 2002).

The development impact of FDI depends, however, on more than this. It is also linked to the TNCs' strategies and to the dynamics of the transfer of technology and skills by TNCs. How much upgrading of local capabilities takes place over time, how far local linkages deepen and how closely affiliates integrate themselves to the local learning system depends on the interaction of a number of factors, such as the trade and industrial policy regime, and other policies that effect TNC operations as well as the local factor markets and institutions that determine the absorptive capacity of host economies (Lall, 1996).

A familiar mode of analysis has been to suggest that TNCs transfer their existing competitive attributes, such as the technology and expertise to produce established goods, in order to improve the efficiency of their use through a combination of local, standardized and cost-effective inputs (Hymer [1960] 1976; Vernon, 1966; Kojima, 1977). By allowing a more effective use of the existing competitive attributes of both the TNC and the host country, such behaviour enhances static efficiency through improved resource allocation. TNCs internalize their mature and standardized technologies, in particular, in a certain country based on the cost characteristics of its qualitatively homogenous inputs. Successful local development then changes the host country's input characteristics, i.e. higher prices for qualitatively improved assets, and compels the cost-obsessed TNC operations to migrate to a new, now lower-cost, country (Pearce, 2001). This hollows out part of the development process to which the TNC initially contributed. As such, this line of argument represents a hostage to fortune, and critics can point to an implicit vulnerability of the host country to the footloose exit of the TNC.

However, the footloose perspective focuses only on low cost- or high efficiency-seeking overseas operations in TNCs (Dunning, 1993). It also adopts an extreme view of institutional centralization, with a massively hierarchical organizational structure allocating centrally-generated sources of competitiveness, e.g. technology, for use in the most cost-effective locations through the activity of highly dependent subsidiaries. The presumed inability of subsidiaries to generate any form of locally-derived individuality means that they have no distinctive roots, or what is called 'embeddedness' in their host country.

It has been suggested, in line with extensive recent work on the strategic nature of the TNC and its subsidiaries (White & Poynter, 1984; D'Cruz, 1986; Hood & Young, 1988; Young, Hood et al., 1989; Pearce, 1999; Taggart, 1996, 1999), that there are several alternatives that can be activated through subsidiaries. Such suggestions allow for certain types of localized individualization, which is in line with a wider theme of dispersed responsiveness, learning and creativity in the modern TNC (Håkanson, 1990; Håkanson & Nobel, 1998; Yamin, 1999). Their proponents argue that processes of developmental evolution can emerge at the subsidiary level, based on their differentiated motivation and capability (Birkinshaw & Hood, 1997, 1998; Birkinshaw, et al., 1998; Taggart, 1998; Luostarinen & Marschan-Piekkari, 2001).

This can mitigate the danger of short-term disinvestment and provide potential for the longer-term involvement of subsidiaries within host country development processes. These alternatives can either sharpen the competitiveness of TNCs' existing goods in host country supply channels through responsive market-seeking behaviour, or widen the TNC's product range and technological scope through knowledge-seeking activity. Such subsidiaries may then have the potential and opportunity to escape from strict dependence on the parent company and, instead of almost exclusive reliance on the inward transfer of group technology, may contribute to the transnational group's competence creation. This also embeds these subsidiaries in a mutually dependent and sustainable fashion in the local evolutionary processes.

Research, mainly on industrial countries, has shown that subsidiaries typically evolve along a palette of trajectories. Subsidiaries are established for a variety of motives, e.g., resource, market, efficiency or (strategic) asset (such as knowledge) seeking (Dunning, 1993) and through a variety of modes (e.g., greenfield, acquisition or joint venture), meaning that a single evolutionary process for subsidiaries cannot be readily identified (Rugman & Verbeke, 2001). While this research interest has been directed primarily towards the implications of subsidiary companies achieving ever more strategic roles within their corporate system, subsidiaries may also shrink or die out, as well as expand in larger or more specialized units. There are indeed many different factors that influence such processes.

While there is no shortage of typologies suggesting that subsidiaries vary in their contributory role to the multinational group, they all vary in their perspective on the sources of variation and evolution. In particular, three complementary perspectives can be determined from the TNC subsidiary literature (Birkinshaw et al., 1998). The first perspective consists of subsidiary choice, whereby the role of the subsidiary can to a large extent be defined by local management (White & Poynter, 1984; D'Cruz, 1986; Roth & Morisson, 1992; Birkinshaw & Hood, 1997; Taggart, 1997).

The second perspective is based on head office assignment; i.e., head office is responsible for defining the strategic imperatives of the whole company and is supposed to understand best how subsidiary roles can be assigned to ensure that those imperatives are met (Bartlett & Ghoshal, 1986; Gupta & Govindarajan, 1991, 1994; Roth & Morrison, 1992; Birkinshaw & Morisson, 1995).

The third perspective starts from environmental determinism, and regards the role of each subsidiary in large part as a function of its local environment (Bartlett & Ghoshal, 1986; Ghoshal & Nohria, 1989; Jarillo & Martinez, 1990; Westney, 1990). Moreover, a number of subsidiary typologies explicitly consider the host country environment as a key distinguishing variable (e.g., Bartlett & Ghoshal, 1986; Ghoshal & Nohria, 1989). For instance, Birkinshaw and Hood (2000) specifically research the impact of industry clusters on subsidiary roles and strategy.

In order to come to a complete understanding of the TNC phenomenon, it is necessary to consider subsidiary, corporate, industry and country factors. However, the three perspectives are competing with one another for relative salience (Birkinshaw et al., 1998). Swedish research put the emphasis on embeddedness as a critical factor for subsidiary development (Forsgren et al., 2000; Forsgren & Pedersen, 1998). Subsidiaries thereby have to manage corporate, business and local embeddedness. Corporate embeddedness concerns the relationship with the multinational network. Business embeddedness considers the linkages with important customers, suppliers and other third parties. Local embeddedness refers to links with the national innovation system.

The specific nature of the relationship between the subsidiary and its host country environment is seldom spelled out, however. The most common approach is to adopt the simplifying assumption that the host country environment is more or less given, and that the subsidiary has somehow to adapt to it. A second approach is to see the subsidiary as tapping into or drawing on the host country environment. Examples of this approach are not only Porter's (1990) view that foreign-owned subsidiaries typically tap into local industry (clusters) in order to keep their parent company informed about leading-edge thinking in that cluster, but also studies by Frost (1998) and Almeida and Kogut (1997) that show how subsidiaries draw on local sources in their innovation processes. A third approach, which has not been argued to any great extent in the academic literature, is to see the subsidiary as a contributor to the host country environment. This approach is conceptually and intuitively straightforward, in that many national economies rely to a large degree on foreign-owned subsidiaries to provide employment, investment and exports (Birkinshaw & Hood, 1998). Consequently, there is a need for research that looks explicitly at the impact that foreign-owned subsidiaries have on their host country economy. Factors such as the level of decision-making autonomy, the presence of R&D activities, and the relationship with local suppliers, are all likely to influence the development process of the host country.

The three approaches to modelling the relationship of the subsidiary with its host country are, of course, all partially relevant. When superimposed on one another, they suggest an ongoing process of development, whereby the subsidiary reacts to and draws on the local environment at the same time as contributing to the local economy as a whole as well as to specific business partners. Over time, it is argued, the successful subsidiary coevolves with its environment and gradually plays an increasingly important role in the local economy. The subsidiary itself typically goes through a development process where it gains enhanced value-added scope and greater decision-making autonomy (Birkinshaw & Hood, 1997), and this process is both driven by and a source of benefit to the local economy.

In sum, transnationals decide their strategies according to the characteristics of their technologies and products as well as the characteristics and policies of the host countries. The multinationals' strategic decisions then determine how their affiliates affect the host economy. Most host country governments simultaneously try to influence the behaviour of the foreign TNCs established on their territory, either directly through regulations or indirectly by affecting the environment in which the TNCs operate. To the extent that these interventions affect the behaviour of the foreign TNCs, they also determine the effects on the host economy. It is this intricate interplay between firm and host country strategies that will determine to what extent foreign subsidiaries may contribute significantly to growth and development in some circumstances, but may also have negligible or even negative effects on the local economy in other situations.

2.2   New economic geography

While the observation that firms tend to cluster in particular regions is hardly novel (Smith, 1776; von Thünen, 1826; Marshall, 1890), it has recently been taken up to explain the stickiness of certain locations in an increasingly slippery world (Markusen, 1994). These theories suggest that firms may be drawn to the same locations because proximity generates positive externalities or agglomeration effects (Markusen, 1994, 1996). Economists have proposed agglomeration effects in the form of both static (pecuniary) and dynamic (technological) externalities to explain industry localization (Baptista, 1998).

According to Marshall (1890), the external effects of agglomeration consist of various types of benefits and cost savings obtained outside the market that may lead to increased productivity of a firm. These effects may consist of the availability of skilled labour and the access to specialized suppliers of intermediary goods, but also localized knowledge spillovers. These economic benefits allow an increase in the productivity of firms in a static perspective and augmenting the capacity for innovation and sustained productivity growth in a more dynamic way.

Clusters are characterized as localized networks of production of interdependent firms, knowledge-producing agents and customers, linked to each other in a value adding production chain (OECD, 1999). The use of clusters as a descriptive tool for regional economic relationships provides a richer, more meaningful representation of local industry drivers and regional dynamics than do traditional methods. An industry cluster is different from the classic definition of industry sectors because it represents the entire value chain of a broadly defined industry from suppliers to end products, including supporting services and specialized infrastructure.

Scholars have attempted to classify industrial clusters into different categories on the basis of their scope, density, pattern of activities, growth potential, innovation capability, governance structure and foreign participation (Dunning, 2000).

A variety of empirical and descriptive studies have examined evidence on the cluster phenomenon per se, focusing on different issues, such as initial cluster formation and growth. Some factors, such as a series of historical circumstances, the influence of government actions and legislation, and the development of unique capabilities, were identified that shape the development of the industry and anchor the industry in the region (Cantwell & Glac, 2005). Several studies have put emphasis on dynamic aspects such as the entry of firms into the cluster and firm growth or performance in clusters (Baptista & Swann, 1999).

Saxenian (1994) and Porter (1990, 1998) identified the existence of a number of competitive clusters on the basis of small-sample qualitative studies and documented the existence of agglomeration externality mechanisms. At the industry level, there is also evidence of a positive relationship between agglomeration and competitiveness (e.g. Henderson, 1986; Ciccone & Hall, 1996) in terms of, e.g., increased labour productivity, enhanced human capital (labour quality), rapid industrial restructuring (plant size and specialization), increased competition (international and local) and innovation (investment and capability).

Krugman has emphasized the importance of clustering on economic growth in his writings on trade and geography (Krugman, 1991, 1995; Krugman & Venables, 1995), while Porter stressed the role of clustering in the competitiveness of industries and companies from a business management point of view (Porter, 1990, 1996). The major concern of these studies on linkages between industrial clusters and national competitiveness is to assess enhanced competition and technological spillovers as the mechanism through which the productivity of the host economy is improved. It needs to be stressed that the competitiveness of the individual firm is a very important element in this concept as rival firms make up a competitive cluster and economic self-interest is ultimately the glue that binds the cluster together (Enright, 1996).

As such, different clusters can also be categorized, based on the origin of the industry in a specific location: indigenous versus transplanted. Some industries grew up as indigenous industries and were afterwards exposed to a globalizing economy with increasing levels of international trade and investment. In the first stage, indigenous (hub-and-spoke) clusters are characterized by tightly linked local firms and relatively few foreign-owned subsidiaries (Gray et al., 1996). Over time, the number of foreign subsidiaries in originally indigenous industries increases as a result of the globalizing economy. More specifically, successful industries attract multinationals that set up new firms or acquire local companies in order to access the available strategic assets.

While most research focuses on developed economies, an increasing number of cases from developing countries has come to light where clustering has helped local firms to grow and export, for example, rattan furniture from Indonesia, towels from Turkey, cotton T-shirts from India, surgical instruments from Pakistan, jewellery from Thailand, computers from Taiwan, wood products from Chile or ceramic tiles from Brazil. While not an automatic outcome, clustering helps small enterprises to grow. The significance of clustering lies in facilitating growth, enabling small firms to overcome the growth constraints which are common in developing countries (Schmitz, 1997). Once grown, successful firms sometimes decide to move out, although they usually do not do so (Nadvi, 1997). The reasons for this are summed up in the concept of collective efficiency.

Other industries originate as a direct result of the growing levels of international trade and investment between countries and regions. These transplanted (satellite platform) industries are initially characterized by (relatively many) foreign branch plants that are rather weakly embedded in the local economy. At first, there are only a limited number of local firms. Transplanted industries are likely to continue to depend on their parent company back home or *keiretsu*-type members abroad for key supplies or core technologies for some time, and will only slowly develop 'local' ties, set up R&D units and grow to become clusters (De Beule & Van Den Bulcke, 2001). Alternatively, the virtuous circle of economic development by embedding foreign plants in the local economy does not materialize and the agglomeration of firms remains a satellite district.

Several empirical studies have also found evidence of temporal as well as spatial concentration in the location of FDI (Knickerbocker, 1973; Vernon, 1974; Wheeler & Mody, 1992; Florida & Kenney, 1994; Smith & Florida, 1994; Head et al., 1995; Braunerhjelm & Svensson, 1996; Ford & Strange, 1999). This 'bunching' is a self-reinforcing process in which initial FDI accounts for additional FDI (Arthur, 1990; Markusen, 1990; Wheeler & Mody, 1992).

3 Reciprocal impact of TNCs and clusters

3.1 Impact of TNCs on clusters

The discussion about the impact of TNCs on foreign industrial clusters is derived from the literature about the relationship between TNCs and the host economy. It suggests that the major impacts of TNCs on the host country are related to employment, transfer of technology, knowledge spillovers, balance of payments, exports, foreign exchange, demand expectations, competition and entrepreneurship stimulation. Extending from this literature, Dunning suggests that foreign TNCs play a major role in the formation, structure and development of industrial clusters, especially for knowledge-based clusters, exports processing zones and technology parks (Dunning, 2000).

The impact of TNCs on industrial clusters depends on the nature and form of assets of the investing company, the location-bound resources and capabilities of the host clusters and the organizational mechanisms through which they interact (Enright, 2000). This argument is clearly based on Dunning's OLI paradigm which combines ownership, location and internalization advantages and is frequently used in the literature for explaining the phenomenon of FDI. TNCs – which have a wide product mandate, strong export orientation, highly skilled production process and personnel, substantial local content and deep involvement in building up local research capabilities – are most likely to contribute positively to the regional development as 'developmental TNCs' (Young et al., 1994).

Zander and Sölvell (2000) emphasized that TNCs can be considered as a boundary-spanning vehicle, furthering the integration of regions through international trade, foreign direct investment and international knowledge exchange. Cantwell and Iammarino (1997) found that the concentration of technological activity by foreign affiliates is correlated to the concentration of the same activity carried out by local firms. Therefore, TNCs appear especially prone to perform R&D investments in foreign locations with a strong technological activity, and this leads to a further strengthening of indigenous R&D activities, thus illustrating the coevolution of domestic firms and foreign subsidiaries in host country clusters.

While most of this literature refers to the experiences of industrially advanced countries, it has inspired recent work on developing countries. There is a growing body of literature (Humphrey & Schmitz, 1996; Nadvi & Schmitz, 1994) which shows that clusters also matter in developing countries. They are in fact common in a wide range of countries and sectors, even though they take different forms. Clustering has also helped small firms to overcome well-known growth constraints and to sell to distant markets, nation-ally and abroad. These two conclusions concerning developing countries need to be qualified because the growth experiences have been diverse. At one end of the spectrum, there are artisanal clusters that have shown little dynamism and seem unable to expand or innovate (e.g. McCormick, 1999). At the other end are clusters that have been able to deepen their inter-firm division of labour, raise their competitiveness and break into inter-national markets (e.g. Meyer-Stamer, 1995; Nadvi, 1997). Along this spectrum, there are many intermediate cases (e.g. Knorringa, 1996; Rabellotti, 1997).

There is a consensus in the literature that clustering facilitates the upgrading of pro-duction and related activities. It is less clear how this upgrading comes about. Much of the literature (including Krugman, 1991, 1995) assumes that it is a spontaneous process of deepening specialization, of spilling over of know-how and of synergies, a view that can be traced back to Alfred Marshall's discussion of local external economies in indus-trial districts. Some of the recent literature has stressed that there is also a deliberate force at work, namely consciously pursued private cooperation and public support. This came out most clearly in the work on industrial districts in advanced countries (e.g. Brusco, 1990; Pyke, 1992; Sengenberger & Pyke, 1991; Trigilia, 1989), but also in research on developing countries (e.g. Humphrey & Schmitz, 1996; Meyer-Stamer, 1995; Tendler & Amorim, 1996). Recent literature on industrial districts and enterprise clusters suggests that the grouping of enterprises into sectoral and geographic clusters gives rise to a certain collective efficiency that can enhance competitiveness and foster industrialization.

A number of empirical studies have shown that certain clusters have resulted from the agglomeration of the facilities of foreign subsidiaries, especially in the case of 'satellite platform clusters', while other contributions have identified the substantial influence of multinationals on individual clusters located both in industrial and in developing coun-tries. The dominant role of foreign TNCs in cluster formation and development has been illustrated, for instance, by the cases of German and Swiss firms in the New York–New Jersey–Pennsylvania pharmaceutical cluster (Enright, 1991) and foreign TNCs in the development of Venezuela's oil and petrochemical cluster (Enright et al., 1996). Subsidiaries of foreign TNCs may also perform the role of regional headquarters and have strong cluster ties among themselves and with local cluster participants. Yet, in some cases, clusters dominated by foreign subsidiaries are likely to behave as satellites of the foreign parent companies, with few spillover effects accruing to indigenous cluster participants.

Birkinshaw studied the specific link between the process of upgrading in industrial clus-ters and the level of foreign ownership of those clusters in order to emphasize the impor-tance of FDI on industrial clusters at different levels of cluster maturity (or life-cycle) and cluster dynamism (Birkinshaw, 2000). His empirical survey on the Stockholm IT cluster showed that foreign investment has an important role to play in shaping the potential for upgrading in a cluster, especially in rapidly growing industries with considerable scope for expansion. Yet, in mature industries that are consolidating, the relative positions of various clusters and their strengths and weaknesses are well known and foreign owner-ship may have little impact on the cluster dynamics.

Enright (2000) developed an interdependent model, as compared to independent and dependent approaches, to analyse the interactions between TNCs and industrial clusters. His empirical study on Hong Kong's financial-services cluster showed that the benefits that foreign TNCs have brought to the local industrial cluster went well beyond the direct benefits of employment, output and skill transfer, as well as the indirect benefits of spillovers into other industries identified with the presence of foreign TNCs. The impact of foreign TNCs was especially related to market creating, cluster creating, infrastructure creating, linkage creating and information creating. Foreign firms in local industrial clusters can be regarded as 'contributing subsidiaries' (Birkinshaw & Hood, 1998) in that they strongly contribute in terms of strategy setting and developing and deploying substantial skills and capabilities. The ability to attract FDI in an emerging cluster, especially from large TNCs with high visibility, may signal at the international level that the cluster is credible; this may result in a foreign investment snowball effect benefiting the cluster as a whole.

To achieve and sustain their ability to compete, many firms increasingly have to rely on their capacity to internationally relocate and disperse their production activities (or some stages of them). The firm's location decisions depend not only on the general (at the country level), but also on the specific (at the regional level) characteristics of the industrial and socio-economic structure of the location, as globalization tends to emphasize the significance of location choices. Moreover, the globalization process can be depicted as a higher degree of interdependency among the geographically dispersed units of global (multinational) firms. This leads to a stronger geographical concentration of both production and technological activities of TNCs, which have been defined as 'the key-ring in the chain from global to local' (Cantwell & Iammarino, 1997). Therefore, as globalization processes are likely to strengthen regional differences, local environments will play an increasingly important role in the TNCs' value-added activities.

3.2   Impact of clusters on TNCs

TNCs are increasingly seeking complementary foreign assets and capabilities of a knowledge-facilitating kind, trying to add value to their core competitive advantages. This is particularly the case as their affiliates are becoming more firmly rooted in host economies. Examples of this approach are the view that foreign-owned subsidiaries typically tap into local industry in order to keep their parent company informed about leading-edge thinking (Porter, 1990; Bartlett & Ghoshal, 1986). Studies by Frost (1998) and Almeida and Kogut (1997) show how subsidiaries draw on local sources to feed their innovation processes. Exceptions to this finding, however, are, for instance, low value-adding activities in the less developed areas of the world. Although much of the recent FDI in developing countries is prompted either by traditional market-seeking motives or by the desire to take advantage of lower production and, especially, low labour costs, or the availability and price of natural resources. Yet, even when firms have a choice, the physical and human infrastructure, together with the macroeconomic environment and the institutional framework of the host country, play a more decisive role than they did before.

Consequently, TNCs have increasingly invested in foreign industrial clusters to augment their knowledge base through obtaining direct access to foreign pools of skilled human resources and knowledge (Dunning, 2000; Rugman & Verbeke, 2001). FDI by TNCs has been driven by knowledge-seeking and/or strategic asset-seeking motivation, while foreign subsidiaries have been more and more considered as 'asset-augmenting investments' (Dunning, 1998b), 'scanning units' (Bartlett & Ghoshal, 1986; Westney, 1990) and 'transplanted home bases' (Porter, 1990).

From the TNC perspective, participation in a foreign cluster may lead to several benefits: the access to knowledge, which otherwise would have remained out of reach; the potential leveraging of this knowledge throughout the firm's internal network; the transfer of global best practices; the monitoring of rivals active in the foreign clusters, etc. The positive impact of foreign industrial clusters on the asset creating and competitiveness of TNCs has become the focus of several researchers (Birkinshaw & Hood, 1998; Birkinshaw, 2000; Birkinshaw & Hood, 2000; Enright, 2000; Peters & Hood, 2000). These studies provide a rich set of conceptual and practical insights into the contribution of foreign industrial clusters in general and foreign subsidiaries in particular to the competitive position of TNCs. The importance of TNCs in foreign cluster formation, functioning and upgrading constitutes an interesting segment of the literature, which focuses on the dependent, independent and interdependent relationships between foreign clusters and TNCs (Enright, 2000; Cantwell & Santangelo, 1999). Yet, the dynamic interaction and coevolution between indigenous clusters and foreign subsidiaries is a complex phenomenon, whose causality and sequential development are difficult to identify.

The impact of foreign clusters on TNCs can be analysed at two levels, i.e. from the perspective of the subsidiary located in the foreign cluster and from that of the TNC group. From the subsidiary perspective, Birkinshaw and Hood (1998) showed that subsidiaries located in leading-edge clusters tended to have higher value-added activities, to be more internationally oriented and to be better embedded into local environments than subsidiaries that were not located in such clusters. With regard to the spillover effects of foreign clusters on TNC groups – i.e. through foreign subsidiaries located in the clusters to their parent companies or groups, the role of foreign subsidiaries varied according to their function within TNC groups (Enright, 1998), the structural context imposed by the parent company, the entrepreneurial capacity of subsidiary management and the local environment (Birkinshaw & Hood, 2000).

When foreign subsidiaries are set up as 'listening posts', they may be used to collect information and knowledge from the clusters and disseminate it to the parent companies and other subsidiaries in the multinational group. In an advanced stage of development, they can serve as a vehicle to transfer skills and capabilities from the cluster to the rest of the multinational group. In the case of stand-alone investments, foreign subsidiaries often serve as the centre for a particular business segment of TNCs on a global or regional scale, especially within satellite platform clusters. TNC may also benefit from advantages that a foreign cluster might have in developing and producing a particular product or service that can be transferred to the existing business units of the group through its subsidiaries in the cluster (Enright, 2000). In leading-edge industrial clusters, two major functions of foreign subsidiaries have been observed. The first category consists of scanning units that tap selectively into sources of advantage in foreign national industrial clusters. They are often R&D units with limited development capability of their own, which allow them to contribute to, as well as to draw on, the knowledge base of the cluster (Porter, 1990). Their agglomeration effects have been regarded as positive to promote this type of localized innovation processes (Zander & Sölvell, 2000). The second group is composed of transplanted home-bases, which are responsible for top management, R&D activities and major manufacturing operations of an entire production division. In addition to this type of high profile subsidiaries, there are also likely to be many more traditional subsidiaries in leading-edge clusters, for example, market-seeking units that are located in the clusters because the country represents an important market for the TNC's products. Still others may operate as resource-seeking units that are located in the cluster to gain access to specialized inputs, well-trained labour or low-cost factor inputs.

TNCs increasingly tend to perform R&D investments in foreign locations with strong technological capabilities, and this leads to a further strengthening of indigenous R&D activities (UNCTAD, 2005). There is an increase in knowledge-seeking FDI by TNCs, because the intra-firm specialization and the related local embeddedness of know-how make it difficult to launch and maintain international innovation processes within the TNC without participating in foreign clusters. Yet, to be present in a foreign cluster does not necessarily create positive effects on the innovation process of TNCs, for the following reasons. Different subunits within the TNC may have a specialized knowledge base and a specific technological trajectory, which may be inconsistent with the knowledge absorbed in a foreign cluster. In addition, the TNC unit involved in the knowledge-absorption process may be faced with, on the one hand, difficult choices between maximizing convergence of its own operations with the other parts of the TNC network and, on the other hand, maximizing convergence with the functioning of the localized knowledge cluster in which it is physically embedded (Cantwell & Santangelo, 1999).

4 Concluding remarks

The discussion about the impact of TNCs on foreign industrial clusters is derived from the literature about the relationship between TNCs and the host economy. The literature on location factors has shown that TNCs can gain access to a number of specific location factors by concentrating their value-added activities in a particular region/country. The location factors can be determined by natural and created resources, strategic assets, market information and production knowledge. Recent research has applied these approaches to cluster studies and concluded that clusters should be considered as an important variation of the geographic or location-based advantages that influence international production. Asset-augmenting investments have been used to describe the situation in which TNCs invest abroad to gain access to specific capabilities present in a foreign cluster in order to enhance the assets that the corporation already possesses.

TNCs tend to locate their international operations where they may benefit most from suitably specialized factors that are complementary to their own major strengths in order to enjoy localized spillovers from the dynamic host economy. On the other hand, the comparative advantage of the local system is enhanced over time through the presence of foreign-owned affiliates. Consequently, not only chance events but also government inducements of localized clusters can have a lasting influence on the geographical pattern of manufacturing and service industries on a global scale.

The importance of TNCs in foreign cluster formation, functioning and upgrading constitutes an interesting but ambivalent discussion, which focuses on the dependent, independent and interdependent relationships between foreign clusters and TNCs. Although clusters can be either transplanted or indigenous, the dynamic interaction and coevolution between clusters and foreign subsidiaries is a complex phenomenon, whose causality and sequential development are difficult to identify.

The literature seems to suggest that foreign TNCs can play a major role in the formation, structure and development of industrial clusters, especially for knowledge-based clusters, exports processing zones and technology parks.

References

Almeida, P. and B. Kogut (1997), 'The exploration of technological diversity and the geographic localization of innovation', *Small Business Economics*, **9**(1), 21–31.

Arthur, B. (1990), 'Positive feedbacks in the economy', *Scientific American*, **262**, 92–9.

Baptista, R. (1998), 'Clusters, innovation and growth: a survey of the literature', in G.M.P Swann, M. Prevezer and D. Stout (eds), *The Dynamics of Industrial Clustering: International Comparisons in Computers and Biotechnology*, Oxford: Oxford University Press, pp. 13–51.

Baptista, R. and G.M.P. Swann (1998), 'Do firms in clusters innovate more?', *Research Policy*, **27**, 525–40.

Baptista, R. and G.M.P. Swann (1999), 'A comparison of clustering dynamics in the US and UK computer industries', *Evolutionary Economics*, **9**, 373–99.

Bartlett, A. and S. Ghoshal (1986), 'Tap your subsidiaries for global reach', *Harvard Business Review*, **64**, 87–94.

Birkinshaw, J. (2000), 'Upgrading of industrial clusters and foreign direct investment', *International Studies of Manufacturing and Organisation*, **30**, 93–111.

Birkinshaw, J. and N. Hood (1997), 'An empirical study of development processes in foreign owned subsidiaries in Canada and Scotland', *Management International Review*, **37**(4), 339–64.

Birkinshaw, J. and N. Hood (1998), 'Multinational subsidiary evolution: capability and charter change in foreign owned subsidiary companies', *Academy of Management Review*, **23**(4), 773–95.

Birkinshaw, J. and N. Hood (2000), 'Characteristics of foreign subsidiaries in industry clusters', *Journal of International Business Studies*, **31**(1), 141–54.

Birkinshaw, J. and A.J. Morisson (1995), 'Configurations of strategy and structure in subsidiaries of multinational corporations', *Journal of International Business Studies*, **26**(4), 729–54.

Birkinshaw, J., N. Hood and S. Jonsson (1998), 'Building firm-specific advantages in multinational corporations: the role of subsidiary initiative', *Strategic Management Journal*, **19**, 221–41.

Blomström, M. (1991), *Host Country Benefits of Foreign Investment*, Cambridge, MA: National Bureau of Economic Research.

Blomström, M. and A. Kokko (1996), 'The impact of foreign investment on host countries: a review of the empirical evidence', Worldbank, Washington, DC.

Braunerhjelm, P. and R. Svensson (1996), 'Host country characteristics and agglomeration in foreign direct investment', *Applied Economics*, **28**(7), 833–40.

Brusco, S. (1990), 'The idea of the industrial district: its genesis', in F. Pyke, G. Becattini and W. Sengenberger (eds), *Industrial Districts and Inter-firm Co-operation in Italy*, Geneva: ILO, pp. 10–19.

Cantwell, J.A. and K. Glac (2005), 'TNCs, locational clustering and the process of economic development', in L. Cuyvers and F. De Beule (eds), *Transnational Corporations and Economic Development: From Internationalisation to Globalisation*, London: Palgrave Macmillan, pp. 84–101.

Cantwell, J.A. and S. Iammarino (1997), 'Regional systems of innovation in Europe and the globalisation of technology', working paper, University of Reading.

Cantwell, J. and G.D. Santangelo (1999), 'The frontier of international technology networks: sourcing abroad the most highly tacit capabilities', *Information Economics and Policy*, **11**, 103–23.

Christopherson, S. and M. Storper (1986), 'The city as studio, the world as back lot: the impact of vertical disintegration on the location of the motion picture industry', *Environment and Planning D: Society and Space*, **4**, 305–20.

Ciccone, A. and R.E. Hall (1996), 'Productivity and the density of economic activity', *American Economic Review*, **86**, 54–70.

D'Cruz, J. (1986), 'Strategic management of subsidiaries', in H. Etemad and L.S. Sulude (eds), *Managing the Multinational Subsidiary*, London: Croom-Helm, pp. 75–89.

De Beule, F. and D. Van Den Bulcke (2001), 'Industrial clusters and Japanese manufacturing affiliates in the Belgian small open economy', in D. Van Den Bulcke and A. Verbeke (eds), *Globalization and the Small Open Economy*, Cheltenham, UK and Northampton, MA, US: Edward Elgar, pp. 173–205.

Dicken, P. (1992), *Global Shift: The Internationalization of Economic Activity*, London: Paul Chapman.

Dicken, P. (1998), *Global Shift: Transforming the World Economy*, London: Paul Chapman.

Dunning, J.H. (1993), *Multinational Enterprises and the Global Economy*, Wokingham: Addison-Wesley.

Dunning, J.H. (1994), 'Re-evaluating the benefits of foreign direct investment', *Transnational Corporations*, **3**(1), 23–51.

Dunning, J.H. (1998a), 'Location and the multinational enterprise: a neglected factor?', *Journal of International Business Studies*, **29**(1), 45–66.

Dunning, J.H. (1998b), 'Globalisation, technological change and spatial organisation of economic activities', in A.D. Chandler, P. Hagstrom and O. Solvell (eds), *The Dynamic Firm. The Role of Technology, Strategy, Organisation, and Regions*, Oxford: Oxford University Press.

Dunning, J.H. (2000), 'Regions, globalisation, and the knowledge economy: the issues stated', in J.H. Dunning (ed.), *Regions, Globalisation, and the Knowledge Economy*, Oxford: Oxford University Press.

Enright, M.J. (1991), 'Geographic concentration and industrial organisation', Ph.D. dissertation, Harvard University, Ann Arbor, Michigan.

Enright, M.J. (1996), 'Regional clusters and economic development: a research agenda', in U.H. Staeber, N.V. Schaefer and B. Sharma (eds), *Business Networks: Prospects for Regional Development*, Berlin: Walter de Gruyter.

Enright, M.J. (1998), 'Regional clusters and firm strategy', in A.D. Chandler, P. Hagstrom and Ö. Sölvell (eds), *The Dynamic Firm. The Role of Technology, Strategy, Organisation, and Regions*, Oxford: Oxford University Press.

Enright, M.J. (2000), 'Regional clusters and multinational enterprises', *International Journal of Industrial Organization*, **30**, 114–38.

Enright, M.J., A. Francés E. Scott and S. Saavedra (1996), *Venezuela: The Challenge of Competitiveness*, New York: St. Martin's Press.

Florida, R. and M. Kenney (1994), 'The globalization of Japanese R&D: the economic geography of Japanese R&D investment in the United States', *Economic Geography*, **70**(4), 344–69.

Ford, S. and R. Strange (1999), 'Where do Japanese manufacturing firms invest within Europe, and why?', *Transnational Corporations*, **8**(1), 117–42.

Forsgren, M. and T. Pedersen (1998), 'Centres of excellence in multinational companies: the case of Denmark', in J. Birkinshaw and N. Hood (eds), *Multinational Corporate Evolution and Subsidiary Development*, London: Macmillan.

Forsgren, M., J. Johanson and S.D. Deo, (2000), 'Development of MNC centres of excellence', in U. Holm and T. Pedersen (eds), *The Emergence and Impact of MNC Centres of Excellence. A Subsidiary Perspective*, London: Macmillan Press, pp. 45–78.

Frost, T.S. (1998), 'The geographic sources of innovation in the multinational enterprise: US subsidiaries and host country spillovers: 1980–1990', *Sloan School of Management*, Cambridge, MA: MIT Press.

Ghoshal, S. and N. Nohria (1989), 'Internal differentiation within multinational corporations', *Strategic Management Journal*, **10**, 323–37.

Gray, M., E. Golob and A. Markusen (1996), 'Big firms, long arms, wide shoulders: the "hub-and-spoke" industrial district in the Seattle region', *Regional Studies*, **30**(7), 651–66.

Gupta, A.K. and V. Govindarajan (1991), 'Knowledge flows and the structure of control within multinational corporations', *Academy of Management Review*, **16**(4), 768–92.

Gupta, A.K. and V. Govindarajan (1994), 'Organizing for knowledge flows within MNCs', *International Business Review*, **3**(4), 443–57.

Håkanson, L. (1990), 'International decentralization of R&D: the organizational challenges', in C.A. Bartlett, Y. Doz and G. Hedlund (eds), *Managing the Global Firm*, London: Routledge, pp. 256–78.

Håkanson, L. and R. Nobel (1998), *Organisational Characteristics and Reverse Technology Transfer*, International Business Strategies and Middle East Regional Cooperation, Jerusalem, Israel, Graduate School of Business Administration, Bar Ilan University.

Head, K., J. Ries and D. Swanson (1995), 'Agglomeration benefits and location choice: evidence from Japanese manufacturing investments in the United States', *Journal of International Economics*, **38**(3–4), 223–47.

Henderson, J.V. (1986), 'Efficiency of resource usage and city size', *Journal of Urban Economics*, **19**, 47–70.

Hood, N. and S. Young (1976), 'U.S. investment in Scotland – aspects of the branch factory syndrome', *Scottish Journal of Political Economy*, **23**(3), 279–94.

Hood, N. and S. Young (1988), 'Inward investment and the EC: UK evidence on corporate integration strategies', in J. Dunning and P. Robson (eds), *Multinationals and the European community*, Oxford and New York: Blackwell, pp. 91–104.

Humphrey, J. and H. Schmitz (1996), 'The triple c approach to local industrial policy', *World Development*, **24**(12), 1859–77.

Hymer, S. [1960] (1976), *The International Operations of National Firms: A Study of Direct Investment*, Cambridge, MA: MIT Press.

Jarillo, J.C. and J.I. Martinez (1990), 'Different roles for subsidiaries: the case of multinational corporations in Spain', *Strategic Management Journal*, **11**, 501–12.

Knickerbocker, F.T. (1973), *Oligopolistic Reaction and the Multinational Enterprise*, Cambridge, MA: Harvard University Press.

Knorringa, P. (1996), *Economics of Collaboration: Indian Shoemakers between Market and Hierarch*, Thousand Oaks, CA: Sage Publications.

Kojima, K. (1977), 'Transfer of technology to developing countries – Japanese type versus American type', *Hitotsubashi Journal of Economics*, **17**(2), 1–14.

Krugman, P.R. (1991), *Geography and Trade*, Cambridge, MA: MIT Press.

Krugman, P.R. (1995), *Development, Geography, and Economic Theory*, Cambridge, MA: MIT Press.

Krugman, P.R. and A.J. Venables (1995), 'Globalization and the inequality of nations', *Quarterly Journal of Economics*, **110**(4), 857–80.

Lall, S. (1993), 'Multinationals and technology development in host countries', in S. Lall (ed.), *Transnational Corporations and Economic Development*, London and New York: Routledge, pp. 237–50.

Lall, S. (1996), 'Transnational corporations and economic development', in United Nations, *Transnational Corporations and World Development*, London: International Thomson Business Press, pp. 44–72.

Luostarinen, R. and R. Marschan-Piekkari (2001), 'Strategic evolution of foreign-owned subsidiaries in a host country: a conceptual framework', in J.H. Taggart, M. Berry and M. Mcdermott (eds), *Multinationals in a New Era: International Strategy and Management*, Houndmills: Palgrave Macmillan, pp. 180–93.

Markusen, A. (1994), 'Studying regions by studying firms', *The Professional Geographer*, **46**, 477–90.

Markusen, A. (1996), 'Sticky places in slippery space: a typology of industrial districts', *Economic Geography*, **72**(3), 293–313.

Markusen, J.R. (1990), *First Mover Advantage, Blockaded Entry, and the Economics of Uneven Development*, Cambridge, MA: National Bureau of Economic Research.

Marshall, A. (1890), *Principles of Economics*, London: Macmillan.

McCormick, D. (1999), 'African enterprise clusters and industrialization: theory and reality', *World Development*, **27**(9), 1531–51.

Meyer-Stamer, J. (1995), 'Micro-level innovations and competitiveness', *World Development*, **23**(1), 143–8.

Nadvi, K.M. (1997), 'The cutting edge: collective efficiency and international competitiveness in Pakistan', IDS Discussion Paper No. 360, Institute of Development Studies, Brighton.

Nadvi, K.M. and H. Schmitz (1994), 'Industrial clusters in less developed countries: review of experiences and research agenda', IDS Discussion Paper No 339, Institute of Development Studies, Brighton.

OECD (1999), *Boosting Innovation: The Cluster Approach*, Paris: Directorate for Science, Technology and Industry.

OECD (2002), *Foreign Direct Investment and Development: Where do we stand?*, Paris: OECD Development Centre.

Ozawa, T. (1992), 'Foreign direct investment and economic development', *Transnational Corporations*, **1**(1), 27–54.

Paniccia, I. (1998), 'One, a hundred, thousands of industrial districts. Organizational variety in local networks of small and medium-sized enterprises', *Organization Studies*, **19**(4), 667–700.

Pearce, R. (1999), 'The evolution of technology in multinational enterprises: the role of creative subsidiaries', *International Business Review*, **8**(2), 125–48.

Pearce, R. (2001), 'Multinationals and industrialisation: the bases of "inward investment" Policy', *International Journal of the Economics of Business*, **8**(1), 51–73.

Peters, E. and N. Hood (2000), 'Implementing the cluster approach: some lessons from the Scottish experience', *International Studies of Manufacturing and Organisation*, **2**, 68–92.

Porter, M.E. (1990), *The Competitive Advantage of Nations*, New York: Free Press.

Porter, M.E. (1996), 'Competitive advantage, agglomeration economies, and regional policy', *International Regional Science Review*, 1–2, 85–94.

Porter, M.E. (1998), 'Cluster and the new economics of competition', *Harvard Business Review*, **76**(6), 77–91.

Pyke, F. (1992), *Industrial Development through Small-firm Cooperation. Theory and Practice*, Geneva: International Labour Office.

Rabellotti, R. (1997), *External Economies and Cooperation in Industrial Districts*, Houndmills: Macmillan Press Ltd.

Roth, K. and A.J. Morrison (1992), 'Implementing global strategy: characteristics of global subsidiary mandates', *Journal of International Business Studies*, **23**(4), 715–36.

Rugman, A.M. and A. Verbeke (2001), 'Subsidiary-specific advantages in multinational enterprises', *Strategic Management Journal*, **3**, 237–50.

Saxenian, A. (1990), 'Regional networks and the resurgence of Silicon Valley', *California Management Review*, **32**, 89–112.

Saxenian, A. (1994), *Regional Networks: Industrial Adaptation in Silicon Valley*, Cambridge, MA: Harvard University Press.

Schmitz, H. (1997), 'Collective efficiency and increasing return', *IDS Working Paper*, No. 50, University of Sussex, Institute of Development Studies, Brighton.

Scott, A.J. (2002), 'A new map of Hollywood: the production and distribution of American motion pictures', *Regional Studies*, **36**, 957–76.

Scott, A.J. and D. Angel (1987), 'The global assembly-operations of US semiconductor firms: a geographical analysis', *Environment and Planning A*, **20**, 1047–67.

Sengenberger, W. and F. Pyke (1991), 'Small firm industrial districts and local economy regeneration: research and policy issues', *Labour and Society*, **16**(1), 1–24.

Smith, A. (1776), *An Inquiry into the Nature and Causes of the Wealth of Nations*, Oxford: Clarendon Press.

Smith, D.F. and R. Florida (1994), 'Agglomeration and industrial location: an econometric analysis of Japanese-affiliated manufacturing establishments in automotive-related industries', *Journal of Urban Economics*, **36**(1), 23–41.

Taggart, J.H. (1996), 'Multinational manufacturing subsidiaries in Scotland: strategic role and economic impact', *International Business Review*, **5**(5), 447–68.

Taggart, J.H. (1997), 'An evaluation of the integration-responsiveness framework: MNC manufacturing subsidiaries in the UK', *Management International Review*, **37**(4), 295–318.

Taggart, J.H. (1998), 'Identification and development of strategy at subsidiary level', in J. Birkinshaw and N. Hood (eds), *Multinational Corporate Evolution and Subsidiary Development*, London: Macmillan.

Taggart, J.H. (1999), 'US MNC subsidiaries in the UK: characteristics and strategic roles', in F. Burton, M. Chapman and A. Cross (eds), *International Business Organisation*, London: Macmillan.

Tendler, J. and M. Amorim (1996), 'Small firms and their helpers: lessons on demand', *World Development*, **24**(3), 407–26.

Trigilia, C. (1989), 'Small-firm development and political subcultures in Italy', in E. Goodman and J. Bamford (eds), *Small Firms and Industrial Districts in Italy*, London: Routledge.

UNCTAD (2005), *World Investment Report 2005*, New York and Geneva: United Nations Publications.

Vernon, R. (1966), 'International investment and international trade in the product cycle', *Quarterly Journal of Economics*, **80**, 190–207.

Vernon, R. (1974), 'The location of economic activity', in J.H. Dunning (ed.), *Economic Analysis and the Multinational Enterprise*, London: Allen and Unwin.

von Thünen, J.H. (1826), *Der isolierte Staat in Beziehung auf Landwirtschaft und Nationalökonomie*, Jena: G. Fischer.

Westney, E.D. (1990), 'Internal and external linkages in the MNC: the case of R&D subsidiaries in Japan', in C. Bartlett, Y. Doz and G. Hedlund (eds), *Managing the Global Firm*, London and New York: Routledge.

Wheeler, D. and A. Mody (1992), 'International investment location decisions: the case of US firms', *Journal of International Economics*, **33**(1–2), 57–76.

White, R.E. and T.A. Poynter (1984), 'Strategies for foreign-owned subsidiaries in Canada', *Business Quarterly*, **49**(2), 59–69.

Yamin, M. (1999), 'An evolutionary analysis of subsidiary innovation and reverse transfer in multinational companies', in F. Burton, M. Chapman and A. Cross (eds), *International Business Organisation*, London: Macmillan.

Young, S., N. Hood and J. Hamill (1989), *Foreign Multinationals and the British Economy*, London: Routledge.

Young, S., N. Hood and E. Peters (1994), 'Multinational enterprise and regional development', *Regional Studies*, **7**, 657–77.

Zander, I. and Ö. Sölvell (2000), 'Cross-border innovation in the multinational corporation: a research agenda', *International Studies of Management and Organization*, **2**, 44–67.

14 Diversity and the case against specialized clusters
Pierre Desrochers, Frédéric Sautet and Gert-Jan Hospers[1]

1 Introduction

The geographical concentration of related manufacturing and service firms is as old as economic development,[2] but it has drawn renewed attention in the last two decades in the wake of the spectacular growth of regional economies such as Silicon Valley (South San Francisco Bay), Route 128 (greater Boston area) and the 'discovery' of numerous manufacturing districts in locations ranging from Denmark and Italy to Thailand and Japan. While contemporary policy prescriptions that built on geographically localized, related and interdependent firms can be traced back to the 'growth poles' and 'growth centres' strategy of the 1950s and 1960s (Chapman, 2005), the most appealing to policy makers in recent times has been the 'cluster' strategy put forward by Harvard Business School's Michael Porter in his 1990 best-seller, *The Competitive Advantage of Nations* (Porter, 1990). In short, this approach suggests that the geographical concentration of firms working within a particular field raises their productivity, innovativeness, competitiveness, profitability and job creation capacity, and therefore of their immediate and wider geographical areas. This prescription was further repeated, refined and sometimes made more confusing in the following years (Porter, 1998; 2000a; 2000b). Although the Harvard scholar did not invent or even do the most original work on regional economic development, his reputation and well-established status as one of the world's foremost business strategy theorists put him in a unique position to popularize his growth prescription to policy makers worldwide. Indeed, as one observer put it, 'governments and regional development organizations on all continents except Antarctica have come calling' on Porter (Hoffman, 2001).

Despite its widespread adoption, the cluster-based development strategy has been criticized on many counts, ranging from the fuzziness of the concept to its status as a rationale for arbitrary industrial policy (Desrochers and Sautet, 2004; Hospers et al., this volume). Perhaps the main problem with clusters remains, as Chapman (2005:597) points out, the inevitable 'difficulties faced by many formerly successful, but specialized old industrial areas [which] provide clear evidence that territorially based advantages may mutate into liabilities'. Building on insights that have long been known to regional development specialists and on more recent ones, this chapter re-examines the case against regional specialization by pointing out that it is more likely to result in economic downturns, to prevent the spontaneous creation of inter-industry linkages, and to hamper the creation of innovative ideas through the combination of existing know-how and artifacts than a more diversified economic base.

2 Clusters and regional specialization: an overview

In Porter's (2000a) view, clusters are made up of firms *in a particular field* that are linked in some ways and that are *geographically proximate*. More precisely, clusters are geographic concentrations of interconnected companies, specialized suppliers, service providers, firms in related industries, and associated institutions such as universities, standards agencies and trade associations in a particular field that compete and/or cooperate with each other. The fact that these firms and institutions are geographically proximate facilitates the movement of ideas and people between them, which ultimately promotes innovative behaviour.

Porter's conception of clusters, however, is said to be more inclusive than the older notion of 'industrial district' developed by Alfred Marshall (1920) at the turn of the twentieth century. While Marshall focused on very similar firms, Porter's clusters are not limited to single industries, but encompass an array of linked industries and other entities important to competition. They therefore often extend downstream to channels or customers and laterally to manufacturers of complementary products or companies related by skills, technologies or common inputs. Furthermore, their geographic scope can range from a region, a state, or even a single city to span nearby or neighbouring countries: 'The geographic scope of a cluster relates to the distance over which informational, transactional, incentive, and other efficiencies occur' (Porter, 2000a:16). Considering the extent to which all industries ultimately depend on each other, however, it is no surprise that the boundaries of any given clusters are often in the eyes of the beholder. As Porter (2000a:17) puts it: 'Drawing cluster boundaries often is a matter of degree and involves a creative process informed by understanding the linkages and complementarities across industries and institutions that are most important to competition in a particular field.'

While Porter's prescription might seem reminiscent of failed past attempts to 'pick winners', he argues that 'a role for government cluster development and upgrading should not be confused with the notion of industrial policy' and that 'the intellectual foundations of cluster theory and industrial policy are fundamentally different, as are their implications for government policy' (p. 27). In his opinion, industrial policy rests on a view of competition in which some industries and firms offer greater wealth-creating prospects than others and are therefore the target for support. Industrial policy also tends to centralize intervention decisions at the national level. Cluster theory, to the contrary, puts the emphasis on the interconnections and spillovers within a cluster and therefore supposedly rests on a broader and more dynamic view of competition among firms and locations (see Hospers et al., this volume).

In this perspective, all existing and emerging clusters deserve attention and policy makers can then avoid the problems associated with the support of individual firms (which distorts market signals), industries (which presumes that some industries are better than others and distorts market signals) and sectors (which are too broad to be competitively significant). In Porter's words:

> A cluster focus highlights the externalities, linkages, spillovers and supporting institutions so important to modern competition. By grouping together firms, suppliers, related industries, service providers, and institutions, government initiatives and investments address problems common to many firms and industries without threatening competition. A government role in cluster upgrading, then, will encourage the building of public or quasi-public goods that significantly affect many linked businesses. Government investments focused on improving the business environment in clusters, other things being equal, might well earn a higher return than those aimed at individual firms or industries or at the broad economy. (Porter, 2000a, p. 27)

In practice, however, much evidence suggests that policy makers have failed to grasp Porter's subtle distinctions between cluster policy and industrial policy and have often reverted to old-fashioned practices of picking industries that are either trendy or politically powerful (Hospers et al., this volume). Indeed, as Chapman (2005:597) points out, while cluster-based and related policies imply 'the theoretical prospect of regional diversification by exploiting supply-chain and information-based/knowledge-based relationships, in practice they tend to promote regional specialisation', a strategy that has typically proved problematic in the past (Buss, 1999; Hansen, 1996).

While regional specialization has long been thought by economists to be both a logical outcome of market competition and a good setting for innovation, this perspective has been challenged on several counts by local economic development officials, sustainable development theorists and unconventional regional economists. Their arguments will now be examined in more detail.

3   The case for local diversity

3.1   Static externalities

For two hundred years, the vast majority of economists and economic geographers have viewed the geographical specialization of economic activities as a desirable outcome of trade and the division of labour.

In this perspective, the law of comparative advantage applied to geographical areas states that, by specializing in the production of one type of good (e.g. automobile production) or one set of related goods (e.g. automobile and truck), for which they have a relative advantage (in terms of opportunity costs of producing the good), regions or countries would be better off than if they only had access to autarkic production.

The law of comparative advantage is said to be true whether a region or a country disposes of an absolute advantage in only one good (the one it specializes in) or has an absolute advantage in the production of every good – as long as the differences in opportunity costs in production makes it advantageous for countries to specialize. This is the famous case given by Ricardo (1817) between England and Portugal: even when Portugal has an absolute advantage in both the production of cloth and wine, the two countries can gain from trade by specializing in the production of the good for which they have the lowest opportunity cost.

From the early development of comparative advantage, geographical location and specialization of regions have been prominent issues. Spatial analysts have also long described the importance of localization economies that occur when a firm benefits from the close proximity of other related firms through common labour pooling, better access to intermediate inputs and increased face-to-face communication (Rosenthal & Strange, 2004).

Despite the widespread acceptance of the case on behalf of regional specialization, there have always been compelling arguments for local diversity. First is the concept of urbanization economies that relates to the agglomeration of firms in various industries in one location. For example, software engineering firms can serve a different array of customers in an area better and/or more cheaply than if these firms were maintaining all software-related functions within their corporate structure. Transport infrastructures such as ports and airports can also serve a wide array of businesses in a particular location, in the process generating external economies for all lines of work. A diversified local economic structure has also been said to generate a greater 'multiplier' effect when new productions are added to the local economy and provide new potential outlets to local producers.

Many studies have tried to estimate the extent, magnitude and respective importance of local diversity and urbanization economies, but these measurements have always been problematic (Rosenthal & Strange, 2004; Siegel et al., 1995), as has been the development of a workable concept of diversity. As Malizia and Feser (1999:92) point out: 'Economic diversity is the presence of multiple specializations. This definitional point deserves emphasis because the diversity literature is so confusing.'

Another obvious advantage of diversified local economies is the fact that they have long been viewed as more stable and resilient than highly specialized regions that are more prone to abrupt decline if their main line of business is supplanted by competitors or the emergence of new and better substitute products. Indeed, the economic landscape is littered with local areas of industrial specialization that were once prosperous and dynamic but have since gone into relative or absolute decline, from textile producing regions in advanced economies to once-thriving, but specialized, agricultural districts in areas that offered less interesting conditions than other parts of the world that were eventually integrated in the world economy. This was certainly obvious to Alfred Marshall (1920) who observed that 'a district which is dependent chiefly on one industry is liable to extreme depression, in case of a falling-off in the demand for its produce, or of a failure in the supply of the raw material which it uses', but that this problem was 'in a great measure avoided by those large towns or large industrial districts in which several distinct industries are strongly developed".[3] Indeed, as Keir (1919:47) pointed out at about the same time, it was 'true of every town whose industries are not diversified' that there were few places more hard-hit during hard times.

Confronted with this fact, local economic development officials and policy makers have long been concerned with the promotion of more diversified economic bases, especially in declining regions (Siegel et al., 1995). And yet, as Rosenfeld (2001:2) points out: 'Michael Porter's *Competitive Advantage of Nations* (1990) challenged the prevalent U.S. local development objective of very diversified economies.'

3.2   The development of new inter-firm linkages

Cluster-based development policy is to a large extent about creating and reinforcing dynamic linkages between firms and other institutions. In practice, however, the sectoral emphasis of most cluster development projects might be detrimental to the creation of interindustrial linkages between firms. Another policy prescription that has reached a worldwide audience in recent years, the planning of 'eco-industrial parks' (EIPs), is instructive in this respect.

The policy rationale behind EIPs is to colocate very different firms that will feed on each other's waste, in the process turning them into useful inputs. In its current incarnation, this idea first emerged following the 'discovery' of numerous such linkages in the small Danish industrial town of Kalundborg and its surrounding region, where six major industrial plants now engage in water (seven), energy (six) and solid waste (six) exchange projects (Chertow, 2000; Jacobsen & Anderberg, 2004).

Among other things, a power company supplies residual steam from its coal-fired power plant to an oil refinery and in exchange receives refinery gas that was formerly flared as waste. The power plant burns the refinery gas to generate electricity and steam and sends its excess steam to a fish farm, to a district heating system serving 3500 homes and to a pharmaceutical and enzyme manufacturing plant. Sludge from the fish farm and pharmaceutical processes becomes fertilizer for nearby farms. Surplus yeast from the biotechnology plant's production of insulin is shipped to farmers for pig food. The fly ash from the power plant is sent to a cement company, while gypsum produced by the power plant's desulphurization process goes to a gypsum wallboard company. Finally, the refinery removes sulphur from its natural gas and sells it to a sulphuric acid manufacturer.

Similar spontaneous, although less formalized, patterns have also been observed in various regions of Germany, Finland and the United States (Desrochers, 2002). Already familiar with the Kalundborg case, Schwarz and Steininger (1997) set out to investigate if such a network was unique and conducted a 'snowball' survey of the Austrian province of Styria, a much more diversified regional economy. Having identified similar, but much more numerous and complex, recovery linkages, the authors proceeded to map them (Figure 14.1), although it is important to note that, because of their research design, the authors did not document interregional linkages. Despite claims to the contrary, however, such 'industrial symbiosis' has always been a widespread market phenomenon emerging out of entrepreneurial activity and is unlikely to be improved by public planning (Desrochers, 2001b; 2002).

With cluster-led development becoming increasingly prominent, however, the task of promoting industrial symbiosis and, by extension, its spontaneous emergence, is proving increasingly difficult. As one Asian academic involved in the development of EIPs observed: 'In fact, tenants belonging to the same industry are put in the same zone inside the estate. Freedom of choice is also constrained: many investors cannot pick the location they prefer, but similarly many estate managers claim that they cannot select the right industry mix' (Chiu, 2002).

3.3   Local diversity and knowledge combination

Urban theorist Jane Jacobs (1961, 1969) has long argued that the unique asset of cities and what makes their wealth is precisely their diversity. One of her insights that has finally attracted the attention of economists in recent years is that urban development and growth stems in large part from the possibility that individuals are given to experiment with different sources of knowledge and encounter individuals with different experiences and background. As she put it, these circumstances typically pave the way for new combinations that always cut across conventional classification systems (Jacobs, 1969:62). This point has long been obvious to students of past technological change. For example, it is believed that the bow-drill, which was used as much for drilling holes as for starting fires, led to the bow (McNeil, 1996). The concept of a production chain was adapted over several decades in flourmills, slaughterhouses, machine tool works, canning, railroad car and auto assembly factories (Hounshell, 1984; Klemm, 1959). Lasers are now used in, among other things, printers, telecommunication equipment, navigational instruments, textile machinery, surgery, precision measurement, weapon systems, sound systems, and cash registers (Lipsey et al., 1998). Lichtenberg (1960) reports that, during the first half of the nineteenth century, New York's shipbuilding manufacturers diversified to include making carriages, steam engines and locomotives. Hounshell (1991) similarly points out that, during the 1890s' 'bicycle craze', numerous buggy, railroad, toy, agricultural equipment, firearms and sewing machine manufacturers turned to the production of bicycles.

Some recent empirical studies that have attempted to test Jacobs' hypothesis have indeed come to the conclusion that cities with an industrial structure that is more

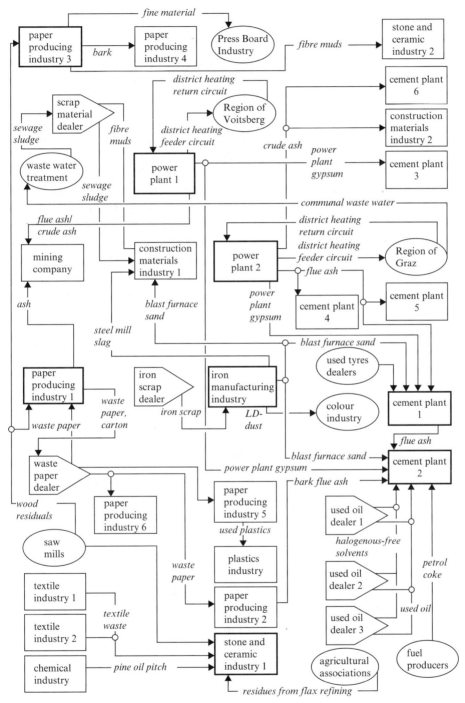

Source: Schwarz and Steininger (1997, p. 51).

Figure 14.1   Industrial recycling structure of Styria

diversified than the national average tend to be more prosperous in terms of economic growth and job creations than more specialized ones (Glaeser et al., 1992; Feldman, 2000). As Duranton and Puga (2000:53) write: 'The link between innovation and diversity seems fairly robust, so that highly innovative clusters cannot be bred in previously specialized environments.' However, these analyses of Jacobs' hypothesis have remained at a fairly abstract level and have not dealt with the processes by which knowledge is actually created and exchanged by and between individuals.

Some anecdotal evidence, such as Gutenberg's invention of the printing press (Figure 14.2), nonetheless provides valuable insight. At the dawn of the fifteenth century, printing was no longer a novelty in Europe. Printing from wooden blocks on vellum, silk and cloth is believed to have come into practice in the twelfth century, and printing on paper was widely practised in the second half of the fourteenth century. Oddly enough, though, the starting-point of Gutenberg's invention was playing cards on which a few words had been printed by way of rubbing wood blocks on a sheet of paper. As he wrote in his correspondence to a clergyman:

> Well, what has been done for a few words, for a few lines, I must succeed in doing for large pages of writing, for large leaves covered entirely on both sides, for whole books, for the first of all books, the Bible. How? It is useless to think of engraving on pieces of wood the whole thirteen

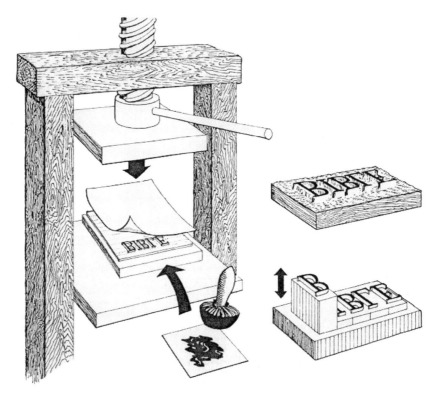

Source: http://lib.nmsu.edu/instruction/lsc311 /beck/ppress.jpg.

Figure 14.2   Gutenberg's printing press

hundred pages . . . What am I to do? I do not know: but I know what I want to do: I wish to manifold the Bible, I wish to have the copy ready for the pilgrimage to Aix-la-Chapelle. (Koestler, 1969:122)

Gutenberg then searched for a device more resistant than wood block, which led him to notice the seals used to authenticate documents, but rubbing them on paper did not give a clear print. He found the solution one day, while attending a wine harvest near his city.

> I took part in the wine harvest. I watched the wine flowing, and going back from the effect to the cause, I studied the power of this press which nothing can resist . . . God has revealed to me the secret that I demanded of Him . . . One must strike, cast, make a form like the seal of your community; a mold such as that used for casting your pewter cups; letters in relief like those on your coins, and the punch for producing them like the foot when it multiplies its print. There is the Bible! (Koestler, 1969: 123–4)

When inventing the printing press, Gutenberg followed a few common transfer mechanisms. In essence, when combining resources in a new way, an individual uses his previous know-how and his capacity of observation and learning. He therefore has only two ways of combining different resources. The first is to incorporate a new type of material/process/product (M/P/P) in a previously unrelated M/P/P, while the second is to find a new use for a M/P/P. Gutenberg thus already knew how to work metal, a skill that he learned as the child of the Archbishop of Mainz's goldsmith. This skill undoubtedly facilitated the transition from wooden to lead moveable types, a process that required steel for letter punches, lead for moulds, a tin–zinc–lead alloy for types and brass or bronze alloys for dies. On the other hand, his observation and subsequent learning about a particular wine press provided the final breakthrough needed for the creation of the first functional printing press.

Another famous case of borrowing ideas from other industries to create new production techniques is the development of the assembly line at the Ford Motor Company. It is thus generally acknowledged that the success of the Detroit manufacturer owed much to previous developments in other industries, such as the production of interchangeable parts, the idea of continuous flow, and the rise of the efficiency movement (Hounshell, 1991; Klemm, 1959). One industry that provided Ford's technical people with a model of efficient material handling was the meat packing industry. According to Hounshell (1991:241), William Klann, head of the engine department at Ford, recalled touring Swift's Chicago slaughterhouse and suggesting to superintendent Peter E. Martin upon noticing a 'disassembly line': 'If they can kill pigs and cows that way, we can build cars that way and build motors that way.' Klann also stressed that the Ford flow production also drew upon the mechanical conveying system of other regional businesses, such as flour milling and brewing firms: 'We combined our ideas on the Huetteman & Cramer grain [conveying] machine[ry] experience, and the brewing experience and the Chicago stockyard. They all gave us ideas for our own conveyors' (idem). According to Hounshell, the process technology employed in food canning might also have inspired some of Ford's employees.

Building on the notion that creative individuals combine existing things in a new way by building on their capacity of using their previous know-how and of observing and learning new things, Desrochers (2000; 2001a) surveyed literature in a number of fields ranging from technology and business history to management and psychology and further interviewed close to 50 individual inventors to suggest that new knowledge combinations in the industrial realm are accomplished by the following means:

- multidisciplinary teams working within a firm;
- employees adding to, or switching, their product line;
- individuals moving from one type of production to another;
- individuals observing a product/process in another setting and incorporating it into their main activity; and
- individuals possessing different skills and working for different firms, collaborating with each other.

Desrochers (2001a) further suggests that a diversified city is likely to increase the probability of combining existing resources in different configurations by offering a greater number and variety of problems to be solved, as well as a much wider pool of expert knowledge and other useful resources to develop new solutions. While local diversity might not necessarily be a prerequisite for these processes, agglomeration economies do tend to reduce the costs necessary to create new combinations, especially for smaller businesses.

Furthermore, communication between individuals that do not have a common knowledge base is often facilitated by geographical proximity and its resulting increased face-to-face communication. Raymond Kurzweil, a pioneer in the field of electronic music synthesizers, thus relates some difficulties in getting linguists, signal-processing experts, VLSI [very large scale integration] designers, psycho-acoustic experts, speech scientists, computer scientists, human-factor designers and experts in artificial intelligence and pattern recognition to work together in his plant:

> Each one of these fields has very different methodologies and different terminologies. Very often a term in one field means something else entirely in another field. Sometimes we even create our own terminology for a particular project. So, enabling a team like that to communicate and solve a problem is a significant challenge. If you look at the entire company, you bring in even more disciplines: manufacturing, material-resources planning, purchasing, marketing, finance, and so on. Each of these areas has also developed sophisticated methodologies of their own that are as complex as those in engineering. My challenge is to provide a climate in which people with different expertise can work together toward a common goal and communicate clearly with one another. (Brown, 1988:243–4)

In the social context of market exchange, this process of combination of unrelated things will be guided by the profit and loss mechanism. As Schumpeter explained, what distinguishes the mere inventor from the entrepreneur innovator is the fact that his invention is socially useful. Through profit and losses, the market system provides the only mechanism enabling individuals in society to distinguish what is socially useful from what is not. Entrepreneurial activity is ultimately guided and sanctioned by the profit and loss mechanism, which selects the projects that are most desired by other individuals in society. In the absence of this mechanism, there is no way to know whether allocating resources to a project is socially useful.

If innovation is understood as the combination of previously unrelated things, it seems obvious that diversified cities will be more likely to generate innovation than specialized ones. This was certainly obvious to Keir (1919:47) almost a century ago when he pointed out the following:

From the point of view of employees, [geographically-specialized] localization is bad because it also tends toward narrowing the minds of the townspeople. A young man brought up in Fall River, say, has but little choice of occupation; he must become a weaver or a loom-fixer or some other artisan connected with cotton manufacture, because by upbringing, education and example he is forced into that path, and furthermore he goes to work at an early age. It may happen that many a square peg is rammed into a round hole in this way, or a life constricted which might under better conditions have expanded. There is something deadening to the human mind in uniformity; progress comes through variation, therefore in a town of one industry a young man loses the stimulus for self-advancement.

Porter (2000a:24) himself seems to have caught on to this rationale when he argues that, when a cluster 'shares a uniform approach to competing, a sort of groupthink often reinforces old behaviors, suppresses new ideas, and creates rigidities that prevent adoption of improvements'. 'Clusters', it turns out, might also 'not support truly radical innovation, which tends to invalidate the existing pools of talent, information, suppliers, and infrastructure.' While in these circumstances a cluster participant might not necessarily be worse off than an isolated firm because both can outsource, 'the firm in an established cluster might suffer from greater barriers to perceiving the need to change and from inertia against severing past relationships that no longer contribute to competitive advantage'.

4   Conclusion

Clusters development has become an important article in policy makers' and government advisers' toolboxes. Indeed, as Lagendijk and Cornford (2000) have put it, cluster-based development strategies have led to the growth of a 'regional development industry' that is oriented towards the production and circulation of knowledge in the form of reports, conferences and seminars.

The idea that specialized clusters are beneficial to economic development ultimately finds its roots in the work of Ricardo (1817) and his law of comparative advantage. Because of the dynamic and generally unpredictable nature of economic life, however, no policy maker is really in a position to decide which region should specialize in which industry. It is only through the information generated by local actors that the best geographical setting for the prosperity of an economy will be found at any given point in time. It may be the case that an emerging or undeveloped region might benefit from regional specialization in an early stage of development, but a deliberate emphasis on such specialization by policy makers is certainly self-defeating in the long run. As much evidence suggests, regional specialization leaves regional economies more subjected to experience economic downturn, and is less likely to promote positive externalities such as inter-firm linkages (including recycling linkages) and new technology combinations. A better setting for innovation would then seem to be a diversified city made up of many specialized clusters – which is historically what most thriving cities have spontaneously been. While it might be impossible to create local diversity successfully, its spontaneous emergence through the entrepreneurial discovery process should not be hindered by counterproductive policies such as cluster-based development.

Notes

1.   University of Toronto, George Mason University and University of Twente, respectively.
2.   For example, Alfred Marshall refers to an essay on the various industrial districts of England that was published in the thirteenth century (Marshall, 1986 [1920]:223).

3.   From the non-paginated version of Marshall's (1920/1890), *Principles of Economics*, 8th edn, Book IIV, Chapter X (http://www.econlib.org/library/Marshall/marP.html).

References

Brown, K.A. (1988), *Inventors at Work. Interviews with 16 Notable American Inventors*, Redmond, WA: Tempus Book of Microsoft Press.
Buss, T.F. (1999), 'The case against targeted industry strategies', *Economic Development Quarterly*, 13(4), 339–56.
Chapman, K. (2005), 'From "growth centre" to "cluster": restructuring, regional development, and the Teeside chemical industry', *Environment and Planning A*, 37(4), 597–615.
Chertow, M. (2000) 'Industrial symbiosis: literature and taxonomy', *Annual Review of Energy and the Environment*, 25, 313–37.
Chiu, A.S. (2002), 'Ecology, systems, and networking. Walking the talk in Asia', *Journal of Industrial Ecology*, 5(2), 6–8.
Desrochers, P. (2000), *De l'influence d'une Ville Diversifiée sur la Combinaison de Techniques: Typologie et Analyse de Processus*, Ph.D.dissertation (geography), Université de Montréal.
Desrochers, P. (2001a), 'Local diversity, human creativity and technological innovation', *Growth and Change*, 32(3), 369–94.
Desrochers, P. (2001b), 'Cities and industrial symbiosis: some historical perspective and policy implications', *Journal of Industrial Ecology*, 5(4), 29–44.
Desrochers, P. (2002), 'Regional development and inter-industry recycling linkages: some historical perspective', *Entrepreneurship and Regional Development*, 4(1), 49–65.
Desrochers, P. and F. Sautet (2004), 'Cluster-based economic strategy, facilitation policy and the market process', *Review of Austrian Economics*, 17(2/3), 233–45.
Duranton, G. and D. Puga (2000), 'Diversity and specialisation in cities: why, where and when does it matter?', *Urban Studies*, 37(3), 533–55.
Feldman, M. (2000), 'Location and innovation: the new economic geography of innovation, spillovers and agglomeration', in G.L. Clark, M.P. Feldman and M.S. Gertler (eds), *Oxford Handbook of Economic Geography*, Oxford: Oxford University Press, pp. 373–94.
Glaeser, E., H. Kallal, J. Scheinkman and A. Shleifer (1992), 'Growth in cities', *Journal of Political Economy*, 100(6), 1126–52.
Hansen, N. (1996), 'Regional development policies: past problems and future possibilities', *Canadian Journal of Regional Science*, 19(1), 107–18.
Hoffman, W. (2001), 'Professor Porter goes to Washington', *The Doric Column*, 31 December (http://mbbnet.umn.edu/doric/michaelporter.html).
Hounshell, D. (1991/1984), *From the American System to Mass Production, 1800–1932*, Baltimore: Johns Hopkins University Press.
Jacobs, J. (1961), *The Death and Life of Great American Cities*, New York: Random House.
Jacobs, J. (1969), *The Economy of Cities*, New York: Random House.
Jacobsen, N.B. and S. Anderberg (2004), 'Understanding the evolution of industrial symbiotic networks', in J. van den Bergh and M.A. Janssen (eds), *Economics of Industrial Ecology. Materials, Structural Change, and Spatial Scales*, Cambridge, MA: MIT Press, pp. 313–35.
Keir, M. (1919), 'The localization of industry. How it starts; why it grows and persists', *The Scientific Monthly*, 8(1), 32–48.
Klemm, F. (1959), *A History of Western Technology*, New York: Scribner.
Koestler, A. (1969/1964), *The Act of Creation*, London: Hutchinson of London.
Lagendijk, A. and J. Cornford (2000), 'Regional institutions and knowledge – tracking new forms of regional development policy', *Geoforum*, 31, 209–18.
Lichtenberg, R.M. (1960), *One-Tenth of a Nation: National Forces in the Economic Growth of the New York Region*, Cambridge: Harvard University Press.
Lipsey, R.G., C. Bekar and K. Carlaw (1998), 'What requires explanation?', in E. Helpman (ed.), *General Purpose Technologies and Economic Growth*, Cambridge, MA: MIT Press.
Malizia, E.E. and E.J. Feser (1999), *Understanding Local Economic Development*, New Brunswick, NJ: Center for Urban Policy Research, Rutgers University.
Marshall, A. (1920/1890), *Principles of Economics*, 8th edn, London: Macmillan (http://www.econlib.org/library/Marshall/marP.html).
McNeil, I. (1996/1990), 'Introduction: basic tools, devices and mechanisms', in I. McNeil (ed.), *An Encyclopedia of the History of Technology*, London: Routledge, pp. 1–40.
Porter, M. (1990), *The Competitive Advantage of Nations*, London: Macmillan.
Porter, M. (1998), 'Location, clusters and the "new" microeconomics of competition', *Business Economics*, 33(1), 7–17.

Porter, M. (2000a), 'Location, competition, and economic development: local clusters in a global economy', *Economic Development Quarterly*, **14**(1), 15–34.

Porter, M. (2000b), 'Location, clusters and company strategy', in G.L. Clark, M.S. Gertler and M.P. Feldman (eds), *The Oxford Handbook of Economic Geography*, New York: Oxford University Press, pp. 253–74.

Ricardo, D. (1963 [1817]), *The Principles of Political Economy and Taxation*, Homewood, IL: R.D. Irwin.

Rosenfeld, S. (2001), 'Backing into clusters: retrofitting public policies', paper presented at the 'Integration Pressures: Lessons from Around the World', John F. Kennedy School Symposium, Harvard University, 29–30 March (http://www.rtsinc.org/publications/Harvard4%20doc%20copy.pdf).

Rosenthal, S.S. and W. Strange (2004), 'Evidence on the nature and sources of agglomeration economies', in V. Henderson and J. Thisse (eds), *Handbook of Urban and Regional Economics*, Vol. 4, Amsterdam: Elsevier, pp. 2119–172.

Schwarz, E.J. and K.W. Steininger (1997), 'Implementing nature's lesson: the industrial recycling network enhancing regional development', *Journal of Cleaner Production*, **5**(1/2), 47–56.

Siegel, P.B., T.G. Johnson and J. Alwang (1995), 'Regional economic diversity and diversification: seeking a framework for analysis', *Growth and Change*, **26**(2), 261–84.

PART FOUR

SECTORAL CLUSTERS

15 Clustering in financial services
Naresh R. Pandit, Gary A.S. Cook and G.M. Peter Swann

1 Introduction

The primary function of the financial services industry is to intermediate profitably between savers and borrowers in an economy, in effect distributing funds accumulated by savers to meet the demands of borrowers. Two second-order functions are risk pooling and management, and facilitating payments. When considering the *location* of financial services, it is useful to distinguish between retail and wholesale services. On the whole, retail financial services are directly offered to the general public and the small firm sector. Examples include interest-bearing savings accounts, loans to enable the purchase of residential property, and overdrafts. Such services tend to follow population and so are dispersed in line with the dispersal of the general population. Wholesale financial services, on the other hand, are offered to large companies and governments. Examples include bond and equity issues, help with mergers and acquisitions, and sophisticated financial risk management products such as financial derivatives. In most developed economies, such wholesale services tend to cluster, concentrating in a small number of places (Bindemann, 1999; Davis, 1990; Poon, 2003). Begg (1992) provides a useful typology of such wholesale financial services clusters. At the global level, three clusters are in a leading class of their own: London, New York and Tokyo. These clusters provide a wide range of financial services and are where the headquarters of major financial services firms and institutions are located (Andersson, 2000; Sassen, 1991). Second-order clusters are also diversified but serve *regional* economies and include Hong Kong, Frankfurt, Paris and Singapore. A third category consists of specialist or niche international centres such as Edinburgh, Luxembourg and Zurich. Next come national centres with limited international business such as Rome, Hamburg and Barcelona. Penultimately, Begg identifies within-country diversified regional centres such as Leeds and Bristol in the UK and, finally, there are within-country specialist centres which, for the UK, would include Norwich and Bournemouth.

This chapter considers the leading type of wholesale financial services clustering focusing on the City of London,[1] the oldest and the largest relative to its national economy of the three in this group. There are two major differences between the City of London and the other two (Nachum, 2003). First is the share of financial services activity controlled by foreign ownership which is much lower in New York and Tokyo (for example, the number of foreign banks in the City, New York and Tokyo was 573, 275 and 93, respectively in 2000). This situation partly arises because the UK and so the City of London has a more liberal policy attitude to foreign ownership (Morgan, 1997). Second, the City of London is more international in its outlook with a much higher percentage of foreign business. In contrast, New York and Tokyo's strength relates to the strength of their domestic economies and currencies. London's unique position is that its strength is *independent* of its domestic economy and currency. Both of these differences mean that the City of London is the world's foremost *international* wholesale financial services cluster.

The outline of the chapter is as follows. The next section describes *how* wholesale financial services production clusters in the City of London. This is followed by the chapter's core section which examines *why* wholesale financial services production clusters in the City of London. Extant theory on the reasons for financial servicing clustering is tested against the findings of a large-scale empirical study of financial services clustering in the City of London. A final section relates the discussion to the 'end of geography' thesis in financial services (O'Brien, 1991) and concludes regarding the likelihood of continued financial services clustering in the City.

2   The City of London financial services cluster
The rise of the financial services industry in the City is fundamentally linked to the rise of the UK as a major trading and commercial nation with the industry *facilitating* trade and commerce both within the UK and between the UK and the rest of the world. As such, its origins date back to the late seventeenth century, when goldsmith-bankers began to provide monarchs and merchants with the money they needed to fund their ventures around the world.[2] At that time, Amsterdam was more important than the City as a financial centre and it was only towards the end of the nineteenth century, when the UK emerged as the world's most important trading nation, that the City emerged as the world's most important financial services centre (Kynaston, 1994; 1995). Since then, except for a decline in the inter-war years (Kynaston, 1999), the City has gone from strength to strength and is now undisputedly the world's most important international wholesale financial services cluster (Coggan, 2002; Kynaston, 2001; Poon, 2003).

The modern City has core activities in banking, insurance and fund management, supported by a panoply of activities including legal services, accounting, management consultancy, advertising, market research, recruitment, property management, financial printing and publishing, and the provision of electronic information (IFSL, 2005). Geographically, there are five distinct sub-concentrations of activity, all of which are north of the River Thames (see Figure 15.1). First is Canary Wharf to the east which is the home of some of the largest investment banks. Second, is the very dense 'square mile' that is the original City of London featuring banks, insurance and law firms. Third is, a less dense West End concentration featuring banks near Mayfair and advertising in Soho. Fourth is, an incipient concentration north of the City featuring services such as architecture and business support. Finally, a concentration lies in-between the City and the West End, consisting of law firms located in close proximity to the law courts. Together these *interdependent* sub-concentrations make up the City of London financial services cluster.

The cluster employs some 316 000 people (IFSL, 2005) in a very tight space. Indicative location quotients of UK financial services employment, calculated by dividing the proportion of regional financial services employment by the proportion of national financial services employment, show that London's quotient is twice the national average and almost twice as large as Scotland, the region with the second-highest quotient (see Table 15.1).[3] The concentration of the industry in London is further demonstrated in Figure 15.2, which gives data on UK and London financial services employment and shows that roughly one-third of national employment is located in London.

The City's domination of the international wholesale financial services industry is remarkable. It holds the top rank for cross-border bank lending, foreign equities turnover,

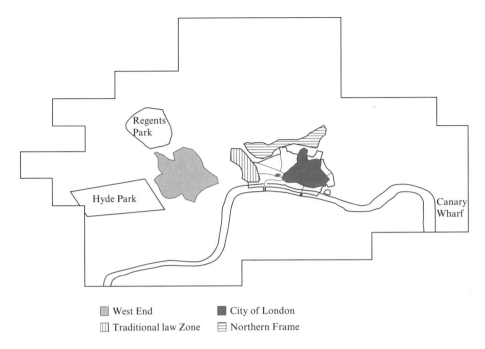

West End   ■ City of London
▥ Traditional law Zone   ▤ Northern Frame

Source: Taylor et al. (2003, p. 15).

Figure 15.1   The City of London financial services cluster

Table 15.1   Location quotients of British financial services employment

UK = 1.00	1996	1997	1998	1999	2000	2001	2002
London	2.23	2.19	2.07	2.01	2.03	2.01	1.96
Scotland	0.84	0.88	0.90	0.93	1.01	1.07	1.09
UK	1.00	1.00	1.00	1.00	1.00	1.00	1.00
South West	1.05	0.96	0.98	0.98	0.97	0.96	0.94
South East	0.99	0.99	1.01	0.97	0.95	0.92	0.91
East	0.84	0.91	0.91	0.93	0.88	0.84	0.83
Yorkshire & Humberside	0.78	0.85	0.89	0.85	0.79	0.78	0.79
North West	0.78	0.75	0.78	0.81	0.80	0.80	0.78
West Midlands	0.72	0.71	0.72	0.75	0.73	0.74	0.75
Wales	0.60	0.59	0.59	0.60	0.65	0.73	0.74
Northern Ireland	0.49	0.47	0.48	0.49	0.52	0.54	0.56
North East	0.52	0.49	0.48	0.52	0.50	0.54	0.54
East Midlands	0.55	0.54	0.56	0.53	0.50	0.49	0.46

Notes: 2002 data are for January – June only.
Quotients calculated as the ratio of the share of financial service employment in total employment for the
region to the share of financial service employment in total employment nationally. Financial services defined
as item J in the Labour Force Survey, 'financial intermediation'.

Source: ONS and HM Treasury calculations.

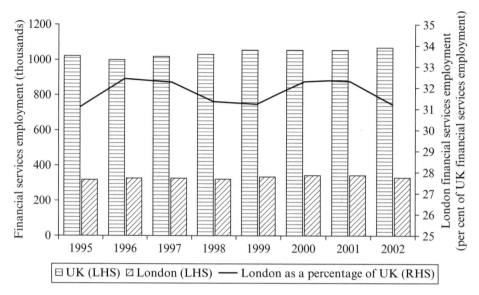

Note: 2002 data are for January–June day.

Source: ONS.

Figure 15.2   UK and London financial services employment

foreign exchange turnover, over-the-counter derivatives turnover, marine insurance net premium income, and secondary market international bonds (see Table 15.2). Among the top five world economies, it also contributes the largest trade surplus (see Figure 15.3).

3   Reasons for the clustering of financial services in the City of London

Why does wholesale financial services production cluster so densely in the City of London? Drawing from over 20 theoretical studies of clustering and financial services, HM Treasury's (2003) extensive study of London as a financial centre begins by identifying eight general 'centripetal forces' that give rise to wholesale financial services clustering (2003, p. 25):

- colocation near to a variety of complementary firms and related services,
- a large pool of skilled labour,
- liquidity and size of markets,
- access to financial infrastructure,
- physical infrastructure, especially office space, telecommunications networks and international transport links,
- localized information and technology spillovers,
- 'thick' institutional structures, including regulatory approach,
- initial conditions.

The study proceeds to suggest which of these general forces apply to London, and finds that London's most 'significant strengths . . . in terms of centripetal forces' are:

Table 15.2   Share of international financial markets

% share	London	US	Japan	France	Germany	Others
Cross-border bank lending	20	9	8	8	11	44
Foreign equities turnover	44	31	–	–	3	22
Foreign exchange turnover	31	19	8	3	5	34
OTC derivatives turnover	43	24	3	10	3	17
Marine insurance net premium income	16	11	14	8	10	41
International bonds – secondary market	70	–	–	–	–	–
Fund management (as a source of funds)	8	46	12	5	4	25
Hedge funds assets	20	69	1	2	–	8

Source: Adapted from IFSL (2005).

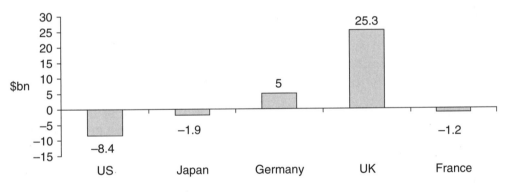

Source: International Monetary Fund.

Figure 15.3   Financial services trade balances

- 'a critical mass in financial expertise, offering a wide range of complementary services to the international investor;
- market infrastructure which can support high levels of activity, offering liquidity to traders, which thereby encourages other traders into the market;
- a pool of skilled labour, and flexible labour markets relative to other financial centres.' (HM Treasury, 2003, p. 26)

Another, more empirical study, examining the reasons for wholesale financial services clustering in the City involved two of this chapter's authors and is reported in Taylor et al. (2003). The study collected primary data from a postal questionnaire survey and a set of 39 face-to-face interviews. With respect to the former, 1500 questionnaires were posted to financial services companies known to be operating within and up to 500 metres beyond the boundaries of the City of London and Canary Wharf. The sample was selected using a stratified method. 100 per cent of the largest 350 firms were selected. These were identified primarily from a database supplied by the specialist information provider *Market Locations*. The remaining 1150 firms were drawn at random from the rest of the *Market Locations* database (using a random number generator). The original mailing went out in April 2002, with a follow-up in June 2002. A third mailing was considered but rejected in view of the good response rate to the first two mailings. A total of 310 usable questionnaires were returned, a response rate of just over 20 per cent.

Respondents were asked to rank the importance of a potential benefit of a City location from 1 (not important) to 5 (very important). The findings of the postal questionnaire survey are presented in Table 15.3. Benefits are presented in total score rank order which is the sum of recorded scores for a given benefit. A benchmark for interpreting these total scores is the average of the total score across all factors in the questionnaire, which was 855. The 95 per cent confidence interval around this average is 808–901. Accordingly, when comparing the relative importance of each benefit, any total score below 808 is relatively unimportant and any total score above 901 is relatively important. The table divides benefits into groups where there is no statistically significant difference in the total score within groups but there is a statistically significant difference between groups (based on the 'conservative' sign test).

The importance of a credible address stands apart at the head of these benefits. It was also among the most consistently mentioned benefits in the interview survey where interviewees stated that a firm's address signalled that it was a serious player and, as such, its *address* acted as a strong brand. The second-highest rated benefit of a City location is the ability to tap into a strong, skilled labour supply. This is of course unsurprising, being in line with the classic work on industrial location by Marshall ([1920] 1927). Of course, the defining characteristic of a cluster is the close proximity of related firms and institutions and this is reflected in the finding that proximity to customers, in the physical sense and in the sense of being on the beaten track, are the number three and four benefits. Proximity to professional bodies is the number five benefit and the knowledge spillovers that occur when physically close to related firms and institutions is the number six benefit. All four of these proximity-related benefits score higher than the benchmark of 901 and, taken together, rack up a sizable score of 3838. In the questionnaire, Taylor et al. (2003) asked *why* proximity was advantageous (Table 15.4).

The paramount importance of maintaining personal contact and being able to interact face-to-face is evident. In the questionnaire survey as a whole, these were the second and third most highly ranked factors. The importance of face-to-face contact was underscored by the interview survey, which cast light on why it is important. Several firms emphasized the importance of a face-to-face meeting for conducting complex transactions where it was important to fashion agreement while reducing the chances of misunderstandings or creating antagonism. A face-to-face meeting had the advantage that more information is conveyed, including important non-verbal signals, for example in trying to judge whether someone is honest and trustworthy or in gauging whether someone is unhappy or becoming upset. At the stage when deals are being transacted, a crisis can emerge at any time and there may be a need for a meeting to sort the matter out quickly and satisfactorily. One firm suggested that this requirement meant that it was important for senior staff to be based in London. Similarly, several firms cited the need to be close to regulators, including the Bank of England, in order to have the ability to meet face-to-face to resolve important issues and to cement an ongoing relationship. The overall impression gained in

Table 15.3   General benefits of a City of London location

How important are each of the following benefits of your location?

	1	2	3	4	5	0	Total
Your address is important to being perceived as credible	18	23	63	111	91	2	1152
You benefit from a strong, skilled labour supply	21	22	62	95	85	22	1056
You benefit from being close to market-leading customers	18	46	66	88	77	12	1045
Your customers external to London find it easier to locate you	32	42	72	98	46	15	954
You benefit from being near professional bodies	36	59	79	68	52	11	923
Knowledge transfer from the City's 'financial atmosphere'	28	45	75	72	57	28	916
You benefit from being near leading competitors	49	58	63	73	41	23	851
Customers external to London find it easier to interact with you	45	58	87	62	35	19	845
Ability to find firms who will supply bespoke services	34	75	83	56	36	22	837
It is the best place to be to take market share from rivals	37	60	74	65	39	32	834
Proximity to a relevant exchange or physical marketplace	55	36	70	44	57	45	798
Ability to benchmark against competitors	67	68	72	43	23	33	706
Local rivalry amongst competitors is a powerful spur	63	70	69	44	18	42	676
Ability to access real-time information on market trends	80	65	49	44	27	41	668
Support from local government	119	66	33	13	11	64	457
Access to venture capital	113	46	31	13	11	90	405

Source: Taylor et al. (2003, p. 29).

Table 15.4   The importance of close proximity to other firms

How important are each of the following reasons for having a location in close proximity to other firms in London?

	1	2	3	4	5	0	Total
It is easier to build and maintain personal contacts	12	15	46	123	101	7	1177
The ability to have face-to-face contact	14	15	37	108	117	12	1172
It is easier to build relationships of trust and cooperation	17	33	71	98	73	13	1053
It is easier to communicate because we have a common understanding of the business	27	33	67	108	51	17	981
We generally have complementary expertise with such firms	24	47	10	80	34	19	911
Multidisciplinary teams can be assembled more quickly	30	46	73	86	41	27	890

Source: Taylor et al. (2003, p. 40).

the interviews is that there is a deep-rooted need to conduct certain wholesale financial services business face-to-face.

Proximity also enabled a greater *frequency* of meeting because time and money costs were lower compared to the case when people had to travel long distances. In turn, being able to meet more frequently helped team building. A number of firms in banking and legal services commented on the need to have adequate space for large meetings because the size of meetings had grown as transactions had become larger and more complex. Several firms emphasized that, while there had been a burgeoning use of e-mail and video conferencing for intra-firm and inter-firm communication, neither of these media would ever replace the need for physical face-to-face meetings. Several respondents commented that e-mail and video conferencing work much better with people they knew, so face-to-face meeting will continue to be important in forming relationships that can subsequently rely on more remote communication media. Finally, the interview survey highlighted that being able to walk between firms, institutions, professional bodies, bars, gyms etc. was of great significance in sustaining face-to-face contact especially in the compact geographical area of the City.

To what extent do the findings of Taylor et al. (2003) corroborate the three centripetal forces suggested by the Treasury study? The first centripetal force, the critical mass of complementary financial services expertise, is fully endorsed. Taylor et al. (2003) find that the production of complex financial services in the City often requires the formation of teams drawn from related firms and institutions. Furthermore, it is vital that the members of such teams are able to engage in frequent and sometimes impromptu face-to-face meetings. On the demand side, customers are more likely to find related suppliers and value the ability to compare producers' prices and products when they are concentrated in a tight geographical space. Once united, the quantity and quality of supplier/buyer interaction again increases within a tight geographical space. Buyers' search for quality suppliers can be affected by market signals such as the reputation of a production centre and location can perform a valuable economic role by transmitting a credible signal of a firm's history and quality.

The second centripetal force, market infrastructure, receives good but not compelling endorsement by this study. International transport links and high-speed telecommunications networks are clearly important, particularly with respect to interaction with customers that are external to the cluster. Also, London's time-zone, which allows incumbent firms to manage their daily trading from east (Tokyo) to west (Chicago, San Francisco) on the same day (Golding, 2001) is an advantage. However, these features are hardly unique to London and so cannot be fundamentally differentiating. Similarly, buildings with large floor plates that can accommodate large trading floors is an undoubted strength of Canary Wharf (particularly for large investment banks (Clark, 2002), which drive the cluster) but again such sites and such buildings can be found in many large cities. Finally, the importance of proximity to a relevant exchange in order to access liquidity has diminished as exchanges have become computerized and automated and so accessible from a distance.

The third centripetal force, the skilled and flexible labour supply, is fully endorsed. Four key advantages stand out. Firstly, labour is attracted into the market because the size of the market provides a better chance of continuity of employment. Secondly, the sheer size of the market provides an incentive for people to invest in highly specific skills. Thirdly, the movement of people between firms in the cluster helps to spread a network of contacts and facilitates knowledge spillovers. Finally, compared to other European financial centres, labour laws are less stringent, enabling financial services firms to hire and fire with relative ease in response to the natural cyclicality of the industry.

Taken together, the Treasury study and Taylor et al. (2003) point strongly to the importance of *relationships* in wholesale financial services production and proceed to demonstrate that such relationships fundamentally require frequent face-to-face contact and therefore fundamentally require physical proximity. Other important work on wholesale financial services clustering reaches a similar conclusion. Davis (1990) and Cobham (1992) categorize the benefits of financial services clustering as exogenous (national-level) or endogenous (cluster-level) and conclude that exogenous benefits (such as government regulation), are *less* important than endogenous benefits. Clearly, the Treasury study and Taylor et al. (2003) support this proposition. Eccles and Crane (1988) also concur and identify five *firm*-level production characteristics in investment banking that benefit from clustering. Thrift's (1994, p. 333) excellent summary of these characteristics is worth quoting at length:

> First, much of the production of financial products and services takes place at the boundaries of the firms. Firms tend to be client- rather than task-centred and to rely on repeat business. Second, firms tend to be flattened and non-hierarchical. Responsibility is often diffuse and vague with results coming from the efforts of small teams of relationship and product specialists . . . Third, as a matter of course, firms need to cooperate with one another as well as compete, for example in syndicated lending or the placement of securities. Fourth, firms often find it difficult to judge their performance accurately. They can only be sure of how they are doing through comparison with other firms' successes and failures . . . Fifth, it is difficult for financial services firms in international financial centres to build up the equivalent of inventories to buffer the firm. The result is that the employees of these firms have to be constantly 'on the go' to find new business. They must be able to work in a crisis mode, dropping everything to complete a task on time or to get work. (Thrift, 1994, p. 333)

Thrift (1994) concludes that physical proximity, both to competitors and to suppliers and buyers, is critical in wholesale financial services production. This conclusion resonates with Agnes' (2000) analysis of the Australian interest rate swaps industry which finds that 'dealing by necessity involves the revelation of proprietary trading information, so the formation of relationships characterised by trustworthiness, rapport, and confidence assumes great significance; these features develop through face-to-face meetings and social interaction, facilitated by spatial proximity' (p. 348). Tickell (2003) corroborates this. His review of the literature on finance and localities concludes that, 'Despite the phenomenal transformations in the nature of finance in the latter third of the twentieth century . . . the business of finance still thrives upon close inter-firm and inter-personal relationships' (p. 236).

4 Conclusion

Whilst the City of London's initial advantage may have been one of historical legacy, as 'the centre of Empire' (Clark, 2002) and the home of the Industrial Revolution, a London location continues to be important not only in spite of the costs associated with strong demand for a limited supply of highly centralized space (Cook et al., forthcoming), but also in spite of four major developments since financial services deregulation in the UK in 1986 (i.e., post 'Big Bang'). Firstly, the *structure* of the cluster has changed. Firms are much larger and are active in many sectors (Clark, 2002). Chief amongst these are the so-called 'Universal Banks' or 'Bulge-Bracket firms' the exemplar of which is Citibank. Clark (2002, p. 446) observes, 'whereas the old City of London was characterised by networks of similarly located smaller firms, the new model of firm organisation and management is one based upon huge office towers of many thousands of employees'. Secondly, the City has undergone significant *cultural* change which has been labelled 'Wimbledonisation' by Kynaston (2001): just as Wimbledon is the home of tennis and yet British champions are rare, so the City of London is the home of finance and yet the cluster is dominated by foreign-owned firms. Philip Augar in his book, *The Death of Gentlemanly Capitalism*, (2000) further documents the cultural change that the City has undergone post-deregulation by suggesting that the environment in which business is done has moved from that reminiscent of a 'gentleman's club' to one characterized by intense competition and hard work. The third and fourth major developments post 'Big-Bang' are that the City has been disproportionately subject to rapid technological change in the form of the 'ICT revolution' and that the City has been subject to increasing globalization. On the basis of these two changes, O'Brien, writing in 1991, predicted the 'end of geography' in financial services:

> The end of geography, as a concept applied to international financial relationships, refers to a state of economic development where geographic location no longer matters in finance, or much less than hitherto . . . For financial firms, this means that the choice of geographical location can be greatly widened, provided that an appropriate investment in information and computer systems can be made . . . There will be forces seeking to maintain geographical control . . . Yet, as markets and rules become integrated, the relevance of geography and the need to base decisions on geography will alter and often diminish. (1991, pp. 1–2)

Whilst this predication may have great applicability to *retail* financial services, regarding *wholesale* financial services, the substance of this chapter indicates that it is exaggerated.

For example, Tickell (2003) observes that, while these changes have had an impact on the location of financial services production, this impact has been limited, applying more to low-value, back office activities and less to the high-value knowledge-intensive activities of the City that critically benefit from clustering. Corroborating, Martin (1994) first states:

> In principle, modern telecommunications technologies render the need for financial centres increasingly obsolete: new banking and trading technologies, such as local area networks (LANs), on-line transaction processing (OLTP) and electronic data interchange (EDI), not only increase the range of financial services, but also confer considerable locational freedom on institutions. Market participants no longer have to be in the same centre, the same country or even the same continent for trading to take place. (Martin, 1994, p. 262)

He then continues to observe that such developments have indeed led to the dispersal of financial services activity away from established clusters, but concludes, 'Much of this, however, has been of back offices, leaving the head offices and primary business within the national capitals' (ibid., p. 263). This line of thinking resonates with Enright (2000) who states,

> as transportation and communications improve, as technology becomes more widely dispersed, and as barriers to trade and investment fall, some industries become more dispersed over geographic space. In other industries and activities, however, the same forces foster geographic concentration by allowing firms and locations to exploit specific sources of competitive advantage over even wider geographic areas . . . This logic concludes that as competition globalises, the geographic or location-specific sources of competitive advantage will tend to become more, not less, important. (Enright, 2000, pp. 115–16)

In summary, despite radical change post deregulation in 1986 in the form of changing structure, changing culture, rapid technological change and increased globalization, geographical proximity remains essential for wholesale financial services production in the City of London. As Thrift (1994) succinctly puts it: 'International financial centres will continue because they satisfy essential communicative/interpretive needs that cannot be met through electronic communication. There will be no 'end of geography'. (Thrift, 1994, p. 352)

Acknowledgements

This research was partly funded by the UK Economic and Social Research Council and partly funded by the Corporation of London. We would like to acknowledge input from Jonathan Beaverstock, Kathy Pain and Peter Taylor. None of these is responsible for any remaining errors.

Notes

1. Technically, the 'City of London' refers to the 'square mile' around the Bank of England. Although this remains the geographic core of the cluster, developments to the east, west and north have extended the centre to the extent that the term 'the City' is now generally used to refer to the cluster as a whole and not just the square mile (Golding, 2001). This chapter will follow this convention.
2. One such business, Barclays bank, was founded by John Freame and his partner Thomas Gould in Lombard Street, London, in 1690. The UK's central bank, the Bank of England, was founded in 1694.
3. The location quotient for London declines from 2.23 to 1.96 over the period 1996–2002, not because of a decline in financial services employment in London, but rather because, over the period, growth in UK financial services employment exceeds growth in London financial services employment.

Bibliography

Agnes, P. (2000), 'The "end of geography" in financial services? Local embeddedness and territorialisation in the interest rate swap industry', *Economic Geography*, **76**, 347–66.

Andersson, A.E. (2000), *Gateways to the Global Economy*, Cheltenham, UK and Northampton, MA, US: Edward Elgar.

Augar, P. (2000), *The Death of Gentlemanly Capitalism*, London: Penguin.

Begg, I. (1992), 'The spatial impact of completion of the EC internal market for financial services', *Journal of Regional Studies*, **26**(4), 333–47.

Bindemann, K. (1999), *The Future of European Financial Centres*, London: Routledge.

Clark, G.L. (2002), 'London in the European financial services industry: locational advantages and product complementarities', *Journal of Economic Geography*, **2**, 433–54.

Cobham, D. (Ed.) (1992), *Markets and Dealers: The Economics of the London Financial Markets*, London: Longman.

Coggan, P. (2002), *The Money Machine: How the City Works*, London: Penguin.

Cook, G.A.S., N.R. Pandit, J.V. Beaverstock, P.J. Taylor and K. Pain (2007), 'The role of location in knowledge creation and diffusion: evidence of centripetal and centrifugal forces in the City of London financial services agglomeration', *Environment and Planning A*, **39**(6), 1325–45.

Davis, E.P. (1990), 'International financial centres – an industrial analysis', *Bank of England Discussion Paper*, 51.

Eccles, R.G. and D.B. Crane (1988), *Doing Deals. Investment Banks at Work*, Boston, MA: HBS Press.

Enright, M.J. (2000), 'Regional clusters and multinational enterprises', *International Studies of Management and Organization*, **30**(2), 114–38.

Golding, T. (2001), *The City: Inside the Great Expectation Machine*, London: Prentice-Hall.

H.M. Treasury (2003), *The Location of Financial Activity and the Euro*, London: H.M. Treasury.

International Financial Services London (2005), *International Financial Markets in the UK*, May (available at www.ifsl.org.uk).

Kynaston, D. (1994), *The City of London: Volume I: A World of its Own 1815–1890*, London: Pimlico.

Kynaston, D. (1995), *The City of London: Volume II: The Golden Years 1890–1914*, London: Pimlico.

Kynaston, D. (1999), *The City of London: Volume III: Illusions of Gold 1914–1945*, London: Pimlico.

Kynaston, D. (2001), *The City of London: Volume IV: A Club No More 1945–2000*, London: Pimlico.

Marshall, A. (1920), *Principles of Economics*, London: Macmillan.

Marshall, A. (1927), *Industry and Trade*, London: Macmillan.

Martin, R. (1994), 'Stateless monies, global financial integration and national economic autonomy: the end of geography?', in S. Corbridge, R.L. Martin and N. Thrift (eds), *Money, Power and Space*, Oxford: Blackwell, pp. 253–78.

Morgan, G. (1997), 'The global context of financial services: national systems and the international political economy', in G. Morgan and D. Knights (eds), *Regulation and Deregulation in European Financial Services*, Basingstoke, Macmillan Business, pp. 14–41.

Nachum, L. (2003), 'Liability of foreignness in global competition? Financial service affiliates in the City of London', *Strategic Management Journal*, **24**, 1187–208.

O'Brien, R. (1991), *Global Financial Integration: The End of Geography*, London: Pinter.

Poon, J.P.H. (2003), 'Hierarchical tendencies of capital markets among international financial centers', *Growth and Change*, **34**, 135–56.

Sassen, S. (1991), *The Global City: New York, London, Tokyo*, Princeton: Princeton University Press.

Taylor P.J., J.V. Beaverstock, G.A.S. Cook and N.R. Pandit (2003), *Financial Services Clustering and its Significance for London*, London: Corporation of London.

Thrift, N. (1994), 'On the social and cultural determinants of international financial centres: the case of the City of London', in S. Corbridge, R.L. Martin and N. Thrift (eds), *Money, Power and Space*, Oxford: Blackwell, pp. 327–55.

Tickell, A. (2003), 'Finance and localities', in G.L. Clark, M.P. Feldman and M.S. Gertler (eds), *The Oxford Handbook of Economic Geography*, Oxford: Oxford University Press, pp. 230–47.

16 Spatial clustering of culture
David Emanuel Andersson and Åke E. Andersson

1 Introduction

Spatial concentrations of activities that are economically related are often referred to as clusters. Clusters are the most obvious examples of agglomeration economies. Agglomeration economies exist because of various types of spatial friction, which give rise to spatial transaction costs such as transport and communication costs. These spatial transaction costs explain not only the emergence of clusters, but also the emergence and growth of all spatial concentrations of humans, such as cities, towns and villages.

In agglomerations, both consumers and producers benefit from lower costs of transporting conventional inputs and outputs. Even more significant are benefits associated with less tangible knowledge inputs into production processes. Good access to other producers and consumers is associated with good access to new and tacit knowledge. The agglomeration economies that derive from the production and dissemination of knowledge exist in all industries, but tend to be especially important in the production of goods and services with high knowledge content. And cultural industries, such as those that supply art or entertainment products, typically involve both creativity (new knowledge) and learning-by-doing (tacit knowledge).

The location of the film industry in a very small number of metropolitan areas is an illustration of agglomeration economies in a cultural industry. The most important spatial clustering of film industry are in Hong Kong, Mumbai and Los Angeles. The analysis of the film industry cluster and its causes is concentrated on Los Angeles with its employment of close to 180 000 persons in the Motion Picture and Video Industries (Camors, 2005). This corresponds to direct spending of $2.8 billion.

The impact on the economy is far greater and implies an indirect film industry expenditure of $1.3 billion on hotel services, $0.2 billion on real estate services, $0.2 billion on professional services, and $ 1.25 billion in all other industries. The multiplier is thus close to 2.

The role of the film industry cluster of Los Angeles is projected to be unchanged in the nearest future. The most important factor for generating agglomeration economies in the film industry and other 'performance industries' is the demand for a specialized local labour market (i.e. embodied knowledge). Most actors, directors, scriptwriters, photographers and technicians are hired for the duration of the production of a film negative or for even shorter time periods. The short employment contracts imply greater labour mobility among film-making firms than among firms in most other industries. Film industry workers can only achieve long-term employment by being permanently accessible to potential short-term employers.

When workers move between different firms they both learn and disseminate knowledge, which is a further source of agglomeration economies. Such learning and knowledge dissemination are impeded if workers are restricted to one firm, and thus to one set of firm-specific routines. This is one reason why open clusters with high labour turnover rates and other types of informal interaction among firms have a creative edge: open clusters both *create* and *disseminate* knowledge at a faster rate than 'closed clusters' of secretive corporations (Saxenian, 1994).

Cultural clusters encompass geographical concentrations of cultural production and consumption. Culture is, of course, a vague and ambiguous term, but in this context we refer to goods and services that offer different kinds of aesthetic experiences to the consumer. In other words, cultural clusters are centres for the production or consumption of art and entertainment experiences in the widest sense of those terms, which means that we include tourism, gaming and sports in our understanding of culture.

In one way, all consumption is consumption of experiences. When a consumer of sandwiches is eating her sandwich, she is subjectively experiencing and evaluating various attributes, such as the taste, smell and visual appeal of the sandwich. A sandwich is thus in this sense not qualitatively different from a cultural product. Nevertheless, cultural products usually exhibit greater complexity, in that they both consist of a much greater number of potentially valued experience attributes, and most cultural products additionally include *uniqueness* vis-à-vis other similar products as an attribute that consumers value in itself. It makes much more sense to speak of an optimized or standardized sandwich than it does to speak of an optimal standardization of music.

For some cultural products such as concerts, theatre performances, football games or guided tours, there is an additional element of simultaneous production and consumption of the experience service in question. We may also express this as the consumer's assumption of the role of co-producer. The response of the audience is in itself a valued and inseparable attribute of the cultural product, so that a live concert and a playback of a recording of the same concert may be two distinct and unequally valued cultural products.

2   Cultural infrastructure

In the short run, the emergence of cultural clusters is far from random. It is extremely unlikely that the next cluster of the film industry or the music industry will appear in a small isolated town in western Australia or northern Brazil. The reason for this is that the emergence of new clusters is supported by an infrastructural arena that itself emerges at a much slower pace. Therefore, 'activity clusters' and 'infrastructural clusters' – to coin two new terms – evolve on different time scales.

The infrastructure consists of any object, rule, activity or other phenomenon which is both collective (i.e. shared among a group of people) and durable (i.e. more durable than one or more shorter-term activities against which the infrastructure is contrasted). The infrastructure is therefore not given once and for all, but may change as time scales and communities are redefined. For example, the routines of a firm are part of the firm's non-material infrastructure, and are at the same time also relatively short-term activity patterns which a more durable and more collective ('more infrastructural') legal infrastructure supports. Likewise, buildings are material infrastructural assets that support day-to-day production activities, but are at the same time relatively short-term and disaggregated expressions of even more infrastructural, but non-material, architectural composition principles. Thus, not only can the infrastructure be divided into a multitude of material and non-material types, but each type of infrastructure is, further, part of a multi-layered structure where the layers reflect differences in durability and collectiveness.

The conventional notion of the 'material infrastructure' makes us think of highways, factories and power plants, but there is also a *cultural* material infrastructure which is as physical, durable and collective as any highway or factory. Temples, churches and palaces are components of a cultural material infrastructure that may support cultural production and consumption for decades, centuries, or even millennia. The same Roman amphitheatre – in various stages of disrepair – may have supported gladiator shows 2000 years ago, trade fairs 500 years ago and opera performances today.

The cultural material infrastructure, generally speaking, comprises the aesthetic attributes of the general material infrastructure. The aesthetic attributes are economically significant if there are some people who are willing and able to pay for them. And these attributes are, in accordance with our definition, infrastructural if they are durable and jointly consumed by a group of people. Architectural composition principles as they manifest themselves in buildings and the architectural–aesthetic characters of neighbourhoods are perhaps the most obvious link between the non-material infrastructure of ideas and the material infrastructure of their physical manifestation.

Aesthetically valued buildings and neighbourhoods tend to be visible (i.e. consumable) not only to the formal owners, but also to other residents and to visitors, and this is indeed a necessary condition for regarding such buildings and neighbourhoods as infrastructure. Therefore, the economic value of the aesthetic attributes of the infrastructure will be capitalized not only in the price of the aesthetically valued buildings, but also in the price of land with good access to the aesthetic services embodied in the cultural infrastructure. The total market price of an aesthetic attribute of a building is therefore not only a part of the total price of the building itself, but it is also a part of the price of other buildings which bidding consumers value for their perceived good access to those attributes. In other words, the aesthetic value of a view of a building that is perceived as beautiful is not only an attribute of the building, but is also an infrastructural *neighbourhood attribute*. The spatial extent of the relevant (attribute-impacted) neighbourhood depends on consumers' (i.e. potential buyers and renters of real estate) perception of superior access to a valued aesthetic service. The relevant 'neighbourhoods' of specific aesthetic services are as wide-ranging as the variability in consumers' perceptions of accessibility benefits: they can range from a small part of a city street to an entire metropolitan region.

In most city regions, there are a number of buildings, places and neighbourhoods that have the character of cultural infrastructure. When the agglomeration of such infrastructure is sufficiently large in a region, we can speak of the region as a 'cultural infrastructure cluster'. In such clusters, the cultural infrastructure is usually both an input into the production of more rapidly depleted cultural goods and services as well as constituting a number of attributes that are valued consumer services in their own right. The consumption of spatially concentrated cultural infrastructure services often takes the form of cultural tourism, and normally involves consumption of complementary products as well, for example hotel and restaurant services.

Every year, the French tyre manufacturer Michelin publishes guides to Europe's cities. These guides are well known for their restaurant awards, where exceptional restaurants are awarded one, two or three stars. Perhaps it is less well known that Michelin's panel of tourism specialists also awards one, two or three stars to exceptional attributes of Europe's cultural infrastructure. Arguably, we may refer to regions with a substantial total number of such infrastructural culture stars as cultural infrastructure clusters. Table 16.1

Table 16.1   *Cultural infrastructure as measured by the number of cultural Michelin stars, 10 top-ranked metropolitan areas of Europe, 2003*

City	Rank	Total number of culture stars	Architectural stars	Museum stars
Berlin	1	208	89	119
Rome	2	197	174	23
London	3	179	142	37
Florence	4	156	119	37
Vienna	5	156	96	60
Lisbon	6	135	95	40
Paris	7	121	89	32
Barcelona	8	119	99	20
Prague	9	86	73	13
Edinburgh	10	81	69	12

Source: Michelin Guide Rouge (2003).

presents Europe's 10 leading cultural infrastructure clusters according to this way of measuring aggregate collective and durable culture. The resulting measure mostly reflects architecture as expressed in buildings and neighbourhoods as well as those agglomerations of smaller cultural artifacts that museums make available to the public.

Table 16.1 shows that five European cities have more than 150 stars each, comprising four capitals as well as the smaller but historically significant cultural centre of Florence. The overall index of aggregate cultural infrastructure consists of two components: architecture (individual buildings, streets, squares and neighbourhoods) and museums. Architecturally, Rome's extremely long history as a cultural centre has bequeathed an unparalleled architectural infrastructure, as has London's more recent centuries as a global economic centre.

Museums make up a part of the cultural infrastructure that is specifically aimed at tourists in their role as consumers of cultural services. The ranking of museum (sub-) clusters is somewhat different from the ranking of architecture clusters. Most of the highest-ranking and none of the lowest-ranking regions are national capital cities. Berlin's status as the greatest museum cluster in Europe may be attributable to the size of Germany as well as Berlin's period of being divided into the capital of East Germany and the largest city of West Germany, which made the political leadership of each half of Berlin compete for cultural superiority and prestige.

Hedonic price models can be used to estimate the overall effect of cultural clustering on land and other real-estate prices. However, different real estate markets have different spatial impacts. For example, housing markets tend to be geographically segmented in accordance with practical commuting possibilities. A real estate market with a much more extensive spatial impact is the market for hotel rooms, which concentrate on tourists, conference organizers and business travellers on globally or continentally competitive markets.

Andersson and Andersson (2006) used a cultural cluster index based on the agglomeration of cultural Michelin stars by analysing the impact of cultural cluster index magnitudes on hotel rates in a sample of 1278 hotels in 68 European regions. To avoid

Table 16.2   Hedonic price function for the European market for hotel rooms, 2003,
dependent variable: natural logarithm of published single room rate (€)

Variable	Estimated coefficient	t-value
Intercept	3.055	
Cultural cluster index (logs)	**0.080**	**5.67**
Population (logs)	−0.027	8.10
Published SCI papers in region (logs)	0.134	−2.01
Downtown location	0.150	6.69
Airport location	0.171	3.55
Hotel with at least two stars	0.253	8.56
Hotel with at least three stars	0.315	14.81
Hotel with at least four stars	0.271	10.53
Hotel with five stars	0.188	4.92
'Pleasant' hotel	0.279	8.11
Gymnasium in hotel	0.119	5.63
Adjusted R^2=0.642; n=1278.		

Source: Andersson and Andersson (2006).

potential confounding due to other accessibility factors, the model also included a number of control variables such as downtown and airport location, metropolitan area population and an indicator of general economic development (i.e., published Science Citation Indexed (SCI) papers in the region). Even so, the cultural cluster index had a statistically significant impact on published hotel rates. The estimated mean elasticity of the cultural cluster index on hotel rates was 0.08 (see Table 16.2). If we compare this elasticity with real cultural clusters in Europe we can express this finding as follows: a region with Barcelona's level of cultural infrastructure can be expected to have single rooms that are twice as expensive as a city with Birmingham's level, other things equal.

The estimated price of the cultural cluster index attribute is an estimate of the implicit price of regional cultural infrastructure. As such, it is an estimate of the overall impact of a regional cultural cluster on regional land prices. It is thus a partial indicator of the value of the cultural infrastructure to consumers, both directly as durable consumer goods and indirectly as durable inputs into various production processes. But the regional cultural cluster index *does not* approximate the total value of the regional cultural infrastructure to consumers, either directly or indirectly. This is because the effect only measures *region-wide* impacts, not localized ones. An example of localized cultural infrastructure effects is provided by the variable 'Pleasant' hotel in Table 16.2. Hotels are denoted as 'pleasant' if Michelin's assessors consider a hotel to be aesthetically appealing in a general sense. This is thus a price effect that represents more localized infrastructure: durable edifices which are shared among sub-sets of (temporary or permanent) regional residents. The price of 'pleasantness' may typically be capitalized in hotel rates (represented by the hedonic attribute price) as well as hotel meal prices and land values of adjacent buildings with attractive views (i.e. effects that the hedonic price function does not estimate).

3 Infrastructure and cultural services

Not only tourists and other consumers value cultural infrastructure of the type mentioned above. In some cases, such infrastructure constitutes durable capital goods that are used as inputs in the production of more 'perishable' cultural services. For example, the Sydney Opera House is a part of the infrastructure that is both directly consumed as well as being a capital input that may be used in the production of operas, musicals, concerts and plays as well as, possibly, also for conferences, conventions and other large-scale meetings. Museum buildings are also good illustrations of the multiple roles of the cultural infrastructure: a museum building may be considered sufficiently attractive to be a consumption good in itself, but it may also help produce smaller-scale infrastructure (e.g. durable sculptures that are consumed among the group of museum visitors) and serve as an input in the production of short-term activities such as exhibitions and the sale of cultural souvenirs.

But it is not only the *cultural* infrastructure that co-produces less durable cultural services. All types of infrastructure may serve as capital inputs in cultural production processes. Non-material infrastructures such as languages and social institutions are necessary social capital inputs in all production, including cultural production. Unlike large-group social institutions, however, more localized non-material infrastructure does not primarily affect the general level of transaction costs, but instead simultaneously reduces transaction costs and facilitates learning processes in specific localized production arenas such as firms, production teams and relatively durable networks of firms and individuals.

Extracultural material infrastructure is the final type of infrastructure that influences short-term cultural service production. On a fundamental level, transportation infrastructure such as roads and airports influences accessibility and the cost of transporting inputs and outputs in well-known ways. But there is also the impact of urban design and land-use patterns on learning and creativity, which Jane Jacobs discussed in *The Death and Life of Great American Cities* (1961). Drawing on her observations on what made Greenwich Village such a creative milieu for artists, writers and other cultural creators, Jacobs proposed four neighbourhood characteristics that contribute to dynamic agglomeration economies associated with creativity and innovation.

First, 'primary uses' such as offices, residences and stores should be mixed, so that there are large numbers of people at different times of the day. The resulting mixture of land uses tends to increase the use of 'secondary uses' such as restaurants, cafes and parks, in particular supporting the use of such facilities during non-peak periods such as afternoons and late nights.

Second, blocks should be short, in order to mix people who work or live on a street with the spontaneous movements of passers-through. This facilitates spontaneous encounters among people and further increases the demand for 'secondary use' services.

Third, neighbourhoods should have a mixture of new and old buildings, since creative entrepreneurial start-ups benefit disproportionately from a diverse urban milieu, while at the same time finding it difficult to obtain funding for high property expenditures:

> As for really new ideas of any kind – no matter how ultimately profitable or otherwise successful some of them may prove to be – there is no leeway for such chance trial, error and experimentation in the high-overhead economy of new construction. Old ideas can sometimes use new buildings. *New ideas must use old buildings.* (Jacobs, 1961, emphasis added)

Fourth, the population density should be high, since a high density reinforces the likelihood of unexpected encounters and the opportunities for establishing profitable secondary uses. In addition, a high population density has been found to increase the personal safety of neighbourhood users, thanks to greater informal social controls.

It is important to keep in mind that most neighbourhoods that fulfil Jacobs' criteria have evolved spontaneously, rather than being the results of conscious planning. And even though these unplanned neighbourhoods are conducive to creative and innovative pursuits, there is no guarantee that all such neighbourhoods will in fact constitute creative clusters. However, there are many instances where conscious urban or regional planning has aimed at the exact opposite of Jacobs' recommendations: the single land-use, low-density neighbourhood with new buildings and large blocks was often the dominant ideal among modernist planners.

Fortunately, Jacobs' book has influenced many urban planners from the 1970s onward, and mixed land uses and 'organic' development policies have become more popular in recent decades. However, it is still common for planners to believe that it is more desirable to plan creative clusters in politically favoured industries than to have the more modest aim of facilitating cluster development in whatever industry entrepreneurs experiment with in a particular location. The most ambitious attempts at designing creative clusters are the numerous comprehensive development strategies known as 'science parks' or 'technopoles', but these parks have been almost everywhere unsuccessful if assessed according to their original aims, whether located in France (Sophia-Antiopolis), China (Suzhou) or Japan (Tsukuba). The small number of successful science parks were either spontaneous unplanned developments (Silicon Valley) or planned without detailed goals as to which firms or which industries they should specialize in (e.g. Hsinchu in Taiwan).

Typically, however, creative clusters have emerged in dense urban settings without any preconceived urban or neighbourhood plan. Instead, cultural and other creative clusters have been the outcome of successful discovery processes. These discovery processes are cumulative entrepreneurial processes where a pioneering entrepreneur first discovers a profitable location for engaging in a new land use, and whose profits are later signalled to other market participants. These other market participants may then engage in imitative behaviour, which over time has a tendency to compete away the original entrepreneurial profits (Andersson, 2005).

Webster and Lai (2003) describe how one such entrepreneurial process created a cultural cluster in a neighbourhood that exhibits Jacobs' four recommended conditions. The dense, mixed, short-block area in question is Hong Kong's Lan Kwai Fong and Soho neighbourhoods near that city's financial district.

Only a few decades ago, Lan Kwai Fong consisted of conventional residential streets with a few simple Chinese restaurants and a single supermarket. The entrepreneurial trigger of its future development was the opening of a traditional English pub in the late 1970s, which turned out to be sufficiently profitable to attract imitators. Complementary services, such as ethnic restaurants and nightclubs, soon followed. This emerging nightlife cluster in turn attracted more artistic activities to co-locate, such as a jazz club and an avant-garde theatre, café and exhibition combination known as the Fringe Club. Its website alludes to some of Jacobs' principles:

The Fringe Club is recognized as a lively and dynamic contemporary arts space, not only in Hong Kong but throughout the region, and is often cited as a successful example of how to make positive re-use of a derelict building and thus revive a rundown neighbourhood.

In December 1983, the Fringe moved into a dilapidated and uninhabitable building. Over the years, the building has been restored with care and given entirely new functions. There have been no fewer than eight major renovation projects, undertaken as we continued to work and present shows despite the dust, debris and noise.

The building now houses two theatres, two gallery spaces, a photo gallery, two cafe-bars, a rehearsal room, a pottery studio and showroom, a roof garden and the award-winning 'M at the Fringe' restaurant. In 2002, the Fringe Club won the Hong Kong Heritage Award for the innovative and creative transformation of the old Dairy Farm Cold Storage Warehouse into a lively contemporary arts space. (www.hkfringe.com.hk, 2006)

Lan Kwai Fong's development process also spilled over to the adjoining Soho neighbourhood, where it resulted in a mixture of antique shops, art galleries, and restaurants. The volumes of pedestrians that the area came to attract on a regular basis eventually resulted in the shop-owners persuading the government to convert Lan Kwai Fong's D'Aguilar Street into one of Hong Kong's very few pedestrian streets.

4   Probability-based cultural clustering

Creativity and randomness are important reasons for cultural clustering. Many of the cultural activities are creative in the sense that the output of the production process is an original and not a copy. A new film is called a 'negative' when completed and this negative is then used for a copying process used in the distribution of the film to the potential viewers. Most of the costs of making the film are incurred before the copying/distribution stage. Negative production can be subdivided into a number of consecutive stages with various durations. The probability of success at each stage of the production process is dependent on the success of preceding stages.

The expected net returns on a film project depend on the probability of market success, which in its turn depends on the success of the whole negative production process, on the sunk costs of the production process and finally on the impacts and costs of the marketing process. Assuming that the producer of a film has succeeded in achieving a 90 per cent probability of success at each successive stage of a 20-stage production process, then the total probability of success is $(0.9)^{20} = 12.16$ per cent. Such a low success probability is clearly a rationale for large-scale production, especially considering the large fixed as well as sunk costs that movie production involves. The corporate structure of the industry with very large firms such as Disney and Sony is to a considerable extent a consequence of the need to compensate for the low probability of success of a costly creative project by forming a large portfolio of film projects from different genres with different expected returns and risks.

The implication of all these – to some extent random – factors is that the planning of film production must simultaneously consider multi-stage sunk cost accumulation, incentive structures and revenue probabilities in order to account for the incurred costs of the creative production process plus marketing costs. Three factors are of crucial importance in the planning of film production:

1.   The capacity and accessibility of the different types of skilled labour to be hired for an often short time and with short notice. There is thus a need for accessible spot

markets for highly educated specialists, and these markets are needed at each stage of production. Especially crucial are the markets for directors, editors, script writers, photographers, sound experts and actors.

2. The accessibility of services needed at short notice and low transaction costs.
3. The availability of 'stars' to perform in the leading roles of the script.
4. A conception of emerging tastes (or trends) among fashion leaders in the culture and entertainment industries.

5 The importance of stars as a clustering factor

Experience goods are exchanged in art and entertainment markets. For consumers such goods have inherently uncertain expected utilities. These uncertain expectations make the consumers depend on the views of other consumers with prior consumption experiences as well as on different professional certifiers. In recent years, Internet information has also become increasingly important in this pre-evaluation process. The following list (Table 16.3) of all-time top movies is of importance both for producers and for consumers in their decisions to produce and to consume. Most of these movies were produced by firms based in Hollywood, the movie cluster of the Los Angeles region.

However, the most important certifier (or uncertainty reducer) is the reputation of the principal artists. An actor or actress who has managed the transition from B-films to

Table 16.3   Top 20 movies as voted by regular voters in Earth's Biggest Movie Database users

Rank	Rating	Title
1	9.1	The Godfather (1972)
2	9.0	The Shawshank Redemption (1994)
3	8.9	The Godfather: Part II (1974)
4	8.8	The Lord of the Rings: The Return of the King (2003)
5	8.8	Shichinin no samurai (1954)
6	8.8	Schindler's List (1993)
7	8.7	Casablanca (1942)
8	8.7	Pulp Fiction (1994)
9	8.7	Star Wars: Episode V – The Empire Strikes Back (1980)
10	8.7	Star Wars (1977)
11	8.7	Buono, il brutto, il cattivo, Il (1966)
12	8.7	One Flew Over the Cuckoo's Nest (1975)
13	8.7	The Lord of the Rings: The Fellowship of the Ring (2001)
14	8.7	Rear Window (1954)
15	8.6	Cidade de Deus (2002)
16	8.6	The Usual Suspects (1995)
17	8.6	The Lord of the Rings: The Two Towers (2002)
18	8.6	Dr Strangelove or: How I Learned to Stop Worrying and Love the Bomb (1964)
19	8.6	12 Angry Men (1957)
20	8.6	Raiders of the Lost Ark (1981)

Source: www.imdb.com.

subsidiary roles in A-films can command a substantially higher price than before. A progression to the higher ranks of recognition among actors in A-films further decreases perceptions of uncertainty among potential viewers, thereby increasing their willingness to pay for tickets. The importance of uncertainty-reducing reputation effects is a reason for the prevalence of top-10 ranking lists in the various entertainment industries. One example is the following top-10 list of actors:

Rank	Actor
1	Al Pacino
2	Robert de Niro
3	Tom Hanks
4	Kevin Spacey
5	Harrison Ford
6	Jack Nicholson
7	Anthony Hopkins
8	Sean Connery
9	Ewan McGregor
10	Cary Grant

Source: www.TV4.com.

Table 16.4   Top 20 movies by cumulative worldwide box office revenue

Rank	Box office revenue	Title
1	$1 835 300 000	Titanic (1997)
2	$1 129 219 252	The Lord of the Rings: The Return of the King (2003)
3	$968 600 000	Harry Potter and the Sorcerer's Stone (2001)
4	$922 379 000	Star Wars: Episode I – The Phantom Menace (1999)
5	$921 600 000	The Lord of the Rings: The Two Towers (2002)
6	$919 700 000	Jurassic Park (1993)
7	$883 780 682	Harry Potter and the Goblet of Fire (2005)
8	$880 871 036	Shrek 2 (2004)
9	$866 300 000	Harry Potter and the Chamber of Secrets (2002)
10	$865 000 000	Finding Nemo (2003)
11	$860 700 000	The Lord of the Rings: The Fellowship of the Ring (2001)
12	$848 462 555	Star Wars: Episode III – Revenge of the Sith (2005)
13	$811 200 000	Independence Day (1996)
14	$806 700 000	Spider-Man (2002)
15	$797 900 000	Star Wars (1977)
16	$789 458 727	Harry Potter and the Prisoner of Azkaban (2004)
17	$783 577 893	Spider-Man 2 (2004)
18	$783 400 000	The Lion King (1994)
19	$756 700 000	E.T. the Extra-Terrestrial (1982)
20	$735 600 00	The Matrix Reloaded (2003)

Source: www.imdb.com.

Table 16.5   Top 20 actors by average box office gross revenues

Rank	Actor	No. films in leading role	Average B.O. gross revenue for leading role (US$ million)	All movies: gross revenue (US$ million)	No. of movies	Over $100 million
1	Orlando Bloom	4	204	1 580	8	6
2	Mark Hamill	14	182	1 139	24	3
3	Mike Myers	11	136	1 500	12	6
4	Will Smith	14	128	1 797	15	9
5	Tobey Maguire	11	124	1 142	16	3
6	Harrison Ford	27	112	3 231	33	11
7	Billy Dee Williams	18	108	938	29	3
8	Hugh Jackman	8	106	637	8	3
9	Jim Carrey	17	105	1 903	25	9
10	Tom Hanks	30	102	3 083	32	14
11	Tom Cruise	24	100	2 358	26	12
12	Ian McKellen	18	98	1 545	27	5
13	Eddie Murphy	30	97	2 917	30	11
14	Elijah Wood	17	96	1 774	25	6
15	Tim Allen	11	90	989	13	4
16	Alan Rickman	17	86	1 325	20	4
17	Leonardo DiCaprio	15	81	1 142	16	3
18	Viggo Mortensen	23	79	1 592	34	3
19	Judge Reinhold	18	76	1 084	31	5
20	Adam Sandler	14	73	1 051	18	5

Source: www.imdb.com.

Most top-ranking actors and actresses live in the Los Angeles region. Their location in the region attracts aspiring actors and actresses who want to audition for various film and television roles, while supporting themselves by finding temporary jobs in the region's general labour market. There is thus in that region a large supply of potential talents, which is immediately available at a low cost.

The 'star factor' seems to be generally important for the size of revenues in most art and entertainment industries. Actors commanding a high rank on any of these lists usually attract greater demand at all stages of the distribution process. One consequence of this demand effect is a high correlation between actor income (wealth) and actor popularity ranking. Most actor contracts in the film industry are based on revenues rather than profits, which contributes to the general lack of cost consciousness among creative artists in the film industry. However, after more than half a century, *Gone with the Wind*, with its substantial 'star factor' still generates large revenues each year in the last stage of an impressive syndication process. The importance of stars to the long-term economic viability of films should therefore not be underestimated.

First, a reputation as a high-ranked artist leads to a substantial increase in expected revenues. Second, it is also important to be in the right location, in that artists benefit from global accessibility, regional production and consumption agglomerations and sometimes also a location in a dominant language region.

A high rank in the right location provides the artist with a monopolistic position, which generates monopoly rents from the ownership of a unique knowledge resource. But monopolistic benefits are always constrained in time by changes in rankings and the shifts of consumers' demand schedules among partially substitutable art and entertainment niches. The market form is not a pure form of monopoly but rather *temporal monopolistic competition*. The amounts of creativity and innovation as well as the relative speed of changes of fashions and general consumer demand determine the speed of change in artists' market positions.

6   Conclusions

Spatial clustering is an example of agglomeration economies that has been common in a great variety of industries. One case of cultural clustering is especially prominent in Europe, with its long history of architectural investments. Over three millennia, a remarkable cultural infrastructure has been created in cities like Athens, Rome, Florence and Venice, to name a few examples. The architectural infrastructure has been further reinforced by the creation of globally attractive museums. Around the cultural infrastructure of such cities tourism, conference and congress activities and many kinds of consumer services have grown and shaped integrated culture and experience clusters. The economic attraction of these cultural clusters is reflected in the price level of hotels of these cities. Econometric estimates reported in this chapter are substantial and statistically significant.

However, there are good reasons to assume that spatial clustering is even more important in the sort of creative production that characterizes the many different art and entertainment industries. One reason for this is the learning that is facilitated through large and flexible local labour markets. Such labour markets as can be found in Hong Kong, Mumbai and Los Angeles are both specialized and constantly changing, since the individual workers only remain for a limited time within each specific entertainment production project. In the process of being employed in a specific project, the knowledge of the worker changes, so that he or she will become a transformed human capital input upon re-entering the local labour market. The film industry, and especially the pre-eminent film production cluster in the Los Angeles region, is used to illustrate typical clustering processes in a cultural industry. It is seen that the underlying decision making in the cultural industries is analogous to decision making among rational financial investors. The combination of large and irreversible costs of multi-stage production and marketing and the low probability of success of each creative film project leads to substantial economies of scale of the firms involved in this branch of the entertainment industry. The film-producing firms are large and surrounded by a multitude of smaller and flexible firms generating the necessary services needed at each consecutive stage of production of a film negative. At the centre of the cluster is the limited market of film stars, reaping a large share of the profits. This centre of stars is surrounded by a very large number of prospective actors and actresses, often living on incomes from their arts which are far below subsistence level. As a consequence the distribution of income and wealth is extremely skewed among the participants of this type of entertainment cluster.

References

Andersson, D.E. (2005), 'The spatial nature of entrepreneurship', *The Quarterly Journal of Austrian Economics*, **8**(2), 21–34.

Andersson, Å.E. and D.E. Andersson (2006), *The Economics of Experiences, the Arts and Entertainment*, Cheltenham, UK and Northampton, MA, US: Edward Elgar.

Camors, C. (2005), 'The motion picture industry in Los Angeles', prel. version, IAURIF.

Jacobs, J. (1961), *The Death and Life of Great American Cities,* New York: Penguin.

Saxenian, A. (1994), *Regional Advantage: Culture and Competition in Silicon Valley and Route 128*, Cambridge, MA: Harvard University Press.

Vogel, H.L. (1998), *Entertainment Industry Economics. A Guide to Financial Analysis*, Cambridge, UK: Cambridge University Press.

Webster, C. and W.-C. Lai (2003), *Property Rights Planning and Markets – Managing Spontaneous Cities*, Cheltenham, UK and Northampton, MA, US: Edward Elgar.

17 Clustering in the broadcasting industry
Gary A.S. Cook and Naresh R. Pandit

1 Introduction

It is a commonplace that creative industries, of which broadcasting is an important example, are principally urban phenomena and have a strong tendency to be highly agglomerated within particular cities (Florida, 2002; Hall, 2000; Landry, 2000; Scott, 2000). This chapter will analyse the causes and effects of such agglomeration. Scott (2000) identifies New York, Los Angeles, London, Paris and Tokyo as the leading examples of privileged centres for the production of cultural artefacts, not least due to the interactions between a broad range of agglomerated cultural industries within them. Within television broadcasting, including programme production specifically, Hollywood is dominant, with London and Tokyo being other major global centres.

The chapter focuses on television broadcasting, which is far more highly concentrated than radio broadcasting. In the course of the chapter there will be reflection on a number of key issues and debates in the economic geography literature in respect of which the broadcasting industry offers some relevant evidence. These debates are briefly set out in the literature review. The evidence reported thereafter relating to the UK broadcasting industry is based on three sources: a large-scale econometric study of cluster dynamics using financial data on 1213 broadcasting firms throughout the UK; an interview survey consisting of 72 interviews conducted mainly with firms in the three cities, London, Bristol and Glasgow, between 2001 and 2002; a questionnaire survey of firms in London conducted between January and April 2004, resulting in 204 usable replies.

UK broadcasting clusters may be compared with the large literature regarding Hollywood (Christopherson & Storper, 1986; De Fillippi & Arthur, 1998; Miller & Shamsie, 1996; Scott, 2000, 2002; Storper, 1997; Storper & Christopherson, 1987). While this literature focuses on film production, it is important to be aware that employment related to television in Hollywood is double that related to film and has been less subject to geographic dispersal (Verrier, 2005). The evidence presented in this chapter indicates that the nature of clustering in broadcasting is akin to that identified in Hollywood and typical of that claimed to be characteristic of cultural industries more generally (Scott, 2000).

2 Literature review

The literature abounds with different typologies of geographic concentrations of economic activity (McCann & Sheppard, 2003). These typologies are important because they bring into sharp focus that not all clusters are alike. Moreover, the nature of the cluster has implications for its potential value in the context of a regional development strategy as well as indicating what types of policy action are likely to prove most of value. A number of important ideal types have been identified by Markusen (1996), each of which manifests a certain type of economic logic:

1. The Marshallian (Marshall, 1920, 1927) New Industrial District (NID), of which the Third Italy is identified as an important variety, is emphasized by many leading authors (Best, 1990; Piore & Sabel, 1984; Porter, 1990; Saxenian, 1994; Scott, 1988). The 'Italianate' version differs from the original Marshallian conception in that there is argued to be a high degree of conscious cooperation among firms and also important support from local organizations and institutions. Similarly, Gordon and McCann (2000) distinguish between pure agglomerations, which do not involve substantial interaction, and social network type concentrations which do.
2. The hub-and-spoke district, where regional structure revolves around one or several major corporations in one or a few industries.
3. The satellite industrial platform, comprising chiefly branch plants of multinational corporations. Such districts are typified by a lack of interaction among the firms located there. Firms are above all dependent on corporate parents.
4. The state-anchored district, where a major government tenant anchors the regional economy.

Is any of these descriptions adequate as a description of the broadcasting industry? There has been a degree of dispute regarding the nature of Hollywood as a cluster. The dominant view is that it is a flexibly specialized industrial district (Christopherson & Storper, 1986; Scott, 2002; Storper, 1997; Storper & Christopherson, 1987). Against this, Aksoy and Robins (1992) have claimed that Hollywood is (though they do not use this language) more akin to a hub-and-spoke district, with major studios calling the tune and independent production companies being highly dependent.

The idea of promoting clusters has become central to regional policy in the UK and more widely, yet it is an open question how robust the clusters concept is in this regard. Policy thinking has lighted upon two particular ideas about clusters. The first is the ideal type exemplified by Silicon Valley (Saxenian, 1994) and the idea of flexible specialization exemplified by the Third Italy and Baden Württemberg (Best, 1990; Piore & Sabel, 1984; Scott, 1988). The second is the cluster concept developed and popularized by Porter (1990) in which the idea of flexible specialization again features prominently. There have been two general criticisms of the flexible specialization model: firstly, that it is not an accurate representation even of Silicon Valley, Baden Württemberg and the Third Italy (Malmberg & Maskell, 2002); secondly, that this type of concentration is not the most common and that other types exist which also have a distinct rationale (Gordon & McCann, 2000; Markusen, 1996). A particularly trenchant critique of Porter has been advanced by Martin and Sunley (2003). The nub of their critique is that the concept is too vague and elastic, failing to be specific about either what the spatial limits to a cluster should be, or which sets of industries ought to be linked within a cluster. Martin and Sunley (2003) round their critique off with a trenchant discussion of the shortcomings of the cluster concept as a guide to regional development policy. All firms, whether clustered or not, may benefit from support, and diversity rather than specialization may be more important to cluster development and regional adaptability.

Several authors have championed the region as the most important spatial scale over which clustering processes operate (Coe & Townsend, 1998; Cooke & Morgan, 1998; Scott, 2001; Storper, 1997). Amin and Thrift (1992) argue persuasively that the emphasis on local production complexes is overdone. Models which are locally based do not recognize the importance of emerging global corporate networks and interconnected global city regions. They argue that centres are needed within which to generate and disseminate discourses, collective beliefs, stories about what world production filières are like and to develop, track and test innovations.

The relationship between the city and economic advantages of colocation is of particular relevance to the broadcasting industry which is almost everywhere an urban and specifically large city phenomenon. The relationship between cities on a global scale is also relevant given the presence of multinational media companies in a number of key cities. Finally, the relationship between (generally) capital and lower-level cities in the national city hierarchy is also relevant, given the policy trend in several countries towards spreading broadcasting activity among the regions.

The idea that improvements in transportation, communication and information technologies is leading to a frictionless world, where distance is irrelevant and the need to physically colocate is of diminishing importance, has been both widely aired (e.g. Cairncross, 1997) and strongly criticized (Morgan, 2004). Broadcasting appears a prime candidate for the 'geography is dead' thesis because it produces a 'weightless' product/service which can be delivered quickly, cheaply and reliably on any spatial scale. Morgan (2004) has recently produced a vigorous rebuttal based on a number of key arguments. His first argument is that the 'death of geography' perspective conflates spatial reach with social depth. Being able to receive data is not the same as being able to understand it. By extension, face-to-face communication carries highly important non-verbal expression which augments the spoken word. ICT can be useful for maintaining communities, but much less for building them. Secondly, competitive advantage is based, among other things, on tacit knowledge, which, being person-embodied and context-dependent, is spatially sticky. Gertler (2003, p. 91) argues that effective creation and sharing of tacit knowledge 'depends on institutional proximity – that is, the shared norms, conventions, values, expectations and routines arising from *commonly experienced frameworks of institutions*'. Such institutions will be in part locally and in part nationally constituted.

Malmberg and Maskell (2002) argue that current theorizing on knowledge transfer does not explain why colocated firms are better at creating and transferring knowledge than either one large firm or a network of firms spread across a range of locations. This is matched by a dearth of empirical evidence illuminating how, in practice, knowledge is created and transferred. Malmberg and Maskell suggest that the *vertical* dimension of clusters has been overemphasized and that the *horizontal* dimension, the colocation of firms at the same stage in the value chain, may be more important. A similar claim regarding media industries specifically is made by Bathelt (2005). They suggest that more avenues will be pursued by a set of independent firms than in one large firm and, secondly, that colocated firms tend to be well informed about what their rivals are doing.

3   Some economics of television broadcasting

Television broadcasting may be broken down into four broad vertical stages: programme production; bundling programmes into channels; physical distribution; final consumption and revenue collection. The predominant model for public service broadcasting, and to a somewhat lesser extent commercial broadcasting, has been a high degree of vertical integration. Television programme production has traditionally been broken down into three broad activities: pre-production which involves idea development, scriptwriting, casting, costume, location finding, set construction, financing and insurance; production; and post-production (editing, laying of sound track, titling and special effects). Programme production is essentially a project-based technology in which these disparate sources of input and skills are pulled together for the life of the project. This project-based characteristic is shared with many industries, particularly in cultural and media industries (Grabher, 2002). Two important characteristics are that these disparate activities, which often entail highly specialized skills and equipment, can be hard to coordinate under what are typically tight constraints of time and money (Jankowski & Fuchs, 1995) and that the chain is only as strong as its weakest link (Caves, 2000). A very high premium is placed on those who have the reputation of at minimum being reliable and at best able to make a show a sound prospect for success (Shew, 1992). This, according to Caves (2000), places a premium on mechanisms which certify talent.

Demand for television programmes in terms of viewers tuning in has the very important property that it is fairly stable and predictable, if slowly changing, in terms of total hours viewed, but very uncertain in terms of the popularity of new offerings (Dunnett, 1990). As Scott (2000) argues, the organization of production is becoming more geared to flexibility and innovation in order to cope with constantly changing and unpredictable consumer tastes. Collins (1988) suggests that the strongly ephemeral character of much broadcasting output means that the pace of innovation is much faster than in most consumer industries.

Economies of scale in programme production are not pronounced (Cave, 1989). Economies of scale are significant in what may somewhat loosely be called 'distribution', which relates to the acquisition of broadcasting rights and bundling them into packages, typically in the form of a channel offering. Large distributors are able to absorb a large number of programmes which may be barely commercial and recoup on the relatively small numbers of hits, making major media companies important agents organizing financing, deal making and distribution. The existence of these large economies of scale and scope is of first-rank importance. Firstly, the fact that broadcasters (and studios in the case of Hollywood) are large will create a natural physical agglomeration (Ellison & Glaeser, 1997). Secondly, the large scale of broadcasters relative either to (most) independent production companies or to final consumers brings elements of both monopsony and monopoly power, a feature given high prominence in Aksoy and Robins' (1992) account of Hollywood.

4   General trends and influences in the broadcasting industry

An obvious point about broadcasting is that in every country it is subject to heavy government regulation, which has generally had an influence on the location of broadcasting activity. The UK exemplifies general trends replicated the world over, not least since many national television broadcasting systems were set up to ape the British Broadcasting Corporation (BBC). Firstly, the state broadcaster was set up in the capital, which remains an important strategic centre in the industry. Exceptions to this trend are countries which have political capitals other than in major economic centres. Secondly, when independent television was set up in the UK, a deliberate policy of ensuring that network production (i.e. the production of television programmes that would be screened nationally) took place in the regions was pursued. Other countries have been more or less *dirigiste* on this point, but many have attempted it (Euromedia, 1997). Some countries have from the outset encouraged substantial broadcasting and programme production activity at a regional level, the prime examples being Germany (Kleinsteuber, 1997) and Austria (Trappel, 1997), reflecting their federal structures, and Switzerland (Meier, 1997) which likewise has a decentralized system of political governance as well as distinct linguistic regions.

Attempting to spread broadcasting activity around the regions, once a highly concentrated industry has been established in the capital, has proved difficult. The UK has imposed quotas for regional production, which have to a substantial degree been circumvented by independent companies from London setting up branch offices outside the capital to win business under the quota, but still essentially orchestrating operations from London. At the same time, many independent production companies in the regions have felt it necessary to set up offices in London in order to help secure commissions from the major broadcasters. This centripetal force of the capital is also exemplified in the case of Japan, where, despite attempts to spread activity around the regions when independent broadcasting was set up, activity quickly gravitated toward Tokyo (Brown, 1989; Ito, 1978; Kuratani & Endo, 2003). This impulse toward concentration in a single centre has also been demonstrated by the way Los Angeles has progressively drained activity away from New York in the post-war period (Storper & Christopherson, 1987) as has Glasgow in respect of Edinburgh in the post-deregulation era in Scotland since 1990. Moreover, attempts to woo film and television productions away from Hollywood to other centres in the USA have largely resulted in failure (Scott, 2002). The strong centripetal power of major broadcasting centres the world over is telling testimony against the 'death of geography'.

A second state policy, which has been important around the world, and is again exemplified by Britain, is privatization and deregulation. The major impetus for broadcasting deregulation in Britain came with the Peacock Report (Home Office, 1986). The report led directly to the Broadcasting Act 1990 which aimed at promoting consumer sovereignty (Collins, 1990). Among the major provisions of the Act, (a) The BBC, the Independent Television (ITV) companies and the future operator of Channel 5 were all required to ensure that at least 25 per cent of their total programme output was contracted to independent producers; and (b) a system of competitive bidding was introduced for ITV franchises, with the franchise being awarded to the highest bidder, subject to a quality threshold.

The requirement for competitive tendering led to radical downsizing among the ITV companies, some of whom nevertheless failed to retain their franchises. The creation of new ITV companies as a result of this process, which made few programmes, acted as a further stimulus to independent production (Renton, 1994). The impact of the Peacock Report on the BBC was even more immediate (BBC, 1992) and between 1986 and 1993 the Corporation shed approximately 7000 staff (which represented just over a quarter of employees). Many of those made redundant from both the BBC and ITV companies established themselves as freelance operators or formed independent companies in the vicinity of these major broadcasters. Roughly coincident with these developments has been the rise of cable and satellite broadcasting, which now constitute roughly one-third of broadcasting activity in the UK. This has to some extent undermined the market dominance of the BBC and the ITV companies and has created further demand for independently produced programmes. These two developments bear analogy with the *Paramount Decision* of 1948, which forced Hollywood studios to divest cinemas, thus enforcing vertical *dis*integration, and the rise of television in the 1950s, which led to the demise of the mass-production, highly vertically integrated Hollywood studio model in the post-war period in the USA (Scott, 2002; Storper & Christopherson, 1987). Both were fundamental processes underpinning the development of a highly vertically and horizontally disintegrated and specialized agglomeration in Hollywood which, once started, continued under its own self-reinforcing dynamics.

5 Evidence on the UK broadcasting industry

5.1 Some stylized facts

Broadcasting is highly agglomerated, with an estimated 70 per cent of employment in film and television concentrated in London, which also produces almost three-quarters of independent television programmes. Within this, there is a very strong concentration on an area of approximately one square mile in Soho. Programme production is dominated by the BBC, which is responsible for around 36 per cent of programme production. The independent television broadcasters account for around another 25 per cent. Another 25–30 per cent of the market is accounted for by about 50 medium-sized, mainly London-based independent production companies (many of which are owned by larger media concerns) and the remaining 10 per cent is accounted for by around 500 very small companies. The dominance of London, compared to other regional centres in the UK, is indicated in Tables 17.1 and 17.2, which show, respectively, absolute numbers of employees and location quotients in broadcasting and related media industries. On the one hand, London is much smaller than Hollywood (which has an estimated 132 000 employed in television-related activity), but on the other also more geographically concentrated. Central London includes Soho and West London is dominated by the headquarters of the BBC.

Recent econometric research conducted on the British broadcasting industry (Cook et al., 2001) has yielded results which indicate that the dynamics of industrial clustering are subject to positive externalities of colocation which are generated in a highly asymmetric way. This research broke the UK down into 14 socioeconomic planning regions and took a broad view of the industry which was decomposed into eight broad sub-sectors, each typified by relatively distinct lines of activity and associated technologies and knowledge bases. Briefly, these eight sub-sectors were television broadcasting, radio broadcasting, programme production, post production (e.g. editing, special effects, titling), manufacture of broadcast transmission equipment, manufacture of broadcast programme production and post-production equipment, programme distribution (including physical distribution and trade in intellectual property) and artistes (including talent agencies and theatre companies). These groupings reflect standard ways of disaggregating the industry. This decomposition was done in order to group together like firms, to gauge the spillovers both within particular lines of activity and between different sub-sectors. Two types of model were estimated. The first, a growth model, estimated the extent to which cluster strength, measured in terms of employment in both the firm's own line of activity (own employment) and in related lines of activity (other employment), either impeded or enhanced the growth rate of firms located within the cluster. In almost every case, cluster strength in the firm's own line of activity *enhanced* the firm's growth rate, whereas strength in related lines of activity *diminished* firm growth, suggesting a

Table 17.1   Numbers employed in the audio visual industries, by sector and region

	Wales	Scotland	Central London	West London	London ALL	South East	South West	West Midlands	North West
Broadcast TV	1 300	1 400	5 400	6 900	12 300	1 300	1 100	1 100	1 900
Cable and satellite television	0	0	1 500	1 100	5 300	400	0	0	0
Independent production (television)	1 200	500	5 400	700	8 200	1 500	800	200	1 100
Broadcast radio	700	1 500	4 600	5 200	10 000	3 300	1 100	1 100	1 300
Animation	200	100	900	200	1 400	200	400	200	400
Post-production	100	100	3 700	300	4 500	500	100	100	200
Digital special effects	0	0	600	0	600	100	0	0	0
Facilities (studio/equipment hire)	100	300	300	1 200	2 100	800	300	100	200
Web and Internet	1 100	600	12 100	2 200	20 100	6 100	1 000	400	400
Electronic games	0	800	600	500	1 400	3 400	200	1 000	900
Offline multimedia	1 300	300	1 000	400	2 400	3 200	300	200	200
Commercials production	0	0	2 100	0	2 500	100	0	0	200
Corporate production	200	100	600	200	1 100	900	200	0	100
Film distribution	0	0	400	100	500	0	0	0	0
Processing laboratories	0	0	400	0	400	200	0	0	0
Other	0	0	300	600	1 000	200	100	100	100

Source: Skillset.

280

Table 17.2   Location quotients in the audio visual industries, by sector and selected region

	Wales	Scotland	London ALL	South East	South West	West Midlands	North West
Broadcast TV	1.3	0.7	3.4	0.4	0.6	0.5	0.7
Cable and satellite television	0.0	0.0	6.0	0.5	0.0	0.0	0.0
Independent production (television)	1.9	0.4	3.6	0.7	0.6	0.2	0.7
Broadcast radio	0.7	0.8	2.9	1.0	0.6	0.6	0.5
Animation	1.5	0.4	3.0	0.5	1.5	0.7	1.2
Post-production	0.4	0.2	5.1	0.6	0.2	0.2	0.3
Digital special effects	0.0	0.0	5.6	1.0	0.0	0.0	0.0
Facilities (studio/equipment hire)	0.5	0.8	3.0	1.2	0.8	0.2	0.4
Commercials production	0.0	0.0	5.6	0.2	0.0	0.0	0.6
Corporate production	1.8	0.4	2.7	2.3	0.9	0.0	0.3
Film distribution	0.0	0.0	6.5	0.0	0.0	0.0	0.0
Processing laboratories	0.0	0.0	4.4	2.3	0.0	0.0	0.0
Other	0.0	0.0	3.4	0.7	0.6	0.6	0.5

Source: Skillset.

congestion effect. The second type of model was based on firm entry and investigated the extent to which cluster strength in sub-sectors within each industry either appeared to attract or to repel entry of firms into each sub-sector. Entry into a given sub-sector is almost always *deterred* by existing cluster strength, in that sub-sector and entry attraction typically emanates from *other* sub-sectors.

In terms of growth dynamics, the strongest positive effects of cluster strength in a firm's own line of activity appear in programme production and the manufacture of broadcast transmission equipment. These are followed by post-production and programme distribution. The centrality of programme production and post-production in cluster dynamics is reinforced by entry dynamics. Programme production is the only sub-sector in broadcasting where cluster strength within the sub-sector attracts entry of like firms. Programme production and post-production also exert strong positive entry attraction on each other. Thus there is a powerful virtuous circle, where cluster strength in each of these sub-sectors not only attracts entry but also leads to faster growth. Both of these sub-sectors attract entry from firms in other sub-sectors within the industry.

5.1.1   Social capital and knowledge transfer   Figure 17.1 indicates the top 10 benefits of locating in London according to the questionnaire survey. Scores were based on a simple summation of the Lickert scale responses ranging from 0 (not applicable) to 5 (very important). This leads to a maximum potential score of 1020 (204 replies × 5). This figure immediately indicates the importance of social capital based on face-to-face interaction.

The ability to have face-to-face contact emerges as the single most important factor, closely followed by the ability to build and maintain personal relationships. Why should these two things be so important? Here the interview evidence across all three cities was strong and consistent. In large part, it is due to the fact that what is being created is, most

Figure 17.1   Top 10 benefits of a London location

importantly, an image and sound which will convey meaning. These are cultural artefacts whose most important qualities are the extent to which they convey meaning, emotion and information. This makes it of paramount importance that those who are engaged in their production understand the meaning which is to be conveyed. In order to come to that understanding, communication with the maximum 'bandwidth' is required, i.e. face-to-face contact (Pratt, 2000; Scott, 2000). A network of personal contacts allows teams to be assembled quickly in order to carry out what, by most industry standards, is a short-term project, with the assurance that those engaged will be able to understand and produce what is required. Physical proximity in London promotes rich circuits of information about particular individuals which can be (and are) tapped into when assembling a team. These facts are salient reminders that the ability to produce is a vital influence on location decisions, whereas much of the literature places emphasis on 'ideas' and innovation, as if they were disembodied from production. Moreover, as Pratt (2000) argues, 'death of distance' arguments ignore the fact that many media products have a physical form, which in the case of broadcasting is highly significant, as it must meet exacting technical, as well as creative, standards.

The advantage of physical proximity in promoting trust and cooperation with other companies was highly rated, ninth out of 67 factors in the questionnaire survey. Trust looms particularly large in the relationship between production and post-production and provides an important part of the reason why they are almost always colocated. To hand over the 'rushes' (raw film or video which has been shot) for post-production is to entrust another with a valuable asset in which you have invested heart and soul. To reduce this uncertainty, people like to work with those whom they can trust to 'get it right'. The extent to which this potential advantage is seen to be important in practice is associated with location, rather than with line of business, with the strongest association being location in Soho and, to a lesser extent, a wider definition of central London (important because advertising has a different centre of gravity from broadcast and film). This evidence is consistent with the transaction cost approach to explaining the value of proximity (Storper, 1997), subject to the qualification that what is feared is incompetence rather than opportunism, although Banks et al. (2000) do produce evidence that cultural entrepreneurs do get cheated and fear being cheated. The path of production is sometimes smoothed by personal favours. A common scenario, which was often repeated during the course of the interviews, was where, for example, an independent production company would be strapped for cash for post-production work and would be able to arrange for a 'special fee' from a post-production company, with the promise that, on some future occasion, the favour would be returned by paying a little over the odds. Another example would be engineers within the post-production community lending each other equipment, usually on the implicit understanding that the favour would be returned should such a situation arise in the future. Such behaviour has to be underpinned by trust, a system for establishing and maintaining reputations and norms of reciprocity.

The questionnaire evidence indicates knowledge spillovers are locationally specific within London. The importance of knowledge transfer is moderately high, and again, the degree of importance is differentiated among various types of firm. Post-production companies and firms in Soho are significantly more likely to rate this factor as important. One interpretation is that denser concentrations of firms will experience larger amounts of knowledge spillovers because of greater frequency of interaction. Firms in Soho and in central London were significantly more likely to cite meetings in the street among their three most important types of informal interaction (over seven times more likely to cite if in Soho and four times more likely to cite if in central London, compared to firms outside those areas). Firms in Soho and central London were also significantly more likely to cite meetings in restaurants, wine bars and pubs than firms outside these areas. On the other hand, firms outside central London were significantly more likely to cite interaction via telephone, e-mail and professional bodies. Thus the general pattern is that, the closer firms are to Soho, the more likely it is they will find exchanges with colleagues at informal social settings or simply meeting by chance in the street to be beneficial. The significantly higher importance attached to colocation by firms in post-production tallies with Coe's (2001) observation that post-production has been spatially sticky in Hollywood even at a time when production, at least for more standardized output, has been increasingly moved to Vancouver. Glasgow differs from Bristol in some important respects. The degree of cooperation and informal interaction among its independent companies is palpably lower, the lack of 'untraded interdependencies' being remarked upon by Turok (2003). One possible reason for this is the much lesser degree of physical propinquity in Glasgow compared to Bristol. What these results again indicate is that, firstly, dense communication is important, but where and how that communication takes place is influenced in a fine-grained way by precisely where companies are located and what line of activity they are engaged in.

An important word used repeatedly in the London interviews was 'community'. The same word was used somewhat less frequently in the Bristol interviews and far less frequently in Glasgow. There are several important facets to the existence of this community. Firstly, there are overlapping communities, a wider broadcasting community and a more specific community relating to a particular craft or profession to which an individual will belong. Secondly, access to the community is granted by certain rites of passage, typically a year or two doing menial work for little or no pay as a runner, during which commitment, competence and attitude are assessed. This ensures appropriate socialization, imbuing the individual with attitudes, norms of behaviour and linguistic competence as well as formation of particular craft skills. How to behave and interact with others is a highly important dimension of this inculcation and testing for suitability (Grabher, 2002). Membership of the appropriate community is an important foundation of trust. The desire to establish reputation among peers is an incentive to effort and innovativeness (Heydebrand & Miron, 2002). Norms of information sharing and egalitarianism within communities are also important contributors to innovation.

5.1.2   The labour market   Labour market pooling is highly important. A pool of talented labour with relevant skills stands as the pre-eminent local factor helping firms innovate, according to the questionnaire survey. This is the third-highest ranked factor across the whole questionnaire. From the employer's point of view, London is an attractive location, despite the obvious congestion, because it offers such an exceptional pool of creative talent relative to other areas of Britain. There is clearly a dynamic at work where the reputation of particular regional centres, above all London, attracts talent which makes the centre a more desirable place to do business and so on (David & Rosenbloom, 1990; Nachum & Keeble, 1999). The strong pull of London on highly skilled labour is indicative of a much wider trend (Dorling & Thomas, 2004; HM Treasury, 2001). An important counter-example is Bristol, which is the premier location for natural history producers, based around the Natural History Unit of the BBC (Bassett et al., 2002). Anyone who aspires to work at the highest level in this genre has to operate in this location.

Labour market flexibility was generally viewed as being a source of advantage in a variety of ways. The most important advantage was seen as the ability to recruit good people at short notice, which stood apart from the other advantages of a flexible labour market. This is clearly important in media businesses which have a predominantly project-based mode of operation. Reputation mechanisms are essential in such labour markets as labour is highly differentiated in terms of both skills and ability, which is something well beyond labour pooling benefits based on lower risk of rationing on either side of the labour market. As DeFillippi and Arthur (1998) argue, social capital (knowing each other) and human capital (knowing your trade) are intertwined in the labour market and both matter in a project-based industry.

5.1.3   Vertical and horizontal linkages   The production of moving images and sound is a creative process and a premium will often be placed on the ability to understand and realize the idiosyncratic creative vision of the customer, whoever that may be, from channel controller at a major broadcaster, to account executive for a major corporate client in the advertising world. Accordingly, all types of production companies are significantly more likely to rate the ability to find firms who will supply bespoke services as important. The broad mix of media industries concentrated in London supports the fine-grained division of labour which, it has been argued, is a crucial dynamic of productivity growth and innovation. Highly specialized firms are viable in some cases because they can supply their goods/services to a range of different types of media company (Christopherson & Storper, 1986).

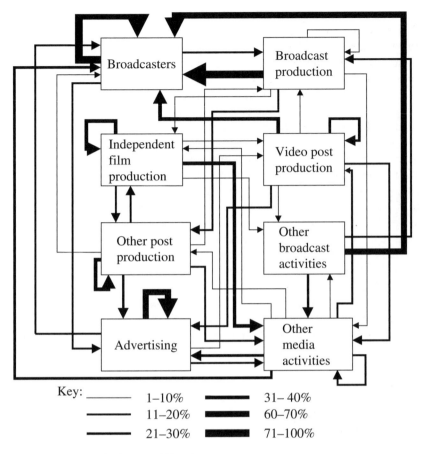

Key:

———	1–10%	▬▬	31–40%
———	11–20%	▬▬	60–70%
———	21–30%	▬▬▬	71–100%

Note: No observations arose in the 41–60% band.

Figure 17.2   Firm ratings of important interdependencies, by line of activity

Figure 17.2 gives an impression of which sectors are most closely interrelated. The figure was constructed by first allocating each firm to a sector on the basis of what it classed as its most important line of activity. The next step was to examine which sectors those firms stated were the most important with which it had interrelationships. The arrows show the direction of the relationship, with the arrow entering the sector rated as most important. The thickness of the lines gives a crude indication of the percentage of each sector's number 1 rankings being accorded to each sector.

A number of features stand out. Firstly, the broadcasters appear to be at the hub of the cluster, which is only to be expected. It is also intuitively correct that broadcast production should value being close to broadcasters, who are their clients. In this respect it is important to note that 'other broadcast activities' includes a number of freelance production managers and directors. Advertisers also emerge as being an important part of the cluster, which is unsurprising, given that they are high budget clients of broadcasters and parts of the post-production community. Post-production itself emerges as being quite central to the cluster, providing essential services to all forms of production, some of which are subsumed in the other media category (corporate video and commercials production). Other media appears to be central too, but this simply reflects the fact that a wide number of other activities have been rolled up into this catch-all category.

Companies do benchmark against each other in a way entirely consistent with the accounts of Porter (1990) and Malmberg and Maskell (2002). A close eye is kept on what commissions rivals win, who they engage on their production projects and the quality of the finished work, always with an eye to learning something of future competitive advantage. There is a conscious rivalry whereby firms and individuals strive to outdo their peers, raising standards and promoting innovation. Companies scrutinize each others' financial information to evaluate whether or not they are earning better margins on their work, again with a view to emulating their performance. Rivalry tends to be less among the smaller companies, which were widely seen as offering each other mutual support. Rivalry is also tempered by the allegiance of individuals to their particular craft community. It is also evident that the plethora of small independent production companies is able to pursue a broader range of ideas than would occur within a single integrated broadcaster–producer (see Storper, 1997, for similar observations regarding Hollywood). This wide experimentation is an important way in which major broadcasters cope with the vagaries of demand. The existence of a web of small, low-cost independent companies is also a means of lowering programme costs. In both respects the structure of the London broadcasting cluster mirrors the strategy adopted by the major studios in Hollywood for coping with the implications of more fragmented and unpredictable demand (Storper & Christopherson, 1987).

As Bathelt (2005) suggests, hub firms play a number of important roles within a particular agglomeration. They establish basic ground rules for programme formats. They attract new businesses as they are important customers, not least since they favour local suppliers both of programmes and of broader services. Traditionally, the BBC, and to a lesser extent the ITV companies, have been important trainers and there is current concern that many high-level skills are being lost as the BBC in particular has scaled back on this training role. Both the BBC and ITV companies have also, since 1990, provided sometimes considerable assistance to fledgling independent companies. On the other hand, as Aksoy and Robins (1992) identify in respect of Hollywood, large broadcasters do have a considerable position of power relative to much of the independent production sector, in the majority of cases offering cost plus contracts for programmes which entail the independent company signing over the whole or the majority of the intellectual property rights to the broadcaster. This perpetuates the dominance of the larger media firms and comparatively few have broken through to become anything like large-scale, independent producers.

London is home to many major overseas media multinationals and is important as a global node for a variety of reasons. It is a primary cultural metropolis which makes it attractive to creative individuals as well as being a melting pot of ideas (the two are interrelated). It can provide firms not only with ideas, but also with production capability sophisticated and flexible enough to meet any demand. The UK in particular, and Europe, are highly important markets for US exports and the UK is a useful beachhead for penetrating Europe. Glasgow has not been able, to date, to establish itself either as a major focus for demand or for production for overseas broadcasters and media conglomerates.

Bristol has done so only to a very limited extent relative to London, the exception being the natural history genre, where Bristol is the leading global centre.

5.1.4 Innovation It is important to appreciate that London is a vital global node in both technological and creative innovation and that these two innovation systems are intertwined. The Soho production and post-production and the Thames Valley manufacturing clusters have the common distinction of being important nodes in a global industry. Indeed the entire broadcasting complex forms a neo-Marshallian node in Amin and Thrift's (1992) sense. For example, when new equipment is being developed it is typically beta-tested in a number of top post-production companies. Where a multinational company such as Sony is concerned, these test sites will be located in key centres around the world, of which London is of prime importance. This on-site testing is important for two reasons, both salient in their ways for the innovation process. Firstly, very good feedback is obtained on how to develop the product, ready for market. Secondly, the fact that a piece of equipment has been tested by a leading facility and endorsed by them is very important in driving sales for the product. Being a test site also has important advantages for the post-production facility. They get 'first go' with the latest equipment, before it is available to some of their rivals. Moreover, they have the opportunity to shape the development of the product closer to their own requirements. The ability to work on cutting-edge equipment also attracts top creative talent and helps retain them.

Social capital is highly important in the innovation system, and is exemplified by considering the role of engineers. Engineers form a highly important network. Particularly among engineers there are examples of knowledge trading, as analysed by von Hippel (1988). Engineers have two important professional affiliations. One is to their profession, the other is to the cluster. Both of these transcend narrow company loyalties and lead to cooperative behaviours which help sustain the cluster and drive its creative and innovative dynamism. Engineers, for example, within the post-production play a pivotal role. They understand the technical side, but also have great insight into the creative side of the business, therefore they can articulate what the customer is really after in a way it would be much more difficult to accomplish if engineers from the manufacturing companies were to attempt to talk to creative people directly. Engineers from the post-production houses are able to visit the R&D labs of the manufacturing companies thanks to physical propinquity which is beneficial to both sides. Occasionally this may lead to the post-production engineers going to help out the R&D team in the manufacturing firm. In this respect, occupational, relational and physical proximity are all important in the creation and sharing of tacit knowledge.

6 Conclusion
By way of summarizing the above evidence, a typology of British broadcasting clusters will now be presented. Broadcasting appears to be a blend of three of Markusen's ideal types. Clearly the importance, almost since the inception of the industry in Britain, of the BBC, marks it as falling partly into the state-anchored model. The existence of dominant firms surrounded by fringe suppliers indicates elements of a hub-and-spoke type of cluster. Firms supplying the BBC and the ITV companies have traditionally been in a very dependent relationship. The industry is still dominated by the major broadcasters, even though many new types of broadcaster have entered the market and the major

broadcasters themselves have been forced to disintegrate vertically. The strength of the broadcasters at the hub of the cluster is critical. They will determine the extent and stability of demand for programming which in turn drives the derived demand for labour. As has been argued above, the formation of the labour pool is a vital process in forming a dynamic regional concentration. Programme production appears to have many features reminiscent of a Third Italy variant of the NID (New Industrial District). There is a high level of both vertical and horizontal disintegration, in the independent sector at least. As Storper and Christopherson (1987) have remarked regarding the post-war development of Hollywood, once the process of vertical and horizontal disintegration starts, it becomes a self-sustaining process as the cluster grows. In these respects broadcasting has very strong similarities with what is believed to be known about Hollywood.

National policy was primarily responsible for the formation of this industrial district. Firstly, as has been discussed, the Broadcasting Act (1990) ushered in a massive increase in the scale of independent programme production. Also of critical importance was the establishment of Channel 4, in 1982, as a broadcaster without its own in-house production capability. London was the natural home of this new broadcaster and it helped to develop the independent production and post-production cluster which was therefore able to prosper more easily in the capital after 1990 than it did in the regions (Allen & Miller, 1994; Lambert, 1982).

Broadcasting in the UK has been mapped in an imperfect way onto the typology of clusters identified in the literature review. In contrast to much of the literature, the questionnaire study revealed how important is the 'microclimate' within the cluster, calling further into question how well any single model or typology can reflect the particularities of a given cluster. All seem to imply a greater homogeneity within a cluster than has been revealed to be the case here. The importance of particular cluster benefits, such as informal knowledge flows and personal interaction, vary significantly by precise location and line of activity. There are strong asymmetries regarding which companies generate positive externalities within the cluster.

Regarding the suitability of the cluster concept for policy, the evidence here supports the considerable scepticism voiced by Martin and Sunley (2003). Firstly, the idiosyncrasies of the cluster are too marked for broad-brush nostrums to be useful. Secondly, classic business support has been effective in Glasgow, and the absence of a 'cluster policy' has been of little obvious detriment in London and Bristol. Thirdly, it is manifestly the case that local policy has been much less important in shaping the overall national dispersion of activity than national policy. Moreover, London has such powerful advantages, given its status as a world city, and as a key node in the global broadcasting industry, that local policymakers have to be realistic regarding what can be achieved in second-tier cities.

Finally, the evidence presented here is not only that geography is not dead, but that it is probably more powerful than imagined, centripetal forces being much in evidence. Firstly, knowledge transfer and information sharing, as well as the formation of social capital, have been shown to be powerfully centred on the very dense heart of the London cluster in Soho, and a rapid decay with distance is indicated. Trust, interpersonal relationships and face-to-face contact have been shown to be of abiding importance. Buzz matters for all the reasons articulated by Storper and Venables (2004) and its effect rises with geographical density. Secondly, labour market dynamics are centred on London and exert a very powerful growth dynamic. Propinquity does facilitate benchmarking, as

Malmberg and Maskell (2002) suggest, but many of the important horizontal externalities take place across organizational boundaries within particular craft communities, where trust looms larger than they imply. Contrary to Malmberg and Maskell's claim, vertical linkages appear dense and fundamentally important to cluster strength.

Acknowledgements

This research was partly funded by the Economic and Social Research Council, award number R000223258, and the British Academy, award number SG-36816. The authors would also like to acknowledge the contribution of Peter Swann and Skillset, who provided employment census data.

References

Aksoy, Asu and Kevin Robins (1992), 'Hollywood for the 21st century: global competition for critical mass in image markets', *Cambridge Journal of Economics*, **16**, 1–22.

Allen, Rod and Nod Miller (eds) (1994), *Broadcasting Enters the Marketplace*, London: John Libbey.

Amin, Ash and Nigel Thrift (1992), 'Neo-Marshallian nodes in global networks', *International Journal of Urban and Regional Research*, **16**, 571–87.

Banks, Mark, Andy Lovatt, Justin O'Connor and Carlo Raffo (2000), 'Risk and trust in the cultural industries', *Geoforum*, **31**, 453–64.

Bassett, Keith, Ron Griffiths and I. Smith (2002), 'Cultural industries, cultural clusters and the city: the example of natural history film-making in Bristol', *Geoforum*, **33**, 165–77.

Bathelt, Harald (2005), 'Cluster relations in the media industry: exploring the "distanced neighbour" paradox in Leipzig', *Regional Studies*, **39**, 105–27.

BBC (1992), *Extending Choice. The BBC's Role in the New Broadcasting Age*, London: BBC.

Best, Michael, E. (1990), *The New Competition*, Cambridge, MA: Harvard University Press.

Broadcasting Act (1990), Eliz 2, Ch. 42.

Brown, Donald R. (1989), *Comparing Broadcast Systems. The Experience of Six Industrialised Nations*, Ames, Iowa: Iowa State University Press.

Cairncross, Frances (1997), *The Death of Distance*, London: Orion Business Books.

Cave, Martin (1989), 'An introduction to television economics', in Gordon Hughes and David Vines (eds), *Deregulation and the Future of Commercial Television*, Aberdeen: University of Aberdeen Press, pp. 9–37.

Caves, Richard, E. (2000), *Creative Industries: Contracts between Art and Commerce*, Cambridge, MA: Harvard University Press.

Christopherson, Susan and Michael Storper (1986), 'The city as studio; the world as back lot: the impact of vertical disintegration on the location of the motion picture industry', *Environment and Planning D: Society and Space*, **4**, 305–20.

Coe, Neil M. (2001), 'A hybrid agglomeration? The development of a satellite-Marshallian Industrial District in Vancouver's film industry', *Urban Studies*, **38**, 1753–75.

Coe, Neil M. and Alan R. Townsend (1998), 'Debunking the myth of localised agglomerations: the development of a regionalised service economy in South-East England', *Transactions of the Institute of British Geographers*, **23**, 385–404.

Collins, Richard, E. (1988), *The Economics of Television*, London: Sage.

Collins, Richard, E. (1990), *Television: Policy and Culture*, London:Unwin Hyman.

Cook, Gary A.S., Naresh R. Pandit and G.M. Peter Swann (2001), 'The dynamics of industrial clustering in British broadcasting', *Information Economics and Policy*, **13**, 351–75.

Cooke, Philip and Kevin Morgan (1998), *The Associational Economy. Firms, Regions and Innovation*, Oxford: Oxford University Press.

David, Paul A. and Joshua L. Rosenbloom (1990), 'Marshallian factor market externalities and the dynamics of industrial localization', *Journal of Urban Economics*, **28**, 349–70.

DeFillippi, Robert J. and Michael B. Arthur (1998), 'Paradox in project-based enterprise: the case of film making', *California Management Review*, **40**, 125–39.

Dorling, Daniel F.L. and Bethan Thomas (2004), *People and Places. A 2001 Census Atlas of the UK*, Bristol: The Policy Press.

Dunnett, Peter J.S. (1990), *The World Television Industry. An Economic Analysis*, London: Routledge.

Ellison, Glenn and Edward L. Glaeser (1997), 'Geographic concentration in US manufacturing industries: a dartboard approach', *Journal of Political Economy*, **105**, 889–927.

Euromedia Research Group (1997), *The Media in Western Europe*, 2nd edn, London: Sage.

Florida, Richard (2002), *The Rise of the Creative Class*, New York: Basic Books.
Gertler, Meric S. (2003), 'Tacit knowledge and the economic geography of context, or the undefinable tacitness of being (there)', *Journal of Economic Geography*, **3**, 75–99.
Gordon, Ian R. and Philip McCann (2000), 'Industrial clusters: complexes, agglomerations and/or social networks?', *Urban Studies*, **37**, 513–32.
Grabher, Gernot (2002), 'The project ecology of advertising: tasks, talents and teams', *Regional Studies*, **36**, 245–62.
Hall, Peter (2000), 'Creative cities and economic development', *Urban Studies*, **37**, 639–49.
Heydebrand, Wolf and Annalisa Miron (2002), 'Constructing innovativeness in new-media start-up firms', *Environment and Planning A*, **34**, 1951–84.
HM Treasury (2001), *Productivity in the UK: 3 – The Regional Dimension*, London: HM Treasury.
Home Office (1986), *Report of the Committee on Financing the BBC*, Cmnd, 9824, London: HMSO.
Ito, Masami (1978), *Broadcasting in Japan*, London: Routledge & Kegan Paul.
Jankowski, Gene F. and David C. Fuchs (1995), *Television Today and Tomorrow. It Won't Be What You Think*, New York: Oxford University Press.
Kleinsteuber, Hans J. (1997), 'Germany', in Euromedia Research Group (ed.), *The Media in Western Europe*, 2nd edn, London: Sage, pp. 75–97.
Kuratani, Masatoshi and Yukihiko Endo (2003), 'Tokyo's central role in the knowledge-based economy', *Nomura Research Institute Paper No. 65.*
Lambert, Stephen (1982), *Channel Four. Television with A Difference?*, London: British Film Institute.
Landry, Charles (2000), *The Creative City*, London: Earthscan.
Malmberg, Anders and Peter Maskell (2002), 'The elusive concept of localization economies: towards a knowledge-based theory of spatial clustering', *Environment and Planning A*, **34**, 429–49.
Markusen, Ann. (1996) 'Sticky places in slippery space: a typology of industrial districts', *Economic Geography*, **72**, 293–313.
Marshall, Alfred (1920), *Principles of Economics*, London: Macmillan.
Marshall, Alfred (1927), *Industry and Trade*, London: Macmillan.
Martin, Ron and Peter Sunley (2003), 'Deconstructing clusters: chaotic concept or policy panacea?', *Journal of Economic Geography*, **3**, 5–35.
McCann, Philip and Stephen Sheppard (2003), 'The rise, fall and rise again of industrial location theory', *Regional Studies*, **37**, 649–63.
Meier, Werner A. (1997), 'Switzerland', in Euromedia Research Group (ed.), *The Media in Western Europe*, 2nd edn, London: Sage, pp. 229–43.
Miller, Danny and Jamal Shamsie (1996), 'The resource-based view of the firm in two environments: the Hollywood film studios from 1936 to 1965', *Academy of Management Journal*, **39**, 519–43.
Morgan, Kevin (2004), 'The exaggerated death of geography: learning, proximity and territorial innovation systems', *Journal of Economic Geography*, **4**, 3–21.
Nachum, Lilach and David Keeble (1999), 'Neo-Marshallian nodes, global networks and firm competitiveness: the media cluster of central London', ESRC Centre for Business Research, University of Cambridge, working chapter no. 138.
Piore, Michael and Charles Sabel (1984), *The Second Industrial Divide: Possibilities for Prosperity*, New York: Basic Books.
Porter, Michael E. (1990), *The Competitive Advantage of Nations*. London: Macmillan.
Pratt, Andy C. (2000), 'New media, the new economy and new spaces', *Geoforum*, **31**, 425–36.
Renton, Timothy (1994), 'Broadcasting enters the marketplace: the keynote address', in Rod Allen and Nod Miller (eds), *Broadcasting Enters the Marketplace*, London: John Libbey, pp. 1–6.
Saxenian, Annalee (1994), *Regional Advantage: Culture and Competition in Silicon Valley and Route 128*, Cambridge, MA: Harvard University Press.
Scott, Allen J. (1988), *New Industrial Spaces: Flexible Production, Organization and Regional Development in North America and Western Europe*, London: Pion.
Scott, Allen J. (2000), *The Cultural Economy of Cities*, London: Sage.
Scott, Allen J. (ed.) (2001), *Global City-Regions*, Oxford: Oxford University Press.
Scott, Allen J. (2002), 'A new map of Hollywood: the production and distribution of American motion pictures', *Regional Studies*, **36**, 957–75.
Shew, William B. (1992), 'Trends in the organization of programme production', in Tim Congdon et al. (eds), *Paying for Broadcasting*, London: Routledge, pp. 64–91.
Storper, Michael (1997), *The Regional World: Territorial Development in A Global Economy*, New York, Guildford Press.
Storper, Michael and Susan Christopherson (1987), 'Flexible specialization and regional industrial agglomerations: the case of the U.S. motion picture industry', *Annals of the Association of American Geographers*, **77**, 104–107.

Storper, Michael and Anthony J. Venables (2004), 'Buzz: face-to-face contact and the urban economy', *Journal of Economic Geography*, **4**, 351–70.

Trappel, Josef (1997), 'Austria', in Euromedia Research Group (ed.), *The Media in Western Europe*, 2nd edn, London: Sage, pp. 1–16.

Turok, Ivan (2003), 'Cities, clusters and creative industries: the case of film and television in Scotland', *European Planning Studies*, **11**, 549–65.

Verrier, Richard (2005), 'Movies, shmovies – T.V.'s taking over L.A.', *L.A. Times*, 19.8.05.

von Hippel, Eric (1988), *The Sources of Innovation*, Oxford: Oxford University Press.

18 Tourism clusters

Ewen J. Michael

1 Introduction

Tourism research is a relatively new field of academic endeavour, having established its identity only over the past three decades. Tourism is a vast and complex field of social and economic activity that encompasses the issues relating to people's travel and visiting from one place to another. Tourism research, then, is multidisciplinary by necessity, for it must deal with the production of its related services, the location of its places, the psychology and choices of its consumers, the marketing of its products, the management and administration of its businesses, the planning for its infrastructure, and for the policy implications that tourism creates for the communities and regions where it occurs. More important, perhaps, are the questions about its role in enhancing economic growth and opportunity in particular environments.

One of the initial problems confronting the tourism researcher is that what constitutes *tourism* as a separable form of human behaviour has proved difficult to define. In the social sciences, tourism concerns the activity of people when they travel – what they do and why – but in economics and the management sciences, analysis focuses on tourism as an industrial process. These disciplines normally assume a careful delineation of boundaries, to establish a degree of certainty about what distinguishes one industrial activity from another. Flow-on and spillover effects are part of what they want to identify; but when an activity is labelled as *tourism*, there is often confusion and ambiguity. For example, part of a business function may be tourism but part of it may not; or worse, from the analyst's viewpoint, the same product or service may be tourism for one consumer but not for another (at what point, for example, do you distinguish business travel from tourism?). While tourism researchers have contributed to the refinement of this problem, the precision of definition remains wanting and is often a matter of individual perception.

In these circumstances, there is value in rehearsing the arguments about what constitutes a *tourism* activity and the issues that confront its development, before considering how the principles of clustering have been interpreted for application in this field. This chapter, then, draws attention to the work by tourism analysts in *micro-cluster* formations and the linkages they have established with *network* theory. It concludes with some consideration of how these principles are now being applied in practice.

2 What is tourism?

The original approaches to tourism analysis stem from concepts of travel, where transport economists and statisticians recognized aspects of visiting that were not related to commerce or migration. They clearly needed to separate classes of travellers and differences in travel markets for broad industry studies, but their attempts to define tourism solely by movements over arbitrary distances or for convenient time-periods has proved inadequate, if not redundant, for continents like Africa or Australia, where the concepts of time and distance have different implications. It has proved more useful, perhaps, to bring the *purpose* of travel into the assessment, to emphasize that tourism is a leisure or non-working activity, which '*a person chooses to perform*' (Aronsson, 1994: 79). This establishes the notion that tourism is a non-pecuniary activity determined by an individual's own motivations, and so provides at least one means of distinguishing what is *tourism* from what is not. This assumes, of course, that the economic consequences of the activity are not forgotten: for, at the end of any analysis, the *tourist* is still a consumer, albeit in some specific form of market (Michael, 2002: 119).

Tourism is also about locations. It is about the places that people visit and the experiences they gain from travel. The study of *place* and the *authenticity* of the tourism experience provide a focus that has captured the attention of sociologists, social psychologists and marketing analysts to better comprehend the purpose of travel. From a different perspective the same issues raise new questions for geographers and economists whose concern lies with the development of these locations. For them, interest rests in explaining why locations develop as destinations, how they emerge and grow, and what opportunities they create for enhancing social and economic well-being – if, indeed, they do. It is within this context of *place* that many tourism activities can be observed occurring in *cluster* formations, where bundles of separate activities are combined to produce the experience that tourists wish to consume.

3 Tourism and development

Arguably, there are many approaches for examining tourism development, though no single framework yet appears to have the consensus of support that casts it as a paradigm for analysts. Clustering theory has a role here, and one with some relevance for communities that seek to build or enhance a tourism function as part of their economic choices. Given the impacts from changing markets and the globalization of trade, there has been an inexorable shift in the development profile of tourism around the world. International tourism receipts now represent around 6 per cent of world exports (goods and services) and, despite the impacts of changing global security requirements, the growth in tourism continues to outstrip the world's growth in real GDP (WTO: 2005). In short, tourism is a global growth industry that is generating substantial economic benefits for many countries, but the opportunities are unequally distributed according to the amenity of destinations and the potential to capitalize on the prospects for growth.

Nowhere is the disparity in tourism development more apparent than in the emerging economies of Asia and South America and amongst the rural communities who live in the peripheral regions of the industrialized Western states. For many who live in these areas, the tenor of global change is not necessarily perceived as being to their benefit, and so they perceive inequities in the opportunities afforded them to share in this potential. Rural decline is a vexed issue in this context, but visible in many countries as a declining resident population and as a falling share in the value of rural outputs. The consequences include the loss of employment opportunities, particularly for younger workers, which has led to a drift of population to urban centres that has made an impact on the capacity of many communities to maintain their lifestyles. This process has contributed to an increasing sense of social and political dissatisfaction, but the issue is not so much that economic wealth is declining, but rather that the opportunities for future employment, growth and resurgence are perceived to be diminishing. Hence, there are now new demands for approaches to policy that can rebuild the platform for regional growth (Michael, 2007).

In this context, the potential for expanding tourism is often perceived as one element of the package of solutions that will contribute to regional growth, for tourism is based on local resources and, as a service industry, generates both strong employment and income multipliers. Tourism offers multiple externalities (both positive and negative) that may deliver multiple solutions in some local circumstances. They can be incorporated as part of holistic approaches to development, particularly where tourism is recognized as a dynamic for change in those localities for which a competitive advantage exists. In this sense, tourism policy concerns the means to enhance *visitations*, to locations rather than the sponsorship of *icon* activities; but, such a proposition calls on policy makers to acknowledge the benefits and impacts from growth stemming from myriad micro-economic sources rather than from single centrally planned projects. The argument, as summarized succinctly by the OECD (Hugonnier, 1999), is that the older models of regional equalization and sporadic investment have given way to new concepts based on the competitiveness of regions and the decentralization of resource allocation decisions to provide the basis for regional communities to reverse the trends of declining employment and economic opportunity. It may be an overstatement, but it is within this changing framework that tourism analysts are exploring the potential of cluster theory as a mechanism to enhance growth in ways that expand social *opportunity* to deliver positive outcomes consistent with existing community needs and values.

4   Clusters: contexts and applications
Because tourism analysis is multidisciplinary by nature, it is not surprising that cluster theory has been applied in widely different ways, for different issues and for different purposes. Many of these applications reflect the discussions elsewhere within this *Handbook*, but they can commonly be found in four distinct fields of tourism research, as indicated below.

4.1   Economic growth (strategic planning)
One of the key issues in tourism research concerns the potential for analysts and public sector planners to contribute to an understanding of the way tourism destinations and business activities evolve and develop. The aim, here, is to enhance the capacity for broad strategic planning both within the industry and within regions, guided perhaps by Porter's (1991) approach to cluster analysis in major industrial regions. However, the difficulties in trying to interpret a descriptive framework for prescriptive applications on a smaller scale has meant that much of the work remains focused on building the supporting structures that might encourage the growth of existing or potential tourism clusters (Nordin, 2003: 34).

4.2   Geography and location analysis
Location remains a key concept in tourism research, and a number of studies have pursued aspects of clustering theory as a means to explain the effectiveness of some locations in comparison to others (see, for example, Jackson & Murphy, 2002). In essence this stream of research remains focused on the benefits and synergies of geographic proximity or co-location. Some have extended this to include comparisons between regions to identify differences in competitive advantage, as Jackson (2006) suggests in her study of regions in China to find avenues for greater participation by local firms in tourism development.

4.3 Marketing

The widest use of clustering theory within the tourism research literature relates to the common benefits that regional associations of firms can extract through co-operative marketing programmes. In this application, co-located firms offering similar products or experiences join in co-operative ventures to promote their services, usually to consumers outside their own region. In some forms, this interpretation lends itself to government participation, where tourism or local development agencies take up the role of convenors to act as focal points or as sponsors of the common aims of firms. Examples of these practices are myriad, and can be found across a range of divergent activities in different countries. Just for illustration, these include the sponsorship of national, thematic and local clusters to promote tourism in South Africa (South Africa, 2005), the grouping of different agricultural activities for promotion to tourists in Alberta, Canada (Alberta, 2005) or, as an example at a local level, the 'Healthy Lifestyles Tourism Clusters' project in East Sussex, England. At a more sophisticated level, the strategic plans of some state authorities with responsibilities for tourism development incorporate elements of clustering to promote and market co-located specialist services, where groups of firms may offer niche activities as different as wine-tasting and adventure holidays. There is perhaps no better example than the '*jigsaw*' strategy in Victoria, Australia, which established individual marketing plans for each region in the State based on distinct clustered segments to appeal to different visitor interests, emphasizing the idea that each piece of the *jigsaw* is needed to make up the whole picture (Tourism Victoria, 2002).

4.4 Microeconomic management

It is in the field of microeconomic management and community development that tourism analysis has made an original contribution to Cluster Theory in recent times. This interpretation stems from a series of tangential findings in a number of earlier niche market studies – antique retailing in Southwestern Pennsylvania (Grado et al., 1997); antiques as a tourism market in Australia (Michael, 2002), or Seaton's (1996, 1999) analyses of *Book Towns* – all of which pointed to the possibility that some niche markets, particularly those that generate a demand for travel, are amenable to clustering in regional areas. The hypothesis that arose suggested that micro-markets of this type, when operating in a cluster formation, produce a range of accelerated economic and social benefits for some local communities, and might possibly lead to the formation of new tourism destinations. The intriguing element in this proposition lay in its application at the *micro* level, where small communities remain in control of the development process, thus adding a political dimension to the resolution of development possibilities.

While the empirical evidence for tourism cluster formations seemed substantial, the theory needed to explain these effects in small community settings was inadequate. At the time, it could be said that the notions of location and clustering were well understood in strategic planning, but the underlying paradigm derived from the economies-of-scale that could be leveraged in large-scale regions and these dynamics could not be assumed to exist in many tourism locations. In the search for solutions, tourism researchers have explored the role of complementary service providers to create *diagonal* value-chain relationships in cluster formations (Poon, 1994), and re-examined the nature of demand for tourism to explain how firms add value to their products by participation in a cluster process. In micro-environments, of course, the benefits from clustering remain both constrained and asymmetric, but the integration of *network* theory explains how both firms and communities can interact to share these gains (detailed in Michael, 2007).

5   The clustering effect

Within tourism research, the discussions of the principles underlying the concept of *clustering* focus on those business activities that derive their commerce from travel and visitations. Despite the wealth of literature detailing the segmented structure of tourism markets, the advocates for tourism development often ignore its predominantly small-scale nature. In many countries, small businesses and local operators are the mainstay of the domestic tourism product (Middleton, 2001). These businesses deliver the tourism reality and provide the platform that makes a region attractive and accessible. They determine the nature of the industry's interaction with its host communities, as well as providing the basis for employment and the potential for growth and innovation. The circumstances in the State of Victoria, Australia, illustrate the point: the data for 2000–2001 quantified total tourism activity, both domestic and international, at 54 million visitor nights and 42 million day trips (Tourism Victoria, 2002: 67), with two-thirds by either measure occurring in regional or rural areas. Apart from a small volume of packaged tour business, most visitors were classified as *independent travellers* making use of the services and products of thousands of small businesses scattered across the State, a pattern of activity that is duplicated in many regions of the world's more developed countries. For tourism analysts, then, this is the real world in which they operate; hence, the potential for cluster development remains focused on these circumstances.

Clustering theory is not a panacea for regional development, but there may be particular market circumstances that favour its formation and, where these apply, they may create *opportunities* for local growth. The potential for policy development, however, is constrained by the absence of a comprehensive understanding of the processes that lead to clustering and of the impacts it has in particular regions. The problem, here, is to identify the dynamics that lead to the successful clustering of regional niche industries, and the social implications that stem from this location concentration.

5.1   Forms of clustering

In a traditional schematic framework, there were said to be two distinct types of cluster formation, derived from the co-location of like firms at the same level of a production process (horizontal clustering), or from the co-location of firms at different stages in a value-chain (vertical clustering). This understanding of clustering became an entrenched part of post-war economic analysis, for it assumed that each form of economic co-location could extract the synergies and economies-of-scale for participating firms in a market: 'Generally, the more industries that are located in a given area the greater the external economies that become possible' (Mountjoy, 1966: 107).

This approach had its weaknesses, for there was as much empirical evidence to support the effectiveness of clusters as there was to contradict it. Porter's (1991) model breathed new life into this framework, which was extended still further with the inclusion of a third type of cluster formation that recognized the concentration of co-located complementary activities (diagonal clustering). In very recent times, this model has taken on a new analytic dimension with the realization that what matters for strategic planning purposes is the way these forms of clustering come together; for, while it is the *structure* of the cluster

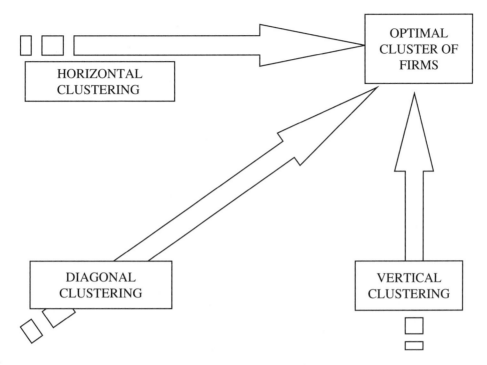

Figure 18.1   Optimal cluster development for micro industries

that generates the synthesis between firms to increase the collective market size, it is the relational dynamics between firms that leads to commercial success and, perhaps more importantly, leads to the prospects for optimizing the potential for growth in regional environments. Figure 18.1 provides an abstract model of the concept.

The concept of *horizontal* clustering is easiest to understand. It refers simply to the geographic co-location of like firms operating at a similar level in a value-chain. While the firms are *competitors*, in that they sell a like product using similar productive resources, their co-location pools the potential customer base to increase total sales. Sometimes such co-location generates other advantages in terms of labour supply, shared information and infrastructure to reduce costs or the effects of externalities. Routine examples are apparent in the distinct precincts of retail or manufacturing activity in every sizeable city. In Figure 18.1, the arrow for horizontal clustering can be read from left to right to indicate an increasing concentration of co-located firms.

Vertical clustering identifies the relative co-location of firms in an industry's supply chain. Here, the relationship between firms depends on the linkage between stages in a production process that enhances specialization. The geographic proximity between firms minimizes logistics and distributional costs, and may offer other benefits in the form of concentrated labour skills and market information. A simple example within the tourism industry might comprise a group of vineyards, with a co-located winery, warehousing and distribution facilities, perhaps with a local retailing outlet and consumer information service: the chain is complete from grower to consumer. (Figure 18.1 demonstrates this relationship as an increasing level of integration between firms as the arrow rises).

However, it is the inclusion of the concept of *diagonal* clustering that makes the framework pertinent to tourism analysis. It refers to the concentration of *complementary* (or symbiotic) firms, where the separate activities of each firm add value to the activities of other firms, even though their products may be quite distinct. In this sense, diagonal clustering brings together firms that supply separate products or services, packaging them into bundles that will be consumed as though they were one item. In the tourism industry, and perhaps for many other service industries, the co-location of many complementary providers adds value to the consumer's total experience. In a sense, this is routine, for a tourism destination requires firms to supply activities, transport, hospitality, accommodation, etc. to deliver the experience the visitor seeks. The converse may also be true, because the absence of key services will restrict the potential of other firms to develop. The direction of the arrows in Figure 18.1 imply a growing concentration of complementary service providers, and hence an expansion in the bundle of values to be derived from the destination's activities.

5.2   Complementarity

Poon (1994) explored diagonal clustering (the grouping of complementary firms) and diagonal integration (the grouping of complementary activities within a single firm) as new approaches for tourism business strategists seeking to add value to a firm's activities by integrating complementary services into the final product offered to consumers. In effect, this provides a diversification of services to better meet the needs of a target group of consumers and allows firms to tap the economies-of-scope and the synergies between products, rather than the economies-of-scale that are the focus of horizontal and vertical clustering (Poon, 1994: 224). Collections of firms, then, align themselves with each other to deliver integrated products, which contain sets of attributes that are perceived by the consumer as a single entity. For example, a day tour to a tourism destination might be sold with transport, meals and information services as a single package even though it is a production process that comprises the activities of several different suppliers.

The economic rationale for diagonal clustering stems from the notion that a complementary product or service adds value to an existing product by enhancing its utility through an expansion of the range of attributes when both products are consumed jointly. In this sense, the products of complementary firms play a critical role in the consumer's decision process by making the product more attractive. On the other hand, a substitute product can replace the original: hence the suppliers of substitutes become the true competitors in a market segment. As a consequence, Brandenburger and Nalebuff (1997) have suggested there is an obvious strategy for business growth (which they label as *co-opetition*) based on co-operative practices amongst complementary providers who compete in the market with the suppliers of substitute or alternate services. In short, diagonal clustering is about the processes that build the alignment between complementary providers to expand the scale of production by making the products themselves more attractive 'rather than fighting with competitors' (Brandenburger & Nalebuff, 1997: 14).

For tourism, the focus of cluster analysis is to provide a framework for industry participants and regional communities to identify and extract the gains inherent in the clustering process that can be applied to their individual local needs, rather than with the more traditional analyses based on market competition. Nonetheless, if this approach is applied as a strategy for tourism development, it still requires the kinds of assessments identified by Porter (1991) of the customer base (demand behaviour) and of the local capacities to produce a tourism product that will match those needs. It also requires an assessment of a region's *related and supporting* industries and the likely responses to new entrants from existing firms, to determine whether geographic concentration can be converted into more strategically sophisticated clustering relationships. More importantly, cluster analysis must establish the existence of any symbiosis between like firms and the alignments for complementarity that will affect their potential for growth.

6   Co-location or clustering

The principles of cluster analysis have their origins in the traditional theories that were established more than 40 years ago, although they have been substantially revised as a consequence of Porter's analyses (1991, 1998). In smaller-scale environments, however, there is perhaps a need to distinguish between the effects from clustering compared with those that accrue from simple co-location. This is particularly relevant for tourism because much of the industry encompasses a plethora of small communities, towns and villages with their own sense of place and identity, and where the different scale of activities raises questions about the dynamics that are assumed to drive a cluster's formation. For example, the notion embedded in clustering is that the economic and social benefits derive from either or both the *horizontal* or *vertical* integration of firms, because they allegedly have the potential to extract the economies-of-scale inherent from their *co-location*. While these can be significant in some larger regions or cities, the reality is that the sum of these gains is often too small to be detected as visible outcomes at a micro level. Although this form of location analysis might work in some small-scale environments, it often does little more than illustrate the effects of economic specialization. However, where the effects of *diagonal* clustering are included in the analytic framework, in the form of complementary activities that add value to the existing local production, it becomes possible to recognize an increasing level of benefits through economies-of-scope. This creates the potential to expand the market's size and the opportunity for local wealth creation, even for small communities (Michael, 2003).

Tourism analysts often find it difficult to adapt the principles that have been identified in studies from other industries when they deal with the development issues in very small communities. In part, this is because the dynamics of scale are such that the interactions between people are more clearly visible and the vagaries of individual behaviour can be seen to affect the outcomes more significantly. It is also because tourism encompasses a broad range of industrial activities and processes, where the relationships between firms become substantively different from that found in single industry formations. It could be argued, of course, that tourism firms often find themselves in close proximity to each other from the necessity to be situated within the natural feature that makes up a destination's attractiveness, and hence tourism analysts assume the existence of those fixed effects that arise from co-location and concern themselves only with the elements of clustering that remain discretionary.

Small-scale analysis, however, does have its advantages. It brings to the fore those arguments that demonstrate the benefits of localization, and particularly the advantages that accrue to local operators from their embedded knowledge about *the place* where tourism occurs. Gertler (2003: 78) notes that 'tacit forms of knowledge can only be acquired through experience', and knowledge about *the place* and the nature of *local practice* is not tradeable, nor is it relevant to those outside *the place* (Maskell & Maskell, 1999).

Micro-clusters based on tourism lend themselves to these hypotheses, as any expansion of the complementary activities at a destination, which is integrated into the local product, adds new attributes and new value to the basket of benefits available to consumers. In the real world, of course, there are myriad circumstances where groupings of co-located firms display elements similar to clustering, even knowledge sharing, but still do not deliver the anticipated outcomes. This does not necessarily contradict the proposition, for the principles of micro-clustering suggest the clustering effect occurs only where the synergies generated by the co-location of firms are actually *captured* and *shared* by those firms. In small economic communities, this might include the mechanisms that enable cost savings and welfare benefits from a cluster's formation to be transferred to both the enterprises and the community that makes up its membership. This does not imply that the distribution of benefits or economic gains will be equal, for it is more likely to be asymmetric, but rather that all the members of a cluster understand and participate in the process and that all are able to gain.

There is also a distinction between the mechanics of *co-location* and those of a *cluster* formation. The concept of *co-location* suggests that the concentration of like industries in a geographic area will produce multiplier effects (economic), along with their consequent social impacts (externalities), as firms extract the gains from economies-of-scale and a pooled customer base. If the firms are genuinely competitive in this environment, they should use the efficiency gains from co-location to reduce their cost structures; but, ultimately, they should also compete away these gains by lowering prices – which may or may not result in increased consumer demand and a larger market, but would certainly reduce the incentives for firms to join the cluster (Michael, 2003). *Clustering*, however, implies that the rate of regional growth can be accelerated by the co-location of symbiotic industries as they learn through co-operative practice to extract the synergies and complementarities that exist between their production processes, which ought to enhance the value of those products or services provided by the cluster's members. In short, policies that enhance the concentration of competitive firms in a given location can aim only at increasing productive activity through the marginal economic gains based on economies-of-scale, whereas those that generate a synthesis and interaction between firms seek a cumulative acceleration of benefits.

Geographic co-location may well be a necessary condition for effective cluster formation to occur, but it is by no means a sufficient condition. The problem, of course, is that, even when complementary firms operate in co-location with each other, this alone will not generate synergies between those firms, nor necessarily lead to greater cost efficiencies. Rather, it creates an *opportunity* for those firms to put in place the mechanisms and strategies to capture those benefits. However, each cluster formation is unique; hence, the business development processes needed to identify those synergies and shared cost benefits differ in every case.

Figure 18.2 represents this concept by suggesting that the mechanics of clustering stem from the process of optimizing the gains from both economies-of-scale and of scope (the large arrow), but the gains for firms come in the form of a continuum based on their increasing ability to co-operate. Co-location offers common marketing advantages, but the benefits from clustering require common business strategies to evolve. The clustering effect, that is

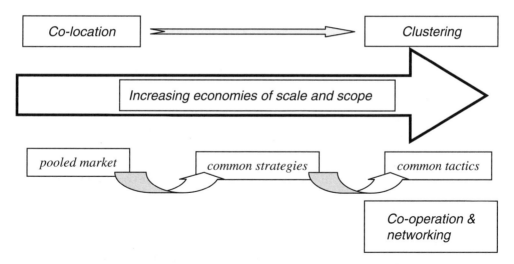

Figure 18.2   A clustering spectrum

visible in truly successful formations, moves still further towards co-operative or common business practices (labelled here as *tactics*), where firms might share resources or communication systems to build a collective relationship with their customers and suppliers.

In tourism applications, a cluster formation has the potential to become an effective force for regional growth because the activities of its firms are based on *visits*, where any increase in the demand for travel brings with it a need for complementary growth amongst the range of supporting industries that service visitor needs. Hence the proposition that a tourism-based cluster formation not only enhances multiplier and externality effects, but *accelerates* the opportunities for new forms of economic wealth by creating a demand for a host of complementary activities which in turn generate their own multiplier effects. Tourism growth, of course, also brings with it new impacts, costs and externalities for a community, not all of which are welcome. The social impacts of clustering based on niche markets in small communities remains a challenging field of research, even if Seaton (1999) provides some guide with his analysis of six specialized *Book Towns* in north-western Europe.

7   Networks: co-operation and trust

Understanding the economic dynamics of clustering and the mechanics of its formation are essential elements for analysing how a successful cluster operates, but still does not explain why some groups of co-located firms are able to optimize the benefits from clustering while others are not. There clearly remains another dimension that considers how some groups of firms are able to co-operate and share their collective outcomes – even though the rewards are inevitably asymmetric. What persuades them to make and sustain such choices?

Economics provides part of the answer. In terms of motivation, firms and their host communities have the potential to gain more through co-operation in a specific location as a means to compete in a broader market. However, such a proposition is only viable if all firms contribute. This implies some form of mutual agreement, whether formal or informal, where all participants know with certainty that each is contributing to the collective outcome (a form of mutual assurance game, Dixit & Nalebuff, 1991: 126). Unfortunately, the flaw is obvious: a co-operative process cannot emerge, or will collapse, if any firm or substantive element of the host community seeks only to extract the immediate synergies and externality gains from the group in pursuit of their own self-interest. A more effective answer is required.

One explanation lies in contemporary *networking* theory, or at least in those variants that have been applied to the social nexus between business and the community in tourism destinations. Dredge (2004: 197) suggests that, while network theory has generally been used as a retrospective tool for policy analysis, it can also explain how and why different interests in small communities interrelate within a network. In small cluster formations, the network of business and community interests needs to handle common problems for its membership to build a consensus, but inevitably there will exist diversity and difference in the aspirations of those members, so successful networks must also be able to resolve conflicts, and that implies a capacity to build and sustain *trust* among the membership.

Networking theory examines the range of reasons for individuals and groups to associate with each other. In their collected summary of the benefits other researchers found with networking, Lynch et al. (2000) demonstrate a raft of issues about 'learning and exchange', 'community' and 'business activity' that go well beyond the short-term gains normally proposed as motivations in economic analyses. These *human* factors imply that network members are motivated by longer-term interests, which include the necessity to build and maintain a sustainable relationship between businesses and their community hosts. If such long-term interests exist, this helps to explain the evolution of trust amongst the members of a cluster. Its weakness, of course, is that this approach is based on relatively small associations of people who are able to communicate and interact with each other on a personal basis, which might not be possible in larger-scale regions. Nevertheless, it reaffirms the micro-clustering approach as a co-operative planning tool for small communities. What is still missing from tourism research is an understanding of the ways that firms initiate and maintain these co-operative networks to operationalize the 'cluster effect'.

8   From principles to practice

For tourism researchers, the analysis of clusters and cluster effects is separate from issues that concern those aspects of business strategy that the firm itself controls, including those decision processes to develop outcomes through *alliances* and other forms of commercial integration (see Dyer et al., 2001). Rather, the concern in tourism is with the industry's development at a community level, and with the distinct economic and social impacts, both positive and negative, that may arise from geographic clustering, particularly in smaller or micro environments. It assumes that the *optimization* of a clustering process can generate the dynamics to enhance both business performance and the growth of market size, and so enhance local economic welfare (Michael, 2003). This approach is distinctive, as it integrates the concept of diagonal clustering (Poon, 1994) and the role of complementary service providers (Brandenburger & Nalebuff, 1997) in the development of *segmented local markets* that public policy processes might encourage.

The tenets of successful clustering, which seems to drive competitive advantage based on the co-operative and mutually supportive linkages among the cluster's industries, have only been tested in areas which are already regionally successful, such as Silicon Valley and Boston Massachusetts (Porter, 1998). For tourism, however, the approach has been made proactive for regional policy by inverting the methodological structure. It seeks to identify the existing market niche industries within a local environment and search for a dynamic alignment of complementary firms that can add value to the total regional product. The desired outcome is a package of attributes delivered by a host of small businesses that the target visitor wants to consume as a single entity. While small-scale, the synthesis and synergy between the co-located firms continues to extract economies-of-scale, but now adds a new dimension through economies-of-scope to increase opportunity and diversification. In combination, the two generate a new pattern of accelerator effects, but the form that growth takes remains directed by the existing community.

Within the global tourism industry, there are increasing examples of states and communities seeking to apply the principles of clustering as mechanisms to guide development. While many of these form part of the plethora of approaches used to enhance the growth of small businesses and many remain limited solely to the development of local or regional marketing programmes, there are still instances where the objectives of policy are focused on building genuine synergies between complementary operators in particular localities. Mitchell and Schreiber (2006), as one example, point to the development of tourism clusters in New Zealand and the role of the Ministry of Economic Development in sponsoring a programme of support to encourage the formation of integrated local networks of clusters based on consumers' perceptions of the complementarities inherent in food, wine and tourism.

Nevertheless, for tourism, there are still a number of issues to be resolved by both researchers and policymakers before clustering can be seen as a reliable tool for local development. There remains, for example, a need to find an effective means of identifying the range of complementary activities most suited to the delivery of a regional tourism product. These complementarities will differ in every application because each regional community is its own *place* with its own specialized and unique product, and, hence, has its own basis for visits. The search for complementarities is much more than the determination of cross-elasticities (albeit one type of indicator); rather, it is about identifying those synergies which actually add value to the total outcome in a specific location. At another level, the search process itself is difficult for local communities, for inevitably they lack the means to acquire the appropriate information. One role for policy, then, is to service these needs, allowing communities to make choices based on their own requirements. Nevertheless, clustering theory appears to have applications for tourism markets, demonstrating a potential to optimize the delivery of sustainable economic, social and environmental benefits for regional communities. For tourism policy, it is an approach focused on creating economic *opportunity*, where business and community development are seen as inextricably linked.

References

Alberta (2005), *Alberta Ag Tourism Directory*, [Department] Agriculture, Food and Rural Development: available at www1.agric.gov.ab.ca/general/agritour.nsf.

Aronsson, L. (1994), 'Sustainable tourism systems: the example of sustainable rural tourism in Sweden', *Journal of Sustainable Tourism*, 2(1–2), 77–92.

Brandenburger, A.M. and B.J. Nalebuff (1997), *Co-opetition*, foreword edn, New York: Currency Doubleday.

Dixit, A.K. and B.J. Nalebuff (1991), *Thinking Strategically – the Competitive Edge in Business, Politics, and Everyday Life*, New York: W.W. Norton & Company.

Dredge, D. (2004), 'Networks, conflict and collaborative tourism planning', *CAUTHE 2004: Creating Tourism Knowledge*, School of Tourism & Leisure Management, University of Queensland, Brisbane, 10–13 February 2004, pp. 195–207.

Dyer, J.H., P. Kale and H. Singh (2001), 'How to make strategic alliances work', *Sloan Management Review*, **42**(1), Summer, 37–43.

Gertler, M.S. (2003), 'Tacit knowledge and the economic geography of context, or the undefinable tacitness of being (there)', *Journal of Economic Geography*, **3**, 75–99.

Grado, S.C., C.H. Strauss and B.E. Lord (1997), 'Antiquing as a tourism recreational activity in Southwestern Pennsylvania', *Journal of Travel Research*, **35**(3), 52–6.

Hugonnier, B. (1999), 'Regional development tendencies in OECD countries', *Regional Australia Summit, Keynote Presentation*, Canberra, 26–29 October (14 pages).

Jackson, J.A. (2007), 'Developing regional tourism in China: the potential for activating business clusters in a socialist market economy', *Tourism Management*, **27**(4) 695–706.

Jackson, J.A. and P.E. Murphy (2002), 'Tourism destinations as clusters: analytical experiences from the New World', *Tourism and Hospitality Research: The Surrey Quarterly Review*, **4**(1), 36–52.

Lynch, P.A., K. Halcro, N. Johns and I. Buick (2000), 'Developing small and micro-enterprise networks to build profitable tourist destinations', *Destination Development Conference*, ETOUR, Mid-Sweden University, Ostersund.

Maskell, P. and A. Maskell (1999), 'Localised learning and industrial competiveness', *Cambridge Journal of Economics*, **23**, 167–86.

Michael, E.J. (2002), 'Antiques and tourism in Australia', *Tourism Management*, **23**(2), 117–25.

Michael, E.J. (2003), 'Tourism micro-clusters', *Tourism Economics*, **9**(2), 133–45.

Michael, E.J. (2007), *Micro-clusters and Networks – the growth of tourism*, Oxford: Elsevier.

Middleton, V.T.C. (2001), 'The importance of micro-businesses in European tourism', in R. Lesley and D. Hall (eds), *Rural Tourism and Recreation: Principles to Practice*, Wallingford: CAB International, pp. 197–201.

Mitchell, R. and C. Schreiber (2006), 'Wine tourism networks and clusters – co-operation and barriers in New Zealand', in E.J. Michael, *Micro-clusters and Networks – the growth of tourism*, Oxford: Elsevier.

Mountjoy, A.B. (1966), *Industrialization and Under-developed Countries*, 2nd edn, London: Hutchinson.

Nordin, S. (2003), *Tourism Clustering & Innovation – Paths to Economic Growth & Development*, Paper No. U 2003:14, European Tourism Research Institute, Östersund.

Poon, A. (1994), *Tourism, Technology and Competitive Strategies*, Wallingford: CAB International.

Porter, M.E. (1991), *The Competitive Advantage of Nations*, London: Macmillan.

Porter, M.E. (1998), 'Clusters and the new economics of competition', *Harvard Business Review*, November–December, pp. 77–90.

Seaton, A.V. (1996), 'Hay on Wye, the mouse that roared, book towns and rural tourism', *Tourism Management*, **17**(5), 379–82.

Seaton, A.V. (1999), 'Book towns as tourism developments in peripheral areas', *International Journal of Tourism Research*, **1**, 389–99.

South Africa (2005), *South African Tourism Cluster Study Summary*, Tourism leadership Group: available at http://www.nedlac.org.za/research/fridge/south_african_Tourism_cluster_st.htm.

Tourism Victoria (2002), *Victoria's Tourism Industry Strategic Plan 2002–2006*, Melbourne: Tourism Victoria.

World Tourism Organization (2005), *Facts & Figures – information, analysis and know-how* (http://www.world-tourism.org/facts/eng/economy.htm). [Note: This is a permanent site with data updated routinely.]

Index

Ablas, L.A. de 153
accessibility measure 51–2
Acs, Z.J. 25, 70
address, credible 254, 255
advertisers 285
agent diversity 124–5, 128
agglomeration 14, 23–38
  clusters, firm types and nature of
    transactions 30–32
  clusters, innovation and 26–30
  importance of clustering and 23–6
  measurement problems 33–5
agglomeration economies 4–7, 15, 25, 26–7,
    133–49, 261
  industrial clusters, growth poles, industrial
    complexes, industrial districts and inter-
    firm networks 135–8
  innovation 140–43
  learning regions 138–40
  localization economies *see* localization
    economies
  urbanization economies *see* urbanization
    economies
Agnes, P. 258
Aksoy, A. 286
Alberta, Canada 295
Allen, J. 97
Almeida, P. 222, 227
Alvstam, C.G. 80
Amin, A. 275–6
Amsterdam 250
Andersson, Å.E. 53, 264–5
Andersson, D.E. 264–5
Andersson, M. 52
architecture 263, 264
Arrow, K.J. 69–70, 71–2, 73
Asheim, B.T. 139, 140
assembly lines 241
asset-augmenting investments 227, 228, 229
asset mass efficiency 120
assignment problem 44
assistance, need/opportunity to seek out 104,
    106
asymmetries 70, 72
Atherton, A. 100, 101, 103, 109
Atkin, R.H. 153, 154, 156
attractiveness of regions 45–6
Audretsch, D.B. 25, 67, 74, 75, 122
Augar, P. 258

Australia
  interest rate swaps industry 258
  state of Victoria 295, 296
Austria 119, 120–21, 278
  Styria 208–9, 210, 238, 239
automobile industry 80, 123, 208, 210, 241
autonomy, loss of 105, 106
average dissimilarity technique 169–70

'Ba' 97
backward linkages Q-analysis 154–67
  Chicago economy 158–67
Baden Württemberg 275
Bairoch, P. 54
Balloni, V. 193
Baptista, R. 195
Barro, R.J. 24
Bathelt, H. 86, 87, 286
Beaudry, C. 61, 195–6
Becattini, G. 191
Begg, I. 249
Bellandi, M. 195
benefits, identification of and agreement on
    105, 106
Bergman, E.M. 116, 119, 120–21, 153
Berlin 264
Betts, J.R. 126
Bianchi, G. 191
Bianchi, R. 193
Birkinshaw, J. 221, 222, 223, 226, 228
Block, F.L. 141
Boissevain, J. 99
Bologna, Italy 195
Boschma, R.A. 125
Boston 130, 303
  biotechnology community 80
  Route 128 75, 93, 128, 130, 141, 234
'bottom up' approaches to cluster formation
    15, 93–113
Boudeville, J.R. 28
box office revenues 270, 271
branch plant syndrome 220
Brandenburger, A.M. 298
breakaway firms 9, 71, 72
Brenner, T. 116, 117, 118, 122
Breschi, S. 50, 61, 195–6
Brioschi, F. 193, 194
Bristol 249, 283, 284, 287
Britain *see* United Kingdom (UK)

British Broadcasting Corporation (BBC) 277, 278, 279, 284, 286, 287
Britton, J.N.H. 80
broadcasting industry 17, 274–91
  economics of TV broadcasting 276–7
  general trends and influences 277–9
  innovation 287
  labour market 284
  social capital and knowledge transfer 281–4
  typology of UK broadcasting clusters 287–8
  UK broadcasting industry 277–89
  vertical and horizontal linkages 284–7
Broadcasting Act (1990) 278, 288
Bröcker, J. 153
Brown, K.A. 242
Brusco, S. 191, 192–3
buildings 262, 263
  architectural stars 263, 264
  museum buildings 266
bundling programmes into channels 277
business embeddedness 222
business groups 190–91, 192–5, 197, 199
  impact on structure and governance of IDs 194–5
  presence and characteristics of business groups within IDs 192–4
buzz, local 86–90

Cainelli, G. 193, 194, 196
Camagni, R. 84
Cambridge 93
Camors, C. 261
Canada 80, 208, 283, 295
Cantwell, J.A. 225
Capello, R. 62
Carpi, Italy 193, 194
central business district (CBD) 53
centralization 221
'centripetal forces' 252–3, 256–7
chains of structural complication 156–7
chance/random events 127
Chandler, A.D. 144
Channel 4 288
Chapman, K. 234, 236
Chenery, H.B. 153
Chicago
  metalworking sector 137, 145
  metropolitan economy 158–67
Chinese coke-making sector 145
Chinitz, B. 28
Chiu, A.S. 238
Christaller, W. 1
Citibank 258

cities 27, 94–5, 276
  European 263–5, 272
  innovation and 34–5
  see also urbanization economies
City of London 16, 249–60
  financial services cluster 249, 250–52
  reasons for clustering of financial services 252–8
Clark, G.L. 80, 258
club (social network) model 2, 31, 32, 33
cluster analysis 169–70, 185
  wavelet transformation *see* wavelet transformation
cluster-based renewal of old industrial areas 16, 206–16
  diversification 206–7, 209–11, 213–16
  incremental change 206–9, 213–16
  radical change 206–7, 211–16
cluster formation 15, 93–113
  as a business dynamic of relational and spatial proximity 94–5
  phases of cluster development 106–7
  policy implications of 'bottom up' dynamics 109–11
  process 100–104
  relational and locational dynamics 95–8
  stages 101–4, 110, 111
  taxonomy of 98–100
  temporal dynamic of 108–9
  thresholds 104–6, 110, 111
cluster intensity 146
cluster life-cycles 15, 114–32
  and phases 114–26
    exhaustion phase 122–6, 128–9
    existence phase 115–18, 127
    expansion phase 118–22, 128
CMI 140
Cobham, D. 257
Collins, R.E. 277
colocation 14–15, 39–66
  or clustering in tourism 299–301
  colocation dynamics as generic phenomenon 60–62
  phenomenon 40–41
colocation–clustering spectrum 300–301
colocation externalities 46–53
  distance sensitivity and scale economies 46–7
  extra-market 49–50
  regional R&D externalities 50–53
  via the market 47–9
common issue/problem, identification of 101, 102, 104, 106
community 283–4
comparative advantage, law of 236

competitiveness 224
complementarities 298–9, 303
congestion costs 121
consumer-driven supply chains 137, 143–4
consumption-related amenities 45–6
contact intensity 3
Cook, G.A.S. 279
Cooke, P. 93, 94, 211
cooperation 197
   recognition of need/opportunity to
      cooperate 101, 102, 104–5, 106
   tourism 301–2
cooperative marketing programmes 295
core and periphery 144–5
Cornford, J. 243
corporate embeddedness 222
Crane, D.B. 257
creativity 29–30
credibility 105, 106
credible address 254, 255
critical mass in financial expertise 253,
   256–7
cultural change 258–9
cultural cluster index 264–5
cultural clusters 16–17, 261–73
   importance of stars 269–72
   infrastructure 262–5
   infrastructure and cultural services 266–8
   probability-based cultural clustering
      268–9
   see also broadcasting industry; tourism
cultural infrastructure clusters 263–5
cultural proximity 141–3
cumulative causation 7
customers
   costs of interacting with 42–3
   distance to 44–5
   taste for diversity 56–8
Czamanski, S. 153

Dalum, B. 120
Daubechies, I. 172, 173
Davis, E.P. 257
De Liso, N. 196
Debreu, G. 39
declining clusters 13–14, 35, 123
deep relationships 100
Dei Ottati, G. 192
delivery spillovers 49–50
demand
   demand factors and IDs 197
   externalities 11
Denmark
   Kalundborg 237–8
   mobile communications cluster 120

deregulation
   broadcasting 278
   financial services 258–9
Desrochers, P. 238, 241–2
Detroit auto cluster 123, 208
developing countries 224, 225–6
development coalitions 139, 140
developmental TNCs 225
Dew, N. 68
diagonal clustering 296, 297, 298, 299
diagonal integration 295, 298
Dicken, P. 220
DiPasquale, D. 136–7
discrete wavelet transform (DWT) 173–5
   DWT-based clustering (DWTBC) 176,
      177–85
   maximal overlap (MODWT) 175
   one-dimensional (1D DWT) 174
   two-dimensional (2D DWT) 175, 182–5
discriminative approaches 169–70
dispersion economies 15, 133–49
   supply chains 133, 137, 143–5
distance sensitivity 6, 46–7
distribution 277
district groups 193, 194, 197, 198
diversification 206–7, 209–11, 213–16
diversity
   agent diversity 124–5, 128
   and the case against specialized clusters 16,
      234–45
   case for local diversity 236–43
   local employment diversity and urbanization
      economies 33–5
   urbanization economies and taste for 55–8
downstream (delivery) spillovers 49–50
Dredge, D. 302
Dridi, C. 153
Dunning, J.H. 221, 223, 225
Duranton, G. 27, 28, 240

Eccles, R.G. 257
Eckhardt, J. 69
eco-industrial parks (EIPs) 237–8, 239
economic decline 237
economic growth 23–5, 71, 294
economic knowledge 71
economies of scale *see* scale economies
economies of scope 105, 106, 300–301
Edinburgh 249, 264, 278
efficiency externalities 10–11
efficient clusters 10–12
electronic proximity 143
embeddedness 221, 222
emerging clusters 106–7, 109
Emilia Romagna, Italy 29, 192, 193

employment
    broadcasting industry 279, 280
    measurement of sectoral employment
        distribution 33–4
    UK financial services 250, 251, 252
employment density 33
'end of geography' 258–9, 276
endogenous entrepreneurship 71, 72, 75
endogenous growth 71
endowments, region's 42, 43
    and attractiveness of regions 45–6
engineers 287
Ennals, R. 139
Enright, M.J. 50, 110, 211, 224, 225, 226–7,
    259
entrepreneurial choice model 68–9
entrepreneurial clusters 75
entrepreneurial technological regimes 118
entrepreneurship 9–10, 67–77, 242
    knowledge spillover theory of 15, 67, 68–72,
        74, 75
environmental determinism 222
established clusters 106–7, 109
established industries, new clusters in 206–7,
    209–11, 213–16
Ettlinger, N. 145
Euclidean distance 169
European cities 263–5, 272
exhaustion phase 122–6, 128–9
existence phase 115–18, 127
expansion phases 118–22, 128
experience, knowledge of 142
experience goods 262, 269
exploitative expansion phase 120–22, 128
exploratory expansion phase 118–20, 128
export-base models 78, 79, 81–3, 89
external economies of scale 5, 7
external market potential 3–4
external threats 14
externalities 10–11
    colocation 46–53
    static 236–7
extra-market colocation externalities 49–50
extraregional accessibility 51–2

face-to-face contact 97, 254–6, 281–2
factor-proportions theory 42
fast location processes 41–3
Feldman, M.P. 62, 74, 122
Feser, E.J. 125, 153, 237
film industry 261, 268–72
    importance of stars as a clustering factor
        269–72
    probability-based cultural clustering 268–9
    top 20 films 269, 270

financial services 16, 249–60
    City of London cluster 249, 250–52
    reasons for clustering in City of London
        252–8
Fine, C. 143
Fingleton, B. 140, 146
firm-centred view of IDs 198
firm entry 281
firm strategies 208, 209–10, 211–12, 213, 214,
    215
firm types 30–32
fixed costs 5, 47, 57–8, 60
flexible specialization 139, 275
Florida, R. 29–30, 208
footloose perspective on TNCs 220–21
Ford Motor Company 241
Fordist system 78
foreign direct investment (FDI) 209–10, 215,
    219, 225, 227, 229
    see also transnational corporations (TNCs)
foreign ownership 249
formalization of group and its collaborative
    activities 101, 104, 105, 106
Fornahl, D. 116
Forslund, U.M. 59
forward linkages Q-analysis 165, 166
France 253
Francis, J. 62
Fringe Club 267–8
Fritsch, M. 75
Frost, T.S. 222, 227
Fujita, M. 2, 40, 53, 54, 56
functional (urban) regions 2–4, 45, 57–8

Gabaix, Z. 23
gain, recognizing or gauging 105, 106
Geographic Information Systems (GIS) 171
geographic proximity *see* spatial proximity
'geography is dead' thesis 258–9, 276
Gereffi, G. 145
Germany 75, 253, 278
Gertler, M.S. 141–2, 142, 208, 276, 299–300
gestation periods 108–9, 110–11
Glaeser, E.L. 25
Glasgow 278, 283, 286, 288
global pipelines 86–90
global supply chains 144–5
globalization 67, 75, 227, 258–9
Goldstein, H. 126
Gone with the Wind 271
Gordon, I.R. 2
Grabher, G. 123, 206
Granovetter, M. 32, 100
Gråsjö, U. 52
Greenwich Village 266

Groupe de Recherche Européen sur les Milieux Innovateurs (*GREMI*) 83
growth
  economic 23–5, 71, 294
  model and broadcasting clustering 279–81
  regional *see* regional development and growth
  urbanization, innovations and 54–5
growth poles 28, 135–8
Gustavsen, B. 139
Gutenberg's printing press 240–41

Haar wavelet 171–2, 173
Hansen, W.G. 3
Harrison, B. 144–5
Hassink, R. 116, 123
head office assignment 222
Healthy Lifestyles Tourism Clusters project 295
Heckscher–Ohlin theorem 40, 45
hedonic price models 264–5
Helsinki 56
Hewings, G.J.D. 153, 165
high-tech clusters 140
  cluster-based renewal in old industrial areas 206–7, 211–16
Hippel, E. von 287
Hoffman, W. 234
Hollywood 219, 272, 274, 278, 283, 286, 288
  employment 261
  nature of cluster 275
  Paramount Decision (1948) 278–9
  stars 271
homogeneity 124
Hong Kong 261
  cultural cluster 267–8
  financial services cluster 226–7, 249
Hood, N. 222, 223, 228
Hoover, E.M. 1, 27, 40, 134
horizontal clustering 296, 297, 299
horizontal diversification 195
horizontal externalities 10–11, 49–50
horizontal linkages 284–7
host countries, TNCs and 219–23, 225
hotel rates 264–5
Hotelling, H. 1
Hounshell, D. 238, 241
housing 45–6
Hsinchu science park 267
hub firms 286
hub-and-spoke clusters 224, 275, 287–8
Hudson, R. 209
human capital 29–30, 284

Iacobucci, D. 193
Iammarino, S. 225

ideal types 274–5, 287–8
  see also models of clustering
import networks 56, 58
income choice model 68–9
incremental change 206–9, 213–16
incubator model 28
Independent Television (ITV) companies 278, 279, 286, 287
indigenous clusters 224
industrial clusters 135–8
  input–output system 15, 153–68
industrial complexes 2, 30–32, 33, 135–8
industrial districts (IDs) 8, 16, 93, 135–8, 189–202, 226, 235, 275
  broadcasting industry 288
  business groups and 190–91, 192–5, 197, 199
  innovation 28, 29–30
  structure and governance 194–5
  technological innovation 191, 195–7
  'traditional' model of 190, 191–2, 198
industrial policy 235–6
industrial symbiosis 237–8, 239
information and communication technologies (ICT) 25, 139, 258–9, 276
information spillovers *see* knowledge spillovers
infrastructure 4, 12–13
  cultural 262–5
  and cultural services 266–8
  knowledge *see* knowledge infrastructure
  market 253, 257
initial collaborative project, development of 101, 102–3, 104–5, 106
innovation
  agglomeration, clusters and 26–30
  agglomeration economies 140–43
  broadcasting industry 287
  and cities 34–5
  innovation dilemma of old industrial areas 205–6
  local diversity and knowledge combinations 238–43
  regional innovation systems 125–6, 204–5
  technological innovation and IDs 191, 195–7
  and urbanization economies 54–5, 58–60
innovation-based adjustment of old clusters 206–9, 213–16
innovation externalities 10–11
innovative clusters 10–12
innovative milieux model 28, 29–30, 83–4, 89
input-buying firms
  clustering 41, 48–9
  taste for diversity 55–6
input–output linkages 6, 40, 79–80
input–output systems 15, 153–68

input spillovers 49–50
input-supplying firms
    clustering 40–41, 48–9
    costs of interacting with 42
    distance to 43–4
institutions
    cluster-based renewal in old industrial areas
        209, 211, 212, 213, 214, 215
    trade 25
interaction
    frequency of 283
    infrastructure 12–13
    intensity 3
interconnectedness of asset stocks 120
inter-firm linkages, local diversity and 237–8,
    239
inter-firm networks 135–8
inter-industry accounts 15, 153–68
inter-industry linkages 6, 40, 79–80
internal market potential 3–4
internal returns to scale 27
internal scale economies 5, 6, 7, 40
internal threats 13–14
international financial markets 250–52, 253
intra-market colocation externalities 47–9
intraregional accessibility 51–2
intraregional market demand 45
Ireland 212
Isard, W. 1, 135
isolating mechanisms 120
Italy
    Emilia Romagna 29, 192, 193
    IDs 16, 189–202, 275
    Marche region 119, 193
Ivarsson, I. 80

Jackson, J.A. 294
Jacobs, J. 54, 56, 95, 238–40, 266–7
Jacobs hypothesis 58, 62
Jaffe, A.B. 25, 73–4
Japan 249, 253, 274, 278
Jarillo, J.C. 69
jigsaw marketing strategy 295
Johansson, B. 3, 4, 10, 46, 53, 54
Johnson, B. 139, 140

k-means algorithm 169–70
Kalundborg 237–8
Karaska, G.J. 79
Karlsson, C. 1, 63
Kebir, L. 114, 115–16, 117, 118, 119, 121
Keilbach, M. 67, 75
Keir, M. 237, 242–3
Klann, W. 241
Knight, F.H. 68

knowledge
    of experience 142
    flows, innovation and urbanization
        economies 58–60
    knowledge/science base 125–6, 128
    local diversity and knowledge combination
        238–43
    social embeddedness 142
    tacit 140, 142, 276, 299–300
    types of 140
knowledge-based clusters 15, 78–92
    limited evidence of regional input-output
        linkages 79–80
    local buzz and global pipelines 86–90
    models of regional development and growth
        80–86
    regional networks and growth 78–9, 89
knowledge centres 97–8
    taxonomy of clusters emergence 98–100
knowledge filter 70
knowledge generation, regional model of
    86–90
knowledge infrastructure
    cluster-based renewal in old industrial areas
        208–9, 210, 212, 213, 214, 215
    overspecialized 206
knowledge-intensity 12
knowledge-intensive clusters 206–7, 211–16
knowledge-seeking FDI 227, 229
knowledge spillover theory of
    entrepreneurship 15, 67, 68–72, 74, 75
knowledge spillovers 6, 15, 25, 26, 67–77, 276
    broadcasting industry 281–4
    colocation externalities 49–50, 50–53
    entrepreneurial clusters 75
    role of geographic proximity 67, 72–4
Kogut, B. 222, 227
Korzeniewicz, M. 145
Krueger, N.F. 69
Krugman, P.R. 1, 2, 24, 46, 73, 115, 117, 224
Kurzweil, R. 242
Kynaston, D. 250, 258

labour
    broadcasting industry 284
    costs 6, 137
    cultural clusters 272
    film industry 268–9, 272
    financial services cluster 253, 254, 257
    knowledge intensity 12
    pool of skilled labour 6, 26–7
Lagendijk, A. 243
Lai, W.-C. 267
Lakshmanan, T.R. 3, 4
Lall, S. 220

Lam, A. 142
Lan Kwai Fong 267–8
land prices 264–5
land values 62
Langlois, R. 192
large firms 144–5
large regions 8–9
lasers 240
Laursen, K. 126
Leamer, E. 143
learning regions 138–40
Lee, C.W.B. 126
Lehmann, E. 67, 75
Lichtenberg, R.M. 238
link effects 10, 11
linkages
    backward linkages Q-analysis 154–67
    forward linkages Q-analysis 165, 166
    horizontal and vertical 284–7
    inter-industry 6, 40, 79–80
    local diversity and inter-firm 237–8, 239
Lipsey, R.G. 238
Lissoni, F. 50, 97
listening post subsidiaries 228
local accessibility 51–2
local buzz 86–90
local diversity 236–43
    development of new inter-firm linkages
        237–8, 239
    and knowledge combination 238–43
    static externalities 236–7
local embeddedness 222
local non-traded inputs 6, 26–7
local skilled-labour supply 6, 26–7
localization economies 5, 6, 27, 40, 54–5, 61,
        133–4, 135, 236
    and colocation externalities 46–53
    measurement problems 33–5
localization hypothesis of knowledge spillovers
        72–4, 75
localized external effects 85
location analysis 14–15, 39–66
    agglomeration and urbanization economies
        53–60
    colocation dynamics as generic phenomenon
        60–62
    colocation phenomenon 40–41
    conditions for location of the firm 41–6
    location and colocation externalities
        46–53
    perspectives on 39
    tourism 294
location quotients 279, 281
lock-ins 123, 128–9, 206
Locke, R.M. 136

lognormal noise 182, 183
London 124, 264, 274
    broadcasting industry 274, 278, 279, 280,
        281–7, 288
    City of London 16, 249–60
Lorenzen, M. 116
Los Angeles 56, 274
    Hollywood *see* Hollywood
Lösch, A. 1
Lösch–Weber landscapes 85
Lucas, R.E. 54
Lundvall, B.Å. 139–40, 143
Lynch, P.A. 302
Lyon, F. 100, 103

Maclennan, D. 46
Maggioni, M.A. 116, 117, 118–19, 121, 122
Mahalanobis distance 169
Maillat, D. 83, 84
Malizia, E.E. 237
Mallat, S. 174, 176
Malmberg, A. 1, 118, 120, 196, 276, 289
manufacturing sector 165, 167
Marche region, Italy 119, 193
market
    colocation externalities via the 47–9
    infrastructure 253, 257
    pooled 300–301
    potential 2–4, 12–13
market-seeking units 228–9
marketing 295
Markusen, A. 28, 135, 136, 223, 274–5
Marshall, A. 1, 5–6, 26–7, 40, 50, 94, 191, 192,
        223, 235, 237, 254, 275
Martin, R. 135, 259, 275
Martini, G. 195
Maskell, P. 1, 114, 115–16, 117, 118, 119, 120,
        121, 196, 276, 289
maximal overlap DWT (MODWT) 175
maximum dissimilarity technique 169–70
McCann, P. 2
McNeil, I. 238
measurement
    agglomeration measurement problems
        33–5
    of aggregation 127
    knowledge spillovers 73, 74
meat packing industry 241
meetings 254–6
Menzel, M.P. 116
Michelin stars, cultural 263–4
Michigan auto cluster 128
microeconomic management 295–6
milieux, innovative 28, 29–30, 83–4, 89
Mitchell, R. 303

model-based approaches to cluster analysis
170
models of clustering 2, 30–32
    see also ideal types
Modena-Reggio Emilia, Italy 195
monopoly 272
Morgan, G. 249
Morgan, K. 93, 94, 97, 276
Moses, L.N. 43
Mountjoy, A.B. 296
multiple joint projects 101, 103, 105, 106
multiplex relationships 99–100
multiplier models, regional 78, 79, 81–3, 89
multi-resolution analysis (MRA) 176
    multi-resolution approximation-based
        clustering (MRABC) 177–85
    two-dimensional 182–5
museums 264
    buildings 266
Myrdal, G. 7

Nachum, L. 249
Nalebuff, B.J. 298
need/opportunity to cooperate, recognition of
    101, 102, 104–5, 106
neighbourhoods 263
    characteristics and creativity and innovation
        266–7
networks
    cluster-based renewal in old industrial areas
        209, 211, 212, 213, 214, 215
    inter-firm 135–8
    regional 78–9, 89
    social 2, 31, 32, 33
    tourism 301–2
new economic geography 1–2
    TNCs 223–5
new growth theory 54, 73
new industrial areas/districts *see* industrial
    districts
new trade theory 58
New York 56, 138, 249, 274
New York–New Jersey–Pennsylvania
    pharmaceutical cluster 226
New Zealand 303
non-traded clusters 115
non-traded local inputs 6, 26–7
North, D. 95, 97
nursery-city model 28
Nuti, F. 193

Oakey, R. 79–80
O'Brien, R. 258
Oh, M.-S. 170
Ohlin, B. 1, 4, 6, 27, 40

Oinas, P. 80
old industrial regions 16, 123, 203–18
    cluster-based renewal of 16, 206–16
    clusters and regional innovation 204–5
    innovation dilemma of 205–6
OLI paradigm 225
one-dimensional DWT (1D DWT) 174
Ontario auto cluster 208
opportunities, entrepreneurial 67, 68–9, 70,
    74
organizational proximity 141–3
Owen-Smith, J. 80

Paramount Decision (1948) 278–9
Paris 249, 274
Parma, Italy 193
patent production function 51
Peacock Report 278
Perroux, F. 28, 135
phases
    of cluster development 106–7
    of cluster life-cycles 114–26
        exhaustion 122–6, 128–9
        existence 115–18, 127
        expansion 118–22, 128
physical proximity *see* spatial proximity
picking winners 235–6
Piore, M.J. 78, 139
pipelines, global 86–90
Pittsburgh 128, 138
poisson noise 182, 183
Polenske, K.R. 133, 144, 145
policy 275
    and broadcasting industry 288
    cluster-based renewal in old industrial areas
        209, 211, 212–13, 214, 215–16
    and cluster formation 109–11
    cluster policy and industrial policy 235–6
    implications of new research perspectives on
        IDs 198–9
    tourism 303
polyvalent technology sources 125, 128
Pontarollo, E. 195
pooled market 300–301
Poon, A. 295, 298
Porter, M.E. 24, 28, 29, 78, 93, 94, 109, 117,
    123, 135, 139, 143, 222, 224, 234–5, 243,
    275, 294, 296, 299
positioning 197
post-production 277, 281, 285–6, 287
potential clusters 106–7, 109
Powell, W.W. 80
Power, D. 196
Pratt, A.C. 282
Press, K. 13

price
  formation and colocation externalities 47–9
  hedonic price models 264–5
printing press 240–41
privatization 278
probability-based cultural clustering 268–9
process technologies 141–2
producer-driven supply chains 137, 143–4
product cycle model 28–9, 52–3
product differentiation 49, 56–7
product innovations
  industrial districts 195–7, 198
  urbanization economies 58–60
production chain 238
productivity 53–4
profit and loss mechanism 242
programme production (TV) 276–7, 281
proximity 10, 11
  cultural 141–3
  electronic 143
  financial services cluster 254–6, 258
  organizational 141–3
  relational 94–8, 109–10
  spatial *see* spatial proximity
  transactional 96–100
Puga, D. 27, 28, 240
pure agglomerations 2, 30, 31, 32, 33
Putnam, R.D. 117

Q-analysis 153–68
  industrial clusters and their augmentation
    163–5, 166
  links with superposition principle 157–63
  methodology 154–7
q-connectedness 156
q-nearness 155–6
questionnaire surveys 253–4, 255, 256, 281–3
Quigley, J.M. 46, 54

radical change 206–7, 211–13, 213–16
Raftery, A.E. 170
rank-size ordering method 157
Reggio Emilia, Italy 193, 195
regional development and growth 78–9
  models 23–5, 80–86
  tourism and 293–4
regional innovation systems (RIS) 125–6,
    204–5
regional multiplier models 78, 79, 81–3, 89
regional networks 78–9, 89
regional specialization 7, 16, 234–45
  and case for local diversity 236–43
  clusters and 234–6
region's endowments 42, 43
  and attractiveness of region 45–6

regulation 277–8
relational proximity 94–5, 109–10
  emergence of clusters 95–8
relationships 257, 258
  multiplex 99–100
renaissance 123–4, 128–9
Renault, C. 126
research and development (R&D) 229
  regional R&D externalities 50–53
research institutes 126
Research Triangle 75
resource-based approach 4, 7
resource endowments 45
resource-seeking units 229
retail financial services 249
Ricardo, D. 236, 243
rivalry 196–7, 286
Robertson, P.L. 192
Robins, K. 286
Rome 249, 264
Romer, P. 69, 73
Rosenfeld, S. 237
Rosenthal, S.S. 236
Route 128 75, 93, 128, 130, 141, 234
routines 50, 262
routinized technological regimes 118
Ruhr area 210
  environmental protection industry 212
rural decline 293

Sabel, C.F. 78, 139
Sala-i-Martin, X. 24
Salter, A. 126
San Francisco Bay area *see* Silicon Valley
San Mauro Pascoli, Italy 193, 194
Sarasvathy, S.D. 68
satellite platform clusters 224–5, 226, 275
Saxenian, A. 29, 141, 224, 262
scale economies 105, 106
  agglomeration and dispersion
    economies/diseconomies 15, 133–49
  broadcasting industry 277
  colocation externalities 46–7
  emergence and growth of clusters 4–5, 7
  internal 5, 6, 7, 40
  tourism 300–301
'scale' of issue 104, 106
scaling coefficients 174
scaling filter 172, 173
scanning units 227, 228
Schätzl, L. 81
Schreiber, C. 303
Schumpeter, J.A. 28, 135, 242
Schwarz, E.J. 238, 239
science knowledge base 125–6, 128

science parks 267
scope, economies of 105, 106, 300–301
Scott, A.J. 24, 29, 84–6, 274, 277
Seaton, A.V. 301
self-organizing maps 169–70
service sector 165, 167
Shane, S. 69
shared faces 155, 156
    shared face matrices 156, 161–3
Sheffield metal-working cluster 80
Shin, D.-H. 116, 123
shopping districts 53, 56–7
Silicon Valley 11–12, 29, 75, 93, 219, 234, 267,
    275, 302
    compared with Route 128 141
    input–output linkages 79–80
    learning region 143
    role of Stanford University 89
simplices of backward linkages 161
    simplicial complex 155
    simplicial families 154–5
        chains of structural complication
            156–7
skilled labour, pool of 6, 26–7
skills transfer 220
slicing procedure 154
    based on decomposition method 157–63
slow location processes 41–3
small businesses 296
small regions 7–8
smallest dissimilarity technique 169–70
social capital 29, 209
    broadcasting industry 281–4, 287
social dimension of IDs 191–2
social network (club) model 2, 31, 32, 33
social usefulness of inventions 242
Soho (Hong Kong) 268
Soho (London) 279, 282, 283, 287
Sölvell, Ö. 225
South Africa 295
spatial impossibility theorem 39
spatial price-equilibrium (SPE) model 44
spatial proximity 234–5
    broadcasting industry 282
    cluster formation 94–100, 109–10
    financial services clusters 257–8
    innovation 141–3
    and knowledge spillovers 67, 72–4
spatial transaction costs 85
specialization
    flexible 139, 275
    local employment specialization and
        localization economies 33–5
    regional 7, 16, 234–45
    too narrow in old industrial areas 206

spillover externalities 49–50
    see also knowledge spillovers
spin-offs 9, 71, 72
stages model of cluster formation 101–4, 110,
    111
    thresholds in cluster development 104–6,
        110, 111
Stanford University 89
Starret, D. 39
stars, film 269–72
start-ups 71, 72, 74
state-anchored model 275, 287
static externalities 236–7
Steininger, K.W. 238, 239
Stevenson, H.H. 69
Stockholm 56
    IT cluster 226
Storper, M. 97, 133, 135, 143
Strange, W. 236
strategic asset-seeking FDI 227
strategic planning 294
structural change 258–9
structural complication, chains of 156–7
structural Q-analysis *see* Q-analysis
structural rigidities 13–14
Styria, Austria 208–9, 210
    industrial recycling structure 238, 239
subsidiaries
    and host country 221–3
    impact of clusters on TNCs 227, 228–9
    subsidiary choice perspective 221
Sunley, P. 135, 275
super-clusters 84–6, 89
superposition principle 157–63
supply chains 137, 143–5, 153
'supply' factors in IDs 196–7
sustainability of clusters 12–14
Swann, G.M.P. 116, 117, 119, 121, 124, 125
Swann, P. 195
Switzerland 278
    watch industry 84, 208–9
Sydney Opera House 266
system-centred view of IDs 198

tacit knowledge 140, 142, 276, 299–300
tactics 300–301
Tampere IT cluster 212
Tappi, D. 117, 119
taste for diversity
    customers 56–8
    input-buying firms 55–6
Taylor, P.J. 251, 253–7
technological advance 25, 258–9
technological innovation 191, 195–7
technology implementation 141

technology transfer 220
Telecom Corridor 12
television broadcasting 17, 274–89
test sites 287
Thisse, J.-F. 40, 53, 54, 56
Thompson, W. 114
thresholds of cluster formation 104–6, 110, 111
Thrift, N. 257–8, 259, 275–6
Thünen, J.H. von 1, 39, 46
Tichy, G. 13, 116, 120, 122
Tickell, A. 258, 259
time compression diseconomies 120
Tokyo 249, 274, 278
'top-down' approaches to cluster formation 93
Toronto electronics firms 80
tourism 17, 292–304
    clustering effect 296–9
    colocation or clustering 299–301
    contexts and applications of clusters 294–6
    and development 293–4
    nature of 292–3
    networks 301–2
Tracey, P. 80
trade 25, 58, 250
trade balances 252, 253
traded clusters 115, 127
trading relations 33
'traditional' ID model 190, 191–2, 198
transaction costs 30–32
    spatial 85
transactional proximity 96–100
transactions, nature of 30–32
trans-local pipelines 86–90
transnational corporations (TNCs) 16, 144–5, 219–33
    impact of clusters on 227–9
    impact on clusters 225–7
    impact on host countries 219–23, 225
    new economic geography 223–5
transplanted clusters 224–5, 226, 275
transplanted home-bases 227, 228
transportation 25
    costs 43–4, 137–8
    infrastructure 266
    problem 44
travel 292–3
    see also tourism
Treasury study 252–3, 256–7
trust 32, 96, 97, 99, 100, 143
    broadcasting industry 282–3
    development of 105, 106
    tourism 301–2
Tuscany, Italy 192
two-dimensional DWT (2D DWT) 175, 182–5
two-dimensional MRA 182–5

uncertainty, knowledge and 69–70, 72
United Kingdom (UK) 140, 210
    broadcasting industry 277–89
    London *see* London
United States (US) 253
    auto industry 123, 128, 208
    see also Boston; Chicago; Hollywood; Los Angeles; New York
universal banks 258
universities 126, 128
upgrading 226
upstream (input) spillovers 49–50
urban planning 266–7
urban (functional) regions 2–4, 45, 57–8
urbanization economies 5, 6, 14–15, 27, 40, 53–60, 133–4, 135, 236
    agglomeration and 53–5
    customers' taste for diversity 56–8
    and dynamics 62
    innovation and 54–5, 58–60
    input-buying firms' taste for diversity 55–6
    measurement problems 33–5
    productivity 53–4

Vancouver 283
Velamuri, S.R. 68
Venables, A. 2, 97
Venezuela oil and petrochemical cluster 226
Venkataraman, S. 68
Vernon, R. 28
vertical clustering 296, 297, 299
vertical externalities 10–11, 49–50
vertical integration 194–5, 276–7
vertical linkages 284–7
Victoria state, Australia 295, 296
Vietorisz, T. 135
Visser, E.-J. 125
Volvo 80

Wales 210
Walker, R. 133, 135
Watts, H.D. 80
wavelet clustering algorithm 176–85
wavelet coefficients 174
wavelet filter 172, 173
wavelet smoothing parameter 176
wavelet transformation 16, 169–86
    examples 177–85
    methodology 171–7
Weber, A. 1, 39
Weber problem 43–4
Webster, C. 267
Weibull, J.W. 51

Wheaton, W.C. 136–7
wholesale financial services *see* financial
    services
Williamson, O.E. 32
willingness to commit resources 105, 106

Winter, S. 118
Wolfe, D. 208
Wolter, K. 116

Zander, I. 225